THE CANDIDATE

"We all went into this thinking it was going to be the Charge of the Light Brigade."

—*Clive Lewis MP*

THE CANDIDATE

JEREMY CORBYN'S IMPROBABLE
PATH TO POWER

ALEX NUNNS

OR Books
New York · London

© 2018 Alex Nunns

Published by OR Books, New York and London
Visit our website at www.orbooks.com

All rights information: rights@orbooks.com

First printing 2016
Second edition 2018

Cataloging-in-Publication data is available from the Library of Congress. A catalog record for this book is available from the British Library.

ISBN 978-1-68219-104-0 paperback
ISBN 978-1-68219-105-7 e-book

Text design by Under|Over. Typeset by AarkMany Media, Chennai, India. Printed by BookMobile in the United States and CPI Books Ltd in the United Kingdom.

TABLE OF CONTENTS

PROLOGUE

"Politics isn't going back into the box where it was before."
—*Jeremy Corbyn*

Jeremy Corbyn has a tiny television. In his house in Islington the Labour leader, his wife, and his closest aides have gathered for the release of the exit poll that will give the first indication of the result of the June 2017 general election. They have no idea what is coming; they will find out when they see it on TV like everyone else. But the television, sitting on a pile of books, is so small that Corbyn and his strategy chief Seumas Milne are forced to stand right in front of it, anxiously awaiting the news.

It is approaching 10 p.m., the moment of truth. Corbyn has given each of his companions a sheet of paper and asked them to predict Labour's result. His chief of staff, Karie Murphy, is the most optimistic—to the amusement of her colleagues she has been talking for weeks about what they will do "when we're in Number 10." The expectations of the others are lower, tempered by experience and by the Labour Party's internal polling, which points to a Tory landslide.

Merely the fact that there is doubt about the result counts as an achievement for the leadership, however. When the snap election was called on 18 April almost every political pundit had written off Labour. Theresa May's gamble was "about the surest bet any politician could ever place," wrote Jonathan Freedland in the *Guardian*. By that point Corbyn had been subjected to nearly two years of ridicule and distortion by the vast bulk of the media. He had been undermined and even bullied by his own MPs and other elements within his party. Opinion polls had suggested the Conservatives' lead was as big as the entire Labour vote.

There followed one of the most remarkable election campaigns mounted by any party in British history. In the seven weeks of the contest, according to some polls, Labour's standing has improved by up to 15 percentage points. But only the official exit poll will reveal if these projected gains have been real.

Big Ben strikes 10 p.m. All eyes are on the small screen. "And what we're saying is the Conservatives are the largest party," announces presenter David Dimbleby. "Note they don't have an overall majority."

There is a sharp intake of breath.

"Hung parliament!" exclaims Milne.

Four hours later a throng of reporters and cameramen is waiting for Corbyn to arrive at the local sports hall where the count for his constituency is taking place. There has already been a false alarm: the media had rushed forward in response to cheers, only to find the hubbub was for the arrival of the Official Monster Raving Loony Party candidate. But the presence of armed police at the door signals that the entrance of the man of the moment is imminent.

A beaming Corbyn strides into the building to a burst of applause. Even some of the other parties join in. It is an acknowledgement of his remarkable, against-the-odds campaign performance. But it also reflects the dignified way in which he has carried himself throughout the election. As he pushes through the scrum of journalists wielding microphones and cameras, one reporter shouts out: "Jeremy, are you the next prime minister?" His status has grown immeasurably in just a few hours.

Once all the candidates for the seat of Islington North are assembled on stage, the returning officer reads out the numbers:

4,946 votes for the Liberal Democrat candidate; 6,871 for the Conservative. Then: "Jeremy Bernard Corbyn, Labour Party, 40,086." A big cheer goes up. Corbyn raises his eyebrows in surprise, an involuntary smile on his face. It is a thumping result; he has taken 73 per cent of the vote. 10,000 more people have voted for him than in the previous general election.

"It's an enormous honour to be elected to represent Islington North for the ninth time and I'm very, very honoured and humbled by the size of the vote that has been cast for me as the Labour candidate," Corbyn says in his acceptance speech. Turning to the broader picture, he declares: "Politics has changed. Politics isn't going back into the box where it was before... People have said they've had quite enough of austerity politics, they've had quite enough of cuts in public expenditure... and of not giving our young people the chance they deserve... People are voting for hope."[1]

· · · · ·

Politics *had* changed. Despite not winning the June 2017 general election, Labour recorded an extraordinary result, experiencing its biggest jump in the popular vote since 1945 and adding seats to its tally in parliament for the first time since 1997. But the numbers reflected something more profound, if less tangible.

The election animated a new spirit. On the night before polling day, Jeremy Corbyn had returned to Islington for the final campaign rally of his marathon tour around the country. The event was being held inside the Union Chapel, but the most remarkable scenes occurred outside. Labour's bright red battle bus crept towards the venue through streets packed with well-wishers. Thronging crowds spilled onto the road, blocking a major London thoroughfare. Some climbed trees and even lamp posts to welcome the Labour leader home. But perhaps more noteworthy were the reactions of less dedicated types—those who came out of pubs with their drinks to join in a chorus of 'Oh Jeremy Corbyn,' the spontaneous election anthem, or people on their way to the tube station who stopped to clap the arrival of the bus. The atmosphere was more like that of a music festival or a dramatic sports final than fuddy-duddy party politics.

This had been no ordinary election campaign. It had signalled a shift in political 'common sense.' Millions of people, especially young people, were no longer satisfied by the narrow menu of options that had been offered up by the political elite for more than three decades. Such a development requires explanation. The story of how the ossified shell of British politics was cracked open goes back to an even more unlikely event two years earlier: the election of Corbyn as Labour leader. Both shock results were expressions of the same underlying phenomenon. The clues were there for those who wished to see them.

1

INTRODUCTION

"We've been through 100 days of the most amazing experience many of us have had in our lives."
—Jeremy Corbyn

"Wow," says John McDonnell, breaking the silence. Everyone in the room expected Jeremy Corbyn to win, but not by this much. The "unelectable" left-winger has just taken 59.5 per cent of the vote in a four-horse race.

The candidates and their campaign chiefs have been cooped up on the third floor of Westminster's vast Queen Elizabeth II conference centre for 40 minutes anxiously awaiting advance notice of the result. Deprived of their phones and iPads to prevent the news leaking out, they have been forced to make small talk. After a summer in which the contenders have whiled away countless hours backstage at hustings up and down the country, there is not much more to say. When the gruelling programme of events began, Corbyn was a 200/1 rank outsider. Today, 12 September 2015, he is about to become leader of the Labour Party.

After Iain McNicol, Labour's general secretary, reads out the fateful figures, Corbyn's defeated rivals—Andy Burnham, Yvette

Cooper and Liz Kendall—offer their congratulations. Corbyn and McDonnell reciprocate, thanking the others for a comradely contest. There are hugs, but it is all rather restrained. Yet inside, the victors are fit to burst. They are "gobsmacked" at the scale of the win.

When the result is publicly declared downstairs in the conference hall an hour or so later, the discordance of the audience reaction hints at the troubles ahead. There is wild cheering from some sections of the room. People literally jump out of their seats, shouting and punching the air. Hardened trade unionists are standing up chanting "Jez we did, Jez we did!" There is ecstasy and disbelief in the block reserved for Corbyn's campaign team. A few minutes earlier rumours had zipped along the rows that Corbyn had won 60 per cent, an idea his supporters dismissed, saying there was no way that could be right. Until the last moment, some feared the contest could yet be fixed or summarily cancelled. "You can't imagine that they will allow this to happen," said one.

But it has happened. And Corbyn's detractors cannot believe it either. Between the islands of joy there is a sea of dejection. MPs, many of them appropriately grouped on the right hand side of the hall, sit in stony silence, betraying their emotions with the occasional grimace. Party staff wear sullen, sad faces to match the black attire they are sporting, symbolising the death of the party they have known. An incredulous Labour-supporting journalist sits shaking his head repeatedly as he surveys the scene.

Dressed in an uncharacteristically smart dark blue jacket gifted to him by his sons for the occasion—worn without a tie, in keeping with the European anti-austerity look—Corbyn delivers a victory address that heralds a changed party from that represented in the room. He makes a point of welcoming the new recruits who have surged into Labour's ranks over the summer, inspired by the chance to transform national politics. His speech meanders its way to a rousing conclusion: "We don't have to be unequal, it doesn't have to be unfair, poverty isn't inevitable. Things can, and they will, change."

The press pack descends on Corbyn as soon as he steps off the stage. The party staff, whose job it is to look after the new leader, seem paralysed. "Go on, get a grip guys!" Corbyn's campaign press officer tells them, before manhandling his boss through the jostling paps himself, past the TV reporters jabbing microphones in his face.

When Corbyn eventually gets out of the building he heads to a victory party for his team in a nearby pub. In a brief moment of respite in the cab on the way, he and his old friend McDonnell share a knowing look that says: "How the hell did we end up here?"

At the Sanctuary pub it is pandemonium. 16,000 people volunteered their labour to the Corbyn campaign; it feels like they are all squeezed into the building. The bar manager is panicking about health and safety, saying he will have his licence revoked. When Corbyn arrives there is screaming and cheering and hugging. TV crews try to push their way in through the door. Others resort to filming through the window.

A small amplifier and microphone are set up at one end of the room. Corbyn stands on a chair to make a speech. "We've been through 100 days of the most amazing experience many of us have had in our lives," he says. Someone has given him a tea towel printed with an image of his mentor, the late Tony Benn. Corbyn reads aloud the quote: "Hope is the fuel of progress and fear is the prison in which you put yourself." Several people burst into tears.

Nobody has noticed the American family sat at the back. They only came in for a quiet lunch, and find themselves in the middle of a raucous party. "Apologies to this American family that we've interrupted," Corbyn says. "We respect our good friends in America." The room breaks out into a spontaneous chant of "USA, USA, USA!" It is the most unlikely chorus coming from a crowd of socialists celebrating the election of an anti-imperialist. "No one expected to hear that!" Corbyn laughs.

It is a day of incongruities. As Corbyn and his supporters rejoice, a huge demonstration is snaking its way through central London, called in response to horrific scenes of people drowning in the Mediterranean out of desperation to reach a place of safety. Corbyn's attendance would usually be a certainty. But members of his campaign staff have been anxious that he should not go—it is not expected of a party leader, and anyway there is too much work to be done assembling a shadow cabinet. Corbyn, though, will not be bossed. Without warning his team, in his victory speech at the QEII centre earlier he had announced: "One of my first acts as leader of the party will be to go to the demonstration this afternoon to show support for the way refugees must be treated."

It was quite a statement. Three and a half hours later, Corbyn is stood in front of tens of thousands in Parliament Square proclaiming: "Refugees Welcome." Watching on, McDonnell feels proud of his friend's "courage and grit and bravery." Behind the stage, as the new leader's third speech of the day draws to a close, a phalanx of young volunteers in bright red 'TEAM CORBYN' T-shirts forms a protective cordon ready to speed him through the throng of ecstatic supporters and selfie-seekers, and on to a future in which courage, grit and bravery will be in high demand.[1]

· · · · ·

How on earth did Jeremy Corbyn become leader of the Labour Party? He had been doing his own thing as a backbench MP for 32 years, the embodiment of a thoroughly marginalised political tradition. He had as little ambition to lead his party as he had expectation of doing so. It was easier to imagine the famous monkey hitting random keys on a typewriter and producing the complete works of Shakespeare than hammering out a plausible story that ended with Corbyn at the helm of the Labour Party. It would have taken a writer the equal of Shakespeare himself to make believable a plot in which the protagonist went on to defy a coup, a leadership challenge, and a 25-point opinion poll deficit to lead his party to a 40 per cent share of the vote in a general election.

But while Corbyn's rise was unlikely, it was not beyond explanation. It was not, as most commentators and many Labour MPs seemed to believe, the result of a political nervous breakdown in the party. Rather, Corbyn was swept to the leadership by a fluid political movement that cohered around him, burst its dam and became a torrent. It was fed by three discernible tributaries. The largest ran through the party itself, where the members had turned sharply against New Labour. The second flowed in from the trade unions and was the culmination of a 15-year shift to the left. The final stream had its source in the social movements and activists of the broad left, within which the strongest current was the anti-austerity movement.

Before they converged, each of these tributaries had carved out its own course in its own time. But they all sprang from resistance to the dominant economic ideology of the day—that bequeathed by Margaret Thatcher. It was the spectacular implosion of her economic system in the 2008 financial crash that changed everything. Suddenly the Faustian pact underpinning New Labour—in which the City of London was allowed to take ever-greater risks provided it cut the government in on some of the rewards—was exposed as a catastrophic gamble.

This had a profound impact on Labour Party members, yet it took time to be felt. The membership still appeared Blairite in 2010, when David Miliband was its first choice for leader, only to be beaten by his brother Ed thanks to the votes of trade unionists. But by 2015 the party had changed. There was no big moment of epiphany, just an unspectacular drift leftwards. Some of it was down to new recruits joining, attracted by Ed Miliband's more radical policies. Most was simply a realisation that the old formulas had failed. Underpinning it all was the lived experience of Tory austerity, generating a hunger for a more robust, combative politics.

The 2015 general election defeat was a bombshell. Rather than leading to demoralisation and retreat as the Labour right expected and the left feared, it instead galvanised the members, hardening the trends of the previous five years. This blindsided the Labour establishment. The Blairites, in particular, saw the defeat as an opportunity to launch a counter-revolution and reclaim the party. But there was no appetite for a return to a political project scarred by the financial crash, privatisation and war. Members had grown sick of the management techniques developed by Tony Blair that had shut them out of policy decisions and stitched up the party structures. Miliband had allowed some air to flow back into the party. The membership was not willing to be suffocated again.

Labour MPs appear to have had no inkling of this shift in sentiment. The Parliamentary Labour Party (PLP) had become detached from the wider membership, with an insular culture all of its own. The prizing of conformity over talent had produced a lesser quality of MP, reflected in the clutch of mediocre hopefuls initially vying to replace Miliband. The PLP's political centre of gravity meant that, as the 2015 leadership contest got underway, the debate was pulled heavily to the right, leaving a vacuum to be filled on the left.

But in May 2015 the Labour left believed itself to be at the weakest point in its history. John McDonnell pronounced it the "darkest hour."[2] It looked as if there would be no left candidate for leader. Prominent voices such as the writer Owen Jones argued that the left should sit out the contest for fear of being "crushed."[3]

Yet the left's message resonated with the membership from the moment that Corbyn was unexpectedly pushed onto the stage. One of the most persistent myths about his victory is that it was somehow foisted on the party by outsiders. This is fantasy. Corbyn was ahead among party members within weeks of getting his name on the ballot paper. When his campaign team started to canvass Labour members by phone the results were "too good to be true."[4] Corbyn swept up the nominations of Constituency Labour Parties across the country, moving into first place a month into the race. This all happened under the radar of the press, when Corbyn was still unknown to the general public.

Polling at the conclusion of the contest confirmed this description of a profoundly changed party. Corbyn had massive support from newer party members. But most remarkably he had finished 19 points clear among those who joined before 2010.[5] These were people for whom the Labour Party had been a political home when led by Tony Blair and Gordon Brown. Now they wanted "a new kind of politics."

This sea change within the party might never have found an avenue for expression had it not been for developments in the trade unions. Their endorsements helped deliver Corbyn a majority of trade unionists' votes and provided vital funds and staff for his campaign. But most importantly, their backing conferred legitimacy. If the unions, especially the two giants, Unite and Unison, were behind him, Corbyn could no longer be written off as a no-hope, fringe candidate.

There might seem to be nothing remarkable about unions supporting Corbyn. He was, after all, the most pro-trade union candidate imaginable. But in fact it was a highly unusual development.

Unions are cautious beasts. What matters to them is maximising influence. The last thing they could be expected to do was to back an outside chance.

Why did they do it? Within each union there was grassroots pressure from activists. In several, including Unison, this power from below had a profound impact. But there was also a bigger, historic process in train. In the post-war period trade unions had been integrated into British capitalism, given a seat at the table in the running of industry, sometimes treated as partners by government. The unions grew mighty but such corporatist arrangements made for compromised, inert organisations. Thatcher tore all that up. In the 1980s the unions were banished, vilified, broken. The new, aggressive form of capitalism she unleashed had no need for them. Blair, when he arrived in power in 1997, offered no salvation.

This had an effect on Labour politics. The old corporatist system fostered an affinity between the unions and the Labour right. But the rug was pulled from under that alliance. New Labour regarded the unions with thinly-veiled contempt.

Cast out by capital and brought low in their own party, the unions no longer had any reason to stick with the right. They gave the party a good shake when they backed Ed Miliband as the change candidate in 2010. They put resources into the anti-austerity movement that gathered pace with the Tories in power. A new breed of general secretaries were less enamoured of the Labour establishment, less compelled to defend it, less likely to defy grassroots pressure urging them to nominate someone like Corbyn for leader.

But this is only part of the story. In their new role as an internal opposition in the party, the unions came into close combat with the Blairites. A minor skirmish in the Scottish constituency of Falkirk in 2013 blew up into a major national rumpus. Through a bizarre series of errors and miscalculations, the upshot was the adoption in 2014 of a whole new set of rules for electing the leader of the Labour Party—rules which, though no one dreamed it at the time, would open the way for Corbyn.

Two changes would have a momentous impact on the 2015 leadership contest. The most consequential stripped MPs of their disproportionate voting weight. From now on the vote of an MP would be worth no more than that of an ordinary party member.

The old arrangement had effectively given the PLP a veto on any prospective leader who lacked substantial support in parliament. Its abolition was the price the unions extracted for their acquiescence to the rest of the package. Almost inadvertently, the way Labour elected its leader had been radically democratised.

But it was the less significant reform that consumed the attention of the media: the 'registered supporters' scheme by which non-members could vote for a fee, set at £3 in 2015. It was the brainchild of the Blairites, who imagined there was a reservoir of centrist voters just beyond the walls of the party. Allow them the chance to vote in Labour's internal elections and they would pour in, dilute the influence of trade unionists and party activists, and refloat the New Labour ship. It was, to put it mildly, a misjudgement. Although the effect of registered supporters on the 2015 contest has been exaggerated (they accounted for a quarter of the total ballot, not enough to outweigh the members), an incredible 84 per cent of them voted Corbyn.

The '£3ers' had another less quantifiable impact, related to the third great tributary feeding the Corbyn surge. It was the involvement of the social movement activists, campaigners and loosely networked progressives of the broad left that lent the Corbyn campaign its particular character. The rallies, the social media fizz, the burst of young people suddenly appearing on the scene—this looked like movement politics.

All the dynamism on the left over the previous half-decade sprang from resistance to the policies adopted to deal with the legacy of the financial collapse, which had borne down hardest on those least to blame for the crisis. Like the economic ideology that produced the crash, this was an international phenomenon. Widespread anger at elites was reflected in the growth of movements and parties of both the left and the right across Europe and the US. On the left, it gave rise to Syriza in Greece, Podemos in Spain, and Bernie Sanders in the US. In Britain it was seen first in the Occupy movement and UK Uncut, local 'save our services' campaigns and giant union-organised demonstrations. A section of this mobilised constituency rushed into the Greens before the 2015 general election, but found its way blocked by the first-past-the-post electoral system. Whereas in Europe new parties of the left had shot up at the expense of their established social democratic rivals, in Britain the anti-austerity movement saw a sudden opportunity to express itself within the Labour Party.

The offer of a vote for £3 lowered the bar of entry, but it was not certain that movement activists would accept it. Many of them had grown up despising a Labour government shamed by the Iraq War. Only a candidate whose years of campaigning left no doubt about his commitment could have captured their trust. Yet there was something else to it. The breath-taking surge of people inspired by Corbyn's candidacy came after party members had put him in the lead, after trade unions had lent his challenge an air of plausibility. They joined because it looked like he could win. The momentum they generated ensured that he would.

The excitement inherent in the rare chance to actually change national politics was infectious. It took on a viral quality, spreading beyond the usual suspects to young people getting involved in politics for the first time, students, artists, anti-establishment rebels, online petitioners. They combined with socialists who had left Labour under Blair but were now returning to restore the party to what they considered its true values.

When these new recruits came into contact with existing members and trade unionists at rallies in halls, churches and public squares around the country, through Facebook groups and Twitter hashtags, a new political movement was born: the Corbyn movement. Its defining quality was its desire to make history for itself. It wanted to *do* things: volunteer, proselytise, phone canvass, recruit friends, attend events, suggest policies, vote, build a force for change. It was a coming together of people grown tired of spectator politics. It met an echo in the participative ethos and practice of Corbyn and his campaign.

This movement had a powerful tool not available to previous generations: social media. It was a game-changer, fostering a collective identity among people who might otherwise have been unaware of each other's existence. It allowed the Corbyn phenomenon to expand at breakneck speed and was a catalyst for activity in the world beyond the internet. It transformed what might in the past have been shattering attacks from the press into opportunities to galvanise supporters.

Online, Team Corbyn was streets ahead of its rivals. Instead of seeing social media solely as a platform from which to broadcast, it sought to unlock the democratic potential of the technology by encouraging engagement, debate and participation. Its strategy was geared towards making people feel "like actors in this campaign, rather than consumers of it," as Corbyn's social media coordinator put it.[6]

"A movement, not a man" was one of the unofficial slogans shared by Corbyn supporters. As the man himself frequently insisted, it was about 'we' not 'I.' "Our campaign—it's not me, it's our, it's a lot of people together—is changing things and I happen to be in a position where I'm asked to speak on behalf of it," he said.[7]

But the movement also made the man. Corbyn gained confidence throughout the contest. The mass rallies in every corner of the country helped the reluctant candidate to "grow into the role" of leader, "though not in a conventional sense," according to his friend Jon Lansman.

Though he might deny it, without Corbyn's particular personal qualities it is much less likely that the movement would have got off the ground. Ironically, it was his reticence to push himself forward that enabled his rapid advance. He stood only from a sense of duty to the left. He could scrape together the required 35 nominations from MPs precisely because they perceived him as no threat. A more forceful figure such as McDonnell would have found the door slammed in his face. "Jeremy's the nicest man in politics; he hasn't got any enemies," was the pitch an ally made when arguing that Corbyn should be the left's candidate.[8]

Corbyn's great achievement in the subsequent months was to liberate the Labour left from its ghetto, to appeal across the party and beyond. His brand of socialism—critical of the top-down model of nationalisation associated with old Labour, advocating instead cooperative management—sounded fresh to a new generation. His anti-austerity message was on trend with the anger electrifying the left across Europe. His promise to democratise the party and invest power in the members was an offer both open enough to appeal widely, and radical enough to create excitement.

Yet Corbyn managed to present a vision that felt both contemporary *and* like a return to Labour's core values. Though his opponents cast him as a 'hard left' throwback who had not changed his mind since the 1980s, aspects of his programme were, in his own words, "depressingly moderate."[9] His economic policies could be judged to be to the right of those proposed in 1983 by the SDP—the rightist splitters from Labour.[10]

The MP Clive Lewis describes Corbyn as "a Christian socialist without the Christian. He's an ethical socialist." When, at a pivotal moment in the contest, Corbyn became the only candidate to vote against the Welfare Bill, he was at one with the majority of Labour members on what they considered to be a moral issue—that the government should not deliberately increase poverty. The PLP, meanwhile, seemed to have discarded its moral compass. While the chasm dividing MPs and members offered Corbyn the opportunity to gather broad support, his character eased the way. He embodied the left's usual unbending resolve but combined it with a personal warmth and generosity that proved attractive.

That Corbyn does not exhibit the characteristics traditionally expected of a leader continues to confound his critics. He has neither the rousing oratorical skills of Tony Benn nor the slick presentational gifts of Tony Blair. Yet he possesses a rare ability to connect with an audience by articulating deeply held shared values. According to a close ally, "He's not an ideologue; he's not a strategist; he's not an organisation builder." He provides a different type of leadership, the ally says, drawing on other strengths: his integrity, his adherence to principle, his moral force. He is an example. And he is an enabler.

People determine the course of history, but in circumstances not of their choosing. The financial crash of 2008 was like an earthquake that rattled the buildings above but did not quite bring them down. Since then, joists and walls have tumbled, concrete dust has been falling from the ceilings, and some structures have toppled. Corbyn is a product of this precarious historical moment.

For all the twists and turns of agency and chance along the way, only in such extraordinary times could the left take the leadership of the Labour Party three months after proclaiming its own nadir. It was a stunning victory but it seemed to come too soon. Corbyn became the leader of a party he could not control. The old guard in the upper reaches recoiled at the tens of thousands of new recruits rushing in at the grassroots. A failed coup against Corbyn in the summer of 2016 advertised to the electorate that Labour was dysfunctional. Neither side was powerful enough to get its way, but each had the strength to thwart the ambitions of the other.

How could the Conservatives resist exploiting Labour's troubles? Theresa May's decision to call a snap election in April 2017 was taken against a backdrop that looked as bleak as could be for Corbyn. Labour was over 20 points behind in the polls. The EU referendum had transformed the political landscape. The Tories' reinvention as the party of Brexit had enabled them to consume UKIP and unify the right. The prime minister was enjoying an extended honeymoon with a fawning press.

But the deep, tectonic shifts that brought Corbyn to the fore had not been addressed. That mainstream opinion was in denial about this meant that Labour appeared to come from nowhere. Its astonishing performance in the June 2017 general election dumbfounded all those who had been determined not to understand what had happened two years earlier.

There are echoes of a previous period of tumult, when the political and economic orthodoxy appeared incapable of responding to a changed world and parties contorted as the terrain beneath them shifted. An unlikely figure from outside the consensus became Leader of the Opposition. Margaret Thatcher acted not so much as a midwife to a new era, but as a surgeon performing a caesarean section without anaesthetic. It is the orthodoxy she established which appears to be teetering.

The obstacles facing Corbyn as a leader of the left are orders of magnitude greater than those that confronted Thatcher. Even if one historical era is giving way to another, that provides no guarantee that Corbyn or the left can succeed. As intimidating as the task seemed from the vantage point of 2015, winning an election is the easy part. Any attempt to use government to wrest power from the elites is sure to meet ferocious resistance. But when such a rare chance arrives, there is only one option available: to seize it. If Corbyn's rise demonstrates anything, it is that politics is only predictable until it is not.

2

LED BY ED

"I am afraid we are going to have to keep all these cuts."
—Ed Balls

Could it really be about to happen? Could an underdog, an insurgent candidate, become the leader of the Labour Party?

The atmosphere is electric in the conference hall as the moment of truth approaches. Labour's leadership contest has spanned the summer, from the party's desperate defeat at the general election in May to today's tense declaration in September.

On stage, the announcer reads off a blizzard of numbers. Assembled delegates hold their breath. There are gasps from the crowd as some anticipate the result using mental arithmetic.

And then, before the announcer can finish, the hall erupts into applause. Labour has a new leader: a candidate no one expected to win when the race began.

A candidate who took on New Labour from the left.

Ed Miliband.

· · · · ·

It is easy to forget the extent to which Ed Miliband's victory over his brother David in 2010 was seen as a break from New Labour. In case there was any doubt, the best evidence was the immediate, vitriolic reaction of the Blairites. Ed's win was "the doomsday scenario," according to one anonymous briefer to the press. Another disturbed Labour figure described it as "a gothic horror."[1]

Anyone who could provoke so much fury from such bad losers must have been doing something right. From the intensity of the response it was as if the party had elected a radical outsider (heaven forbid). Yet Ed Miliband was part of a New Labour establishment that had splintered in the 2010 leadership contest. He represented a minority fragment but had skilfully appealed over the top of the party machine. As a result, he was something of an enigma. Was he the militant 'Red Ed' portrayed by the press, or was his victory, in the words of a Labour insider at the time, "a Brownite coup dressed up as an Obama insurgency"?[2] Ambiguity—paradoxically—would be the defining characteristic of his tenure.

Miliband's five years in charge was a tale of two trajectories. The leadership began with a blaze of left rhetoric then became progressively more cautious. But the party moved in the other direction as the membership shifted left and the unions set about reshaping Labour. The collision of these two vectors triggered a shakeup of party structures. As a result, Labour's leadership election rules were radically recast. No one knew it at the time, but this would open the door for Jeremy Corbyn.

· · · · ·

First trajectory: the leadership

Compared to the 16 years of Tony Blair and Gordon Brown that preceded him, Ed Miliband represented a departure. Cynics may have accused him of tacking left in the leadership contest in a shameless bid for votes, but once in the job he could easily have tacked right again. Instead, in his debut conference speech as leader, he overturned New Labour's first article of faith that markets are sacrosanct, rebuked the Blair-Brown dependence on the City, reintroduced inequality as a cause for concern, renounced the Iraq War, criticised Israel, and denounced authoritarian attitudes to civil liberties.

He won the leadership by clearly articulating that the deal at the heart of New Labour was over, swept away by the tide of history. That deal, in the view of New Labour's creators, was based on a simple calculation: if Labour accommodates itself to the powerful forces which drive the British economy and state, those forces will tolerate the party doing enough progressive stuff to make it worthwhile. This meant accepting the economic legacy of Margaret Thatcher and going further: making the Bank of England independent, weakening regulations on the City, and killing off the idea that governments can protect their citizens from global markets. In return, New Labour got the backing of influential sections of the media and big business along with a licence to spend the taxes gleaned from the City on public services and a measure of redistribution.[3]

It did not end well. The pact was destroyed by the crash of 2008. For all the years that it kept the show on the road, with election victories and investment in schools and the NHS (coupled with increasing privatisation and wars), the dénouement was economic crisis, defeat at the polls, long-term cuts in public services and greater inequality.

Miliband knew that the deal could not be revived in the new circumstances. But without its protection Labour could expect to be battered by a storm of opposition from powerful interests. In the early stages of his leadership Miliband appeared to appreciate that just as a tree withstands buffeting winds by stretching its roots through the soil below, so the best chance of success for a party of the centre-left would be at the head of a wide network of alliances reaching deep into society: a movement. Speaking to Labour's National Policy Forum a year after his election, Miliband said: "Let's be honest, the [New Labour] leadership believed its role was to protect the public from the party. It never really believed the party could provide the connection to the British people. And we didn't build a genuine movement... We cannot change Britain in the ways we want to unless we become a genuine movement again."[4]

If Labour wanted to be, as one of Miliband's allies put it, "the fulcrum of the wider progressive left," the burning issue on which to prove its credentials was cuts to public spending.[5] In March 2011 Miliband addressed the massive 'March for the Alternative' protest in Hyde Park, London, attended by 400,000 people. Despite his speech passing off reasonably well, some booing from the crowd betrayed that not everyone was convinced—possibly including Miliband himself, who did not look entirely comfortable.

By the start of 2012 Miliband was retreating. In a speech described as a relaunch of his leadership he talked about the "difficult choices" arising from the supposed fact that a future Labour government would have no money to spend. His shadow chancellor, Ed Balls, followed up by effectively announcing Labour's shift to an austerity-lite position, saying: "I am afraid we are going to have to keep all these cuts... At this stage, we can make no commitments to reverse any of that, on spending or on tax." Opposing a pay freeze hitting public sector workers was "something we cannot do, should not do, and will not do."[6]

The trade unions were furious at this "sudden embrace of austerity."[7] But the two Eds had chosen their path, and in summer 2013 they advanced further. Miliband committed the party to a welfare spending cap, while Balls announced that Labour would follow rigid fiscal rules.[8] The following January, the shadow chancellor gave a commitment to eliminate the deficit and run a surplus by 2020.[9]

"The party's triangulation strategy wasn't based on economics," John Cassidy in the *New Yorker* magazine would later write. "It reflected a political judgement by Miliband and other Labour leaders that the British electorate, which blamed the party for the collapse in public finances after 2008, wouldn't listen to anti-austerity arguments."[10] According to one Miliband advisor, the success of the Tory propaganda line that Labour had maxed out the nation's credit card "led us to conclude early on that there was no point in trying to contest their account of the past—that we had to be future-oriented."[11] It was a catastrophic decision.

The party's austerity-lite agenda might have seemed sophisticated to the political insiders who crafted it, but to the public it was either baffling or irrelevant. Labour was opposed to cuts in the abstract, but would make them in practice. It accepted that reducing the deficit was imperative, but said the Coalition was doing it too fast. Miliband posed both as a man sent to banish a failed economic model, and a safe pair of hands. Many Labour members were left cold. "We had hope with Ed that he'd take the party in a different direction," says Michelle Ryan, who voted for Miliband after joining Labour in 2010, and went on to become a Corbyn supporter in 2015. "But I always felt that everything he wanted to do was watered down and it was a very incoherent message in the end. He'd talk about a cost of living crisis, then Ed Balls would say we're going to cap child benefit and freeze public sector pay. So we've got a cost of living crisis but we're going to add to it."

There was a view on the left that Miliband was unable to chart his own course, that he was boxed in by Blairites. But some of his constraints were self-imposed. He was "the epitome of the unity leader model, anxious to manage divisions," according to Luke Akehurst, a one-time supporter from the right of the party.[12] But it was difficult to combine a unifying role with Miliband's other aim of conjuring a movement. It even precluded him from building a powerbase within his own party, making his position as leader seem more vulnerable than it ever was.

The story of Miliband's political journey as leader, one of his senior aides told the *Guardian*, was a gradual shift from his more radical instincts to "the cautious tactical politics he had learned during his long stint under Gordon Brown at the Treasury."[13] It was an approach that was found wanting at the ballot box and that left an uncertain legacy. Everyone could find something to hate: the right could decry the mansion tax; the left could express disbelief at the "Controls on immigration" merchandise mug. The scene was set for rival camps with competing explanations of why Labour lost the 2015 general election to fight it out. But they would be appealing to a party that, under the radar, had changed fundamentally.

• • • • •

Second trajectory: the party and the unions

A striking feature of Miliband's leadership election, one that would haunt him, was the split sympathies of party members and trade unionists. Ed was famously elected on the votes of the latter, while the membership backed his brother—by 54.4 per cent to 45.6 in the final round of voting.[14] But between 2010 and 2015 the divide between party members and trade unionists was bridged—and the members were the ones to move.

The Labour right's strength in 2010 was not as great as David Miliband's result implied. Although he was the favoured choice of the Blairites, he was also the most high profile candidate on offer. His support was solid among long-standing members who had stuck with it through the Blair-Brown years. But this old party was dying. By the end of Gordon Brown's tenure the total membership was less than 40 per cent of its 1997 peak of 405,000, having fallen to 156,000 in 2009.[15] Many members were inactive and the average age was on the rise.[16] Over the following years, according to one former aide to Ed Miliband, "Lots of Blairites left in a sulk because David Miliband wasn't leader."[17]

They were replaced by new blood. A membership surge in 2010 saw 46,000 people join, bringing the total to 194,000.[18] The level then stabilised, before another spike saw membership top 200,000 on the eve of the 2015 election.[19] Anecdotally, the new members were drawn to Ed Miliband's more radical rhetoric and policies like the energy price freeze, the 50p tax for high earners, a higher minimum wage, the mansion tax, restrictions on zero-hours contracts and the promise to put a brake on NHS privatisation. His unexpected stand against bombing Syria in 2013 was another attraction. According to Miliband's aide, "It is generally the case that those that… joined [were] sympathetic to the leader."[20]

There was also a deeper process going on. The economy had changed since the crash, making life hard and bleak for many. This shaped the views of old and new members alike. "It was a journey that all of us were on over five years, with the austerity and seeing how that's affected people, including in our own lives," says party member Michelle Ryan. "My husband's a police officer and it has affected his work. My ex-husband is a fire-fighter and he talks about things that have changed for him."

The leftward shift could be seen in internal elections. Every two years members vote to fill six seats on the party's National Executive Committee (NEC). In 2012, the left slate won 47 per cent of the vote, while the right got 33 per cent.[21] By 2014, the left had increased its share to 55 per cent—the "best left result since the 1980s" according to Jon Lansman, a linchpin on the party's left.[22] Christine Shawcroft, one of the committee members re-elected with an increased vote, said at the time: "Members voted by a clear majority for candidates opposed to austerity and austerity-lite."[23] This sentiment was confirmed by a survey of party members in May 2015 (before the surge of support for Jeremy Corbyn). Over 90 per cent thought cuts to public spending had gone too far. When asked to place themselves on a left-right scale (where 0 was left wing and 10 right wing) the average result was 2.39.[24]

While the membership was moving left, some of the unions were getting organised. A pivotal date was 21 November 2010: Len McCluskey's election as general secretary of Unite, Britain's biggest union. McCluskey was a left general secretary who was not sentimental about Unite's ties to Labour. "Len, when he was campaigning, visited about 100 different work sites and everywhere he went shop stewards were saying, 'Why the hell are we spending money on the Labour Party when it ignores us and acts against our interests?'" remembers Martin Mayer, a Unite delegate on Labour's NEC. "He knew we couldn't just carry on as before with a blank cheque. But it didn't seem right that we should disaffiliate from the Labour Party when we hadn't actually been fighting to change it."

The union set about developing a new 'political strategy' to reshape Labour, officially adopted in summer 2012. The idea, McCluskey explains, was "to get our members, activists and shop stewards to join the Labour Party" and then encourage them to endorse union-supported candidates to stand for parliament. Just like the Blairite pressure group Progress, Unite began identifying, mentoring and training potential candidates.[25] They were chosen according to whether they shared "our values of collectivism, solidarity and community spirit," McCluskey says. Unite's political strategy soon became a lightning rod for press opprobrium, but the union was not alone. The GMB had a programme to get its people into parliament, and TULO (the Trade Union and Labour Party Liaison Organisation), which brought together Labour's affiliated unions, provided some of the infrastructure.

The selection of parliamentary candidates has always been a Labour flashpoint. The choice of who stands for Westminster determines the political balance of the parliamentary party. The unions were not the first to focus their efforts there: in New Labour's heyday, vetted Blairites were 'parachuted in' to safe seats while strong left hopefuls were excluded. Party workers were tasked with personal lobbying for preferred candidates, or were even told to chase up certain postal votes but not others.[26] Although on many occasions candidates of the right won fair and square, a number of high profile, egregious cases sent the message that it was barely worth trying to get selected against the will of the New Labour machine. The most notorious example was that of Liz Davies who found herself at the centre of a media storm in 1995 when Tony Blair went "ballistic" at her selection for the seat of Leeds North East. Davies was smeared and deselected. By the time she prevailed against her accusers in court her chance had passed.[27] Even sitting members of the NEC like Mark Seddon had candidacies blocked.[28] The parliamentary party that Corbyn inherited as leader was a testament to the success of this operation.

Miliband had neither the control-freak inclinations of New Labour nor the infrastructure necessary to stitch-up selections. In the resultant vacuum, contests became straight fights between different sections of the party.[29] Unite, with its new political strategy, was ready. "We'll be fighting the right wing in the constituencies to get trade union candidates selected," said Dave Quayle, the chair of Unite's national political committee, in July 2012. "We want to shift the balance in the party away from middle-class academics and professionals towards people who've actually represented workers and fought the boss." The new strategy got results. By mid-2013 the union reckoned half the candidates it had supported had been selected.[30] The GMB also found success.

In the event, Labour's poor result in the 2015 general election meant that much of this effort came to nothing—but not all of it. "The 2015 intake [of MPs] is probably the most pro-trade union cohort for decades," wrote Andrew Harrop of the Fabian Society that year. "Many are former union officials... and others are unquestionably on the left." This was not to say they were out of sync with the membership. On the contrary, "The composition of the new intake reflects the general sentiment of Labour Party members under Ed Miliband's leadership, with constituency parties keen to signal a break from the Blair/Brown years."[31]

Had Miliband known the true weakness of the Blairites' position within the party during his leadership, perhaps history would have been different. As it was, they retained an aura of power, and were not finished yet.

· · · · ·

Trajectories collide: Falkirk

The two great trajectories of Ed Miliband's tenure collided in the Scottish constituency of Falkirk in 2013—in the predictable form of a selection row. Miliband, the unity leader, was faced with a stark choice: side with Unite or the Blairites. He chose the latter. The consequences were historic, but precisely the opposite of what the right intended. Features of the 2015 leadership election that would be crucial to the left's victory—£3 votes, a reduced role for MPs, the number of nominations needed to get on the ballot—were all a legacy of the Falkirk "scandal."

A story that ended up having national implications began at the level of the hyper-local, with a man asking friends and relatives in the Broomhill Inn pub in the village of Bonnybridge if they wanted to join Labour. He asked his colleagues at the oil refinery in Grangemouth, too. In a short time around 100 new members were brought into the Labour Party.

The man on the recruitment drive was Stephen Deans, chair of both Unite in Scotland and Falkirk West CLP. The local party needed a candidate to stand for Westminster, so Unite put its political strategy into action. Driving it forward was Karie Murphy, a former chair of the Scottish Labour Party and a member of the union's political committee north of the border (Murphy would later become Jeremy Corbyn's chief of staff). When Deans decided not to stand himself, Murphy stepped up to become the candidate.

Unite's efforts ruffled feathers. The legacy of New Labour in Falkirk was a party so small—with only around 100 members—that a sudden influx of new recruits resembled a steamroller coming to crack a nut.[32] The departing MP was the violently Blairite—and simply violent—Eric Joyce. His political career ended in shame after thumping and head-butting several MPs in a House of Commons bar in 2012, which is why the constituency had a vacancy. Suspension and resignation from the party did not stop Joyce decrying Unite's recruitment drive as "infiltration."[33]

While these events were simmering in Falkirk, far away in London the enmity between Unite and the Blairites was coming to the boil. Unite's continuing grievance was Labour's adoption of an austerity agenda. The problem, Len McCluskey said in an interview in April 2013, was that Miliband was listening to the "siren voices" of the Blairites: "If he is brave enough to go for something radical, he'll be the next prime minister. If he gets seduced by the Jim Murphys and the Douglas Alexanders, then the truth is that he'll be defeated and he'll be cast into the dustbin of history."[34] In response, Miliband accused McCluskey of being "disloyal."[35]

A rift had opened and the Blairites had the perfect wedge to drive into it: the issue of selections. Sensing that the unions were getting better organised, the right complained of "stitch ups" when its candidates missed the cut.[36] "Our political strategy was pitting Unite candidates for election face to face with Progress' candidates, and we started to win," says Martin Mayer from Unite. "Falkirk was really the high noon of all that; it was a showdown."

On 11 May 2013, at Progress' annual conference in London, Lord Mandelson, the grandfather of New Labour, launched the opening salvo. Jon Lansman was observing proceedings:

> The final plenary had an absolutely horrible panel consisting of Mandelson, David Aaronovitch, Oona King and [Stephen Twigg]… Falkirk at that point still hadn't been in the English press. And they went for McCluskey. They went for him big time. There was a real anger and hatred in what both Mandelson and Aaronovitch said.

Mandelson made some statement... and Aaronovitch immediately after said, 'Well, I think you've got tomorrow's headline.'

The following day the *Guardian* reported Mandelson's allegation that "a cabal" of union members was manipulating Labour's parliamentary selection procedures (with callous disregard for irony, given that Mandelson owed his own original selection to friends in high places).[37] Claims of "mass recruitment of Unite members... with their fees being paid *en bloc* by the union" were perfectly true, and perfectly within the rules. This was, in fact, the purpose of the 'union join' scheme under which unions could cover the first year's subs of members brought into the party from their own ranks—a scheme introduced by none other than Tony Blair.[38] But soon there was another allegation that, if true, would amount to a breach. The *Herald* reported that some recruits had been signed up without their consent.[39]

As the press latched on to the story, Labour halted the Falkirk selection and ordered an internal inquiry. When the report came back in late June it set off a chain reaction of political explosions. First, the CLP was put into "special measures"—run from Labour HQ—and Karie Murphy and Stephen Deans were suspended from the party. But because Labour refused to publish the report, these actions only deepened the press' suspicion of some dark conspiracy. The Tories piled on the pressure, taunting Miliband for his supposed dependence on McCluskey. Next, Tom Watson resigned from the Labour frontbench for no apparent reason. He had links to the affair—Murphy was his office manager and he had approved some of the Unite membership applications—but his crime was unclear. Blairites shed no tears at Watson's demise, still furious at him for organising the 2006 'Brownite coup' that forced Blair from office.

With the press feverous, the story convulsing Westminster, Miliband's next step was startling: he called the police. On 5 July Labour passed its internal report to Police Scotland and asked it to investigate the events in Falkirk. Miliband then briefed the press that the allegations amounted to "malpractice, bad practice or even corrupt practice."[40]

Miliband held McCluskey responsible for what he considered an affront to his democratic principles in Falkirk. But the clash was "personal psychodrama as much as political dispute," according to Declan McHugh, a Labour advisor.[41] "I am incredibly angry about what has happened," Miliband told the BBC. "Certain people have let down this party and I am not going to let it happen."[42] For his part, McCluskey says he can "never forgive Ed Miliband. He reported my union to Police Scotland. It was quite extraordinary."

Miliband chose to escalate the row into a full-scale offensive against the trade unions. Whatever was in the report (which was still secret), he gave the impression it was abominable—so bad that Labour's whole relationship with the unions was at risk. The line from the leader's office was that trade unions were a "powerful vested interest" on a par with "banks, energy companies and Rupert Murdoch," and Miliband would confront them.[43] He let it be known that he was planning "bold reforms" and, as a down payment, immediately scrapped the 'union join' scheme.

Some Blairites were quick to raise the stakes with calls for a complete severing of the historic link between the unions and the party. One anonymous "former cabinet minister" (Mandelson's voice is almost audible in the words) said: "We need to have a commission that looks at the union link... We need to get to a place where you simply have one category of Labour Party members. There should no longer be a formal union affiliation. Of course, if unions want to donate to the party they can. Ed is not there yet. But he will be. He acts in a deliberative way. But when he makes a decision he moves very rapidly."[44]

Miliband did move rapidly—too rapidly. On 9 July 2013, following a panicked weekend spent cobbling together a sufficiently dramatic response to the self-made crisis, he gave perhaps the most consequential speech of his leadership. He announced that he would require individual trade unionists to 'opt in' if they wanted to contribute money to the Labour Party through their union's affiliation fee. Previously, union members were often automatically affiliated by a collective decision of their organisation unless they chose to opt out. This proposal had no relevance to the situation in Falkirk, but that passed without much comment since no one was too sure exactly what had happened there.

The potential consequences of the change were huge. Far fewer trade unionists would be affiliated. That could undermine the legitimacy of the unions' position within the party in all kinds of areas: the 50 per cent share of the vote they wielded at Labour's annual conference, the number of seats for union delegates on committees like the NEC, and the third of the vote reserved for trade unionists in leadership elections. These types of structures had been designed to bond together the distinct mass-membership organisations of the Labour *Movement*. They had enabled the party to set down roots in society strong enough to secure its place as the hegemonic force on the British left for nearly a century. But they had been in the Blairites' sights for some time. "Really, it was only Progress that was pushing it," says Lansman. "It was a concession by Miliband to the right." The leader's stance was even sold in Blairite terms as a "Clause IV moment." And Miliband's speech gained the seal of approval of the man himself, as Blair told Sky News: "It is bold and strong. It is real leadership."[45]

A battle with the unions would, Miliband hoped, allow him to shed the 'Red Ed' moniker and dispel his caricature as a union puppet. He even had it briefed that the crisis was "a chance to show his mettle as leader."[46] According to Lansman, Miliband "didn't like union power, and in particular he didn't like Len McCluskey's power." He thought it preferable for the party to have a direct relationship with individual trade unionists than one mediated by union leaderships. He hoped union members would be more engaged that way—better to have 100,000 active participants than several million passive onlookers. "With this change I invite you to be at the centre of what this party does, day in day out, at local level," he told them in his speech.[47]

But perhaps there was a simpler explanation for Miliband's actions: maybe what happened in Falkirk really was that bad. As Labour still refused to publish its internal report it was difficult to tell. But given the fuss Miliband had kicked up, there was surely substance to the allegations.

The first sign that this might not be the case came when the police announced later in July that there were insufficient grounds for an investigation. Then, in September, in a dramatic but under-reported turnaround, a further Labour Party investigation into Karie

Murphy and Stephen Deans exonerated them of any wrongdoing and lifted their suspensions.[48] Extraordinarily, it emerged that the Blairite candidate in Falkirk, Gregor Poynton, had done the very thing of which Unite was accused. He had recruited 11 new members to the party *en masse* and paid their fees with a single cheque—which was against the rules. Two of those recruits said they were signed up specifically to vote for him—which was even more against the rules. Yet this time, no one called the police.[49]

It took until February 2014 for the original report into Murphy and Deans to finally be leaked. When it came it was astonishing—not for the evidence it contained, but for the lack of it. The main conclusions were stark enough, and familiar from all the briefings. The report's eight findings were bullet pointed on the front page, among them: "There is evidence that members were recruited without their knowledge"; "There can be no doubt that members were recruited in an attempt to manipulate party processes"; "Deliberate attempts were made to frustrate the [investigation's] interviews."[50]

But the report was a strange document, because the subsequent 19 pages contained very little. An analysis by the *Guardian*, which had obtained the leak, found "there is only limited evidence in the report which supports [its] conclusions." Of the eight bullet points, the *Guardian* thought that just two could be sustained.[51] Only one was significant—that some members had been recruited without their knowledge. But by this time, even that allegation had been withdrawn: later investigations asserted that the memberships (which numbered fewer than 10) had been given as gifts. Incredibly, neither Murphy nor Deans had been interviewed for the original report.[52] "At no stage in any of this did the party ever speak to me or Stevie, not once," Murphy says. "Not one letter, not one email, not one phone call, ever."

If he read past page one, Miliband must have realised that the report was at best thin and at worst, in the characteristically measured words of McCluskey, a "shoddy fraud."[53] The Unite general secretary had called for the document to be published all along, confident that it would damn itself. It was "lazy and amateurish," he says, "because the Labour Party had been able to get away with being lazy and amateurish in the past. No one challenged them when they were doing individuals in. But doing Unite in was a step too far."

Miliband's aggressive handling of the affair had real consequences for the people involved. The reputations of Murphy and Deans were trashed in the press. Deans' employer, Ineos, suspended him from work at the Grangemouth oil refinery, sparking an industrial dispute that nearly shut down the facility for good. He was labelled a "rogue operator" by David Cameron at prime ministers questions and eventually had to resign from both his job and his position as chair of Falkirk West CLP.[54] Murphy, meanwhile, tried to stand as a candidate in another constituency but was excluded from the selection.[55] Despite all this, the pair did not receive an apology.[56]

There is a final ironic twist in the tale. All the heat and fury over Falkirk was due to there being something of consequence at stake: a safe Labour seat. But at the 2015 general election the SNP took the constituency with a 24 per cent swing and a majority of 19,701.

· · · · ·

The Collins Review

In his big speech of July 2013 Ed Miliband tasked Ray Collins, a former general secretary of the Labour Party, with turning his words into reality. There followed a mammoth negotiation between party elites and the trade unions that spanned the autumn and winter of 2013-14. The resultant Collins Review not only brought about a fundamental change to the way unions related to the party, but also introduced new rules for electing Labour's leader that would have spectacular unintended consequences. The left bitterly opposed the Collins Review at the time; without it, Jeremy Corbyn could never have become leader.

Collins' main objective—because Miliband had announced it in his speech—was to introduce the 'opt in' system for affiliation fees. But this was not quite as it seemed. The change had nothing to do with Falkirk but a great deal to do with paving the way for state funding of political parties. The aim was to 'free' Labour from its financial dependence on the trade unions. Miliband was following Winston Churchill's dictum: "Never let a good crisis go to waste."

Ever since the New Labour days, what could have been a cause for pride—that the party was funded by the collective contributions of working class people—had instead been regarded as a source of embarrassment for the leadership, even though the alternative—semi-corrupt donations from the super-rich—was, by any measure, much worse. In 2006 Tony Blair was hit by the cash for honours scandal. It was alleged that he had given seats in the House of Lords in exchange for loans to the Labour Party. In the wake of the furore, which saw a sitting prime minister interviewed by the police for the first time, Blair commissioned the former civil servant Hayden Phillips to produce a report on party funding. It was a classic establishment move: a moment that threatened to rock the system of governance to its core was diverted into a dry and technical debate designed to bore people to death. Suddenly it was neither the politicians accused of selling influence nor the wealthy people suspected of buying it who were the problem, but—who would have guessed?—the trade unions.

Phillips proposed that the state should give political parties some of their funding, which could be supplemented with private donations of less than £50,000. That was potentially catastrophic for Labour as it would outlaw the large affiliation payments it received from trade unions. So Phillips suggested a solution: Labour could still benefit from affiliation fees as long as they could be shown to be little gifts from individual trade unionists, not big collective payments from their organisation. The unions would still be able to gather up and pass on the fees, but there had to be a paper trail—unions could no longer just say, "Here is the money we have agreed to give you." Instead, individual trade unionists would have to sign a form declaring that they wanted a specific portion of their union subs to be donated to the Labour Party.[57] In other words, they would have to opt in.

Phillips' ideas were never implemented because it proved impossible to get cross-party agreement. So Labour continued to depend on trade union affiliation fees and the Conservatives somehow managed to scrape along on the generosity of their millionaire and billionaire friends. But for the Blairites the idea of state funding remained enticing. They dreamed of no longer having to be answerable to what they saw as the outdated, unpopular and uncontrollable (i.e. democratic) representatives of labour, leaving them free to get on with the business of serving business.

When Miliband was elected leader with trade union support this dream seemed to be over. But in the heat of the Falkirk frenzy Miliband himself revived it. Declan McHugh, a former advisor to Jack Straw who negotiated on behalf of Labour in the unsuccessful party funding talks, was brought in to assist Collins. The model he helped devise would bring Labour broadly into line with the Phillips proposals.

But there was a problem. An 'opt in' system could cost Labour up to 90 per cent of its affiliation income.[58] In the absence of any kind of deal with the other parties, "the sudden pronouncement to upturn affiliation fees was seen by many in the party as an act of unilateral political disarmament," McHugh wrote afterwards. "A Lib Dem representative who had sat opposite me during months of cross-party talks on political funding emailed to ask why we had done it."[59] It was a good question. People involved in the negotiations from the trade union side are convinced that the purpose was to introduce the changes necessary to get the Liberal Democrats on board for a post-2015 vote on party funding under a Labour or Labour-led coalition government.[60]

The 'opt in' system could not just be imposed on the unions because they had the power to veto it and embarrass Miliband. And if Labour did not want their money, they could withhold it and the party would go bankrupt. That was deliberately underlined when, in September 2013, the GMB announced it was cutting its annual affiliation fee by over a million pounds to just £150,000, the amount it expected to raise under the proposed scheme.[61]

Paul Kenny, the general secretary of the GMB, was reportedly furious with Miliband for endangering the union link.[62] Dave Prentis of Unison wanted nothing to do with the reforms—his union's existing affiliation arrangements were similar to those being suggested anyway.[63] But to everyone's surprise, the most enthusiastic supporter of the proposals was Len McCluskey of Unite. He had confounded expectations on the day of Miliband's speech in July 2013—at the height of the Falkirk furore—by taking to the airwaves to welcome the Labour leader's words. "I had no intention of being the big, bad, dinosaur union boss so the media could play me off against Miliband," he says. "When Miliband said that, rather than a block affiliation, he wanted individual Unite members to say 'Yes,' I agreed with that in principle... I believed the million members Unite affiliated to the Labour Party was untenable. We knew that a substantial proportion of them didn't even vote Labour." McCluskey thought an 'opt in' system would make the unions engage with their members, who would be encouraged to "commit to Labour, so that we can have some vibrancy at the grassroots."

McCluskey had other, more prosaic, motives. "I'd taken over as general secretary on the basis of a growing discontent in Unite about why we were giving all this money to the Labour Party," he says. Opposition to the affiliation was building within the union. Meanwhile, dealing with Miliband and Ed Balls had left him frustrated with Labour. "I'd started to lose faith," he admits. He wanted to cut Unite's huge affiliation fee, but was worried about being cast as a "splitter." Suddenly Miliband's proposal gave him the perfect excuse. "I was able to reduce our affiliation by half without being accused of undermining the party. It saved us £1.5 million a year."

When the leaders of the 'big four'—Unite, Unison, the GMB and the CWU—first met to discuss their response to Miliband's speech, McCluskey's opposite numbers were miffed at his support for the 'opt in' idea. "To say they attacked me is too strong but they said, 'Lenny, what's going on?'" McCluskey recalls. Billy Hayes, then general secretary of the CWU, remembers: "There was a bit of frostiness towards Len... because it had been seen as him contradicting the approach of TULO [the affiliates' collective body]."

Without Unite, the other unions were not going to fight to the death over the 'opt in' system, even though they believed it was a long-term threat to their position in the party.[64] It would still be possible to give money to Labour on top of affiliation fees in the absence of a law to cap donations. This would potentially make the relationship between the party and the unions more transactional—a something-for-something arrangement rather than the something-for-nothing deal some trade unionists felt they got from affiliation payments. Not everyone in the unions was unhappy about that.

For the Blairites, the 'opt in' model was a stepping-stone to a bigger ambition. "We all knew what they were after, which was to limit the voting power of unions," says Martin Mayer of Unite. With no chance of the unions agreeing, Collins did not even try to negotiate a reduction of their 50 per cent share of the vote at conference. But it was understood that this was next on the Blairites' hit list. "[Reforming] conference comes later, when we see how many levy payers join," the Blairite advisor John McTernan commented.[65]

In one area, though, the unions' vote share was put on the table: in the election of the leader. Labour used an electoral college for its top job, giving a third of the vote to MPs and MEPs; a third to party members; and a third to affiliated members, the vast majority of whom were trade unionists.[66] Establishing the electoral college had been a great victory for the left in 1981 (the choice of leader had previously been the preserve of MPs alone) but it did result in some absurdities. People who were members of several organisations could vote multiple times. As there were far fewer MPs and MEPs than party members, and far fewer party members than trade unionists, the votes in each category had different weights. In the 2010 leadership contest the first preference vote of one MP was worth that of 477 party members and 794 affiliated members.[67]

Miliband had made no mention of the leadership election rules in his July 2013 speech. But now they were centre stage. In McHugh's telling, this was simply a logical consequence of the other changes. "The move to an 'opt in' system of affiliation fees was bound to dramatically reduce the number of trade unionists eligible to take part in a leadership election," he wrote. "That undermined the claim of affiliates to hold a third of the electoral college. It would have to be reformed."[68] What this account misses out is that the unions *wanted* to overhaul the electoral college as a way to weaken the power of the Parliamentary Labour Party (PLP), the great fortress of the right. Trade unions are good at nothing if not negotiating. This would be their countermove.

The plan Collins and Miliband put forward involved merging the affiliates' and members' sections of the electoral college while preserving the MPs' golden share. The unions would not have that. To bring them on board the whole electoral college would have to be abolished and replaced by a one-member-one-vote system in which an MP's vote would count for no more than anyone else's.

This was unusual territory for the unions. They were historically the main detractors of the one-member-one-vote principle within Labour, which they regarded as an attack on the collectivist arrangements through which they exerted power—an attack that was almost always advanced by the right. But their attitude had been evolving over a number of years.

The rise of New Labour had seen the unions, traditionally the praetorian guard of the Labour leadership, cast out. Suddenly in opposition within their own party, they had to exploit every available mechanism to win policy concessions. This led them to team up with the left in 2009 to push through a rule change mandating the use of one-member-one-vote to elect constituency party delegates to Labour's policy-making body, the National Policy Forum. It was a small victory that went almost completely unnoticed by commentators. But for the unions, it broke the one-member-one-vote taboo.[69]

When Miliband launched a review of party structures called 'Refounding Labour' in 2011, the unions went for the jugular. Via TULO, under the chairmanship of Kenny, they proposed scrapping the electoral college all together.[70] The *unions*, of all people, were arguing for the leader of the Labour Party to be elected by one-member-one-vote. This proved too radical a suggestion for party elites in 2011. But two years later, when everything was put up for grabs in the Collins negotiations, the unions made it a critical objective. Miliband was not the only one to see opportunity in a crisis.

For McCluskey, "the principle of one-member-one-vote, cutting out the PLP who were a drag anchor on everything we were doing," was "absolutely irresistible."

> We had the most right wing PLP in my memory who were giving up 33 per cent of the vote. It was extraordinary. On the basis that the unions would give up their 33 per cent of the vote. But we didn't have 33 per cent! Ours had

been one-member-one-vote since John Smith [in 1993]... It wasn't as if I could say 'Unite's share is going to Jeremy Corbyn' or whoever. For example, our members voted for Tony Blair for leader in 1994 rather than following our recommendation.

If the MPs' third was scrapped, a leadership candidate with a strong powerbase in the PLP would find that support translated into just a hundred or so votes—less than a rival could glean from their own constituency party. Inversely, contenders with little support among MPs could no longer be written off. The ability of MPs to kill a candidacy by ensuring it seemed hopeless was their most potent weapon, and it was being taken from them.

To compensate MPs for this huge diminution, Collins proposed a large hike in the number of nominations a candidate would need to secure from parliamentary colleagues in order to enter a leadership contest. Under the old system, the threshold was 12.5 per cent of the PLP. This was too high a bar for John McDonnell to clear when he tried to run for leader in 2007 and 2010. But now Collins wanted the proportion raised to 20 or 25 per cent. That would make it impossible for a left candidate to get enough nominations—which was precisely the point.[71] In exchange for ceding power over the actual election, MPs were being given greater control over the choice of candidates on offer. They would be the gatekeepers.

The suggestion of a 20 or 25 per cent threshold did not survive the negotiations. It was strongly opposed by the unions. Fascinatingly, there was also resistance from the Blairites.[72] Although their access to the media and penchant for mouthing off gave them an aura of dominance, Blairite MPs were acutely aware of their numerical weakness. (This would be exposed in the 2015 contest when they could only muster enough support to get one of their three candidates onto the ballot, and even then with just six nominations to spare.)[73] In the end a compromise was reached with the threshold set at 15 per cent—still way too high as far as the parliamentary left was concerned, but not completely out of reach, as would be shown. For Andrew Berry, who sits on Unison's Labour Link committee, reducing the threshold was "the key element." "That goes down in history somewhere: had Collins won on that nomination level, well…"

The Blairites came to the discussion about the electoral college with their own ingredient to add to the mix: registered supporters. These were envisaged as average Labour voters who were not about to join the party but who would be given a say in who leads it. This was a pet project of the Blairites, who were besotted by American primaries and the system used by the French Socialist Party to select its presidential candidate in 2011, when members of the general public could vote for €1. The Blairites thought that opening up Labour's internal elections would diminish the influence of union members and plant the party on the fabled centre ground. They assumed that those availing themselves of the opportunity to vote would naturally be to the right of quixotic political activists. Quite why none of them considered the possibility that quixotic political activists would be the most likely to take up the offer remains a mystery.[74]

An earlier incarnation of the scheme betrayed the purpose. During the 'Refounding Labour' review of 2011, an attempt was made to add registered supporters to the affiliates' section of the electoral college, to dilute the voting power of trade unionists. The unions managed to see that off, but now the idea was back in a modified form.[75] Once again, McCluskey's view differed from that of his colleagues. "I was in favour of registered supporters," he says. Convinced that the party had been "hollowed out," McCluskey saw the scheme as a way to re-engage former members who had walked away. "To suggest that I foresaw what was going to happen with Corbyn is going too far," he says, but "I don't care if people believe me or not, I saw the prospect, if we could get into a situation where there was a credible left candidate, of appealing to those thousands of people that we'd lost."

With everyone's cards on the table, there was a bargain to be made over the electoral college. The unions conceded registered supporters and the dissolution of their third of the vote, but only in exchange for what they wanted—the abolition of the MPs' third. That was the deal by which Labour adopted one-member-one-vote (or more accurately, given the inclusion of non-members, one-person-one-vote) to elect its leader.

During the 2015 leadership contest a huge amount of attention would be focused on registered supporters (dubbed '£3ers' after the fee that was levied—an important detail that ensured only the motivated took part). A full-scale panic erupted at the conjured spectacle of mass entryism by tens of thousands of imaginary Trotskyists. But in fact the loss of the MPs' third of the vote was the much more significant change.

With the negotiations finally concluded, Miliband had won on 'opt in' affiliation fees; the Blairites had won on registered supporters; and the unions had won on the MPs' third of the electoral college (although McCluskey was happy with all of it). From the perspective of Labour MPs—apart from those on the left—all three outcomes would prove calamitous within a year-and-a-half of the deal.

But at the time it looked very different. It was the left, largely shut out of the process, that regarded the Collins Review as a catastrophe.[76] The journalist Owen Jones, for example, was "despondent" at the result. "The point about fighting in the Labour Party is the trade union link" which the Collins Review "consciously watered down," he says. A last-ditch effort was made to persuade union leaders against endorsing the final package. Tony Benn was even dispatched to lobby McCluskey personally, but to no avail. "Collins is a disaster for the unions," says Jon Lansman, referring to the 'opt in' system in particular. "Unite bloody voted for the thing! They all voted for it in the end but they only voted for it because Unite had basically lost the argument for them. If Len had spoken against it then we would have defeated the Collins Review and Jeremy Corbyn would not be leader of the Labour Party, which is obviously an irony." McCluskey sees it differently. "I never lost any argument," he says. "I got everything I wanted out of Collins... I saw it as an opportunity to save the Labour Party because it was dying."

The package was put to the vote at a special conference in March 2014. Even on the day "it was by no means certain that it was going to go through," remembers Hayes of the CWU. His union, like others, "wasn't keen on it at all," but eventually decided not to break "TULO discipline." With only the bakers' union and some constituency delegates voting against, the Collins Review passed by 86 per cent to 14. Miliband was cast as the victor, but the Blairites felt they were the real winners. For Progress it was "history in the making."[77] Much later, once the full horror of what they had done dawned on them, the Blairites would disown Collins and hang it around Miliband's neck.

Critical praise for the Collins Review:

"I have said it before, and I'll say it again—Ed Miliband is more Blairite than Blair on party reform."

—John McTernan, Blairite advisor, 31 January 2014.[78]

"Ed has shown real courage and leadership on this issue. It is a long overdue reform that... I should have done myself. It puts individual people in touch with the party and is a great way of showing how Labour can reconnect with the people of Britain."

—Tony Blair, 28 February 2014 [79]

"Miliband's reform is the real thing, and it will have real and welcome consequences—whatever the result of the next general election. If Miliband loses, it means that the next Labour leader will be a Blairite."

—John Rentoul, Blairite journalist, 2 March 2014.[80]

"One of Ed Miliband's great legacies as leader of the party was the reforms to party organisation which mean that actually lots of people can be involved in picking the new leader."

—Tristram Hunt, one-time Blairite MP, 8 May 2015.[81]

3

THE JAWS OF DEFEAT

"This is an analysis that's going to appeal to a lot of people in Labour, the idea that Labour lost because it was too left wing."
—Helen Lewis, deputy editor, the New Statesman

It is 9.59 p.m. on 7 May 2015—general election night. In his constituency in Doncaster, Ed Miliband, leader of the Labour Party, is nervously waiting to hear the results of the exit poll. He thinks he will be prime minister. In Labour headquarters in London, they think he will be prime minister. In Labour-supporting households throughout the country, they think he will be prime minister. Even many political pundits think—however messy the election aftermath—it is likely that Miliband will emerge as prime minister.

It has been a tight election. The polls have shown Labour and the Conservatives tied. But the maths look hopeful for Miliband. Even if the Tories win a few more seats, Labour stands a better chance of being able to cobble together a coalition with other parties.

Big Ben strikes 10 p.m. "Conservatives Largest Party," says the message flashed up on BBC One. That is not a disaster. And then, presenter David Dimbleby says: "Here are the figures... Quite remarkable, this exit poll." Cut to a graphic of David Cameron, hologram-like, standing on a podium that says 316 seats. Miliband's hologram is smaller, further away. His podium says 239. He is miles behind.

Hundreds of thousands of Labour supporters are thumped in the chest at once. Time slows, air is short. For a moment the world ceases to make sense, as if it has become pixelated—like interference on a satellite signal. But Dimbleby is still talking. It is real. Labour has *lost* seats.

Next morning, College Green is a high tech jungle, a mess of tangled cables, studio lights, microphones and laptops beneath a canopy of cluttered gazebos and marquees. The world's media has descended on this small patch of grass in the shadow of the Houses of Parliament, transforming it into an open-air broadcasting complex resembling some kind of classified government test facility, complete with military helicopters buzzing overhead. Expecting days of protracted coalition talks between the parties, the media has come prepared for the long haul. The BBC has even built a huge two-storey temporary TV studio, jet-black except for a large curved window bulging out towards parliament, giving it the appearance of a spaceship that has crashed in Westminster.

There is no need for any of it. The only change from the exit poll of the night before is that the Tories have done even better, with 330 seats, and Labour even worse, with just 232. The Conservatives have an absolute majority. Meanwhile, the Scottish National Party has surged to 56 seats, leaving Labour with just one MP north of the border.

In the tent-studio of BBC Radio Five Live, two men are discussing the implications for Labour. One is a veteran MP from the left of the party, Jeremy Corbyn—re-elected to represent Islington North for the eighth consecutive time, with 60 per cent of the vote and a massive, increased majority of 21,194. The other is Tony Blair's former spin-doctor Alastair Campbell, best known for selling an illegal war.

They do not agree on much, but there is a surprising convergence on one point: Labour should *not* have an immediate leadership election. Corbyn believes the party needs a year or two to understand the defeat and have a full policy debate. Campbell concurs that plunging into a personality contest is a bad idea. Neither has any inkling that Corbyn will be part of such a contest, much less win it.

"What I will say about that encounter," Campbell will later recall, "is that he is likeable, sincere." But Blair's spinner is annoyed that Corbyn is "beginning immediately to stake out" a position that says "Labour lost because we were not left wing enough." In fact, Corbyn's analysis is more specific than that. For him the real issue is austerity, and Labour's failure to oppose it. While chancellor George Osborne's decisions have created terrible inequality and poverty, his opposite number Ed Balls "was in essence saying that the only difference in Labour's policy was that his economic strategy would simply take longer to deal with the deficit."

Making this argument on 8 May 2015, Corbyn is swimming against the tide of politico-media opinion. But it will not be long before he is riding the crest of a wave coming in the other direction.[1]

· · · · ·

One reason why the 2015 general election result provided such fertile ground for argument was that it was a mess, a collection of local, regional and national battles with conflicting dynamics. Because of the first-past-the-post electoral system, aspects of the outcome were perverse. It was easy to forget that Labour actually increased its vote share—albeit by just 1.5 percentage points. Yet this translated into a loss of 26 seats due to the SNP's spectacular surge north of the border. Even in England, a 3.6-point increase in Labour's vote share gained it 15 constituencies, but the Tories added 21 English seats with a 1.4-point improvement.

That the Tories emerged with a majority was a freak, a consequence of the massive haemorrhage of support suffered by the Liberal Democrats. In two-thirds of Liberal Democrat constituencies the Conservatives happened to be in second place.[2] The Tories needed to gain 23 seats to secure a majority; 27 just fell into their hands as Liberal Democrat incumbents were washed away.[3] It would make a better story if this had been the result of a merciless Tory strategy to devour their erstwhile coalition partners, but the fact is in most of these constituencies the Conservative vote barely increased—their opponent simply vanished.[4]

The cruellest irony of all was that in several seats the Conservatives were able to win because Labour took votes from the Liberal Democrats. Labour's vote *gains* helped the Tories to a majority.[5] In constituencies where Labour was the main competitor to the Liberal Democrats it took seats too, there were just fewer of them.[6]

The Tories gained seats because of the fall of the Liberal Democrats; Labour lost seats because of the rise of the SNP. Bizarrely, amid these convulsions the two main parties held steady against each other—Labour won 10 seats from the Tories and the Tories won 8 from Labour; the parties swapped roughly equal numbers of votes.[7] Had the Liberal Democrats and the SNP remained static, the Conservatives' defensive success in holding off Labour in marginal seats would have prevented the latter achieving a majority; the result would have been another hung parliament.

Things become really confusing when the focus zooms in on the nitty-gritty of who took votes from whom. Labour's level pegging against the Tories is, at first sight, bewildering considering that it won far more votes from the Liberal Democrats and lost far fewer to UKIP than the Conservatives did. Analysis by the polling company Survation suggested that 31 per cent of people who voted Liberal Democrat in 2010 switched to Labour in 2015, while 17 per cent defected to the Conservatives. (Why some Liberal Democrat voters chose to punish their party for going into a coalition with the Tories by voting Conservative was one of life's great mysteries.) Though Labour lost 5 per cent of its own 2010 vote to UKIP, the Conservative Party lost 12 per cent of its more numerous supporters.[8] These shifts failed to translate into a loss of seats for the Tories because of a countervailing trend in Labour-Conservative marginals.[9]

The voters that Labour lost to UKIP were fewer than many had feared and probably did not cost it any seats.[10] Where UKIP did eat into Labour's support it did so from both the right and, surprisingly, the left.[11] People who voted Labour in 2010 but switched to UKIP in 2015 reported that they were worried about immigration, but also thought there should be no more public spending cuts. They tended to be working class and said Labour no longer stood for people like them.[12] The party also lost support to the Greens, who broke through the 1-million-vote mark for the first time.[13]

The inescapable fact for Labour was that it simply did not do well enough in the popular vote. It finished 6.5 points behind the Tories, whose slender improvement of 0.8 points across the UK was an impressive achievement for a governing party. A host of theories for why Labour fell short was soon forthcoming. One group in particular was determined to foist its view upon the party.

• • • • •

Competing interpretations of Labour's shock election defeat super-charged the leadership debate that raged throughout the summer of 2015, beginning with a self-serving and erroneous explanation advanced by the Blairites. They hoped their intervention would allow them to reclaim the party; instead it provoked a backlash that prepared the ground for a successful challenge to the Labour elite.

In the days and weeks following the election, in the newspapers and over the airwaves, the Blairites attempted to establish a new orthodoxy around a single word: "aspiration." The reason for Labour's defeat had been its failure to appeal to "aspirational" voters. Leading the charge was none other than Tony Blair, writing in the *Observer* on 10 May 2015 that "Labour has to be for ambition and aspiration as well as compassion and care."[14] Former foreign secretary David Miliband said in an interview that "unless Labour is able to embrace a politics of aspiration and inclusion... then it's not going to win." Shadow education secretary Tristram Hunt wrote that Labour needed "an inclusive vision of the future built around personal aspiration..." Former home secretary Alan Johnson told the BBC that Labour's problem was "the issue of aspiration in people's lives; we can no longer relate to them as a party of aspiration."[15] And David Cameron spoke passionately of an "aspiration nation" (except that was in 2012 and he is a Conservative).[16]

The Blairites, who had volubly predicted that Ed Miliband's 'soft left' approach would be a disaster, thought their time had come again. Their "analysis of what makes a winning Labour Party has essentially been vindicated," said Helen Lewis, the deputy editor of the *New Statesman*, on the BBC's *Andrew Marr Show* on 10 May. "This is an analysis that's going to appeal to a lot of people in Labour, the idea that Labour lost because it was too left wing," she thought, adding that "we'll definitely be hearing more about"—wait for it—"aspiration."[17]

What did they all mean by aspiration? In reality, it was a code word for a return to New Labour. But politicians needed to know how to use it in a sentence, so for most of them "aspirational" became a synonym for middle class. On the same edition of the Andrew Marr programme, shadow business secretary Chuka Umunna put it like this: "In terms of why we lost, in my view the Labour Party succeeds and does best when it marries together its compassion for people who can't provide for themselves—the vulnerable, the poor—with others' ambition and drive and aspiration to get on and do well... For middle-income voters there wasn't enough of an aspirational offer there."[18]

Whenever Blairites attempted to be more specific they risked sounding ridiculous. Such a fate befell Tristram Hunt when he gave a vivid description of the people he thought Labour should appeal to: "John Lewis couples and those who aspire to shop in Waitrose."[19] This was aspirational in the sense that the marketing industry uses the word—an "aspirational product" is one you want, but cannot afford.[20] It went against the grain of progressive politics, which usually seeks to collectively change people's circumstances so they can fulfil their potential, not make them feel bad for shopping at Aldi. Coming from Hunt it was a particularly brave electoral strategy. If adopted in his Stoke-on-Trent constituency it could have seen him out of a job: Waitrose reportedly refused to open a store in the town because "residents are not upmarket enough."[21]

For many Labour members who had been out canvassing, the claustrophobic obsession with aspirational middle class voters as the cause of defeat felt wrong. There was a good reason for this—it was. Labour's vote among the middle class had actually held fairly steady since 2005, even recovering slightly under Miliband compared to the result achieved by Gordon Brown. But Labour had failed to rally the support of working class voters after a dramatic collapse in 2010.

Data from the House of Commons Library showed that among voters in social grade "AB" (taken by polling companies to mean middle and upper-middle class people, although the use of these grades as a proxy for class has been criticised) Labour's share of the vote in 2005—at a general election it won—was 28 per cent; in 2015, despite a bad defeat, it was still 27 per cent.[22] Among "C1" voters (supposedly lower-middle class) 32 per cent voted Labour in 2005, and still 30 per cent did in 2015. But the proportion of "C2" voters (skilled working class) backing Labour fell from 40 per cent in 2005 to 30 per cent in 2015, and for "DEs" (working class and non-working people) a 48 per cent share tumbled to 37 per cent. As the shadow cabinet minister Jon Trickett wrote as early as 13 May, there was "not a shred of evidence" for the argument that Labour had scared away middle-income voters by neglecting "aspiration." "The truth is that Labour recovered among middle class voters but has suffered a cataclysmic decline among working class voters... Labour's electoral base last Thursday was by far the most middle class we have secured in our history."[23]

There was an even simpler way to find out whether "aspiration" had cost Labour the election. A poll conducted in the immediate aftermath of the ballot asked people what put them off voting for the party. Just 9 per cent of participants chose, as one of their top two reasons, the statement "They are hostile to aspiration, success and people who want to get on," making it the least popular of seven options. Even among people who considered voting Labour before backing the Conservatives (some of whom must have lived in towns with a Waitrose) this explanation came last.[24] The idea that Labour lost because it failed to appeal to aspirational voters was unsubstantiated.[25]

· · · · ·

While aspiration was the signature tune of the Blairites' post-election revue, they had other songs in their repertoire.

Tony Blair, writing in the *Observer* in August 2015, gave the best rendition. "I have analysed all the different published polling and focus group evidence about Labour's defeat," he announced.

> They all say the same. Labour lost because it was considered anti-business and too left; because people feared Ed in Downing Street with SNP support; and because he didn't have a credible deficit reduction plan. They didn't vote Tory because they thought he was 'austerity-lite' but on the contrary because he didn't seem committed enough to tough economic decisions. That is the evidence. Does this make any difference to the Corbynistas? Absolutely not.[26]

Of course, no one would ever accuse Blair of lying. But the evidence, and his summary of it, were—on this occasion—rather different. There is a first time for everything.

First, consider the assertion that Labour lost support because it came across as anti-business. In a poll conducted immediately after election day, respondents were asked whether they considered Labour too tough or too soft on big business and the banks. 19 per cent said Labour was too tough; 41 per cent believed it was too soft. People, by a large margin, thought Labour should be *less*, not more pro-business.[27] But for most people a party's attitude to business was not a priority—it was ranked the 10th most important issue out of 13 tested.[28]

Second, Blair claimed: "Labour lost because it was considered... too left." In fact, voters did not think Labour was particularly left. Work by Professor Ed Fieldhouse of the British Election Study showed that the Conservatives were perceived as being further from the centre than Labour.[29] The fact that they nevertheless secured a majority is evidence that, contrary to the cliché beloved of political pundits, elections are not always won on the centre ground. The party considered by voters to be closest to the centre was the Liberal Democrats, and its vote collapsed.[30]

Further academic work from the British Election Study by Professor Jane Green and Chris Prosser looked at the probability of people voting Labour based on how left they perceived the party to be. Their conclusion was stark: "Generally, our data shows that people were more likely to vote Labour in 2015 when they thought the party was more left wing." Although the authors argued Labour would not necessarily be more successful if it moved left, they found that when the party was perceived to be in the centre "support really drops off." "There is very little to the argument that Labour was *too* left-wing to attract voters," they wrote.[31] Moreover, Labour's most left wing policies, such as the energy price freeze and the mansion tax, were its most popular, as the party's official election inquiry made clear.[32]

If at the UK level Blair's claim was wrong, it was outright complacent when applied to Scotland. According to Professor John Curtice, the UK's pre-eminent psephologist, it was the SNP's ability to articulate a vision of an egalitarian Scotland during the 2014 independence referendum that prised away a huge chunk of Labour's support—the party was outflanked on its left.[33] Since Labour's loss of 26 seats was almost entirely down to its collapse in Scotland, it was bizarre to argue that the party's problem was being too left wing.[34]

There appeared to be more evidence for Blair's third contention that "people feared Ed in Downing Street with SNP support." One poll found that 60 per cent of English and Welsh voters said they "would be very concerned if the SNP were ever in government."[35] The issue was certainly on people's minds, but its impact on their votes was unclear.[36] Based on a deep analysis of how voting intention changed in battleground seats, Green and Prosser argued that the "SNP threat" thesis was a "red herring."[37]

The fourth assertion handed down by Blair was that Labour lost because it "didn't have a credible deficit reduction plan." It was true that voters considered the deficit a priority—it was ranked the fourth most important issue in one poll.[38] But that was not the whole story. By an 11-point margin, voters favoured growing the economy by boosting productivity and investment over cutting the deficit, taxes and red tape.[39] Asked if Labour "should cut public spending faster... to get the deficit down more quickly," or "cut public spending slower... to protect public services," more people chose the latter option.[40] Among the crucial group who thought about voting Labour but decided against it, there was a

24-point difference in favour of slower action.[41] Whatever stopped them backing the party, it was not the supposed lack of "a credible deficit reduction plan."[42]

Blair's fifth and final assertion was that people "didn't vote Tory because they thought [Miliband] was 'austerity-lite,' but on the contrary because he didn't seem committed enough to tough economic decisions." Strictly speaking, it was true that *Conservative* voters favoured more austerity.[43] But among the wider electorate attitudes were very different. A major election day survey by Lord Ashcroft found that 46 per cent of voters thought that austerity should continue, but that the greater part, 54 per cent, believed either that it was time for austerity to stop or that it had never been necessary in the first place.[44]

The split in the electorate between Conservative voters, most of whom favoured austerity, and supporters of all the other parties who, by majorities, opposed it, was a significant fact.[45] The Blairite response was to argue that Labour should mimic the Tories' austerity policies in order to win over Conservative voters. But such a strategy would not be cost free. New Labour's instinct had always been to move to the right, safe in the knowledge that Labour's traditional constituency had nowhere else to go. But the 2015 general election demonstrated that the party faced competition for the votes of the economically disaffected from UKIP, the Greens and, most damagingly, the SNP.[46]

There was, at the very least, a debate to be had about how Labour should navigate this dilemma. But in the first weeks after the election the Blairite prescription was the only one under discussion. In the view of Labour MP Emily Thornberry, this triggered a reaction that contributed to Jeremy Corbyn's rise. "There was a feeling after the [2015] general election that the right of the Labour Party was trying to use it as an opportunity to yank the party to the right," she said. "There was a feeling that the Tories had won the election so everything the Tories say is good and everything that Labour says is bad, and that we should look into our souls and worry about why we're on the left, almost... People really didn't like that. They felt that was an affront."[47]

· · · · ·

There were two big, looming truths behind Labour's 2015 election defeat. One was that voters did not trust the party with the economy. The other: they did not know who or what Labour stood for.

Only 23 per cent of voters thought Labour best on the economy, compared to 41 per cent for the Conservatives—the widest gap on any of the top issues.[48] But this was not, as the Blairites spun it, because of Labour's mythical opposition to austerity, its policy on the deficit, or its supposed anti-business rhetoric.

The reality was much simpler. Voters distrusted Labour on the economy because they blamed the party for the economic crash of 2008. That year, the Conservatives took a poll lead on economic competence. Then, over the course of the 2010-15 parliament, two important things happened. First, the Tories—with media help—successfully convinced the public that not only had the crash been Labour's fault, it had somehow been due to overspending. Second, shadow chancellor Ed Balls gradually moved towards the Conservative position on the need for more cuts, giving ground to the Tory narrative in a quest for credibility. But as he did so, polling shows Labour lost trust on the economy and the Conservatives gained it. This widening of the gap began *before* the shallow economic upturn arrived.[49]

To the extent that there was a rational basis for Labour being blamed for the crash, it related to a central tenet of New Labour strategy: its pandering to the City, which resulted in 'light-touch' regulation of the banks. But mostly Labour was held responsible because it happened to be in office at the time. "Some events realign parties with crucial issues," wrote Professor Jane Green and Chris Prosser. "The economic crash in 2008 appears to have done for Labour what the exchange rate mechanism crisis did for the Conservatives more than 20 years earlier: it fundamentally altered the public perception of which party could be trusted on the economy."[50] There could not have been a clearer demonstration of this than Ed Miliband being laughed at on the BBC's pre-election *Question Time* programme for saying that Labour had not spent too much in government. It was the reason David Cameron brandished former Labour Treasury minister Liam Byrne's spectacularly stupid letter saying "I'm afraid there is no money" at every possible opportunity during the campaign.[51]

Miliband and Balls were not rejected because they moved too far from New Labour's economic heritage, they were punished because voters saw them as no change. Perhaps this was unavoidable soon after such a huge crash. But it became inevitable with the failure to offer a clear and distinct economic message. To many Labour members it seemed nonsensical that in the weeks after the defeat the party elite were arguing for a return to New Labour orthodoxy.

The second, related, big truth was that voters no longer knew who or what Labour stood for. Fifty-six per cent of people said they were unclear what Labour was about. Only 33 per cent said they were clear. In contrast, 68 per cent knew what the Tories stood for.[52] Even Labour voters were not sure what their party would have done in government. In focus groups with Lord Ashcroft they "often complained that Labour had been 'remote' and had failed to offer anything impressive or distinctive." The upshot was a palpable lack of excitement about the party. "Few of those who voted Labour said they had done so with any enthusiasm," reported Ashcroft. "If there was any enthusiasm at all, it was at the prospect of getting rid of the Conservatives."[53] Energising supporters may not automatically translate into a majority, but when even a party's loyal voters see nothing to get animated about it is unlikely the wider public will. To underline the point, 70 per cent of people who did not vote Labour in 2015, but said they would consider doing so, thought the country was going in the wrong direction.[54] Despite presumably wanting change, they did not believe Labour would deliver it.

To a growing constituency within the party rank and file, these two big truths were linked: Labour had failed to offer anything distinctive because it had vacillated on economic policy. So taking a strong stance against Tory austerity would give Labour a clear message. This seemed to offer a chance of success for three reasons. First, there was already support among the public for an anti-austerity position after five years of cuts.[55] That sentiment had emerged spontaneously despite Labour refusing to make an anti-austerity argument. By putting the case forcefully, Labour could appeal to that majority and try to expand it. If enough of those people could be fused into a coalition with middle class progressives, they could make a powerful electoral force.

Second, Labour's missing voters were mostly people on the receiving end of austerity. In 2015, against a backdrop of austerity *and* a limited economic recovery, the Conservatives gained support among the affluent but lost votes among those bearing the brunt of the cuts.[56] Labour might have expected its result to be a mirror image. But while the Tories picked up the votes of 64 per cent of people who said they were "already feeling some of the benefits of an economic recovery" (a sentiment most common among the well-off, or ABs), Labour only gathered the support of 43 per cent of those who were neither feeling nor expected to feel those benefits (predominantly DEs).[57] As Professor John Curtice wrote, "Rather than a failure to win over the support of relatively affluent, more 'aspirational' middle class voters, the Achilles' heel of Labour's campaign appears to have been a failure to convince those who were sceptical about the Conservatives' economic record that Labour offered an attractive alternative."[58]

Lastly, Labour would disproportionately benefit if it could engage non-voters.[59] A third of those eligible to vote in 2015 chose not to—outnumbering the entire Labour vote. Turnout was lowest in the parts of the electorate where Labour should have done best. Only 57 per cent of predominantly working class DE voters cast a ballot, compared to 75 per cent of ABs. This class differential was not a law of nature but a recent development. Before 1987 working class people were just as likely to vote as those from the middle class. The emergence of a turnout gap coincided with the dropping of class from the language of mainstream politics and the abandonment of significant social change as a goal. For many years, studies had found a growing feeling among working class people that Labour no longer stood for their interests. Many asked why they should vote when politicians were 'all the same.'[60]

Labour had a large lead over the Tories among another group hit by austerity: 18-24 year olds. People of this age bracket thought the cost of living crisis was a bigger problem than the deficit.[61] But only 52 per cent of them voted. The Conservative victory, meanwhile, was delivered by the over-65s, 79 per cent of whom turned out.[62] (Labour actually won the 2015 election among under-50s, but lost very heavily with the old.)[63]

According to polling company Ipsos MORI, nearly 3 million people who identified as Labour supporters did not cast a ballot.[64] These people needed to be given a reason to vote. Promising them more hardship through further cuts was not going to do it. Offering the prospect of change might. A strategy of mobilising non-voters is a difficult thing to pull off, but it looked worth a try.[65]

Of course, the two big truths that hurt Labour—distrust on the economy and a lack of clarity about what the party stood for—were not the whole story. This account is not a comprehensive analysis of the election loss but a summary of how the politics of defeat shaped up. Other issues contributed to Labour's plight, particularly immigration, welfare and voters' perception of Miliband—although on all three the picture was more complex than is commonly thought.[66]

Following the election, there was no question that the scale of the task facing Labour was formidable. Its poor performance in 2015 meant that to win a majority at the next election it would have to gain 94 seats. Making things harder, the result left far fewer marginal seats for the taking.[67] But the fact that the odds were stacked against Labour strengthened a sense that it needed to do something dramatic. It had been playing a losing game, competing on an economic pitch defined by the Conservatives. Unless it could change the game, it would lose again.

4

FROM DESPAIR TO WHERE?

"This is the darkest hour that socialists in Britain have faced since the Attlee government fell in 1951."
—*John McDonnell*

"We've done the calculations—myself and Jeremy—of the number of potential nominations and we can't get it above 19 or 20," says John McDonnell. It is the Tuesday after the general election, Ed Miliband has resigned as Labour leader, and McDonnell is explaining that it is "highly unlikely" a left candidate can secure the backing of the 35 MPs needed to claim a place in the contest to succeed him.

McDonnell is addressing a meeting of the Left Platform, a new umbrella group for the Labour left. Originally convened to agree demands to put to a possible Labour-led coalition government, the Conservative victory means the group is instead discussing the left's desperate position within the party.

The point is strongly made from the floor that, although there is little chance of a candidate clearing the nomination threshold, someone should at least try. Even a doomed campaign for nominations could act as a brake on a post-election debate careering alarmingly to the right. But McDonnell rules himself out, having failed to get on the ballot paper in 2007 and 2010, and wary of risking his health after suffering a mild heart attack in 2013. The meeting delegates Jeremy Corbyn and fellow MP Kelvin Hopkins to find other candidates. And then the agenda moves on to the more hopeful terrain of "extra-parliamentary struggle."[1]

·····

On the eve of its greatest ever success, the Labour left perceived itself to be at the weakest point in its history. This incongruity contains within it all the drama of Jeremy Corbyn's victory—a rags-to-riches tale (without the riches, and with the rags retained); politics-as-film script. But the left's certainty of its own weakness in May 2015 is more than just a charming irony. In a killer plot twist, it is what made Corbyn's candidacy possible. Doors were opened to the left that would certainly have been slammed shut had the threat it posed been appreciated. And it was out of weakness that the left selected an unlikely and reluctant leadership candidate—one who, against all expectations, would prove to be the ideal casting.

The Labour left, a once a mighty force within the Labour Movement—never dominant, but often dynamic—had by May 2015 retreated into obscurity. "It seemed to have ceased to exist," recalls Owen Jones. "Privately some people were suggesting that was it for the left in the Labour Party, and that a new party was now inevitable."

The left's long decline began three-and-a-half decades earlier, with the ebbing of the grassroots insurgency that propelled Tony Benn to the fore. Integral to the Bennite movement was the Campaign for Labour Party Democracy (CLPD), founded in 1973.[2] The CLPD's mission was to wrest power from the parliamentary party and relocate it among rank-and-file members. Its two big triumphs were the introduction of mandatory reselection, which required MPs to win the support of their local party members before every election (a mechanism that was scrapped in 1990), and the electoral college system for electing the leader and deputy leader of the party.

As soon as the electoral college was in place Benn made use of it, challenging Denis Healey for the deputy leadership in 1981. This was the climax of the Bennite revolt, an epic battle that Benn came within 0.8 per cent of winning (Benn's campaign was run by Jon Lansman, then a young CLPD activist, now an older CLPD activist and the founder of Momentum). The contest split the Tribune Group, the primary organisation of left MPs in parliament. Led by Neil Kinnock, a section of the group turned against the Bennites and made common cause with the right—an alliance that would eventually lead to New Labour. Benn and his comrades, meanwhile, founded the Socialist Campaign Group of MPs. The two sides were unflatteringly labelled the 'soft left' (Tribune) and 'hard left' (Campaign Group). The legacy of this division runs through the decades.[3]

As the tide of Bennite activism receded after 1981, the Campaign Group found itself politically marooned in parliament. Its size and influence dwindled. By 2007, when Tony Blair resigned as prime minister, the group comprised just 24 of 353 Labour MPs.[4] This explains why Gordon Brown faced no leadership contest that year. Two MPs from the Campaign Group—Michael Meacher and John McDonnell—sought to stand, but neither could scrape together the 45 nominations needed to get on the ballot paper.[5] Commentators gleefully declared the death of the left. "It's pathetic," presenter Andrew Neil said to Diane Abbott on the BBC show *This Week*. "Your lot can't even muster 45 backers."[6] (Three years later Abbott herself did make it into a leadership contest after being 'lent' nominations from MPs, but her campaign did not take off.)

In the run-up to his 2007 leadership bid McDonnell had attempted to rebuild the left at the grassroots level with nearly a year of travelling and speaking to countless meetings. Much of the energy he generated was channelled into the Labour Representation Committee (LRC). Set up in 2004 by McDonnell, Jeremy Corbyn and others, the LRC had the architecture to be a serious force, with affiliations from several unions.[7] But in subsequent years it became bogged down in bureaucratic micro-conflicts, including a bizarre battle over control of the magazine *Labour Briefing* that resulted in two versions of the same title existing simultaneously. Owen Jones remembers "going to the LRC conference in 2013 and there was a pathetic number of people who turned up. Generally people were older, without sounding ageist... I remember John [McDonnell] turned to me and said 'It looks like a funeral.'" For LRC national committee member Michael Calderbank, the organisation "didn't have the capacity to reach out to a new audience. It had the politics to do it... But it didn't have the organisational reach."

The CLPD was still plugging away inside the party, concentrating on rule changes, preparing motions for conference, and exposing the abuses of the party machine. This was vital work. But while the CLPD was a reliable presence on the left, it was far from the dynamic element that it had been in the 1970s and 1980s. It was, though, the driving force behind the Centre Left Grassroots Alliance, a slate of candidates that stood in internal party elections and regularly won, much to the leadership's annoyance.

Meanwhile, a new internet-savvy generation of Labour left activists was making its presence felt online. Red Labour, described by organiser James Doran as "a cheeky and assertive digital Bennite social media project," emerged as a humble Facebook page in 2011. It was a hit, picking up 20,000 subscribers in a few years, making it the biggest Labour-related page on Facebook bar the party's official one.[8] At the heart of Red Labour were people like Ben Sellers who had come out of the LRC in order to "move on... into the 21st century." The secret of Red Labour's success, according to Sellers, was that it was "always seen as a serious intervention into the party, but we weren't prepared to play by the rules which seemed to have been set out by those on the left and right of us. It wasn't quite so earnest as either—it was explicitly populist and accessible."[9] But while a following of 20,000 was impressive, clicking "like" on Facebook was a much lower bar of commitment than paying an annual membership fee to a traditional organisation.

On the eve of Corbynsim, the CLPD, the LRC and Red Labour were the three organisational nerve centres of the Labour left. Each came with drawbacks, but they were all that activists had. For some, that did not inspire confidence. "I was very pessimistic about the Labour left, despite being an active member," says Max Shanly, who was involved in all three groups. "I thought everybody was fucking useless." ("I feel bad about that," he adds, "I was wrong.")

With hindsight, things were not as bleak as they seemed. Red Labour had an optimistic aura and a coterie of creative young activists. Both the CLPD and the LRC retained important assets, including mailing lists, know-how, and an extensive network of contacts in local Labour parties across the country. The three organisations would later coalesce in the Corbyn campaign, their distinct cultures shaping discrete parts of the operation. The campaign machine would be infused with CLPD organising skill; its political centre of gravity would owe much to the LRC; and Red Labour would effectively become the 'Corbyn For Leader' social media team. But, in reaching that point, these groups' most valuable contribution was simply their determination to keep on keeping on. It mattered that the left remained "a legitimate force in the party," as Shanly puts it. "We might have been a bit of a useless force, but we were a legitimate force."

The same could be said of the Socialist Campaign Group in parliament. For former member Alan Simpson, the heavily depleted group remained "the only bolt-hole of real political thought" in the PLP, a collection of politicians "who set out to explain that we always had bigger and better choices open to us."[10] As they clung on to their place in the PLP by their fingernails it often seemed scarcely worth the trouble. Many colleagues regarded them as irritants or worse; friends on the broader left thought they were deluded in their fealty to a lost party. But in preserving their political strand within parliament, they kept alive the microscopically small likelihood of a resurgence. Only in retrospect can the significance of their stubbornness be appreciated.

Having endured to 2015, suddenly the left had a glimmer of hope on the horizon. The general election, despite its disappointments, yielded "about a dozen" new left MPs, adding "quality and younger people we can rely on for a number of years" to the parliamentary left, in the view of Lansman. But with others losing their seats—including Katy Clark, Corbyn's future political secretary—the left was "still at a very weak point in the PLP."

Such was the situation confronting John McDonnell as he gave his pessimistic prognosis to the Left Platform meeting on 12

May. "At that stage Jeremy and I were arguing very, very strongly that we would never be able to get anyone from the left onto the ballot," he recalled later. "Please do not take any racing tips from me."[11]

· · · · ·

The Corbyn phenomenon of summer 2015 was fused from a nebula of diffuse activity. One of the earliest elements to become visible to the naked eye was an online petition calling for an anti-austerity candidate to stand for leader. Like so much of the later Corbyn explosion, it was a spontaneous initiative from the grassroots. But it was inspired by the new left MPs.

Alarmed at the early direction of the leadership debate, a group of newly-elected parliamentarians published a letter in the *Guardian* on 15 May calling for "a new leader who looks forward and will challenge an agenda of cuts, take on big business and will set out an alternative to austerity."[12] Signed by 10 MPs—most of whom went on to become familiar names among Corbyn supporters, including Richard Burgon, Clive Lewis, Rebecca Long-Bailey, Kate Osamor and Cat Smith—the letter did not call for a particular colleague to stand, but merely expressed support for the idea of an anti-austerity candidacy.[13] Though an unusual intervention from new MPs, it was not headline news—but it had a powerful effect on one particular Labour Party member. Michelle Ryan, an aromatherapist living in Worthing in West Sussex, was inspired to action.[14] "It jumped out at me," she says. "I thought, 'That's such a good idea, we need to support them... The members should back them up.'"

Ryan posted on a new pro-Labour Facebook page she had joined, suggesting members write a letter of their own in solidarity with the MPs. She was soon collaborating with Rebecca Barnes, a railway worker from Orpington in Kent, who offered to write it. "I started the letter at the end of my shift and put it together on the train home, on my phone," says Barnes. "It was a very productive train ride. It's only about 12 minutes as well."[15]

Ryan and Barnes enlisted the help of Red Labour to spread the word. Working with Naomi Fearon, a Lancashire-based Red

Labour organiser, they put the text online in the form of a petition hosted by the campaigning network 38 degrees. It went live on 20 May under the title: "We want an Anti-Austerity Labour Leader Candidate to Stand."[16]

"The three musketeers," as Ryan describes the group, set about promoting the cause on social media. While Fearon had the Red Labour networks at her disposal, Ryan and Barnes were Twitter novices. "I just started tweeting at anyone who said, 'Oh God, these candidates are awful,' or 'I hate Andy Burnham,'" says Ryan. "Any moaning—I just scoured Twitter all day." The trio were thrilled when John McDonnell retweeted them. Ryan was less excited when Jeremy Corbyn signed the petition—he was not as well known to her.[17]

The petition became the main online expression of the desire for an anti-austerity candidate. It attracted 5,000 signatures, a number dwarfed by the size of the later mobilisation for Corbyn, but a signifier of latent support. McDonnell later spoke of "the wisdom of crowds" in identifying the potential of the moment before he did.[18]

Tellingly, Ryan and Barnes were regular, mainstream Labour Party members. Their motivations were a harbinger of the phenomenon that would sweep the party over the summer. "I wouldn't have thought of myself as strongly left wing or anything," says Ryan, who joined Labour to have a say in its 2010 leadership contest. "I voted for Ed Miliband. I suppose a lot of people assume that people who vote Corbyn would have been Diane Abbott supporters."

Barnes first joined the party in the 1990s, before leaving in the Blair era. She then became an active trade unionist "because I was replaced by a machine at one of the stations I worked at." She re-joined Labour before the 2015 election, encouraged by some of Miliband's policies. "I thought, 'I'm going to give them my support, they're starting to move back to where Labour should be.'"

Both Ryan and Barnes initially supported Andy Burnham in the 2015 contest. But when he described the mansion tax as the politics of envy Ryan baulked.[19] "It just sent a cold chill down me," she says. "If you can't tax wealth, you can't tackle inequality."[20]

Barnes had the same reaction: "I quite liked Andy Burnham. I still quite like him but he'd said something about the politics of envy and I thought, 'Really? I don't sit comfortably with that.' It's not the politics of envy at all."

It was the sense that the leadership hopefuls were hurtling in the opposite direction to the membership that galvanised Ryan and Barnes to act, just as it had moved the new MPs to write their letter. It was a sentiment that would intensify as the contest developed.

· · · · ·

There was nearly a month between the general election defeat and Jeremy Corbyn's announcement that he would stand for leader. For those with an interest in the top job, the left's absence removed any restraint on what became a race to the right. As the debate all but suffocated in an atmosphere of mandatory Blairism, not only the Labour left was appalled—the contest was widely regarded as a flop. It was "a festival of vacuous waffle," according to the commentator Steve Richards.[21] Labour had "fallen in on itself like a soufflé," thought the *Guardian*'s Aditya Chakrabortty.[22]

It was difficult to find a Blairite who was not considering standing. As well as Liz Kendall, who declared early, speculation swirled around Chuka Umunna, Dan Jarvis, Tristram Hunt and Mary Creagh. Three other names that were in the background— Caroline Flint, Stella Creasy and Ben Bradshaw—eventually stood for the deputy leadership. All of these figures had essentially the same politics, making the Blairites' failure to agree on a single candidate perplexing.

The most hotly tipped of the Blairites was Umunna. The bookies immediately had him as the 2/1 favourite.[23] A vocal Ed Miliband supporter in 2010, he confounded everybody by moving right in the intervening years to embrace Blairism just as it was on the wane.[24] He burnished his credentials on the first post-election edition of the BBC's Andrew Marr programme on 10 May 2015 in which he found himself sat next to fellow guest Lord Mandelson, who was only on the programme to put the boot into Miliband.

In typical style, Mandelson offered Umunna a pointlessly cryptic endorsement: "There's a little wait to go, but I think he'll get there."[25] To many Labour members already despondent at the election result, this was a miserable spectacle.

Umunna and Kendall were described as "behaving like family members taking jewellery off a corpse" for their haste in setting out their stalls.[26] But, no sooner had he arrived, Umunna was gone, mysteriously pulling out of the race, depriving the Blairites of their most plausible prospect. Kendall, a relative unknown, was left to fight for the Blairite crown with Creagh, another unknown, and Hunt. Their jostling had wider consequences. The gravitational pull of the mass of Blairite candidates dragged the entire contest to the right.

The Blairites were the ideal villains. Ideologically they exhibited all the signs of rigor mortis. Their thinking had become inflexible, their presentation stiff. Having once been associated with the future, they now harked back to a past tainted by war, financial crisis and party atrophy. But ideal villains must also be weaker than they look. The nominations process revealed that the Blairites were a diminished force. They could only muster enough support to get one representative onto the ballot with little to spare (Kendall eventually received 41 nominations, only six clear of the threshold). The lack of a standout candidate, demonstrated by the need to turn to the untested Kendall, reflected the declining quality of the surviving Blairite MPs. And the spectacle of so many contenders slugging it out was an embarrassment for a wing of the party that retained a fearsome, but apparently undeserved, reputation for fixing contests.

Crucially, these weaknesses were obscured by the Blairites' last remaining asset—media support. Kendall caught the imagination of the press with her maximal Blairite pitch. At the end of May Michael Crick, the experienced political journalist, encapsulated media sentiment with a prophetic tweet: "Under my law of leadership elections—that the freshest and/or youngest contender usually wins—you should bet on Liz Kendall."[27] With proceedings stuck in the Westminster bubble for the nominations period, no firm evidence was available to contradict the conventional political unwisdom of the commentariat. This led Kendall's opponents to overestimate her, including two challengers hoping to appeal more broadly in the party: Yvette Cooper and Andy Burnham. They responded by moving conspicuously to the right.

Cooper was the Brownite standard-bearer.[28] In her opening intervention on 19 May she attacked the party's election platform as too anti-business and argued that Labour "can't be set against the government's recent cut in corporation tax." Beyond that she spoke only in vacuities, promising to be "credible, compassionate, creative and connected to the day-to-day realities of life"; to "move beyond the old labels of left and right"; and, controversially, to "make life better for families."[29]

Burnham's journey was more dramatic and consequential. Seen as a Blairite in his early career, under Miliband as shadow health secretary he endeared himself to the unions and the membership by opposing aspects of NHS privatisation. He was expected to hoover up leftish votes as the least worst candidate on offer, but also had support on the Labour right and in his home region of the North West. With such apparently wide appeal he became the favourite after Umunna's withdrawal.

Egged on by his two biggest backers among MPs—Michael Dugher, his campaign manager, and Rachel Reeves, an evangelist for massive public spending cuts who was being readied for shadow chancellor—Burnham lurched to the right.[30] He declared Miliband's break with New Labour a "mistake."[31] As well as trashing the mansion tax, he indicated support for the Tories' planned reduction of the benefits cap, despite evidence it would put thousands of children into poverty.[32] He went out of his way to distance himself from the trade unions, saying his campaign would not accept their money. Within the narrow confines of the nominations battle this positioning seemed to work. Burnham scooped up pledges of support from MPs and gained favourable coverage in the press. When he gave his first speech of the campaign at the City consultancy firm Ernst & Young on 30 May, in which he proclaimed businessmen "heroes" and said people on benefits should not get an "easy ride," it earned him a glowing write-up from the *New Statesman*, which declared: "By demonstrating early on that he has learned from the failure of Labour's economic message he has strengthened his candidacy."[33]

On another occasion Burnham "admitted" that in government Labour "didn't prioritise deficit reduction early enough... therefore we weren't in a strong enough position when the crash came."[34] The context for the remark was the strangest spectacle of the early phase of the contest, as the candidates competed over who could denounce Labour's past spending with most conviction. Tristram Hunt was the clear winner, saying on the BBC's *Question Time* programme: "Yes we overspent because we did not leave enough headroom in the public finances to deal with a cyclical banking crisis. And so when the banking crisis hit, what we didn't have was the kind of leeway that we needed."[35] Seeing as the "leeway that we needed" amounted to hundreds of billions of pounds, Hunt appeared to be advocating running a ginormous surplus, just in case it had to be given to the banks. As well as being economically absurd, this line—echoed with varying degrees of subtlety by Kendall, Creagh and Umunna—was politically masochistic, since it validated the myth that public spending had caused the recession. Only Cooper explained that the relatively small pre-crash deficit made no difference to the UK's ability to deal with the financial crisis, although she regretted that there had been a deficit at all.[36] As Corbyn's future policy advisor Andrew Fisher pointed out at the time, these confessions placed all the candidates well to the right of the position occupied by George Osborne and David Cameron in 2007, when, on the eve of the crisis, they pledged to match Labour's spending plans.[37]

Having the backing of fellow MPs was seen as important to candidates for generating momentum and demonstrating authority. The Burnham campaign, which was never in any danger of falling short of securing 35 names, nevertheless ran a "whipping operation" aimed at maximising nominations.[38] By tacking right to attract MPs who may otherwise have chosen Kendall, both Burnham and Cooper also hoped to put a brake on the media momentum building up behind their Blairite rival. But this generated a dynamic pushing them away from the views of the wider membership, as over the years the PLP had developed a political culture all of its own.

Burnham's calculations had consequences. His rightwards swoop created a gaping hole to his left. Traditionally, this is where the 'soft left' would be found. But its failure over many years to establish its own agenda or organisational presence meant that anyone unhappy at the prospect of Labour shifting right (including the unions and much of the party membership) was ready to look elsewhere.[39] In any case, following the election the 'soft left' seemed to have fled the scene along with Ed Miliband, who was spotted recovering from his ordeal in Ibiza. No 'soft left' candidate came forward. Lisa Nandy was the most talked about possibility, but quickly ruled herself out. Sadiq Khan was running for London Mayor. Had a 'soft left' candidate stood, it is unlikely that Corbyn would have been able to secure the required nominations, and doubtful he would even have tried.

Burnham could plausibly have occupied 'soft left' territory. In retrospect, his decision to abandon the ground was a catastrophic strategic error. "He just fucked it up completely," says Michael Calderbank of the LRC. "It was definitely Burnham's election to lose." According to Jon Lansman, Burnham "so quickly collapsed to the right that he just destroyed his credibility" as a 'soft left' option. As Burnham saw it, credibility with the left was a lower priority than scotching the notion that he was the 'continuity Miliband' candidate. And there was a more cynical motivation. Commenting to the *New Statesman* on 3 June, one Burnham ally said of his candidate's disgruntled left supporters: "Where else do they have to go?"[40] He would soon find out.

· · · · ·

The question for the left was: who will stand? Among activists, John McDonnell was the obvious choice as the *de facto* leader of the Labour left. The fact that he instantly ruled himself out presented something of a problem, but supporters were not to be discouraged. Soon after election day Red Labour organiser James Doran set up a Facebook page under the name: "We want John McDonnell as Labour leader." "One friend said you've picked the wrong person," Doran recalls. "In a way, much as I love John, he doesn't suffer fools gladly, and there's a number of them in parliament."

Casting about for an alternative name, activists first focused on Ian Lavery, the former president of the National Union of Mineworkers. As a working class MP and member of the Socialist Campaign Group he had good credentials. Privately, some union figures were urging him to stand. But just a week after the general election he not only ruled himself out but pledged his support to Andy Burnham, prompting a frustrated Jon Lansman to post on the *Left Futures* blog that it was "entirely premature for anyone on the left to wholeheartedly commit" to Burnham. "The left throws away its leverage by settling for too little too soon."[41]

Lansman's annoyance stemmed from the fact that, behind the scenes, he was working frantically to ensure there would be a left candidate. "I was talking to Michael Meacher, John McDonnell, Jon Trickett," he says. "All of them had big disadvantages and none of them wanted to do it." Lansman did not know it at the time, but Meacher was suffering with an illness that would overcome him five months later. Despite having his own health worries, it is tempting to imagine that McDonnell might have gone for it had he known there was a chance to win. But he was painfully aware that, just as in the past, he was unlikely to attract enough nominations to get into the contest. "There was no way they were going to let me on the ballot," he later joked, "I'm amazed I'm still there [in parliament]."[42]

Trickett, a shadow cabinet minister, was on paper the most plausible option. As Parliamentary Private Secretary to Gordon Brown and then a confidant of Ed Miliband, he had carved out a unique role as an informal conduit between the left and the Labour leadership. But this meant there was a distance between him and the activists pushing for a candidate. Some questioned whether he could be a credible anti-austerity campaigner having served in a shadow cabinet that had promised more austerity.[43] There were also some old intra-left tensions with the LRC set.[44] Asked after Corbyn's victory why he did not stand for the leadership, Trickett explained: "I didn't think I could unite the left. I'd been on the front bench for seven years. It needed someone from a completely fresh point of view."[45] He ruled himself out on 14 May 2015.

The left's early attempts to find a candidate had come to nothing. The chances of getting on the ballot were diminishing with every promise of support Burnham picked up. It looked as if most trade unions would back Burnham, too, depriving any left challenger of the networks of influence that could swing nominations their way. A despairing Lansman published a blog on 17 May, despondently declaring:

> There will be no left candidate... and there were no left candidates in a position to win (especially after the party's acceptance of the Collins report) even if they could have found 35 nominators in a parliamentary party which is not significantly to the left of its predecessor. The deliberate exclusion and marginalisation of the left by Tony Blair ensured that this would be the case for at least a generation.[46]

Others thought that standing a candidate would be a mistake even if one could be found. Among them was McDonnell. "My argument, and Jeremy was the same really, was that not getting on the ballot paper would be so crushing that it would set us back," he says. "The last thing you want to do is march people up to the top of the hill and then say to them, 'I'm sorry, we're not going to make it.'"[47]

Owen Jones, meanwhile, favoured backing a 'soft left' challenger. He launched a campaign to encourage Lisa Nandy to stand, but she was not going to do it. He then started planning with Trickett a 'Not The Labour Leadership' tour intended to rebuild the grassroots. Both initiatives were rooted in Jones' conviction that the left was so weak that to stick its neck out was too big a risk: "I didn't originally want a 'left' candidate in the Labour leadership election. My view was that, in the midst of general post-election demoralisation, a left candidate could end up being crushed. Such a result would be used by both the Labour Party establishment and the British right generally to perform the last rites of the left, dismiss us as irrelevant, and tell us to shut up forever."[48]

If those on the inside were giving up, the activists were having none of it. "We did badger John [McDonnell] quite a bit," says Ben Sellers, whose experience with Red Labour convinced him there was a simmering anger at New Labour-style politics. "We had a feeling that if we did have a left candidate, even if it wasn't the ideal candidate, we would tap into some of that... We were saying to John that we wouldn't be relying on just those old networks, we've got this new network which is based around social media."

The case for sitting-out the contest was constantly being undermined as the existing candidates said ever-more alarming things. One of Corbyn's future advisors recalls: "What really drove people like me to push for [standing a candidate] was the whole tenor of the debate. The whole narrative was 'we need to move to the right'... This was getting to the point where you go, 'I'm not sure I'll be able to take this if this is the direction it goes in. We've got to at least have a go.'"

Nobody thought that a left candidate had a chance of winning. The aim was merely to influence the debate. For those with a trade union mind-set the argument was obvious: without a name in the frame the left had no bargaining power over the other runners and no means of securing policy concessions.

Lying behind this imperative was the issue of the Labour left's long-term marginalisation. Had other avenues been available to affect the direction of the party, standing a candidate may not have been a priority. But Labour's internal democracy had been so debased in the Blair years that leadership elections were one of the few remaining opportunities for the left to have its voice heard. A place in the contest would offer a chance to "build the left in the party and give it that organisation that it hadn't had for so long," as Sellers puts it.

By the third week of May a sense of ferment began to overtake those who wanted a candidate. The clock was ticking down to the nominations deadline of 15 June. Behind the scenes frantic calls flew back and forth. "We started thinking about almost anyone," says Lansman. "We felt you couldn't really have anyone who was new, but we thought about Keir Starmer [a new MP but former Director of Public Prosecutions]. We even thought about Angela Eagle at one point, could we back Angela? Would she stand? I made a call, I urged her to stand on the basis that she'd be better than the others... We were desperate."

Activists had no such qualms about the new arrivals to parliament, and were pestering them to run. Michelle Ryan was among many Labour members in communication with Clive Lewis, who had developed an instant rapport with the grassroots. "I actually asked him to stand," she says. "I sent him a message and said 'Can you stand for Labour leader?' And he said, 'I don't even know where the toilets are.'"

The CLPD was now "very actively pushing for someone to stand," Lansman remembers. Over the weekend of 23-24 May it decided to have another go at Trickett.[49] By publicly declaring him its choice for leader, the CLPD hoped to "draft" Trickett into standing.[50] Lansman and Pete Willsman, the CLPD secretary, visited Trickett to try to persuade him in person. But he would not budge.[51]

Meanwhile, John McDonnell was penning an utterly bleak article for *Labour Briefing*, the journal published by the LRC. "This is the darkest hour that socialists in Britain have faced since the Attlee government fell in 1951," it began.

> That the candidates for the Labour leadership so far have failed to mount the slightest challenge to capital shows the abject state of near surrender of the Labour Party. No core Labour principle is safe… Redistribution of wealth through taxation is denounced as 'the politics of envy.' Privatisation of the NHS is acceptable as long as it 'works.' Caps on welfare benefits and toughening the treatment of migrants are supported because they were 'doorstep issues.'[52]

"Everybody was tearing their hair out, there was despair," recalls Michael Calderbank. "The situation was so desperate people were thinking 'Why am I in this party anyway? Not only has it just fucked up and failed to challenge Cameron, but it's likely to compound that by drawing the wrong lessons.'"

A wacky idea now took shape within the CLPD. "Could we find someone who would be a caretaker leader, who would do it in order to have a debate about the future direction of the party and then have another leadership election two years later?" Lansman recalls. "It was in that context that we began to think about people like Jeremy." Remarkably, Lansman says, until this point the idea of Jeremy Corbyn running "never entered my head." "We suffered from a blindness to anything other than a conventionally acceptable candidate. I thought John McDonnell was credible, Michael Meacher was, Jon Trickett was for conventional reasons."

On 26 May, Lansman attended a drinks reception for new Labour MPs hosted by TULO, the Labour-union liaison organisation. There he spoke to TULO's national officer, Byron Taylor. Lansman—who had adopted an optimistic attitude despite everything—approached Taylor and said: "I think we can get 35 nominations but the question is who's the candidate?" Lansman ran through the list of names and the obstacles to each of them standing. Taylor's answer was instant.

"It's got to be Jeremy," he said.

"Jeremy? Really Byron? Why?" Lansman replied, taken aback at Taylor's certainty.

"Look, he's got all the right policies," explained Taylor. "People will vote for Jeremy. They like him. They respect him. Jeremy's the nicest man in politics. He hasn't got any enemies."

The last line struck Lansman. "I'd never thought of it like that," he remembers. "I'd never thought of looking for a candidate without enemies... That really sold me on the idea. That was when I started really arguing for Jeremy."

The following day, 27 May, saw the first of two fateful meetings of the Socialist Campaign Group—the body that would decide whether to stand a left candidate.[53] The MPs who gathered in Westminster debated if it would be wise. "There were some who thought that we'll be humiliated, that we'll look weak," recalls Clive Lewis, "and I remember saying: 'If we don't stand anyone we'll look even weaker.'" They discussed the alternative of backing an existing candidate in return for concessions, but there was no agreement. Overshadowing it all was the problem that, if they did wish to run a candidate, there were still no volunteers. McDonnell and Diane Abbott affirmed that neither of them would run—the latter because she was seeking to become Labour's candidate for London mayor.[54]

And then, tentatively, Corbyn raised a suggestion: "What about if I stand?"

According to Lewis, there was "silence around the room. There were some people, for a variety of reasons, who weren't keen on it—some, I think, because they were worried about what would happen to Jeremy."[55] The meeting ended inconclusively, but the idea was now under consideration.

As an integral member of the Labour left, Corbyn had been in the middle of the agonising search for a candidate all along. As early as 12 May he had said it was "essential that there is a left anti-austerity candidate in the leadership election," even as he shared McDonnell's scepticism about the numbers.[56] All of the organised groups—the LRC, the CLPD, Red Labour and others—had come to the same view. Thousands were signing the petition calling for an anti-austerity contender. Here was a problem that Corbyn could solve.

With a firm Bennite conception of his role as an MP ("I always try to encourage people in what they are trying to achieve; MPs can't do everything themselves, we're not gods, but if an MP says 'I will support you,' that is probably a help") Corbyn felt a sense of duty to step up.[57] Explaining his motivations later on, he framed the decision as a "response to an overwhelming call by Labour Party members who want to see a broader range of candidates and a thorough debate about the future of the party."[58] He insisted he put himself forward selflessly "because people asked me to," saying: "I am much too old for personal ambition."[59]

Though Corbyn was standing out of duty, on 27 May it seemed like a relatively small sacrifice. Despite Lansman's optimism, the chance of getting 35 nominations looked slim. In all probability Corbyn was volunteering for a couple of weeks of lobbying and media appearances, a chance to raise the issue of austerity and, when he failed to make the ballot, to demonstrate that the leadership election rules were rigged against the left.

Nevertheless, the silence that greeted Corbyn's offer at the Campaign Group suggested that not everyone thought it was a good idea. Another meeting was scheduled for the following week, 3 June. In the interim, discussion raged within a small group at the heart of the Labour left over the merits of a Corbyn candidacy. Pete Willsman of the CLPD argued that to have any hope of getting on the ballot Corbyn would need to make a public promise to serve for only two years to oversee a policy debate.[60] The sceptical Owen Jones, meanwhile, thought Corbyn was the wrong candidate:

> I've known Jeremy for years and I'm very fond of him but I wasn't convinced he'd be the best spokesperson for the left... We often called him the foreign secretary of the left because he was so interested in international causes from Palestine to Kurdistan... He's so used to speaking to people who are left wing activists that I was worried that during a leadership campaign he wouldn't be able to communicate all his ideas in a way that would inspire people outside of left wing political milieus.

Jones was swimming against the tide. "Basically Jeremy began to gather various people lobbying for him," says Lansman, "mainly CLPD people and Byron [Taylor]." He also picked up momentum among MPs, with Michael Meacher, Cat Smith, Clive Lewis and others becoming strong advocates.

But the man himself was still weighing it up. On the eve of the all-important 3 June Campaign Group meeting he met an ally, later to take up a senior position in his campaign, who recalls: "We were sitting on the terrace at the House of Commons. We were talking with John [McDonnell] and Jeremy and a few other people. John was still quite anti-standing a candidate at all. John was talking to somebody else for a moment, and Jeremy said, 'John doesn't want to do it, Diane doesn't want to do it again, do you think I should?' I said, 'Yeah, I think you should.'"

As they spoke the ally got the impression Corbyn was quite keen on the idea. "He had no expectation of getting on the ballot paper but I think he, like me and everyone else, was just despairing at the state of the debate within the party and wanted it to change." With Abbott and McDonnell out of the picture "he knew it fell to him" to change it.

The following day, before Corbyn went to the Campaign Group, he was scheduled to speak at the Labour Link meeting of Unison's Islington branch.[61] Attendees, including Unison activist and LRC member Andrew Berry, used the chance to raise the question of the leadership: "We lobbied him that we needed an anti-austerity candidate, and he gave a rather cryptic answer which I only really got later. It was something like 'There's still time. We'll have to see.'"

Corbyn then headed to parliament for his date with destiny. With time running out, that day's Campaign Group would be the decisive meeting.

5

GETTING ON THE BALLOT

"Why are you bothering because you're frankly not going to win, are you?"

—Mark Mardell, presenter, BBC Radio 4

In room W1 off Westminster Hall in the Houses of Parliament the Socialist Campaign Group is meeting to decide whether Jeremy Corbyn should stand for Labour leader. There are no journalists outside with their ears to the door. There are no camera crews on standby, no breaking news alerts, and there is no *Guardian* live blog. No voices from the right of the party are issuing dark warnings of impending doom. Simon Danczuk is not yet aware that he should be angry. In fact, there is virtually no anticipation at all—not even from the Labour left, most of which is unaware that the meeting is taking place.

It is 3 June 2015. There are just 12 days left until the deadline for nominations. Any candidate that has not been endorsed by at least 35 MPs when Big Ben strikes twelve noon on Monday, 15 June will not be allowed to take part in the leadership contest. The other runners have been campaigning for nearly a month. They have staff, offices, money and strategies. Some of them have been lobbying colleagues for support since election night. Most

Labour MPs have already decided whom they will back. If the left is serious about taking part, it needs to get on with it.

Since Corbyn indicated that he might be willing to stand he has been canvassing opinion and taking advice from a small circle of allies, receiving a largely enthusiastic response. Cat Smith, the young MP, has arrived at the meeting confident that her friend will run "after much nagging from me and others." Jon Lansman has come into the room determined that Corbyn should stand and, unbeknown to Corbyn himself, has been busy persuading people to attend the meeting to back him. Michael Meacher, for one, is "completely on board."

The attendees—who also include John McDonnell, Diane Abbott, Kelvin Hopkins and Clive Lewis—are under strong pressure from activists to put forward a candidate. The prevailing view is that there must be a left presence. The question is whether they truly have a willing volunteer.

McDonnell, who is chairing the meeting, confirms that he will not stand. "I've done it enough times, I'm not doing it again," he says. Abbott echoes the sentiment, saying she does not fancy it after running in 2010.

McDonnell turns to Corbyn, who is sitting at the end of the table, and says flatly: "It's your turn."

Suddenly the whole room is looking at Corbyn. "All right," he says to his colleagues. "I'll stand if I've got your support."

"OK, if you're going to do it, we'll back you," comes the reply.

Corbyn is a leadership candidate.[1]

· · · · ·

Jeremy Corbyn was propelled to the head of the Labour Party by big historical trends years in the making. But there was nothing inevitable about it. During the tense 12-day effort to cobble together enough MPs' nominations for a place in the contest, his fate was agonisingly dependent on the nitty-gritty of PLP politics. This was the most difficult stage of the entire campaign—it had been designed to be so. The newly raised threshold requiring a candidate to be nominated by 15 per cent of Labour MPs—a result of the Collins Review—was intended to prevent someone like Corbyn joining the field.[2] "Fifteen per cent was judged to be a safe barrier to any outsider—especially someone from the hard left," wrote Declan McHugh, who worked on the reforms.[3] That the embryonic Corbyn campaign nevertheless cleared this hurdle was down to a combination of ultra-modern digital lobbying—inconceivable before the social media age—and behind-the-scenes parliamentary networking of the old-fashioned kind.

The job began immediately. Cat Smith, who counts Corbyn as her "closest friend" among MPs having worked for him before being elected to parliament herself, began making a list of names on her iPad and assigning lobbying duties to the others present at the Campaign Group meeting. "Cat was immediately right down to business," remembers Jon Lansman. "She's still an activist, Cat, basically." Smith's partner, Ben Soffa, was an IT techie who worked for the railway workers' union TSSA. She gave him a call as the meeting wound up. "Right, Ben, what are you doing?" she said. "We need a website now for Jeremy. He's going to run for leader of the Labour Party." Then, turning to Corbyn, "Do you want Jeremy For Leader? Jeremy4Leader?" On the other end of the phone, Soffa registered the chosen domain name and began building the site. The campaign was born.

"I did feel really excited," remembers Smith. "At that moment it felt like everything clicked into place... Because once we'd got a campaign going I know how to run a campaign, Ben knows how to run a campaign, Jeremy knows. We all know how to run a campaign. It was just, 'Right, we're doing this, get on to it.'"

The group's first bit of planning—to wait until the following day to announce Corbyn's candidacy—was immediately scuppered when an excited Diane Abbott tweeted the news. Corbyn's phone started ringing. As he fielded a call from a journalist, Smith and Clive Lewis headed off to begin lobbying colleagues: "Clive and I went onto the terrace outside Strangers' Bar [in the Houses of Parliament]. It was summer so everybody was out. There were loads of MPs sat out there. I'm not a frequenter of the bar. It's not my comfort zone. But I remember working the room with Clive trying to persuade people." As far as Lewis was concerned, it was "in for a penny, in for a pound," even though "we all went into this thinking it was going to be the Charge of the Light Brigade."

Meanwhile, Corbyn made his first appointment, asking his old friend John McDonnell—who remained sceptical of the wisdom of standing—to run the campaign. As the division bell rang calling MPs to vote, McDonnell replied: "I'll do it. Tactically I think it's a mistake, but I'll do it, don't worry." Rather than take on the executive role of campaign manager, McDonnell agreed to be Corbyn's agent and chair of his campaign committee, overseeing the general strategy while others were brought in to "do the legwork."

McDonnell immediately began pulling together a small team to coordinate the lobbying effort. Everything would be focused on the nominations. A source involved in the venture from its earliest moments recalls: "We explicitly said: 'Let's not waste any time building infrastructure for a mass campaign because we should focus on what we're doing now—getting the nominations in.'"

While direct face-to-face persuasion of MPs would be crucial, the group knew it would not be sufficient. Parliamentarians would need to feel pressure from below. In those first few hours a strategy was formulated that would be pursued without deviation until 15 June. The campaign would ask party members to lobby MPs. It would encourage them to relentlessly push the message that Labour needed a proper debate, which could only be achieved by having Corbyn on the ballot.[4] It sounded unthreatening, democratic and reasonable. But it tapped into frustration at how the party had long been stitched up.

"We knew that it would be an uphill challenge and we thought the balance of probability was he wouldn't get on the ballot," says Lansman, "although some of us were more optimistic than Jeremy himself." According to one of Corbyn's close allies: "Jeremy didn't think he would get 35 nominations. Most of us thought we'll probably only get two weeks until the nominations close but at least in that two weeks we'll be able to shape the debate a bit."

As the news of his candidacy began to spread, Corbyn made an announcement via his local newspaper, the *Islington Tribune*, saying "I am standing to give Labour Party members a voice in this debate."[5] He also spoke to the *Daily Mirror*, characteristically eschewing bombast to explain that he was putting his name forward "to see if there is enough support to have a stab at it. We are taking it step by step, and if we get on the ballot paper that's a good start."[6]

That evening Corbyn attended a meeting of his local Constituency Labour Party (CLP). Addressing the party members that knew him best he confirmed that he would be standing for leader. The room erupted.[7]

· · · · ·

Early the following morning, 4 June 2015, John McDonnell called Ben Sellers of Red Labour to ask if he would coordinate the Corbyn campaign's social media operation. Sellers immediately agreed, excited at the chance to play a small part in history. Sellers had long evangelised to McDonnell about how fluid and fast moving Red Labour's online infrastructure allowed it to be. These were precisely the qualities McDonnell now sought.

As if by way of illustration, at 9.13 a.m. @Corbyn4Leader posted its first tweet: "This is the official twitter page for the #Jeremy4Leader campaign. Please RT [retweet] and ask your Labour MP to nominate Jeremy. We need a debate."[8] By midday the account debuted what would become the political slogan of the summer: #JezWeCan, a play on Barack Obama's famous "Yes We Can" refrain.[9] The pun was the brainchild of a Labour councillor who was apparently so embarrassed of it that his identity remains hidden. It was "incredibly cheesy," admits Sellers, "but it did express the idea that it was about us rather than him and that actually this was possible."[10]

The Twitter account was off to a good start but the real action that morning was taking place on Facebook. By lunchtime the Jeremy Corbyn For Labour Leader page had already overtaken the Facebook pages of all the other leadership candidates in its number of subscribers.[11] At the end of the first day 9,000 people had 'liked' the page.[12] Something was stirring.

One reason for the rapid lift-off was that the social media effort began essentially as a side-project of Red Labour, borrowing its reach and methods. "What we did with Red Labour was use populist stuff that we knew would get shared,'" Sellers recalls.

> It was the political equivalent of pictures of kittens... Once we got people interested then we could start talking about policies and the stuff that we knew wouldn't be quite as

popular but that would have more of a political impact. You could get hundreds of people to like a Tony Benn quote, obviously... That is a basic staple of those pages, where you start off thinking 'How can we share this page as much as possible?' We dug through old articles that Jeremy had written on Iraq or whatever, which we knew would be hugely popular, and just made them into memes.

A meme, in this context, is an image overlaid with a striking quote or slogan, designed to be shared. One of the earliest campaign memes, created by young artist Leonora Partington, featured an image of Corbyn being arrested in 1984 wearing a large placard saying: "Defend the right to demonstrate against apartheid." Beside the picture was the message: "You knew what he stood for then. You know what he stands for now. Jeremy 4 Labour Leader."[13]

Sellers established a social media HQ in the People's Bookshop, a store he ran in his home city of Durham, and recruited a group of volunteers including fellow Durham Red Labourite Paul Simpson and Marshajane Thompson, a Unison activist and former co-chair of the LRC based in London. Others were recruited later, but the core group remained tight throughout.

To harness social media for the nominations effort the team produced a list of 49 MPs who, in Sellers' words, "could be seen as either rebels or on the left of the party" and encouraged volunteers to lobby them.[14] "We had a bit of a debate about whether or not we should publish the list because we knew that some MPs may not like that," says Thompson. "But we decided to do it anyway and it went viral."

Sellers was taken aback at how quickly things escalated: "People came out of nowhere and took responsibility for huge chunks of the campaign. At first, there was some apprehension—should we be taking a more centralised approach? But after deliberating for all of a few minutes it became obvious that events had overtaken our plans—it was no longer 'our' campaign, it belonged to those who wanted to contribute."[15]

Meanwhile, a new online petition calling on Labour MPs to nominate Corbyn was started by Stuart Wheeler, a Labour activist in Cornwall. It was featured in the press and quickly accrued 7,000 signatures.[16]

. . . . .

Over four days between 6 and 9 June 2015 Jeremy Corbyn took part in three leadership hustings. The first was at the Fabian Society in London. The debate was notable mainly for Liz Kendall's impressive achievement of being booed, albeit quietly, by *Fabians*—indisputably the politest crowd in the Labour Movement. Kendall's insistence that Labour should be "as passionate about wealth creation as about inequality" provoked their wrath, although the boos were probably due to the cumulative effect of her other crowd-pleasers, such as her strong commitment to £9,000 tuition fees.[17] Kendall later said she knew she would not be leader as soon as she experienced the reaction of hustings audiences. Corbyn fared better, although one journalist noted that after the event crowds gathered around Kendall, Yvette Cooper and Andy Burnham for selfies but there was "no such luck" for Corbyn or Mary Creagh.[18]

On 8 June the candidates were up before the PLP for an hour-long private hustings. Despite the tough crowd, Corbyn handled himself well. One of his critics even joked on the way out: "On that performance, I think Jeremy Corbyn could do it!"[19] Emily Thornberry told the *Morning Star* Corbyn was "really good, really relaxed." Significantly, although her choice for leader was Cooper, she said she would consider lending him her nomination.[20]

The next day the candidates headed to Dublin for a hustings at the GMB conference, where Corbyn went down a storm. It was now Burnham's turn to be booed—only this time it was proper trade union jeering. In a testy exchange the moderator Kevin Maguire asked for a yes or no answer from all the candidates on whether they supported the Tory plan to reduce the benefits cap to £23,000. He came first to Burnham. "Do you back a £23,000 benefits cap?"

Burnham let out an exasperated sigh. He hesitated. There was an interminable pause as he considered how to wriggle out of the question. There were boos.

"Yes or no?" Maguire demanded.

"Kevin I think that's a little unfair because..."

Loud jeering.

"It's what people want to know," Maguire barked.

"Let me just explain why I think it's unfair, because…" Burnham spluttered.

Voices from the audience shouted out "NO!"

"Is that yes or no?" Maguire attempted again, but got only a politician's answer in reply: "I'm not going to set my face against changes to the benefits system but it depends how they do it and I'm not going to give you an answer like that on a question that is that complicated."

Annoyed, Maguire turned to Creagh, who quickly replied that yes, she did support the reduction of the benefits cap. Perhaps the audience was still distracted by Burnham's ordeal, because her response won some scattered applause. Kendall was up next. She agreed with Creagh but got a rougher time for it, and reacted to boos by saying: "You might not like the answer but I have to say my view."

Maguire moved on. "Jeremy, yes or no?"

"No. I will not back it."

Huge cheers. Whoops. Shouts of "YES!"[21]

Away from the hustings, Corbyn's status as a leadership candidate was affording him unprecedented access to the mainstream media. He swapped his usual *Morning Star* column for an op-ed in the *Guardian* on 8 June. "It's time to rediscover the community basis of the Labour Party," he wrote, "as we need to fight back against the very damaging things this government is planning to do to the most vulnerable in society."[22] That evening he did his first TV interview of the campaign, turning in a fluent performance on BBC *Newsnight*, sailing through questions about the royal family ("I don't know any of them personally, I'm sure they're very nice people"), Sinn Fein and tax rates, all the while looking like he was enjoying himself.[23]

While Corbyn was out and about, in Westminster Jon Lansman was coordinating the lobbying effort. Red Labour may have identified 49 "rebel" MPs but Lansman was working from a more ambitious list of 80 "possibles." The Corbyn camp could count on 10 names from the off: old Campaign Group comrades Diane Abbott, Ronnie Campbell, Kelvin Hopkins, John McDonnell,

Michael Meacher and Dennis Skinner; fresh faces Richard Burgon, Clive Lewis and Cat Smith; and shadow cabinet minister Jon Trickett, who despite not being a member of the Campaign Group threw his weight behind the left candidate without hesitation.

"The problem was a lot of people on the left were already committed to Andy Burnham," says Lansman, "and we were losing them fast." Burnham already had 51 backers.[24] He exerted a strong influence on MPs with constituencies in his backyard in the North West. Cat Smith was one. "I had to have a conversation with Andy, because I'd given Andy the impression I'd probably come in behind him," she says. "In my mind I thought I was pulling out of backing the winner, because I genuinely thought Andy was going to win at this point. Basically sacrifice your parliamentary career. Tell the person who's going to be the next leader of the Labour Party you're not going to back him because you're going to back the person who's probably going to come last."[25]

Burnham's team hinted they were relaxed about Corbyn being on the ballot, but privately they knew it would spell trouble. "Imagine the final contest is Liz, Andy, Yvette, Jeremy Corbyn," one unnamed MP told the *New Statesman* on 5 June with rare prescience. "Liz and Yvette will distance themselves from him—but where does Andy go? Does he condemn him? Support him? Try to set a middle way?"[26] Burnham's inability to answer that question would be the story of his campaign.

Corbyn's team had a secret weapon in the lobbying game: experience. Between them McDonnell, Abbott and Meacher had cajoled and inveigled their colleagues for nominations four times. They had a detailed knowledge of the PLP and a sense of which arguments would work on different MPs. They knew the process and how to make deals. And as long-standing parliamentarians they had relationships that could bring in some unlikely names. Meacher, for example, had a personal connection with Frank Field, the maverick backbencher from the right of the party. When the nominations period officially opened on 9 June many were surprised to see Field nominate Corbyn. "I wouldn't say Michael persuaded him because Frank does his own thing," says Lansman, "but Field became the first MP to 'lend' Corbyn his nomination without intending to vote for him in the subsequent election.[27]

Richard Burgon, Kelvin Hopkins, Clive Lewis and Jon Trickett also threw their efforts into persuading colleagues. "There was a division of labour," says Lewis. "We would have regular meetings. We all had people to go and talk to, people that we'd made friends with through being here, people that we vaguely knew." Lansman himself had been through the process of chasing nominations for McDonnell in 2007. A critical ancillary role was played by Seb Corbyn, Jeremy's son, who worked in parliament for McDonnell and became the linkman between his dad and the campaign.

At the end of the opening day of nominations the Corbyn camp could boast 13 names in the bag, including Grahame Morris and Kate Osamor. Bringing the total to 14 was a certain Jeremy Corbyn, who nominated himself in an uncharacteristic act of self-promotion.[28]

· · · · ·

The social media operation had got off to a roaring start but the question was whether it would sway MPs' decisions. The group Ben Sellers assembled began in the naïve belief that securing 35 nominations from the 49 MPs on their list was manageable. They were soon disabused. "About half of that list got obliterated within days because they were supporting Andy Burnham," says Sellers. "We changed our tactics at that point. We needed to think about other ways of getting people who aren't on the left."

As a crowd-sourced lobbying effort, not all the online pressure was well focused. Even Corbyn supporters like Cat Smith felt the heat: "I got an awful lot of emails asking me to nominate him after I had. A lot. Clogging my inbox. I was like, 'I already have. I've done it. Leave me alone. Go and lobby someone who hasn't nominated yet.' I even got some emails from people saying it was a disgrace that I hadn't nominated him... I was like, 'But, but I'm right at the heart of this and I'm doing everything I can!'"

"We did try to update stuff and call people off," laughs Sellers. "I remember with Cat in particular, there were still people saying, 'Oh, I've emailed Cat and I've really told her!' And you're thinking 'No! Just leave her alone.'" Sellers says the team "stressed that people should be polite... But at the same time we were quite ruthless in that we weren't going to sit back and hope for the best."

Social media was at its most effective when it complemented local constituency pressure. While it was easy for MPs to dismiss messages they received online as unrepresentative, support for Corbyn was made real in the person of party members in their area. Inversely, activists whom MPs may have regarded as marginalised in their constituency suddenly appeared to be on the crest of a wave crashing through social media.

Corbyn's 15th nomination, given by Dawn Butler on 10 June, was partly a result of such multi-layered pressure. Butler—who supported Burnham—was pursued by Diane Abbott and others in Westminster, by activists online, and by party members at the local level. LRC member Michael Calderbank was secretary of Butler's CLP in Brent Central. "There was clearly a body of opinion in the CLP that would have been really angry not to have a horse in the race," he says. "It was good that she did that."[29]

Chi Onwurah's nomination provided the clearest example of online and constituency pressure having an effect. She was always going to be receptive to the democratic argument having previously called for a broad selection of candidates.[30] On 9 June she tweeted: "If you live in Newcastle Central and want a progressive future tell me who you'd like me to nominate."[31] It is not hard to infer the response—her next tweet 24 hours later said: "So to put it another way, do any @UKLabour members or supporters in *Newcastle Central* not want me to nominate @jeremycorbyn for leader?"[32] On 11 June Onwurah became Corbyn's 16th nominator.[33]

No one knows how many people participated in the online lobbying but a sense of the intensity could be gleaned by looking at any tweet from a Labour MP mentioning nominations—it would be followed by a string of replies imploring: "Please, just nominate Jeremy."[34] Michelle Ryan was one of the most persistent: "I must have sent God knows how many emails to MPs. I can't even think how many and that's just one person." The numbers were boosted by the journalist Owen Jones using his "social media firepower" to encourage people to join in. According to Sellers the scale was increasing exponentially: "This now was reaching far beyond our Red Labour group. Here came the Corbynistas!"[35]

The mobilisation was still only a fraction of the size it became later in the summer but it had the element of surprise. It was unprecedented for so much pressure to be exerted on behalf of a candidate. None of the other runners could boast anything remotely similar. There was no people's campaign for Mary Creagh.

Previous leadership elections happened before social media had been fully exploited as a political tool. Sellers ran John McDonnell's digital operation in 2007, such as it was: "It's laughable really but I was using MySpace... We just put up some facts about John and policies and things. It must have been probably 100-200 people that actually saw that. It's amazing, the difference in eight years."[36] The "technological advance of using the mobile phone not just to send texts to your friends but to send text to the general public," as activist James Doran puts it, has had political implications. "People have a lot more access to their MPs now," says Marshajane Thompson. "Social media has opened up democracy to be a lot more transparent and interactive. People that wouldn't dream of going to an MP's surgery can tweet their MP and say 'I think you should do something about the litter on my street,' or, 'Nominate Jeremy for Labour Party leader.'"

Everyone involved in the campaign agrees that social media pressure was decisive in the nomination phase. Thompson says simply: "Without social media we wouldn't have got on the ballot paper." McDonnell believes: "That's what turned it really... We'd never had that before." Thompson and Sellers estimate that more than a quarter of Corbyn's nominators—between eight and 10 MPs—were swayed by digital lobbying.[37]

Social media is not a force in itself but a tool. It does not create the conditions for political movements to arise but it allows them to grow at pace. People at opposite ends of the country who would previously not have known of each other's existence can suddenly be thrown together in support of a cause.

A new community was forged in the battle for nominations. "A lot of online groups started to spring up when [Corbyn] was getting on the ballot," remembers Ryan. "All the messages of people wanting it to happen were so powerful. It was a democratic revolution and people really felt they were part of it. We almost felt like a family, like a proper movement. It was tangible."

· · · · ·

Things seemed to be falling into place as the Monday nomination deadline approached. On the evening of Thursday 11 June 2015 Jeremy Corbyn gained the endorsement of Catherine West, his friend and constituency neighbour to the north.[38] West was generally on the left and opposed to Trident nuclear weapons. The following day Corbyn's neighbour to the south, Emily Thornberry, also a friend, added her nomination.[39] With 18 of the required 35 names, Corbyn was past half way.

There was a bolt from the blue on Friday 12 June. A shock survey by the *LabourList* website revealed that Corbyn was the readers' favourite for leader on 47 per cent. His nearest rival, Andy Burnham, was back on 13 per cent. The respondents were self-selecting and in truth the poll was more a reflection of the online mobilisation for Corbyn than an accurate gauge of opinion.[40] But it strengthened the case that there was a real constituency that should not be excluded.[41]

Mary Creagh polled only 3 per cent in the survey, finishing below 'None of the above,' which must be some kind of paradox. She was doing nearly as badly in nominations. Later that day she bowed to the inevitable and withdrew from the contest. Her campaign had never soared, and neither had her rhetoric. "Labour has become an analogue party in a digital age... it needs to become the Carlsberg party, refreshing parts that other parties cannot reach," she had argued.[42]

Creagh's exit was pivotal, releasing her nine backers to choose afresh. "We must appeal to all her MP nominators to back Jeremy Corbyn in the interests of democracy," tweeted John McDonnell.[43] The social media team put out a list of the names, asking people to lobby them politely.[44] On Saturday 13 June Corbyn picked up two: Jo Cox—who, shockingly, would be murdered a year later—and Sarah Champion, both Yorkshire MPs. Each justified their decision on the now standard grounds of wanting the membership to have a wider choice.[45] A spokesman for the Corbyn camp told the *Morning Star*: "The social media campaign and support from the grassroots has really made a difference. We didn't persuade Champion and Cox, they came of their own accord as a result of the pressure."[46]

A third Yorkshire MP pledged her nomination the same day: Louise Haigh. Though a signatory to the letter from new MPs calling for an anti-austerity candidate, Haigh was a genuine supporter of Andy Burnham.[47] But during a series of conversations over several days with activists online and the Westminster lobbying team, she gradually came round.[48]

There was more good news for the campaign that Saturday. An uncharacteristic editorial in the *Guardian* argued that Corbyn "has a right to a place" in the race.[49] There was now no doubting it: Corbyn's candidacy had momentum.

"By the end of the week before nominations closed we really knew that we could do it," says Jon Lansman. But there was a problem. "Jeremy would not make phone calls." Some MPs expected to be asked personally for their endorsement. Naz Shah, for example, would have nominated Corbyn had she received a call from him, Lansman believes. "We hassled him and hassled him and hassled him," but when Corbyn failed to ring, Shah backed Cooper. "He would not ask people for their support, we lost nominations," Lansman says. "He is not a pushy person." Corbyn's reticence was noticed. The 'soft left' MP Clive Efford tweeted: "It seems that everyone possible has contacted me about supporting @Corbyn4Leader except @jeremycorbyn himself!"[50]

Saturday 13 June was a dramatic day for the core team around Corbyn as they became increasingly concerned that he was having second thoughts about standing.[51] When the group tried to arrange a meeting to raise his morale he refused, saying it would take up a lot of people's time. "It got really serious," says Lansman. "On the Saturday evening John went round to see him at his house... John was actually really worried. That evening John said: 'I think we should call it off, I think we should stop now.' At that point, I thought we were going to stop."

It was not that Corbyn was lazy. He had maintained his usual high level of activism, notably speaking in support of striking workers at the National Gallery on 11 June—indicative of how, right from the off, he refused to play it safe.[52] He had, in fact, been making some phone calls to MPs. And he was continuing with the media appearances. When interviewed on BBC Radio 4 on 12 June, presenter Mark Mardell began by asking—in that sneering, contemptuous tone that seems to be a requirement for a job at the

BBC—"Why are you bothering because you're frankly not going to win, are you?" Corbyn was unfazed.[53]

But Corbyn's lack of enthusiasm could be gleaned from other media interviews. Talking to the *Guardian* on 11 June he gave the impression his work was done. "If we get [on to the ballot paper], great," he said. "We'll see what happens, but as far as I'm concerned we've already—by the action we took a week ago—changed the terms of debate."[54] Speaking to *Total Politics* he discouraged the idea that he should be gifted nominations by other candidates. "I don't want charity," he said. "I want to see a proper debate within the party. Essentially there's going to be that debate anyway because there are many in the party, and many members who joined the party, [who] want to see something different. I will certainly be part of that debate whatever the outcome."[55]

McDonnell believes the trepidation Corbyn felt was "a completely natural reaction." With the nominations in reach, he had to reappraise what he had let himself in for. "That weekend he was worried about what would happen... To a certain extent we'd press-ganged him into standing. He did it out of responsibility and conviction... He's not a careerist in any way."

Ben Sellers has "mixed feelings" about the situation: "He's an absolutely deep down decent bloke and I don't like the idea of him feeling pressured into something. But at the same time if we'd ended up with a different candidate... then I don't think there was any chance."

Despite his reservations about standing, Corbyn decided to press on. Lansman observes that Corbyn subsequently "grew into it... in various stages." But that Saturday evening Lansman was "resigned to giving up."

• • • • •

Jon Lansman woke up at 6 a.m. on Sunday—the last full day before the deadline—with renewed determination. Thus far the lobbying team had been working separately. "I thought if we were all in the same room together... it would boost our morale and we could win this." He texted John McDonnell before 7 a.m. and began rounding up the others—Nicolette Petersen and Jack Bond of Jeremy Corbyn's staff, Seb Corbyn and Lansman's son Max. They arranged to meet at the House of Commons at midday.

Corbyn made an appearance on Sky News that morning. Displaying no sign of any doubts, he gave an upbeat and accurate assessment of the nominations: "We're up to 18 as of Friday and I've had some very nice phone calls... We've got four more names who've already agreed to nominate tomorrow morning so that puts us up to 22."[56]

When the lobbying team got together—without Corbyn— they began calling the 44 MPs who were not yet committed, plus anyone who could influence them. "The whole day Sunday [we were] literally ensconced in one room with telephones phoning every contact we possibly could," remembers McDonnell.

Meanwhile, the social media operation was cranked up another notch. The campaign's Facebook page had grown to 19,000 'likes.' A new list of the undeclared was thrown out to the legions of willing volunteers. "If your MP is listed below, and you haven't contacted them, it is especially important that you do so as soon as possible," the post said. "What we are witnessing here is democracy in action. It's impressive, powerful stuff, isn't it?"[57]

By the end of the day Corbyn had 26 nominations, provided all the promises came good. There were several other "strong possibilities." Seven further MPs told the team that they would hold back their nomination until the final moments in case Corbyn got close enough for one extra to make a difference.[58]

That evening McDonnell went to Shakespeare's Globe theatre to see *King John*, he thinks, "or another blood-thirsty one anyway." Half way through the performance he got a call from Seb Corbyn, saying his dad wanted to know the chances of making the ballot. "I think we're going to do it," McDonnell said.

Many of Corbyn's nominators went on to vote for other candidates. So why did they nominate him? The furious voices of the right bellow an answer: they were too weak to resist the social media and constituency pressure. John Woodcock MP, who helped run the Liz Kendall campaign, said those who nominated Corbyn did so simply because they were "getting grief" from email writers, leaving other MPs to ask "what form of punishment was most appropriate" for them.[59] Alternatively, if they were not too weak, Corbyn's nominators must have been too stupid to understand the process. One strategist for Yvette Cooper patronisingly said: "No one had explained the MPs' role in the new [Collins] system… I'm not saying that's their fault, to be fair to them, no one had made this clear."[60]

These explanations are hardly plausible. MPs are not so weak as to buckle under the pressure of tweets and emails if it involves them acting against their interests. Neither are they incapable of grasping the concept of a gatekeeper.[61] Rather, everyone who lent Corbyn a nomination made a political calculation. This is not to say the lobbying operation made no difference. It was vital—but not sufficient. Engaging in a little political geology, drilling down into the detail of MPs' decisions, reveals several strata of motivation

Beginning at surface level, in their public pronouncements most nominators repeated the line crafted by the Corbyn campaign: the party needed a broad debate. A number were clearly genuine in this, although without the clamour on social media they may not have felt obliged to respond. Where they made a political calculation was in thinking there would be few consequences to their actions, so certain were they that Corbyn would lose. "It was a cost-free thing to do," says one Corbyn campaign source, adding, "it didn't quite turn out that way." On the other side of the ledger, most MPs valued the goodwill of their local left wing party members, whose help they needed to canvass and get out the vote.[62]

Digging down a little deeper reveals a motivation Lansman discovered while lobbying MPs. "This is the critical thing," he says. "There were people who never ever supported Jeremy. They weren't doing it just to get people off their backs. They were doing it because they did want to pull the party to the left. They were worried that it was going to go to the right from where it had been under Miliband." For 'soft left' and trade union-supported MPs, getting Corbyn on the ballot was the only available way to rebalance the contest.

John Prescott, the former deputy prime minister, articulated a loose version of this argument in his *Sunday Mirror* column on 14 June, giving Corbyn a further stamp of legitimacy: "I may not agree with a lot that left-winger Jeremy Corbyn says. But it's important in this debate for the soul of the party that members get to vote on his views... In the rush to get their campaigns up and running and chase nominations, I believe [the other candidates] haven't had the time to develop their own manifestos. My worry is the Tories and their pals in the media will do that for them."[63]

Excavating still further uncovers more self-interested motivations. All four MPs vying to be Labour's candidate for mayor of London nominated Corbyn—Diane Abbott, Sadiq Khan, David Lammy and Gareth Thomas.[64] Abbott was on board anyway. As for the others, "It was surprisingly easy to persuade them," Lansman says. "They all did it because they were after Corbyn votes." The online and constituency pressure had revealed a seam of support worth mining. The pledge from Khan, a big figure of the 'soft left,' provided a particular boost on the eve of the deadline.[65]

Finally, at the bottom of the motivations borehole is the oldest form of politics: deal making. Without the powers of patronage enjoyed by their rivals, the Corbyn camp had little bargaining power. Despite Corbyn's objections, his team was interested in "charity" nominations. But although Andy Burnham claimed to be open to 'lending' some of his supporters to Corbyn, his campaign proffered no help.[66] "They really didn't want us on the ballot paper, for good reason," Lansman says. Cooper's team, in contrast, were "quite interested in having Jeremy on the ballot paper because they thought it would take votes away from Burnham," although in the end they were only "a bit helpful." "They did help with some of the Mary Creagh people who would have gone to them, but they said, 'It's OK if you nominate Jeremy.'" Another case was Emily Thornberry, who back on 8 June said: "I do want Jeremy to be on the ballot paper. If it's needed to have some help on that and Yvette's happy then I will look at it."[67]

The election for deputy leader was being run in parallel to the leadership battle, but the deadline for nominations was two days later. This presented an opportunity. On Saturday 13 June the lobbying team noticed that eight of Corbyn's endorsers had not yet nominated a contender for deputy. "That's when we started trying to do deals with the deputy candidates," Lansman recalls. In exchange for a nomination from a deputy candidate or their supporters, the Corbyn camp offered to reciprocate from its own ranks.

Three of the runners for deputy were out-and-out Blairites with whom Corbyn's team had few ties.[68] Another, Angela Eagle, was not interested in doing deals. Tom Watson, on the Sunday, was non-committal. But one hopeful, Rushanara Ali, was desperately short of nominations. She happened to be Lansman's MP and had been speaking to McDonnell, Abbott and Clive Lewis. A deal was made: Ali would receive two endorsements in return for her nomination.[69]

For all these MPs, there was a common factor that eased the way: they liked Corbyn. Unfailingly affable to his colleagues, he provoked no personal animosity. "He's the most caring, compassionate person I've ever come across in politics," attests McDonnell. "A lot of people said, 'All right, it's Jeremy, I will, I'll give him a chance.' If it had been someone else—like me—they wouldn't have done it."

Corbyn's nominators were not the sea-swept invertebrates of the right's portrayal. But their political calculations erred in underestimating the potential of the Labour left. They saw it as no threat. There were several reasons why. First, Corbyn was a particularly unthreatening candidate—personally unambitious, and with no ministerial experience. Second, some MPs seemed oblivious to the change in mood in the party after five years of Tory austerity.[70] Third, the left had consistently failed to provide any evidence that it could be a threat.

The only available guide to the left's potential in a leadership contest came from Abbott's run in 2010, when she finished last. A Corbyn candidacy would similarly "expose how little support there is for the hard left," thought Luke Akehurst, secretary of the Labour First group on the party's right. But this reasoning was unsound. The voting system had changed. As Abbott herself pointed out, "On a one-person-one-vote ballot in 2010 I would have been third. Not inconsiderable support."[71] Moreover, Abbott's result was not an accurate measure of the left's strength, as she did not have the breadth of goodwill that Corbyn enjoyed.[72] Most important, an Ed Miliband victory represented the only chance to move the party away from New Labour in 2010. Given the voting power of MPs in the electoral college, Abbott could not win; Miliband could.[73]

For all their fury, the right could not blame Corbyn's nominators for assuming he would lose—they believed it even more fervently. The conventional wisdom led Akehurst to come out in favour of Corbyn being on the ballot, writing on 9 June: "As an opponent of the hard left, I am confident enough about the superiority of my own political ideas and policies that I want their ideas taken on democratically and defeated... so we can prove that they are not the direction the vast majority of members want to go in."[74]

What, then, of the lobbying effort? MPs had a range of motivations for nominating Corbyn but few would have done so without a push. It was grassroots pressure that forced the issue onto the agenda. For some MPs it almost provided an excuse to act on their other concerns. It was in this sense that social media played a decisive role. To return to the political geology metaphor, at every level the ground was rumbling with seismic activity. It took activism to get Corbyn on the ballot.

· · · · ·

Monday 15 June 2015. Deadline day. The venue for the drama was the office of the Parliamentary Labour Party, nestled in the lower cloister off Westminster Hall, a kind of gothic corridor built in the time of Henry VIII and previously used as a cloakroom. Officially, Corbyn still had 18 nominations. Every other MP that had promised to help would have to visit the PLP office to submit their signed nomination form in person before midday. As most were returning to parliament from a weekend in their constituencies, one delayed train could scupper Corbyn's chances.

The Corbyn camp had resolved to have a physical presence stationed outside the PLP office throughout the morning to "count them in." Jon Lansman did the early stint, arriving at 8.30 a.m. For a while there was no one. Eventually the first nominator appeared: mayoral hopeful David Lammy.

As he waited for others, Lansman's attention turned to deputy leadership candidate Tom Watson, with whom he was on good terms even though Watson hailed from the old (non-Blairite) right of the party.[75] Lansman had spoken to Watson on Sunday evening but had not got far. The call ended with Lansman promising to phone again in the morning. But from outside the PLP office he instead rang contacts in Unite. Although the United Left, the dominant group on the union's executive council, had called for MPs to nominate Corbyn, Unite had made no systematic attempt to help him onto the ballot.[76] But Lansman now managed to get Len McCluskey to put in a call to Watson (McCluskey and Watson later had a spectacular falling out, but were friends at the time). When, after a suitable delay, Lansman spoke to Watson himself he found him far more amenable.

Lansman's priority was not necessarily to get Watson to nominate Corbyn. Rather, he was interested in the influence that Watson could wield as an experienced party operator (or, as the press would have it, a "fixer," "bruiser," and "low-rent 1970s mafia grunt"). "It wasn't so much that we wanted him to get us support," Lansman explains, "we wanted him to firm up our support, to make sure they actually delivered." In return, some Corbyn backers would nominate Watson for deputy.[77]

According to Lansman, Watson said: "If you're going to get me to make sure people nominate you, I want to be absolutely sure you're not lying to me about how much support you've got, and if I find out you've been lying to me I'll take away two nominations for every one I've given you." Lansman would have to share the names of Corbyn's promised nominators with Alicia Kennedy, Watson's right-hand woman. Kennedy, a former deputy general secretary of the Labour Party, was a formidable force. "You've got to hand it to her, she's very good at her job, which is stitching us up," Lansman jokes.

Before he could speak to Kennedy, Lansman had to leave his position outside the PLP office and head to Hammersmith Hospital for an appointment at 10.30 a.m. He was due to be a kidney donor at the end of the month and was giving blood prior to the operation:

> I was having blood taken out of my right arm and I was having to text with my left hand—and I'm right handed—text Alicia the names [of Corbyn's nominators] as I was having the fucking blood taken out... I came out of the hospital after they'd closed me up and I texted Tom to say: 'The things I fucking do for socialism. It was like Alicia was taking more blood out of my left arm than they were taking out of my right!' He found this very

funny and rang me back when I was on the bus. And I
had a good relationship with him during the campaign
because of that.

While Lansman was sweating blood in Hammersmith, out in
cyber-space the digital operation was at full blast. It was "all hands
to the pump," recalls Michael Calderbank. "On the last day we were
frantically tweeting anybody that knew anybody." Calderbank had
an acquaintance that worked for Neil Coyle MP, who was still to
nominate. "I called him and he said, 'Oh I'm with Neil now and
we're just thinking about whether to nominate Jeremy, what do you
think?' And I said, 'What do I think? Yes! Do it, do it, do it.'" Coyle,
one of Mary Creagh's backers until she pulled out, was already
conducting his own survey on Twitter. Among the deluge of replies
urging him to nominate Corbyn was one from Diane Abbott.[78]

Another Creagh supporter, Tulip Siddiq, was also coming
under vociferous grassroots pressure. She had described Corbyn
as a "legend" when allocated a parliamentary office next to his and
had indicated that she would be open to nominating him if Creagh
dropped out.[79] But campaigners feared she would renege. "After
a lot of persuasion," as Unison activist Andrew Berry puts it, on
Monday morning she finally announced on Twitter: "I'm ready to
offer my nomination to JC."[80]

Back outside the PLP office John McDonnell had taken charge
armed with a clipboard containing a list of the MPs who had
promised to nominate. By 11 a.m. he had ticked off eight names to
bring Corbyn's total to 26. In addition to Lammy there were the
Creagh supporters Jo Cox and Sarah Champion; Huw Irranca-
Davies; and Rupa Huq, a "maverick" nominator whose endorsement was unexpected.[81]

Three signatories to the letter calling for an anti-austerity candidate had filed through the office: Louise Haigh; Imran Hussain;
and Rebecca Long-Bailey, who despite being firmly on the left had
been surprisingly slow to make up her mind.[82] As MP for Salford
and Eccles she was under pressure from Burnham-supporting colleagues in the North West. But when she did commit that morning,
she committed fully. "I'm off to get the lovely Jez on the ballot
paper," she tweeted. "In the words of Arnie... 'do it!'"[83]

Still short of nine names with one hour to go, McDonnell and others from the lobbying team anxiously "paced the flagstones of Westminster Hall outside the Labour Party's parliamentary office. Eyes down and oblivious to the groups of sightseers on guided tours, they fired off texts and emails to Labour MPs"—according to the *Morning Star* reporter Luke James who was on the spot.[84]

Then, at 11.15 a.m., out of the blue appeared Margaret Beckett, the former foreign secretary, to nominate Corbyn. It came as a complete surprise. Beckett later agreed with an interviewer that she was a "moron" and said of her decision: "I probably regard it as one of the biggest political mistakes I've ever made." But Harry Fletcher, who volunteered for the Corbyn campaign in its early stages, believed Beckett's intention was to "shift the tone of the debate and move the other candidates away from the centre." If that was the case, she succeeded beyond her wildest nightmares.[85]

Another big name followed fast on Beckett's heels: Jon Cruddas. According to Marshajane Thompson, "Cruddas was sending emails to his constituents saying he would think about nominating Jeremy. At one point he said he wouldn't, then he would, then he wanted to keep out of it. Through the pressure he got on social media... he backed himself into a position where he couldn't then not say anything."[86]

Next Rushanra Ali, the deputy leadership candidate, delivered on her commitment. There were now around 20 minutes to go and Corbyn was up to 30 nominations, including that of future London Mayor Sadiq Khan.

As the clock ticked down, the PLP office began to get crowded. Lansman was back from hospital. Cat Smith arrived, straight off the train from her Lancashire constituency. But where were the nominators? For a worrying few minutes the forward march of Labour MPs seemed to have halted. "Corbyn's team hit the phones again, scrambling for the numbers of MPs who said they would lend their support if the left candidate was on the line," observed James.[87] Mayoral hopeful Gareth Thomas turned up but said he would only add his name once Corbyn had 34 nominations and needed one more.

And now the candidate himself joined the party, still dressed in his cycling gear, fresh from doing media interviews in which he had repeated—endearingly, given the intensity of the moment—that he would have preferred Harriet Harman to stay on as interim leader for a year or two.[88] With just over 10 minutes to go and a dearth of new nominations it began to look like that would indeed have been the better option.

But then came a breakthrough. The two former Creagh supporters, Tulip Siddiq and Neil Coyle, arrived to transfer their nominations. Corbyn had scooped up a remarkable four of the nine MPs who previously backed the Blairite candidate. "Just confirmed my nomination for @jeremycorbyn," Siddiq tweeted. "Ten minutes to go, come on—let's allow a wide debate for our next leader!"[89]

Clive Efford, the 'soft left' MP, added his name to the list, having recovered from the disappointment of not receiving a personal phone call from Corbyn. As he handed over his paper more parliamentarians filtered into the increasingly crowded cloister. Tom Watson was hanging around, but said he would only nominate Corbyn if it was absolutely necessary. Former cabinet minister Andrew Smith was there, as was Gordon Marsden and the independent-minded Roger Godsiff. Rushing in with just a few minutes to go was Ian Murray, shadow secretary of state for Scotland and Labour's one MP north of the border (making him pretty much unsackable whomever he nominated).[90]

The trouble was all of them refused to commit until Corbyn was within one nomination of the target. The minutes were ticking down and they were all just standing there. The situation was absurd, like something from the mind of Lewis Carroll. There were enough MPs to carry Corbyn comfortably onto the ballot, but none would help until the others helped. If Corbyn did somehow manage to reach 34, he would then have six MPs willing to nominate when he would only need one. Suddenly the mayoral candidate, Thomas, relented. With a few minutes to go, the Corbyn camp declared themselves on 33 nominations and pleaded for just two more backers.

Jon Trickett and Harry Fletcher arrived to check on events and were struck by the "theatre" of what they saw.[91] Watson and others were in the outer section of the PLP office, which occupied part of the cloister, the narrow fan-vaulted gothic stone walkway incongruously filled with modern office desks and computers. Through a doorway was the Chapter House, a small polygonal room set in a bay jutting out into cloister court, which served as the office's inner sanctum. This was where signed nomination papers had to be deposited, and so this was where Marsden, Godsiff, Murray and Andrew Smith were stood, with McDonnell, Lansman and Cat Smith alongside trying every technique of persuasion.

Smith was targeting Marsden, whose Lancashire constituency bordered hers. Just two days earlier they had marched together down Blackpool prom for Pride. Smith had used the occasion as an extended lobbying opportunity. Now she was redeploying the same arguments in very different surroundings. "Give us a contest, give us a chance, let us have a debate," she pleaded.[92]

With three minutes to go the tension for Team Corbyn was almost unbearable. They were within touching distance of an incredible achievement, yet their fate was entirely in the hands of a few reluctant MPs. As soon as Big Ben chimed, PLP secretary Wes Ball advised them, the ballot would close.

Desperate times call for desperate measures. Outside the office Corbyn stopped the passing Conservative MP Stewart Jackson. "Fancy joining Labour for £3?" he asked.[93]

In the inner office, McDonnell's impassioned entreaties were failing to melt the hearts of the MPs. Fearing that it was not going to happen, Lansman left the room to try to fetch Watson. He found him stood in the outer office engrossed in his phone—texting some of the MPs in the inner office, just a few meters away. "He was sweating," recalls Lansman. "He was texting people in the inner office to try and make sure that they nominated because he had guaranteed that he would if he had to." A frantic Lansman told Watson: "But they're not doing it! You've got to come in and do it!"

"I think you've got it, don't worry, they'll do it," he remembers Watson saying. It was later reported that Watson reneged on a promise to nominate Corbyn but, according to Lansman, "He actually did more than anyone else."

With seconds to go McDonnell put his dignity to the sword and literally got down on his knees to beg the four reluctant MPs. "Whether you support Jeremy or not, this is in the interests of democracy," he remembers telling them. "Party members want to be able to vote for a candidate of their choice. We've all got a responsibility here!"

Unbeknown to everyone present, these desperate scenes were entirely unnecessary. Extraordinarily, in a classic example of left wing organising skill, the clipboard on which McDonnell had recorded the nominations was wrong. Corbyn already had 34 names.

Unaware of the true situation, the remaining MPs refused to budge. "I admit it, I was on my knees in tears begging them," McDonnell recalled.[94] "It was all a bit emotional. It was!"[95] When begging failed, McDonnell switched to warning the MPs that members would "not understand or forgive if Jeremy was excluded by just two votes."[96]

"It got to 10 seconds before the close of nominations," McDonnell recounted, probably exaggerating slightly, "and two of them cracked."[97]

Gordon Marsden was first to step forward. His nomination was the 35th, but everyone thought it was the 34th. Andrew Smith then handed over his form and (wrongly) went down as the man who put Corbyn on the ballot.

As Big Ben struck 12, McDonnell came out into the cloister and said: "They've done it!"[98] The relief was immediate. Corbyn grabbed Andrew Smith and gave him a huge hug. Formerly in Tony Blair's cabinet, Smith was an unlikely hero of the left, although along with Corbyn and McDonnell he was strongly opposed to Trident nuclear weapons and the Heathrow third runway. He went on to vote for Yvette Cooper, but had the mettle to stand by his nomination after Corbyn's victory.[99]

Addressing one of a small number of journalists gathered outside the office, Corbyn gave "a big thanks to everyone for supporting me and campaigning for this whisker result. The fight against austerity continues!"[100] To another, he said: "I'm on the ballot as a result of a massive campaign by Labour supporters across the country urging MPs to vote for democracy."[101] A photograph tweeted by one of Corbyn's earlier nominators, Chi Onwurah, shows him looking exhilarated and wide-eyed in the moment.[102]

Far away in Durham, Ben Sellers was "sitting there, waiting for news from John McDonnell, refreshing the twitter account manically." At 12.02 p.m. McDonnell tweeted: "As Jeremy's agent I can confirm that he is on the Labour leadership ballot paper with 35 nominations. Thank you everyone."[103] "I stared at the computer screen and I'm not ashamed to say that I seriously welled up as the enormity of what we had done hit home." Sellers relayed the news to the newly forged social media community. "If it had been a football stadium, the place would have erupted, such was the reaction." They may have only won a place on the ballot, but it had come against such odds that it felt like a glorious victory. "The PLP nominations were a massive hurdle—it had been their veto on real party democracy and we'd beaten it."[104]

6

TEAM CORBYN

"We had our canvass returns but no one was going to believe us, they were too good to be true."

—Jon Lansman

"With respect," says Laura Kuenssberg, signalling that she is about to be disrespectful, "there are Conservatives who are mobilising to get you elected because they think you'd be the easiest one to beat."

"There are some very funny people on the internet you know," replies Jeremy Corbyn, to laughs.

Kuenssberg, the host of this special BBC *Newsnight* hustings featuring all four leadership candidates, persists: "Do you really think you have a chance of winning this contest, with great respect"—here we go again—"because you had to have nominations borrowed even from your other MP colleagues?"

"No, I didn't borrow any," Corbyn corrects her.

"They were lent, put it that way," she says.

"They're not to be paid back," Corbyn asserts. "I'm putting forward a point of view that I believe is shared by a considerable number of people... We are not about personalities and individuals;

we're surely about the strength of a movement. I think people have had about enough of personality politics. They want something much more about movement politics."

The audience applauds enthusiastically. Yet this is not a "movement" audience. It is not even a Labour audience. *Newsnight* is holding this debate—the first televised hustings of the campaign, just a few days since Corbyn made it onto the ballot—in a church in Nuneaton, the constituency that pundits insisted Labour had to win in 2015 if it was to form a government, but which the Conservatives held by 5,000 votes. The church is full of Nuneaton residents "open to the possibility of voting Labour." There are questions from UKIP voters, Tory voters and, confusingly, a student who voted Labour but regards himself as a Conservative.

It is a bellwether audience designed to test whether any of the candidates can appeal to the kind of swing voters in marginal seats that decide elections. By the iron rule of the political commentariat, this should be fertile ground for Liz Kendall, the most 'centrist' candidate. Andy Burnham, as the bookmakers' favourite, is expected to do well. Yvette Cooper cannot be written off. Corbyn, as Kuenssberg demonstrates, can.

But it is not going to script. Something strange is happening. Time and again the answers from Kendall, Burnham and Cooper are met by a churchly hush, while Corbyn receives almost blasphemous applause.

One questioner asks how Labour can overcome the legacy of Tony Blair. He receives a barrage of interchangeable platitudes from the three 'main' candidates:

"We have to be the party that helps everyone get on in life."

"I'm not New Labour or old Labour; I want to be today's and tomorrow's Labour."

"We've got to move on from the politics of the comfort zone."

"We've got to grow in all directions."

But then it is Corbyn's turn. "Why, oh why, oh why did Blair have to get so close to Bush that we ended up in an illegal war in Iraq?"

There is thunderous applause. It goes on for longer than Kuenssberg would like. "But, but, but, but, but, but Jeremy Corbyn, but, but Jeremy Corbyn," she says, competing with the noise.

"Some people might think there's not much point rehashing what happened in 2003." Some people might, but not the swing voters of Nuneaton, it seems.

The expectation-defying moments pile one of top of another. Corbyn even wins loud approval for sternly taking to task an audience member over immigration. "You keep letting people into this country," the questioner says. "I'm not racist, I'm being sensible. I fear for England…"

"If there hadn't been immigration to this country what kind of National Health Service would we have, what transport system would we have, what kind of education system would we have?" Corbyn asks him directly and forcefully. "Migrants that come here actually contribute net to the economy, claim less, pay more in tax, and work. If there's a shortage of school places, a shortage of housing, that is our failure to plan for need in the future."

What is clear to everyone in the church, and everyone watching on TV, is that Corbyn is different. Every time he opens his mouth there is a dangerous possibility that he will say something interesting. People listen. He is actually communicating with the audience using language they understand. Politically he is well to the left of most in the room, but they appreciate that he is expressing clear, jargon-free opinions. And what he says sounds like it makes sense.[1]

· · · · ·

Jeremy Corbyn's message resonated from the off. This is important because several myths and half-truths about the cause of his popularity gained currency later on, when his profile became much higher. Commentators watching mass rallies convinced themselves Labour was being hijacked by assorted Trotskyists or claimed members were in the grip of "summer madness."[2] A common theme was that the Labour Party—which observers usually took to be synonymous with Labour MPs—had somehow been done over. The first month of the leadership contest gives the lie to this notion. Before the mass rallies, before the press hysteria, and before the campaign even got fully up to speed, Corbyn was ahead.

Corbyn had a unique advantage. He was the only candidate to unequivocally oppose the Thatcherite economic consensus that had failed so badly in the financial crash. The rallying cry of anti-austerity allowed him to present his candidacy as being—contradictorily—both absolutely of the moment and a return to Labour's founding traditions. Corbyn could easily situate himself within the anti-austerity zeitgeist sweeping Europe—the bright, dynamic new left, in contrast to the dimming light of social democracy. "That phrase we used about austerity being a political choice rather than an economic necessity really resonated," says one of Corbyn's close advisors, "because it gave people a sense of control. It's like, 'Oh we can do something about it.'" Yet at the same time Corbyn could place his candidacy firmly in the mainstream of Labour politics. Austerity, for many party members, was shorthand for Tory economic policy—the same small state ideology the Labour Movement had opposed for a hundred years. While Corbyn's association with the new anti-austerity movements blunted attacks casting him as a throwback, his espousal of traditional Labour ideals undercut attempts to marginalise him as 'hard left.' It was a devastatingly effective combination.

Corbyn's style was a perfect match for his politics. His outsider vibe set him apart. It began with his appearance, which instantly signalled a rejection of the modern political fetish for presentation. Even his beard—for which he had won the Parliamentary Beard of the Year Award no less than five times—was, he said, "a form of dissent" against New Labour.[3] (It also earned him his first official endorsement of the campaign as the Beard Liberation Front announced its support on 3 June on the basis that Corbyn stood for "no cuts.")[4] Corbyn looked like a man from a time when politics was about substance not spin. But his informal dress and preference for open necked shirts also reflected—in a quirky, British way—the European anti-austerity look sported by Alexis Tsipras, Yanis Varoufakis and Pablo Iglesias.

Corbyn had to fight to maintain his unique dress sense, however. "I made the pitch that we needed to smarten Jeremy up a little bit," says the MP Cat Smith. "At one point I thought about trying to turn him into an Andy Burnham—get him a nice suit, shave the beard off."

Smith was not alone in attempting a sartorial intervention. One morning she was eating her breakfast in Portcullis House in Westminster when Harry Fletcher, a member of Corbyn's campaign team, came over. "Have you seen Jeremy?" Fletcher asked.

"Nah, I've not seen him, are you looking for him?" Smith replied.

"Yeah, he's agreed to meet me here because we're going suit shopping." There was a sale on in House of Fraser on Victoria Street.

"What, and Jeremy knows that's what you're doing?" asked Smith.

"Yeah," Fletcher said.

"Well that's why he's not here then, isn't it!" Smith laughed.

An hour later Smith saw Corbyn "casually walking into Portcullis House with his coat on and his bag on his shoulder... I said to him, 'Harry Fletcher's looking for you.' Jeremy just looked shifty and ran off."[5]

More important than Corbyn's appearance was his demeanour: relaxed, approachable, honest. "The guy is just so bloody decent and nice and genuine," says Martin Mayer, a Unite delegate on Labour's NEC. "He talks without sound bites and rhetoric... He cut through all that disillusionment and even hatred of conventional politicians who are seen to be such a betrayal of people's interests—and that was particularly true of New Labour."

One of the first press clippings shared by the Corbyn campaign's social media team was a piece from the *Islington Gazette* of 8 December 2010, reporting that he was "the lowest expenses claimer in the country—after putting in for just £8.70 for an ink cartridge." The story was, as Corbyn pointed out, slightly misleading—some expenses had been deferred—but it became part of the Corbyn legend. For all the distrust of politicians following the expenses scandal, no one doubted Corbyn's insistence that he was a "parsimonious MP."[6]

Comfortable in his own skin, Corbyn was always at ease talking with the general public. "He's happiest when he's around people," says Smith. "He's happiest if you put him in a community centre in a town in the West Midlands or the North East or

Scotland... I don't think he enjoys speaking to the media or politicians." He was well equipped for the relentless series of leadership hustings arranged by the Labour Party. "He was always really good at the hustings," says Jon Lansman, adding that the format suited Corbyn much better than set-piece speeches. "Jeremy is brilliant, in my opinion, at the questions, because he's calm and relaxed and he doesn't give stock answers and so he's so much more interesting." The same approach set him up well for TV. On 2 July Corbyn appeared on BBC *Question Time* for the first time in 32 years as an MP, turning in a solid, profile-raising performance.[7] Backstage Corbyn received a boost when, according to an aide, David Dimbleby revealed that his son had signed-up to vote for him.[8] Corbyn was finding support in unlikely places.

· · · · ·

Among Corbyn's allies there was a range of expectations of how well he might do. One key member of the campaign persuaded his boss to give him time off work by saying: "I don't want the left to fall flat on its face. The main thing is we don't finish fourth, or even worse than that, a distant fourth." Andrew Berry, who helped set up a Unison For Corbyn group, was more optimistic: "Being ahead of the Blairites was where I expected us to be... Owen [Jones] and others were worried that we'd just be slaughtered. It was quite clear that wasn't going to happen." At the most optimistic end of the spectrum was Jon Lansman, but even he did not consider the possibility of winning: "My expectation was that we'd get somewhere between 30 and low-40s per cent of first preference votes."[9]

The early signs were good. Even before the campaign had a central command things were happening out in the wild. Throughout the summer what was known as the Corbyn campaign was actually an amalgam of spontaneous local activity. The official operation was "at the reins of a runaway horse," as the campaign's press spokesperson Carmel Nolan described it.[10] In the first week of the contest 250 people attended a meeting in Newcastle at 48 hours' notice. In London, an activist gathering in a pub on Tottenham Court Road attracted 300 people. Among them was James Schneider, who went on to be Momentum's national organiser and later Corbyn's head of strategic communications. "There was this pretty immediate groundswell of people," he remembers.

Corbyn's candidacy was a magnet for people used to organising on a shoestring. Marshajane Thompson produced the first batch of Corbyn t-shirts, paying her own money to have 100 printed. From these beginnings she ended up running the official Corbyn merchandise shop, which distributed 75,000 items.[11] Such DIY initiatives happened all over.

The contrast with the other candidates' campaigns was stark. They were top-down affairs with little grassroots energy, presided over by highly-paid professionals obsessed with messaging. Andy Burnham, for example, employed as his campaign director John Lehal, a lobbyist for Big Pharma.[12] His director of communications was Katie Myler, a lobbyist from a firm that advised the chemicals company Ineos in its 2013 industrial dispute with Unite at the Grangemouth refinery in Falkirk (the Scottish town that might as well have run for Labour leader itself given the influence it seemed determined to wield on the race).[13]

The Corbyn campaign started with zilch. The first time John McDonnell and Jon Lansman talked about how the operation might be run was on the Sunday before the nominations deadline. At the first proper campaign meeting, held a few days later in Westminster, it was agreed that to dispel the notion that Corbyn's candidacy was not serious, the outfit needed to look professional. Several people, including Clive Lewis and Cat Smith, suggested that Simon Fletcher, chief of staff to Ken Livingstone when he was mayor of London, should be hired as campaign manager.[14]

Although Fletcher was from a different political milieu to Corbyn and McDonnell (he was "seen as Ken's person," Lansman recalls, and was reportedly a former member of Socialist Action, a small and discreet far left organisation) his skill for messaging and cutting-edge campaigning techniques made him a valuable asset.[15] "None of the rest of us had any experience of the technology," says Lansman. "We'd never run campaigns that really worked the database and ran phone banks."

While Fletcher was negotiating his terms, others were laboriously building the campaign infrastructure. The most urgent task was to raise money, usually a dispiriting grind for any campaigner. This time, though, it was different. "Our first fundraising target was £5,000," remembers a member of the team. "We went from £5,000, to £10,000, to £25,000... over the period of a week or 10 days, from comparatively modest amounts of money to where we could do things that were just not possible previously. That was very encouraging."

Another pressing need was to find an office. Fortunately, one fell into the team's lap. Over the previous seven months TULO (the Trade Union and Labour Party Liaison Organisation) had run its general election campaign from a room in the headquarters of the TSSA union, next to Euston station in London. TULO's national officer Byron Taylor arranged for TSSA general secretary Manuel Cortes to kick TULO out with 24 hours' notice, leaving a fully functioning campaign office at the disposal of Team Corbyn.

Gradually the campaign staff took shape. Carmel Nolan, a journalist from Liverpool who helped found the Stop the War Coalition in 2001, became head of press.[16] She was interviewed for the job on a park bench with Fletcher beside her and McDonnell sat on the ground.[17] Nolan characterised Corbyn's team as "a coalition of the willing and the available."[18] Fletcher's old comrade at City Hall Anneliese Midgley was brought in as his deputy, overseeing the 'grid,' the schedule of campaign activity.[19] Corbyn's 25-year-old son Seb played a critical coordination role between the candidate and the campaign and crafted many of his dad's speeches and articles. Jack Bond, who transferred over from Corbyn's Islington office, took on much of the logistical work.

Developing Corbyn's policy line was Andrew Fisher, working in his spare time while still doing his day job for the PCS union. In his 30s, Fisher was a veteran of McDonnell's 2007 leadership bid and a former joint-secretary of the LRC. His work for the PCS, which represented civil servants in every government department, gave him a broad understanding of policy debates and he had detailed knowledge of the trade unions' positions having liaised with them on behalf of McDonnell in a previous job. Most importantly, he had known Corbyn and McDonnell for 15 years and shared their politics.

Lansman's job title—though he worked unpaid—was director of operations. "I was responsible, supposedly, for all field work and online operations." The technical side of the work was the realm of Ben Soffa, Cat Smith's partner, who worked for the TSSA so could easily pop in to the office (he would later join the team on secondment). His immediate task was to set up the NationBuilder software that provided the digital infrastructure behind the campaign.

An inordinate amount of energy was expended on complying with the rules of the Electoral Commission and the Information Commissioner. This dry-sounding task was crucial to Lansman, who wanted to ensure that data gathered during the contest could be used afterwards. "I was absolutely determined to build a left organisation out of this," he says. "It was all about putting together what became Momentum." The campaign could access the Labour Party membership list only for the purposes of the contest. So the team encouraged people to sign up as Corbyn supporters of their own volition. A company was established in Lansman's name to own the database. With as yet no thought of winning, emerging from the contest with an organisational legacy was the big prize.[20]

Such was the set-up in the TSSA office, but that was only part of the story. The structure of the Corbyn campaign can be visualised as a shamrock. While Simon Fletcher's domain formed the central stem, three leaves reached out to the political surroundings: the regional organisers network; the army of volunteers; and the social media operation.

The regional organisers were the least reported, most undervalued component of the campaign. There were 12 of them, spread across the country, their work coordinated at the centre by Alex Halligan, a talented 26-year-old Unite organiser from Salford.[21] At the height of the Corbyn surge in late July and August, the regional organisers were the people arranging big rallies and harnessing the explosion of grassroots activity. They "spent three months of their lives on very low wages running around making sure that everything was covered," says Marshajane Thompson, a regional organiser herself. "If it had just been run from London... the campaign wouldn't have been the success it was."

The second leaf of the shamrock was the volunteer operation. This was the fiefdom of Kat Fletcher (no relation to Simon). Her experience was ideal, having organised volunteers for Ed Miliband's 2010 campaign. She was also Corbyn's friend, acting as his agent in the 2015 general election, and her politics were radical.[22] Fletcher's 'volunteer centre' became something of a freestanding operation once Unite provided space for it in its head office in Holborn after endorsing Corbyn on 5 July.

Completing the shamrock was the social media team. After their success in the nominations period, a decision was taken to allow Ben Sellers and Marshajane Thompson to continue running the Facebook and Twitter accounts almost independently from the central office. "I had to fight for my space," says Sellers. "I remember having a discussion with Simon Fletcher about him wanting sign-off on everything. And I said: 'It's just not workable, it can't happen because we need to move quickly. The whole point of social media is that it reflects the organic, the grassroots, and if there's centralised control'—I was quite dramatic about it at the time, but I said—'you'll just kill it.'"

The arms-length arrangement gave Sellers and Thompson licence to be more strident than the central campaign could get away with and less formal than the competition. The "corporate, New Labour branding" of the other candidates' online output was "very dull," says Sellers, "as if Andy Burnham had asked somebody in his office to do it and they had never had a creative thought in their life." The Corbyn offering, in contrast, appeared collaborative, spontaneous, "almost like people had sent stuff in." "In fact," Sellers remembers, "especially early on people did send memes in and said, 'If you like this...' and we said, 'Yep, we're going to use that.'" The aim was to create a sense of shared ownership over a campaign growing from the ground up.

· · · · ·

For Team Corbyn, the contest would have three phases. In the first, lasting until 31 July 2015, Constituency Labour Parties (CLPs) across the country would nominate their preferred candidate. The second, overlapping phase was 'voter ID'—canvassing members and supporters to find Corbyn voters. The third phase, once ballots were distributed in mid-August, was 'get out the vote'—contacting those who said they would vote Corbyn to ensure they did.

CLP nominations were extremely important to all the campaigns. They carried no weight in the final tally, yet they told a story of who was doing well—invaluable in a contest that was all about momentum. Only full party members could have a say, and different CLPs used different methods for making their choice. In some cases the decision was taken by the local party's general committee, in others by whoever turned up to an all-member meeting.

For Jeremy Corbyn this looked like tough terrain on which to fight. In the 2010 contest David Miliband won the most CLP nominations with 164, while Diane Abbott got just 20.[23] Nevertheless, Team Corbyn approached the battle with purpose. "It was always going to be psychologically important," says Jon Lansman. "Whatever we did it needed to be as good as it possibly could be." Even as the machinery of the campaign was still being built, it was cranked into action.

The ideal CLP nomination would go like this: the regional organiser would establish when a CLP's nomination meeting was taking place; friendly local contacts willing to make the case for Corbyn would be identified; a speaker from outside, such as a supportive MP, would be lined up to address the meeting; all of this would be coordinated with Alex Halligan at the centre; Kat Fletcher's volunteers would phone canvass local members, encouraging supporters to go to the meeting; on the night, volunteers would greet attendees and hand them leaflets; the CLP would overwhelmingly endorse Corbyn; the social media team would publicise the triumph.

It did not always happen like that. It took time before there was a regional organiser in every area. It proved difficult to discover when CLPs were meeting. Many of the early votes were missed entirely. Speakers were difficult to find. The phone canvassing would sometimes be late or incomplete.[24] Initially there was no literature because it had not been printed.

But the campaign improvised with remarkable effectiveness. The phone canvassing may have been a last minute scramble, but that meant calls were made just before each meeting, which turned out to be a good time to ring. If an MP could not be found speak for Corbyn, the team would fall back on CLPD and LRC comrades. Halligan had experience of working on Unite's drive to increase the number of working class and left MPs. He knew how CLPs worked and how to win votes.[25]

No one was shocked when most CLPs that met early nominated Andy Burnham. What was "pleasantly surprising," however, was that "pretty much immediately" Corbyn's support was much broader than expected, says Lansman. "We started getting nominations from places that we didn't expect and we got feedback saying... some quite surprising people were backing Jeremy." According to another member of the team: "You get the known CLPs which will always support the left candidates... But it was extending beyond that... It was right across the country, from the far South West to Scotland... That was the real thing, where it felt like we're not going to get smashed... That's when I started getting my hopes up. But not of winning!"

What was instantly clear was that the party had no appetite for Blairism. Kendall was nowhere. For the advisor who had told his boss he needed time off to ensure Corbyn would not come a distant fourth, the early reports were electrifying. "Fuck, we're sort of third in this," he said to himself. "After the first 20 or 30 or 40 had taken place, the ones that met early, we're third! And we're only just behind Yvette Cooper."[26]

As the campaign picked up, with regional organisers in post and ever more volunteers, the results got better and better. By 10 July Corbyn had moved ahead of Cooper, with 28 nominations to her 25. Burnham was still out front with 36, but this was already dreamland for the Labour left.[27]

Team Corbyn now raised its sights. "Our perception when we started was that Burnham was the person to beat," remembers Lansman. "It was very important to get as close to him as possible... Then we wanted to beat him in CLP nominations once we got to that point." Reports from the meetings suggested Burnham's support was overstated by the totals. "A lot of his nominations came from those northern strongholds," says Lansman. "And some of them were by quite a small margin. And we were the challengers."

One example was Cat Smith's CLP of Lancaster and Fleetwood. The party nominated early. Smith was not able to exert much influence due to the unconventional way the CLP made its choice—it split up into small discussion circles then had a secret ballot. Burnham won—but by a single vote. Corbyn was second.[28]

There was a different dynamic down in London. Michael Calderbank was the CLP secretary in Brent Central, the seat of Dawn Butler. He invited Ken Livingstone to address their meeting. "His authority helped to swing the vote," Calderbank says. In a meeting of about 100 people, Corbyn won on the second round of voting—"it was quite a good margin."

Burnham must have been hearing the *Jaws* theme in his head as Corbyn closed in. By mid-July the left candidate was winning endorsements from middle-of-the-road CLPs. The advisor who was so thrilled at being third remembers:

> My CLP I would describe as apolitical. It's people who are councillors, mainly... Most of the people in it are not part of Progress, the LRC or anything. They just go out, they deliver leaflets, they don't even really want to talk about politics in the meetings... I remember going to my CLP and there were loads of people there, lots of people I hadn't seen before... I moved support for Jeremy Corbyn and a West Indian woman seconded it and gave a very impassioned, 'This is my politics, this is where I come from' speech. And then it was really weird, you had the councillors going: 'Well, I don't like Liz Kendall, she's too far to the right. I don't like Jeremy Corbyn, he's too far to the left. So I think we have to go for Yvette Cooper or Andy Burnham.' It was at that point in the meeting I just thought: 'If they can't actually decide who their candidate is for a leader—it's someone in the middle—these people haven't got a chance'... And we got [the nomination for Corbyn] through on the first round. I was just astonished. I almost fell off my chair. It was that kind of moment because this is not a left wing CLP and we won it.

By 17 July Corbyn was in first place in CLP nominations, with 55 to Burnham's 51.[29] He would not look back, winning 152 nominations overall. Burnham finished on 111, just ahead of Cooper on 109. Kendall won an embarrassing 18.[30]

The trajectory of the CLP nominations hints at the interplay between the agency of the Corbyn campaign and the appetite for his message. Something changed over the course of the first month of the contest, taking Corbyn from third to first in nominations. This happened with very little media coverage. It is surely not a coincidence that as the campaign machine got into gear Corbyn's position improved.[31] Yet it is evident that Corbyn was not a hard sell. The potential support was already there; it only needed to be alerted to Corbyn's existence.

· · · · ·

While it took until 17 July 2015 for Jeremy Corbyn to take the lead in CLP nominations, in raw support he was already ahead. Some of the campaign staff knew this almost as soon as phase two of the campaign, voter ID, got underway. But they could not believe it.

The Corbyn camp's voter ID operation was state of the art. Buttons and surveys embedded in emails and text messages were sent out to gather data. Volunteers manned phone banks (pop-up political call centres) making thousands of calls a night.

The very first time the campaign deployed its electronic communication tools, in early July, the response was overwhelming. "We sent out a few emails and a text message asking, basically, do you back us?" remembers a member of the team. "That's when I started to go, 'Let's not get carried away at the fact that we've got 15,000 people who have pledged to vote for us at this early stage.'"

Meanwhile, in the 'volunteer centre' at Unite HQ, phone bankers were busy calling Labour supporters.[32] One of those hitting the phones from the beginning was James Schneider: "That first day there were maybe six people building for a phone bank in the evening which had 25-30 people. Kat [Fletcher] was saying that was amazing... She was saying: '30 people on a phone bank for a leadership campaign for a minor candidate is *really* good. This is great.' And then by the end of the thing we'd have 500 people coming in on one day."

Schneider remembers getting five kinds of response on the phones in those early days:

It's either:
- 'Don't know who he is.'
- 'You must be absolutely crazy'—fairly rude.
- 'Hahaha you must be really crazy'—not so rude.
- People politely saying 'No' or politely saying 'I like him, but head not heart.'
- And about a fifth saying 'Yes.' And you think, 'That's pretty good! A left candidate getting a fifth. Pretty pleased with that.'

In fact it was better than a fifth—so much better that a staff member who had an overview of the data being recorded by the volunteers started to think that "either people are just so nice to fellow Labour Party members when you phone canvass them that they're lying, or something really is going on here."

The experience of 18-year-old A-level student Lola May gives an insight into the kind of conversations that were taking place in early July. Asked if she personally won anyone over, May says:

I know that I did. A lot of people would be like: 'Jeremy Corbyn, I've heard stuff about him but what does it actually mean?' It would be really interesting to talk to them and hear them change their mind as you explained to them why you were doing this... They'd be like: 'Not everyone else is left wing enough, no one else will vote for him.' And you'd be like: 'Well, actually people are. I've spoken to people and they will be voting for him'... I think that's why people kept coming back to the phone banks... When you're speaking to people and you can actually change their mind... that's quite special.

The initial results of the canvassing gave the campaign a shaky, incomplete picture of what was going on—like a TV on the blink. Ben Soffa, Alex Halligan and Jon Lansman then tried to work out how best to convert the data into an improvised poll for internal use. Whatever method they used, the picture looked implausibly good. And as more results flowed in, it only improved.[33]

As July wore on, Corbyn moved up towards 40 per cent in the internal poll—miles in the lead. Soffa thought it might be a freak occurrence, that the volunteers were somehow finding all of Corbyn's core supporters.[34] Lansman treated the stats with "a lot of scepticism." But by mid-July those privy to the data were starting to wonder. "We had our canvass returns but no one was going to believe us, they were too good to be true from the very beginning," remembers Lansman. "When we actually saw the figures we were staggered. We didn't tell people in the office! We shared it with Simon, but we didn't share it with Jeremy... it would have scared him!"

The last thing the campaign wanted was for the figures to get out, Lansman says. "What we were worried about was that if people generally knew how well we were doing there would be a lot of pressure—as indeed there then was—for an anti-Corbyn campaign." This strategy was soon blown out of the water. On 15 July the *New Statesman* reported on leaked "private polling" from a rival camp. The revelation was explosive. "One survey has Corbyn ahead by more than 15 points," the magazine said. "Another puts him in what one campaign staffer called 'a commanding position... he is on course to win.'"[35]

The early canvassing results and CLP nominations reveal an important truth about Corbyn's success. Far from being a summer craze, his almost immediate rise to first place can only be explained as the culmination of a much longer process within the Labour Party membership. The transformation of party sentiment since 2010, when at a similar stage in the leadership contest a Blairite candidate was first in both CLP nominations and a poll of members, was dramatic.[36] Some of this was down to new members—between the general election defeat and Corbyn getting on the ballot, 48,000 people reportedly joined the party.[37] It was claimed that around a third of the new members were under 30, and the most common age was 18.[38] Later in the summer, when the Corbyn camp analysed its own canvassing data, it discovered that the more recently a member joined, the more likely they were to support Corbyn.[39]

But that does not fully explain the altered landscape. Michael Calderbank is illuminating on the way sentiment evolved within his CLP of Brent Central:

> There was a shift in our CLP to the left in the Miliband period. But I don't think it was new members joining or a radicalisation of consciousness or anything as dramatic as that. The turn away from New Labour re-legitimised more traditional Labour. There was a decisive belief that the Blair years were behind us and we had to move on from the Iraq War, we had to acknowledge mistakes, we had to recover a sense that Labour stood for something different... Things like the housing crisis there was a developing consciousness that housing in London is just screwed and that needs some sort of serious intervention, you can't just let the market get on with it... None of the answers that were coming through from the party's top were connecting with those basic realities, and suddenly Jeremy was there making the case for rent control, making the case for regulating the banks, and it got an echo.

A significant component of Corbyn's early support came from members who did not necessarily think of themselves as left wing, but knew the economic orthodoxy had failed. This has implications for Labour beyond the question of the leadership. It suggests what happened to the party in 2015 was not an aberration, but a historic turn.

7

A MOVEMENT LOOKING FOR A HOME

"It is not just here; there are equivalent movements across Europe, the USA and elsewhere. It's been bubbling for a long time. It is opposition to an economic orthodoxy that leads us into austerity and cuts. But it is also a thirst for something more communal, more participative."

—*Jeremy Corbyn*

The clattering sound of samba beats echoes off the windowless exterior wall of the Bank of England. The usually grey City of London is today an explosion of colour and creativity. Thousands are pouring from the tube station or arriving on foot, assembling for a demonstration against austerity. Soon the crowd is too dense to move easily.

The march sets off at 1 p.m. A mass of humanity snakes between the buildings. The placards read "End Austerity Now," "No Cuts," "Homes Not Trident," "Cut War Not Welfare." Others are less earnest. "Down With This Sort Of Thing," says one. "Dyslexics Against The Cunts," reads another.

The fire-fighters' union has come with a balloon that says "We rescue people, not banks." The NUT teachers' union has a giant inflatable hand with "Hands up for education" written on it. There is a Keep Our NHS Public contingent, anti-fracking demonstrators, and a group of Sisters Uncut feminists. There is a Green bloc, the Black Bloc, and a large number of people dressed as badgers.

It is Saturday 20 June 2015, five days into the official part of the Labour leadership contest, but few on the demonstration are thinking in those terms. Called in an atmosphere of despondency after the general election, the march is an act of defiance. It has been met with scorn from conservative commentators who say the public voted for austerity. The People's Assembly, the broad umbrella organisation for campaigners and unions which has organised the protest, is briefing the media—more in hope than expectation—that 70,000 people might turn out. It is quickly apparent they have underestimated. As the march winds its way towards Parliament Square it is reported that a quarter of a million are on the streets.

At the rallying point, with the Palace of Westminster as a backdrop, the crowd bunches up to hear speeches from the stage. "If they think that they won the war of austerity on 7 May they better think again," warns Unite's general secretary Len McCluskey. Green MP Caroline Lucas says George Osborne has "no mandate" for cuts, because 76 per cent of people did not vote Tory. The singer Charlotte Church gives a rousing speech, emphasising that everybody needs public services simply by listing every category of person she can think of.

Jeremy Corbyn has addressed this kind of rally dozens of times. This occasion is different. He is a leadership contender. As he steps up to the microphone the crowd gives a huge cheer—the kind of reception that will become familiar later in the summer but which today is completely novel. It is as if the veteran protester is the new kid on the block—to the side of the stage Russell Brand, the headline act of the anti-austerity movement, stops what he is doing to hear what the rising star has to say. This is Corbyn's first big speech of the contest, to a vast crowd, at an event that echoes the central political message of his candidacy. It could not have been better scripted as an unofficial launch for his campaign.

But you would not know it from his speech. He does not even mention that he is standing for Labour leader. He does not tell the tens of thousands before him that they could all vote for £3. It is quintessential Corbyn—self-effacing to a fault. In his only oblique reference to the leadership contest he is more concerned to head off any criticism that he is using the event for his personal advantage. "This anti-austerity movement is a movement," he says. "It's absolutely not about ambitious individuals. This is about a social movement of all of us that can change our society into something good, rather than something that is cruel and divided. You all know the way forward."

It falls to the comedian Mark Steel to follow Corbyn's speech: "To start with I'd like to say that I want to live in a world where Jeremy Corbyn walks on stage and is greeted as if he's a rock star." It is said with sincerity but is meant as a joke, so surreal does the whole thing seem to Corbyn's old allies.[1]

· · · · ·

It was the movement that brought the magic to the Corbyn campaign. Although a process was already underway within the Labour membership, what gave the Corbyn phenomenon its distinctive character was the participation of people from outside the party. It was the sense that Jeremy Corbyn was at the head of a broad movement that made his leadership bid so extraordinary. The excitement; the dynamism; the heady, disorienting feeling of the impossible becoming possible—these were the trappings of movement politics.[2]

There are two sides to the tale of how this dimension of Corbyn's support came about. The first describes a conscious effort by the campaign to reach out to the various causes of the left. The second concerns a process that ran in the opposite direction: the anti-austerity movement was already searching for a vehicle through which it could advance its aims, and found it in Corbyn's candidacy.

There is a historical dimension to the first side of the tale, which explains why it was necessary for the campaign to appeal to existing movements. Over the decades the left had become stratified into myriad separate causes. In the 1960s, 70s and 80s there was a flowering of new movements, such as anti-racism and rejuvenated feminism. These often had an uneasy relationship with the Labour Movement.[3] As the Labour Party then became ever-more remote, and with political pluralism on the rise, many seeking to change society came to see their best chance as being through non-party, single-issue campaigns.

The Corbyn candidacy gave this fragmented left the chance to come back together. But it was not obvious that it would do so. As Young Labour national committee member Max Shanly admits, "A lot of these people have grown up despising the Labour Party." The journalist Owen Jones remembers addressing People's Assembly meetings around the country in the Miliband years: "If I'd stood up and said, 'And that is why you must join the Labour Party because the only way we're going to build a left movement in this country that has any chance of taking power is through the Labour leadership,' there's no question I would have been heckled vociferously and aggressively."

The big change in 2015 was that the bar of commitment for potential voters had been dramatically lowered by the registered supporters scheme. Suddenly non-members could have a say over Labour's next leader for £3. The party viewed the leadership election as a recruitment opportunity—the NEC deliberately set the price low and allowed plenty of time for people to sign up. For the tens of thousands who chose to join as full members instead, no retrospective 'freeze date' was imposed to prevent them voting.[4]

Few thought registered supporters would benefit the left. As a brainchild of the Blairites, the scheme was intended to diminish the influence of activists and trade unionists and cement Labour in the fabled centre ground. "Because they were so convinced I suppose I was quite convinced that it wasn't going to work in our favour," says the MP Cat Smith. Some, though, were eyeing up the opportunities. "One of the reasons why I was so keen to have a candidate was I actually did think that, given that we'd agreed the £3, we would do much better than all the people on the right anticipated," says Jon Lansman.[5]

The consensus in Team Corbyn is that the registered supporter system turned their campaign outwards, making the recruitment of fresh blood central to the strategy (partly, initially, due to misplaced pessimism about Corbyn's chances with full members). The first opportunity to test the approach was at the massive People's Assembly 'End Austerity Now' demonstration on 20 June. The fledgling campaign rushed out a leaflet drafted by Simon Fletcher and Andrew Fisher. The simple wording had one goal—to recruit:

> Jeremy Corbyn For Labour Leader
> Together we can end austerity
> Register today to vote in the Labour leadership election: jeremyforlabour.com/vote or use this form

"We gave out the best part of 20,000 of those leaflets," says a member of the team. "I don't know how many directly resulted in anyone joining... but it sparked the idea that this was actually something that was part of the mass movements. I remember saying to people there, 'If everyone on this demo joins, he'll win!'"

Although Corbyn chose not to plug his candidacy from the stage, other speakers did it for him. "Wouldn't it be amazing if everybody on this march registered and voted for Jeremy Corbyn to be leader of the Labour Party?" asked Mark Serwotka, general secretary of the PCS union, who was not a party member at the time. "If tens of thousands of us pay our £3 and register maybe we can have an anti-austerity voice at the top of Labour."[6] As Serwotka spoke, down in the throng Lansman "passed bundles of leaflets in all directions and the crowd distributed them." He had "never found it easier to distribute leaflets."[7]

James Schneider was also leafleting. "I had two people yell 'Labour are awful,'" he remembers. "And a nice Welsh man heard them and said, 'No, not Jeremy Corbyn, he's brilliant, he's been fighting for people his whole life.' And they were like, 'No, no, he's Labour, he must be terrible.' And he said, 'No, you don't understand, read about him, he's brilliant.'"

There was an obvious explanation for the instant enthusiasm for Corbyn. Along with Caroline Lucas and John McDonnell, he was one of a tiny handful of MPs who commanded near-universal respect among grassroots campaigners. According to McDonnell, "No one [else] in the Parliamentary Labour Party had any time for any of the social movements whatsoever and were embarrassed to be... associated with them at all."[8] Corbyn, in contrast, had addressed so many rallies and meetings over the years on such a range of causes that he could count on a bedrock of support from the off. McDonnell remembers: "Jeremy was touring round the country and he was saying, 'Oh I met so-and-so, we met him 10 years ago when we were involved in that occupation.' Or, 'We did the Chile campaign together.' That sort of thing." Corbyn and McDonnell had even helped set up many campaigns—"One of my primary roles in political life [was] booking rooms at the House of Commons for all these different organisations," McDonnell jokes. As soon as Corbyn needed the reciprocal backing of campaigners, their attitude, McDonnell speculates, was: "These people are talking our politics, they've worked alongside us, we need to support them."

Corbyn's level of commitment was impossible to contrive. It stemmed from his fundamental political belief that, despite being an MP, parliament was not at the centre of the world. "Politics isn't really about, as interesting as it is, the arithmetic in Holyrood, in Westminster, Cardiff or anywhere else," Corbyn has said. "It's actually about what people think and do outside. Political change actually comes from the democratic base of our society."[9]

In the weeks following the People's Assembly demonstration Team Corbyn mobilised for more rallies and events—including several in support of Greece, then at the climax of its confrontation with the European Union.[10] On 27 June, at London's Pride Parade, Marshajane Thompson led volunteers signing up supporters at a "Corbyn and Proud" stall—a perfect illustration of Corbyn being repaid for years of tireless advocacy. Corbyn's commitment to LGBT+ rights stretched back to when it was a deeply unpopular cause. As a councillor in Haringey before becoming an MP he led the defence of a gay community centre attacked by the National Front.[11] In parliament from 1983 he voted for virtually every piece of equalities legislation going. He was the only Labour MP to defy the whip to support a Liberal Democrat amendment to the Human

Rights Bill in 1998 to outlaw discrimination based on sexuality—12 years before the Equality Act was passed.[12]

Now, as he marched through London behind a "Jeremy Corbyn for Labour Leader" banner, followed by a man with an "I heart Jeremy Corbyn" placard, the crowds of people watching from the side of the street started spontaneously chanting "Jeremy."

"They're chanting my name!" Corbyn said to Thompson, with what she describes as a "shell-shocked" look on his face. All along the route the chants kept breaking out. In Trafalgar Square, as Corbyn made his way to the platform to speak, he was mobbed.[13] According to Thompson the day felt "just surreal... It's one of those moments where you think 'This is something different.'"

Corbyn's social media team was also recruiting from the broad left. "We didn't realise the impact of the Collins Review when we started," recalls Ben Sellers. "But then it dawned on us that what we needed to do was win over the supporters and face outwards. We talked about the different groups that Jeremy was incredibly popular with and the stuff that he'd done in the past."

Separately, one volunteer took it upon himself to approach various activist organisations. The effort culminated in a letter published in the *New Statesman* on 29 July signed by an assortment of 25 campaigns and prominent individuals. "As grassroots campaigners and activists working for social change from outside Westminster, we recognise the fundamentally flawed and stagnant state of parliamentary politics in this country," the letter began.

> However, it is foolish to suggest that it doesn't make any difference who is in government or who is the leader of the main political parties... Whether he's been leading anti-war marches, standing up for the rights of disabled people or calling for radical solutions to the housing crisis, Jeremy has always been on the side of social movements. We know a lot of people are sceptical about the Labour Party, for many very legitimate reasons. We urge people, despite those concerns, to back a true campaigner leading the opposition.[14]

Other activist organisations, including the Palestine Solidarity Campaign of which Corbyn was a patron, as well as NGOs and charities, were unable to formally back him due to being non-party political. "It's definitely not the case that any of the big organisations gave their email list to Jeremy or anything like that," says a member of the Corbyn camp. "Some took different views to others in terms of how far they were willing to push it and recommend people join." Pushing it further than most was the Stop the War Coalition, which announced its support for Corbyn—who was its chair—on 16 June and promoted a link to the £3 sign-up page.[15]

It was on international and human rights causes such as peace, nuclear disarmament, migrant rights and anti-racism that Corbyn's work was best known and where support was most fulsome. A considerable chunk of his base was made up of people for whom the Iraq War was the seminal issue of their lives. But he enjoyed goodwill from an incredibly wide spectrum of activists—from environmentalists to mental health campaigners and from the respectable end of activism to the more radical, direct action fraternity. Corbyn's candidacy gave them all a single battle to win.

In these early weeks the Corbyn campaign was appealing to activists, rather than the broader array of progressives it would later attract. "The number of people who actually properly knew the full range of Jeremy's politics [was] probably quite small," says a campaign team source. "We're talking maybe 10,000 people." But these activists formed a core of highly experienced campaigners, vocal on social media, keyed into left networks, and not shy about evangelising. They could "vouch for Jeremy being the real thing, not just another Labour politician tacking leftwards," the campaign insider says. It was an indispensible platform on which to build the "maximal broad left" coalition that would emerge by August 2015.

· · · · ·

"There was a movement looking for a home," says the comedian Mark Steel, reflecting on the anti-austerity sentiment that propelled Jeremy Corbyn to such heights.[16] This was the other side of the tale of Corbyn's relationship to the social movements. Although it was important to attract supporters from, for example, the anti-war or anti-nuclear movements, in 2015 those causes were not the engine of left activity that Stop the War had been in the early 2000s or CND had been in the 1980s. A recruitment drive could take the campaign so far, but only a live process with its own electricity could power the forward motion of the Corbyn juggernaut. The anti-austerity movement provided that energy.

It was no coincidence that politicians of the left rose to prominence around the world at roughly the same time, or that the forces that propelled them had so much in common. "It is not just here; there are equivalent movements across Europe, the USA and elsewhere," Corbyn said in the midst of his campaign, reflecting on the reason for his ascent. "It's been bubbling for a long time. It is opposition to an economic orthodoxy that leads us into austerity and cuts. But it is also a thirst for something more communal, more participative."[17]

As Corbyn's comments suggest, the anti-austerity movement was really a continuation of the broader struggle against the aggressive, free market, finance-based form of capitalism ushered in by Margaret Thatcher and Ronald Reagan and now known by the ugly name of neoliberalism. That struggle, led by the Labour Movement in the 1980s, was initially lost. By the time the Cold War ended in 1991 the advocates of neoliberalism could declare total victory. It was, apparently, "the end of history."[18] This was the era of globalisation. In Britain, Labour became New Labour in 1994, conceding that the fundamental tenets of Thatcherism were irreversible. It seemed there genuinely was no alternative.

Some, though, insisted that "another world is possible." An international alter-globalisation movement emerged around the turn of the millennium.[19] It organised itself on non-hierarchical, 'horizontal' lines and had a very different style from the movements of organised labour—an anarchistic vibe, a DIY aesthetic, and a hedonistic streak. For an intense few years no big gathering of a global institution was spared a mass mobilisation of tens and sometimes hundreds of thousands of demonstrators. But it was a tough ask to take on neoliberalism in its pomp. For all its vibrancy, the alter-globalisation movement had minimal impact on mainstream politics and receded after 9/11 as its energy was diverted into resisting the War On Terror.[20]

The financial crisis of 2008 changed the context entirely. The aftermath of the crash should have been a time of vindication and advance for the left. Yet it was unprepared for its moment of opportunity. It lacked institutional power and intellectual confidence. It had become accustomed to losing. The right suffered from no such doubts. "They were better equipped to be able to turn the narrative of 2008 from one of a failing global financial system and elite into one of a failing social security system and welfare state," explains the MP Clive Lewis. After a brief period of panicked Keynesian fiscal expansion (using public investment to generate growth), neoliberal ideology reasserted itself in international bodies, in the Eurozone and, especially after the election of a Tory-led coalition, in the UK government. The European continent embarked on a journey into the dark tunnel of austerity.

The ethos and methods developed by the alter-globalisation movement transferred easily to the anti-austerity cause. In 2011 the non-hierarchical left burst back to prominence with a fresh tactic: occupation. Beginning with thousands of Spaniards occupying city squares, the phenomenon soon spread to Greece and then New York, where it adopted the name Occupy and the slogan "We are the 99 per cent"—differentiating the vast mass of the population from the tiny fraction at the top hoarding all the resources.

This movement was young, drawn mainly from the generation suffering most under policies adopted to deal with the crash.[21] It was hostile to the party political system and indifferent to trade unions. Although occupiers could take ground, they could not hold it—both literally and figuratively.[22] Once they were physically evicted from the squares much of their cohesion was lost.[23] Yet their enduring achievement was to open up political possibilities.

In late spring 2012, Corbyn visited Greece, then in the midst of a wild economic experiment. He saw the hardship, the despair, the beggars on the streets of Athens. But there was something new in the air—not tear gas, but hope. The anti-austerity movement was desperate for a way to impose its will, having failed to force a change of direction through a series of monster protests that had each been, in one Greek leftist's words, "more than a demonstration but less than a revolt."[24] Frustrated, a restless movement sought an avenue into electoral politics. The party it got behind, Syriza, a rebellious child of the Greek Marxist tradition, had polled just 4.6 per cent in the 2009 legislative election. But in June 2012 its support shot up to 27 per cent, coming in a close second. Shockwaves were sent across Europe.

The flip side of Syriza's rise was the spectacular slump of the traditional centre-left party, Pasok. As recently as 2009 it had won an election with 44 per cent of the vote; in June 2012, after implementing austerity, it fell to just 12 per cent. Pasok's fate was a stark illustration of the crisis of social democracy (the diluted version of socialism that had dominated European centre-left politics for a hundred years with its promise to manage—rather than replace capitalism to make society fairer). Corbyn was inspired by the dramatic developments he witnessed in Greece, writing on his return that Pasok's ignominious demise was a "vivid warning" for social democrats everywhere. Having met Syriza leader Alexis Tsipras and attended one of his election rallies, Corbyn was exhilarated that the vacuum had been filled by a socialist alternative.[25]

As Corbyn predicted, Pasok's woes were echoed in subsequent years in the fortunes of other social democratic parties.[26] The roots of this phenomenon were deep. Social democracy enjoyed its most successful period in the three decades following the Second World War, when it was closely tied to a Keynesian economic consensus. There was an implicit bargain whereby industry was supported to grow but had to accept a commensurate rise in the power of labour, which used its position of strength to deliver—via social democratic governments—benefits for the population like universal healthcare and social security. That arrangement was fatally undermined by the triumph of neoliberalism in the 1980s, which saw the basis of the economy switch from industry to finance and services. Trade unions were beaten back and the institutions of social democracy—above all the welfare state—were gradually eroded.[27] In response, social democratic parties became more neoliberal. New Labour in Britain was the standout example, but a conviction that neoliberal economics was an unchallengeable fact of life infected the worldview of leading social democrats everywhere.

Although it became fashionable to observe that electorates were rejecting social democracy following Pasok's demise, in reality social democracy was no longer on offer. Even the delivery of the most modest social democratic promises—investment in core public services—was impossible while accepting the constraints of austerity. As one of Corbyn's advisors says, "It isn't that social democracy has failed, it's just ceased to exist." Centre-left politicians increasingly resembled a detached, technocratic elite, more loyal to the status quo than to their supporters. Yet their traditional voters were among the hardest hit by austerity. Ideologically bereft, social democratic parties offered no hope of an alternative. Not unreasonably, many of their voters withdrew support.

With most social democratic parties stubbornly defending a bankrupt system, the anti-austerity movement instead flowed into, or created, parties to their left. The form this took varied from country to country depending on the local political traditions. In Greece, where the Marxist left was historically strong with a legitimacy derived from the Second World War and the Greek Civil War, it found a home in Syriza. In Spain it created its very own party from scratch: Podemos, which shot to 20 per cent of the vote in December 2015 less than two years after its formation. The most surprising of all the electoral manifestations occurred in the US in 2015-16 in the presidential candidacy of Bernie Sanders. His campaign drew heavily on the Occupy movement, which had resuscitated the American progressive left.[28]

Of course, discontent with a dysfunctional economic system did not just break to the left, as was vividly demonstrated by the rise of Donald Trump, the Greek Nazi party Golden Dawn, the French National Front, the Swedish Democrats and, in a less extreme form, UKIP.

The scale of austerity in Britain was far smaller than in the worst affected European countries, but that was no consolation to the sections of society experiencing cuts.[29] Tory policy tended to single out particular groups for punishment: millions of public sector workers who had their pay frozen; disabled people whose essential benefits were cut and made harder to access; those living in social housing with a spare room that qualified for the bedroom tax; and so on.

One such targeted group—students—provided the first big expression of resistance. The proposal to triple university tuition fees to £9,000 provoked over 50,000 of them to take to the streets for a series of raucous protests in November and December 2010.[30] The effect was to radicalise student organisations and politicise a layer of young people. "Some of them even went to prison," remembers John McDonnell, who says that he and Corbyn were the only MPs who "stood by them and did meetings with their families." The hardships visited on another group—the disabled—produced opposition that was as vociferous, if on a smaller scale. Corbyn and McDonnell were heavily involved with Disabled People Against the Cuts (DPAC), founded in 2010. "We've now got a radical disability movement in this country that we've never had before," McDonnell says.

Other features of the UK economy resembled the US more than Europe: gross inequality, staggering executive pay, stagnating wages, poor worker protections, an unaccountable finance industry, and untouchable corporations. One response was the direct action approach of UK Uncut, which announced itself in October 2010 by shutting down Vodafone stores to protest the company's tax arrangements.[31] The group was in keeping with the horizontal ethos of the alter-globalisation movement, but focused specifically on corporate tax avoidance and evasion. While its tactics appeared to terrify the establishment, Corbyn was an instant supporter. "Essentially it is a moral force," he said of the group.[32]

In October 2011, as part of the global Occupy phenomenon, an encampment was established outside St Paul's Cathedral in London. McDonnell was there on the first night. Although the numbers involved were relatively small, both Occupy and UK Uncut had a disproportionate influence. Tax avoidance was not a prominent political issue before UK Uncut forced it onto the agenda. Anger at economic inequality became more pronounced in the wake of Occupy. These kinds of protest movements were reflexively ridiculed and declared pointless by the British media, yet through their action they shifted the dial.

Far larger numbers could be mobilised by the trade unions, although the political impact of their traditional A-to-B marches was arguably less. 400,000 people took to the streets for a

TUC-organised protest in London in March 2011—the biggest demonstration Britain had seen since the Iraq War. A series of public sector strikes over changes to pensions followed, in which 2 million workers took part.[33]

The big problem for the anti-austerity movement—both the traditional and new parts of it—was how to keep the momentum. The next national TUC demonstration in October 2012 was half as big as its predecessor.[34] It was three years until there was another comparable round of public sector strikes, called in 2014 against the pay freeze, which involved only half as many workers.[35] Similarly, although UK Uncut and Occupy intermittently reappeared, they never recaptured the energy of 2011.[36]

However, by the mid-term of the Coalition government a plethora of anti-cuts groups and community-level resistance had emerged—'save our hospital' campaigns, protests against the loss of childcare services, battles over the closure of local facilities like swimming pools. Women, who were disproportionately affected, led many of these fights. The campaigns were often given organisational backing by union branches and trades councils and unified into local 'Against The Cuts' groups. At their most radical they involved occupations—threatened libraries, for example, were kept open and run by their communities.

"The political movement that took place in terms of anti-austerity was a complete disillusionment with the way in which the current system operates," says McDonnell. "That was translated into relatively inchoate individual criticisms of it, so UK Uncut on the tax system, DPAC on the way disabled people were being treated." The formation of the People's Assembly Against Austerity in 2013 was an attempt to bring together these disparate forces.[37] It united campaign organisations with big unions (including Labour affiliates like Unite, Unison, and the CWU), and a few political parties including the Greens. Corbyn and McDonnell were among the signatories to the Assembly's founding letter.[38] Local People's Assemblies were formed around the country, building up a constituency at the grassroots.

2014 saw a proliferation in this kind of activity. Gatherings got larger. Local struggles gained greater prominence. The issue of housing in London, for example, was pushed to the fore by groups like Focus E15, which emerged organically from efforts to resist eviction, and a high profile campaign involving Russell Brand to defend residents of the New Era estate in Hoxton. Brand himself became a draw for thousands of young people to get involved in the anti-austerity movement as he used his celebrity platform to amplify the ideas and actions of campaigners.

The movement was then energised by the victory of Syriza in the January 2015 Greek election. Against the odds, an anti-austerity party formed the first radical left government in post-war European history. It felt like it was "time for dreams to take revenge," as one elated Greek activist put it.[39] Suddenly, another world seemed not just possible but tangible.

Around the same time, in Britain, a "Green surge" saw thousands join the Green Party, swelling its membership to 50,000—larger than both UKIP and the Liberal Democrats.[40] The explanation for the influx lay in the party's shift left. "The average member was now as much an anti-austerity activist as she was a climate change campaigner; as keen on defending the NHS as saving the rainforest," wrote the Green activist and journalist Adam Ramsay.[41]

Another party presenting itself as part of the anti-austerity left and experiencing a surge in membership was the SNP. The full reasons for its stratospheric rise are complex, but the anti-austerity movement played a part in the drama.[42] Important to the nationalists' case for Scotland leaving the UK was the idea that independence offered an escape from Tory austerity. So when Scottish Labour lined up with the Conservatives to defend the status quo in the 2014 independence referendum, it was rejecting not just nationalism but the anti-austerity movement too. Just like Pasok in Greece, Labour was perceived to be defending a remote elite enforcing measures that hurt its own supporters.

Outside Scotland, the anti-austerity movement found its path blocked by the first-past-the-post electoral system. For the section of the movement that hoped to express itself through the Greens, Plaid Cymru in Wales, or any of the smaller socialist parties, the 2015 general election was a disappointment. The Greens emerged with just one MP, despite winning over a million votes (four times as many as in 2010). Yet anger at the election of a Conservative government gave an unexpected boost to the anti-austerity movement—evidenced in the giant 20 June People's Assembly demonstration.

In its search for a home, Labour's was the last door this movement knocked on.[43] Surprisingly, it found it not just unlocked, but wide open. First-past-the-post could not completely shield Britain from the historical trends sweeping the Western world. The dramatic collapse of neoliberal-infected social democratic parties around Europe did find an echo in the UK, but it was hidden from view, happening quietly within the Labour Party itself.

Labour was traditionally said to be two parties welded together—one social democratic, the other socialist. However, since 1994 Labour had really been three parties: a neoliberal one (Blairites and Brownites), a social democratic one (with a 'soft left' and an 'old right'), and a socialist one.[44] The neoliberal strand, which reigned supreme for so long as New Labour, had by 2015 collapsed like its European centre-left equivalents, mortally wounded by the crash of 2008. But because this tendency still operated under the shell of Labour, no one knew. It took a leadership election to find out. This meant that when the anti-austerity movement rushed into the Labour Party, there was far less hostility from existing members than might have been expected. Indeed, it found the party had been undergoing its own process of transformation.

The extraordinary coincidence of a historic political shift on the centre-left, a radical rule change, and the surprise presence of a left candidate on the leadership ballot meant that, unlike in Greece and Spain, in the UK the anti-austerity movement had an opportunity to make its home in an established party. The potential advantages were immense: Labour not only had the infrastructure, name recognition, and deep-rooted support to benefit from the first-past-the-post electoral system, but its residual links to the trade unions were the reason why it had always been seen by many socialists as the vehicle for progressive change.

Because the anti-austerity movement had a profound impact on British politics, it is easy when tracing its development to overstate its size and strength. As the Tory victory at the 2015 general election showed, austerity was not a concern for many. But it is impossible to explain what happened on the left and in the Labour Party without recognising the movement that forced the pace.

"There was a climate of opposition that was building up, that moved from opposition to demands for transformation and change," says McDonnell. "We caught the wind of that because we were part of it." Once the Corbyn campaign had been set in motion, it started to draw in a broader range of people than were involved in either the anti-austerity movement or other activist causes. "The largest part [of Corbyn's support] was probably unaffiliated left progressives who weren't associated with any particular campaign that Jeremy had been involved in, but probably were generally anti-austerity, generally anti-war, generally pro-tackling human rights situations," says one of Corbyn's team. As the number of such people grew, the campaign morphed into a political movement in its own right, a 'Corbyn movement.'

8

POWER IN A UNION

"The grip of the Blairites and individuals like Peter Mandelson must now be loosened once and for all. There is a virus within the Labour Party, and Jeremy Corbyn is the antidote."

—Dave Ward, general secretary, CWU

Jeremy Corbyn is unhappy if he cannot do something he has always done. On the third weekend of July he is usually in the village of Tolpuddle in Dorset for the Tolpuddle Martyrs Festival, a celebration of trade unionism with live music, banners and speeches. The event commemorates six men who were transported to Australia in 1834 as punishment for combining to form a trade union for agricultural workers. Known as the Tolpuddle Martyrs, the men became heroes of the Labour Movement. Every year thousands of trade unionists and friends gather in the village for a weekend of fun in their honour.

But in 2015 Corbyn is a busy man. His team tells him he is not allowed to go. On the morning of Sunday 19 July, the day of the traditional rally at the festival, he has the official Labour Party hustings for the London region, 130 miles away from Tolpuddle. He cannot possibly fit it in. "Look up the trains and find me a way," he tells his staff, but they report back that there is no way. The festival finishes at 6 p.m. He will not make it.

But Corbyn has a stubborn streak. "I'm going to Tolpuddle," he texts one of his campaign team, Marshajane Thompson. His usual route involves getting a train to Dorchester with his bike, then cycling the seven miles to the village. "I've worked out," he texts, "that if I get off at one of the stops on the way, if Jack [Bond, another member of the team] drives there two hours before me and meets me at that station, then he can drive me the rest of the way and I'll get there on time."

On the day, the plan works better than clockwork: Corbyn and Bond pull up at the festival earlier than expected, at 4 p.m. It is a glorious day. The sun is out, there is a warm breeze, and the site is awash with colour. Corbyn heads to the 'Jeremy Corbyn for Labour Leader' stall, where a team of volunteers is stationed, including Thompson, giving out information, selling campaign merchandise and getting people registered to vote. Virtually everyone at the festival has a red 'JC' sticker. Corbyn is soon surrounded by people snapping selfies, wanting to chat, to shake his hand. He is among friends.

The *Guardian* journalist John Harris has come along to make a short film. He snatches an interview. "Are you surprised by any of this?" he asks Corbyn. "You can't walk more than two yards without someone wanting a selfie and all the rest of it. It didn't happen to Diane Abbott last time. Do you know what I mean? Something's changed."

"People are looking for hope," Corbyn replies. "Our campaign—it's not me, it's our, it's a lot of people together—is changing things and I happen to be in a position where I'm asked to speak on behalf of it, and I'm happy and proud to do so."

"You're too self-effacing," Harris comments.

"Is that a problem?"

"No."

Everyone is demanding that Corbyn speak. But the Trades Union Congress, which organises the festival, is reluctant to let him address the crowd from the stage because it might show favouritism, as none of the other candidates has been offered the opportunity (not that they are present). Improvising, Thompson asks her own union, Unison, if Corbyn can make a speech outside its tent using its PA system. Although Unison has not yet nominated a candidate for Labour leader, its South West regional secretary Joanne Kaye agrees that, as a Unison member, Corbyn should be given the chance to speak.

A plan is hatched. The singer Billy Bragg is the festival's closing act. Thompson speaks to him before he goes on stage and asks him to let the crowd know that Corbyn will speak from the Unison tent after the show. But a large portion of the crowd is travelling by coach, and are due to depart shortly after the 6 p.m. finish. Some volunteers are dispatched to talk to the coach drivers, to ask if they can leave a little later. It is an easy sell—the drivers want to hear Corbyn speak too.

At the end of Bragg's set he tells the audience: "You might be interested to know that in the white tent over there, the Unison tent, you can probably see it, Jeremy Corbyn is there, he'll be speaking shortly... Meanwhile I want to finish off with a quick verse of an old song. Maybe I'll dedicate it to Jeremy this year."

Bragg breaks into 'The Red Flag,' the Labour anthem. Much of the audience joins in, fists raised in a socialist salute. And then the entire crowd turns around to face the Unison tent. It is a ready-made open-air audience of 3,000 people, all staying late just to listen to Corbyn.

"Tolpuddle is something very, very special to me, I first came here as a 14-year-old boy with my mum and dad," Corbyn begins, before launching into a 20-minute speech with the recurring theme: "Let's be proud of what we are."

"We can win people back but we don't do it by apologising for what we are, we don't do it by treating the trade unions as a rather embarrassing uncle that turns up every other Christmas and you wish they'd go. We do it by being proud of what we are, proud of where we come from, proud of our unions."

Corbyn's speech ranges across his campaign issues: austerity, the environment, peace. But he sets it all in the context of the Labour Movement—not just the party, but the movement of working people whose history stretches back through the Chartists, the Tolpuddle Martyrs and the formation of the trade unions, all the way to the English Civil War. When he urges the crowd to fight the Tories' proposed Trade Union Bill, it is as the latest struggle in that history. "Surely to God we can stand up, as the brave people did in this very village in 1834, for trade unions and workers' rights," he says. "Lift our sights up, lift our spirits up, lift our hopes up for a decent, better world. That is what our forebears fought for, that is what we proudly campaign for. And whatever happens, we're a force, we're a presence, we're a future, we're a hope, we're an inspiration to the next generation. Thank you very much for inviting me today."

The crowd responds with a huge cheer and a long ovation. Nobody cares that he was not really invited.[1]

* * * * *

Contrary to the media's portrayal of the trade unions as an extreme, ideological, left wing menace, they are in fact cautious organisations. Their immediate priority is to improve conditions for their members, who have little choice but to work in a capitalist economy. Historically, this has always tempered grander aspirations to usher in a socialist society. When it comes to choosing a Labour leader, the big unions are expected to be pragmatic, to back the candidate who conventional wisdom suggests is the best bet to be prime minister—as long as it is someone with whom they can work—so as to have a negotiating partner in Number 10. They are not expected to back a wildcard candidate. In 2015, they did.

Nine unions nominated Jeremy Corbyn—six of them affiliated to the Labour Party, including the two giants, Unite and Unison. In contrast, three plumped for then-favourite Andy Burnham, two for Yvette Cooper, and none for Liz Kendall.[2] How did this extraordinary situation come about? Of course, each union was different, with its own organisational culture and internal political dynamics. But they were not islands; they all operated on a shared terrain.

A feature of that terrain is familiar from what was also occurring in the party and the social movements: a groundswell of enthusiasm for Corbyn from below. Yet union bureaucracies had decades of experience of resisting pressure from rank and file activists. Something else had changed: a swing to the left in union leaderships over a decade and a half—partly as a result of shifts in the economy, but also in response to the rise of New Labour which stripped the unions of their traditional role in the party. The upshot was a generation of union leaders and officials who did not feel a strong obligation to defend the Labour establishment; and a Labour establishment, personified by Corbyn's three rivals for the leadership, that felt little obligation to the unions.

"A lot of [union] executives were under so much pressure from the grassroots," says John McDonnell. "In addition to that, their executives had come to the view: 'Actually, why are we supporting someone who we don't necessarily wholeheartedly agree with? Why are we going for second best? Why don't we go for someone who we can actually support?'"

There is a whole world of union politics that very few people know anything about. Since the demise of industrial correspondents on newspapers, the media has displayed only the shallowest knowledge of the workings of these organisations. Dramatic shifts of policies and personalities, with consequences for politics and society, pass unremarked. During and after the leadership contest there was very little attempt to understand what had happened in the unions. This was remarkable given that trade union support was a big factor in Corbyn's success. It helped deliver the votes of union members; it provided his campaign with desperately needed money and resources; and, most importantly, it conferred legitimacy and credibility on Corbyn's challenge. It may have been uncharacteristic for the unions to back an outsider like Corbyn, but with their support he no longer was one.

· · · · ·

The collective weight of the trade union movement was not always positioned on the left. In the 1950s an alliance of right-leaning union leaders and MPs dominated Labour. But from the late 1960s the unions embarked on a historic shift leftwards, signified by the election in 1968 of the 'terrible twins' Jack Jones and Hugh Scanlon to lead two of Britain's largest unions. The trajectory was mirrored in Constituency Labour Parties during the 1970s, leading up to the

Bennite revolt of the early 1980s. The culmination of these trends came in 1981, when co-operation between the unions and the constituency parties stripped MPs of their exclusive right to choose the Labour leader, and instead instituted the electoral college system that split the responsibility between the unions, members and parliamentarians.

No sooner had this alliance achieved success than it began to fracture, as unions took fright at the leftward direction of the Labour Party and positioned themselves as a counterweight to the Bennite constituency parties. The unions came to be seen as the praetorian guard of the Labour leadership.[3]

But the unions' might was weakening. The destruction of industry and the imposition of restrictive labour laws by Margaret Thatcher's government reduced union membership from a 1979 peak of 13 million to 8 million by the mid-1990s.[4] Many of the Labour Movement's centres of power, such as the mining industry, were obliterated. The long integration of the unions into capitalism, through their role as partners in industries that were run on corporatist lines, was put into reverse. Capital no longer had any need for the unions in the new, aggressive, Thatcherite iteration of capitalism.

This was the context for the arrival of New Labour in 1994. Actively hostile to the unions, Tony Blair ripped up the unwritten 'rules' that had governed the relationship between the union movement and the party leadership.[5] Whereas previously this had been a reciprocal arrangement—in exchange for influence over policy, unions exercised restraint in the political sphere and helped to manage the party—now Blair made clear that the leadership was preeminent. "We are making the decisions," he declared. As the academic Labour Party specialist Lewis Minkin has written, "it was a bold and extraordinary attempt to manage the relationship in such a way as to make the unions outsider lobbyists in the party they had created."[6]

While an older generation of union leaders, tamed by the fallout from the 1978-9 winter of discontent, was prepared to play along with Blair's game, meekly accepting public humiliation as the price of a spell in power for Labour, younger officials and rank and file activists were harder to persuade. They noted that the majority of Thatcher's anti-union laws were not repealed, business was feted and favoured, and Blair's acolytes openly talked about severing the party's link with the unions. The realisation that Blair was not, in fact, playing a game, and that the payback unions expected for their submissiveness would never arrive, made it more difficult for right-leaning trade unionists to get elected to positions in their organisations.[7]

A generation of new union leaders elected in the early 2000s was dubbed 'the awkward squad' for their willingness to oppose the Labour leadership.[8] Partly as a consequence of the unions' declining industrial power, these leaders had greater freedom of manoeuvre in the political sphere. Having been spurned as a partner by both capital and the state, the unions had less incentive to uphold the status quo.[9] As Labour edged ever rightwards, the unions swung left. From being the praetorian guard of the leadership, they became the internal opposition.

To be effective in this new role, union leaders had to unify. The Labour machine had long played individual unions off against each other to devastating effect. This became harder to do as unions amalgamated into fewer, larger organisations through a wave of mergers that concentrated power. But the unions also made a conscious attempt to coordinate their efforts. There was better cooperation between the general secretaries of the 'big four' unions, and the role of the Trade Union and Labour Party Liaison Organisation (TULO), which brought together all the affiliates, was beefed up.[10]

The unions embarked on a structural battle with the Blairite machine. It was fought out in committee rooms and on conference floors, in votes at the National Policy Forum and the Labour Party conference. In this fight, the unions were thrown into alliance with the left. TULO coordinated with left groups, particularly the Campaign for Labour Party Democracy, which specialised in navigating the party structures, and the related Grassroots Alliance. It reached out to left-leaning constituency parties, left elements in local government, and socialist societies.

This new strategy had some substantial successes, the biggest of which was the Warwick Agreement in 2004, a wide-ranging deal between the party and the unions that was enshrined in Labour's 2005 election manifesto. The agreement created new labour rights, particularly for women and migrant workers, and extracted a pledge from the Labour government not to privatise the Royal Mail.[11] Such measures were in keeping with the traditional role of the trade unions, using their position within the party to make incremental gains for their members. In past decades, this would not have been considered particularly left at all. But with the 'rules' shredded and Labour positioned so far to the right, the voicing of conventional union demands took on an air of defiant opposition.[12]

Yet when Blair resigned in 2007 the unions were not ready to abandon their characteristic caution in choosing a new leader. Instead of supporting the challenge of John McDonnell, whose programme read like a wish list of union demands, they backed Gordon Brown. "It was very hard-nosed and I understood it," says McDonnell. "Their line was: 'You're not going to win, we've got to back a winner because we've got to then negotiate with that winner'... Then they realised there was no negotiation taking place. I think they learnt that lesson."

Instead, the unions focused their efforts on Jon Cruddas' 2007 run for the deputy leadership on a 'soft left' platform. His surprisingly good result—finishing third of six candidates, but receiving the most first preference votes—encouraged the unions that there was an appetite for their agenda. For the same reason, it set alarm bells ringing on the right. Luke Akehurst, secretary of Labour First (the coordinating group of the non-Blairite 'old right'), wrote prophetically at the time: "If we don't ensure that the successors to the current generation of general secretaries are from the moderate wing of the party, we'll end up in a decade's time with Brown's successor in a contested election being from the left."[13]

Following Brown's defeat in 2010 the big unions again passed over the left candidate for leader, Diane Abbott. They did, however, back the non-Blairite with the best chance of winning: Ed Miliband. This hung like a cloud over his entire leadership. As far as the press was concerned, Miliband was forever in the pocket of the unions.[14] His anxiety to shake this characterisation meant that what might have been a relatively harmonious period for union-party relations instead culminated with the disruption of the Collins Review.[15] In part, this was a consequence of Blair's 'no rules' approach to dealing with the unions. In the absence of a set of reciprocal obligations, the unions took matters into their own hands by intervening politically in the party. Their attempt to change the balance of the Parliamentary Labour Party by getting more union-friendly parliamentary candidates selected brought them into direct conflict with the Blairite Progress faction.

The confected crisis in Falkirk in 2013 was a symptom of this clash. Miliband saw it as an opportunity to prove he was not a union puppet and to manoeuvre Labour into a position where, provided it won the 2015 election, it could introduce state funding of political parties and reduce its reliance on the unions for good. In exchange for their acquiescence, the unions demanded the end of the golden share that Labour MPs enjoyed over the choice of leader through their third of the electoral college.

It was ironic that the electoral college—the legacy of co-operation between the Bennites and the unions in 1981—was abolished at the insistence of the unions, and doubly ironic that it led, within a year and a half, to Labour having a Bennite leader. In practice the college had not worked out as the left had intended. In the 1980s it had actually reaffirmed the alliance between the trade union top brass and the party leadership as they sought to keep the left in check.[16] But that was before Blair tore up the 'rules.' By 2014 the unions had far less to lose. They could play against type by advocating their old bête noir, one-member-one-vote, to elect the leader. This inversion reflected the unions' weakened position in the party. When they were strong, presiding over the party in alliance with the leadership, they were hostile to one-member-one-vote because it threatened the collective arrangements through which they wielded influence. Once they were weaker, they began to see it as a useful tool to circumvent the machine.

Meanwhile, the unions' involvement in the anti-austerity movement during the Miliband period cemented their position to the left of Labour. When a string of general secretaries expressed dismay at the leadership's acceptance of austerity economics at the start of 2012, they were not just mouthing-off, but voicing deep frustration within the trade union movement. The pressure on the Labour-union link from the Blairites on the right of the party was mirrored by activists on the left of the unions, both members of rival left parties who attacked the affiliation on political grounds, and others who just thought it was not good value for money.

The Labour Movement pulled together in the run up to the 2015 general election. But following the defeat Miliband's stuttering journey away from New Labour seemed destined to move into reverse. In the first few weeks of leadership jostling the debate careered wildly to the right. The future of the Labour-union link, and by extension the left's involvement in the Labour Party, looked in real peril. Then Corbyn got onto the ballot.

What came next should have been obvious. The unions' historic sweep leftwards over the previous 15 years had landed them on the same political terrain as the Labour left. The logic of their stance against austerity demanded that they back an anti-austerity candidate. What is more, the lesson many trade unionists took from the Collins Review was that the Labour elite had set a course leading to the downgrading of their role within the party and perhaps ultimately to separation. Why not nominate a leadership candidate who rejected that direction of travel?

Corbyn was among the most pro-trade union politicians in parliament. He had worked for NUPE (a forerunner of Unison) before becoming an MP and had always been a dependable supporter of workers' rights, even when it involved voting against a Labour government.[17] Yet none of this meant that Corbyn was likely to get the support of the big unions. There was no reason to think that they would deviate from the traditional criteria they used to select a leader. Unite, the GMB and others were widely expected to back the favourite, Andy Burnham; Unison was thought likely to endorse Yvette Cooper.

The picture was different among a clutch of smaller unions that were firmly on the left. They were affiliated to the LRC and viewed Corbyn and McDonnell as long-standing allies.[18] Two of them, the train drivers' union ASLEF and the bakers' union BFAWU, each with around 20,000 members, nominated Corbyn almost as soon as he was on the ballot.[19] Two more LRC-supporting unions added their endorsements despite having fallen out with the Labour Party so badly that they were no longer affiliated—the transport workers' RMT (with around 80,000 members) and the firefighters' FBU (40,000 members).[20] It was entirely in keeping with Corbyn's political outlook that he welcomed their support, seeing them as part of the broader Labour Movement that he hoped to bring together.[21] McDonnell felt the same, and had over the years established parliamentary groups for various unions, some of them affiliated, some of them not. "They were all bases of support for us, and resourcing," he says.

But it was at the grassroots level that Corbyn and McDonnell enjoyed their widest support. "For most of the trade unions we have an activist relationship," says McDonnell. "We were involved in every dispute, on every picket line, every demonstration… All the stuff around blacklisted workers I set up. So we had rank and file support." This did not endear the pair to some general secretaries, especially in unions where there was a sharp, ingrained hostility between left wing activists and the bureaucracy.[22] McDonnell, in particular, was unpopular in the highest echelons of the union movement, often because he had supported grassroots trade unionists in internal disputes or elections.

The fight against austerity had energised the activist base of the unions, which had grown frustrated with the Labour leadership. Once Corbyn declared his candidacy, this energy had a focus. The workplace setting of trade unionism naturally lent itself to word of mouth transmission. Activist James Doran remembers how "Lay union activists were going to trade union conferences in the course of the summer and would then feedback what they'd heard about the Corbyn campaign to other members of their union branch." Of course, the scale of this support should not be overstated. Unions have millions of members, most of whom are not interested in politics. But those who are tend to be the ones to take an active role in their unions.

Grassroots support for Corbyn was visible at Labour Movement events throughout the early summer of 2015. The response he received at the Tolpuddle Martyrs Festival had been foreshadowed at the biggest workers' gathering of them all, the Durham Miners' Gala, on 11 July—before Corbyn had any media profile, when he was still last in the bookies' estimation.[23] 150,000 people came out on a beautiful, sun-drenched day to watch the marching of union banners through the city streets to the sound of colliery brass bands. Among them were all four Labour leadership candidates. But only Corbyn, who had been endorsed by the organisers, the Durham Miners' Association, was asked to speak.[24] "I consider it one of the greatest honours of my life to be on the stage here in Durham," Corbyn announced.[25] Doran was in the crowd, giving out leaflets and beer mats—the latter a fun idea from the Corbyn camp sporting slogans such as ~~CHAMPAGNE~~ BEER SOCIALIST and JEREMY CORBYN'S LABOUR: STRONG, NOT BITTER. "Campaigning for Corbyn was the easiest leafleting I've ever done," says Doran. "People would be coming up to you and trying to take leaflets and beer mats off you... You could tell that there was a sort of hope and enthusiasm."

· · · · ·

A week before the Durham Miners' Gala, at the other end of England in Brighton, the executive council of Britain's largest union, the 1.4 million member Unite, met to decide who to nominate for Labour leader.[26] Unite was known as a left union but at the time of the meeting—5 July 2015—Jeremy Corbyn was still a fringe candidate. The nomination was expected to go to Andy Burnham.

Len McCluskey, Unite's general secretary, had previously suggested as much to Burnham in person. The union was hardly going to support Liz Kendall, whose election, McCluskey says, "would have signalled the probable disaffiliation of Unite." Yvette Cooper "was clearly not in the ballpark" either. Until Corbyn made it onto the ballot, Burnham was the only option.

But Burnham's priority was to distance himself from the unions. He had watched Ed Miliband struggle with the legacy of his election. To avoid the same fate he had decided to reject any union funding. "The idea was it would make me stronger if I win it without their support," Burnham was later recorded saying, adding that Miliband had "looked like he was the puppet of the unions at times."[27]

Burnham's attitude to the unions accorded with his political positioning as he lurched to the right. McCluskey remembers talking to him—the two were friends—at a reception in parliament on the day that Corbyn announced he would stand. "Andy, what game are you playing?" McCluskey asked. According to the Unite leader, Burnham explained that he had the left's support in the bag and so could focus on the right. "You do know that Jeremy has thrown his hat into the ring today?" McCluskey enquired. Burnham was not aware. "You understand that changes the dynamics dramatically and if Jeremy gets on the ballot paper Unite will be supporting him?"

The context for Unite's appetite for a left challenger was a deep sense of disenchantment with Labour. After its efforts to reshape the party resulted in the Falkirk furore and a public pillorying from Miliband, there was growing pressure within the union to disaffiliate. In April 2014 McCluskey openly speculated that Unite might back the formation of a new Workers' Party should Labour continue to offer "a pale shade of austerity" and lose the 2015 election.[28]

So as soon as Corbyn entered the leadership race impetus gathered behind him—including among the lay representatives on Unite's executive council. Of the 63 people elected to the executive by the membership, 43 belonged to the United Left faction.[29] "I knew and most of my United Left colleagues knew that Jeremy Corbyn represented the politics that we agreed with, and the politics of the Unite political strategy, and therefore we should back him," says Martin Mayer, chair of the United Left.[30]

According to a version of events common in the media, McCluskey still wanted to nominate Burnham but "lost control of his executive" at the decisive 5 July meeting.[31] It is a narrative McCluskey insists is the opposite of what happened. "This idea that I still hoped for Andy Burnham is just not true," he says. "When Corbyn threw his hat into the ring I said to Andrew [Murray, chief of staff of Unite], 'I'll be supporting Corbyn.'"

But rather than steamroller the decision through, McCluskey says he wanted to "manage the situation" behind the scenes. Although the United Left dominated the executive council, not every member wanted to nominate Corbyn. The United Left representative from the aerospace and shipbuilding division, for example, backed Burnham because of Corbyn's views on Trident. Others had joined the United Left not out of political commitment but as a means of getting on, as it was the dominant electoral machine within the union.[32] McCluskey—a member of the United

Left himself—was also mindful of another more centrist faction on the executive, Unite Now. "I was keen to make certain that we took people with us, that we allowed the executive to arrive at a decision that wouldn't cause any friction within the union," he says. His other concern was to avoid alienating Burnham: "I never thought Jeremy could win. It still looked to me as if Burnham was the favourite. As the leader of the largest affiliate in the Labour Party it was important to maintain a linkage."

When it came to the meeting in Brighton "it was an easy win" for Corbyn, McCluskey recalls, "with those who voted for Burnham quite comfortable in supporting the position." The executive council of Britain's biggest union threw caution to the sea breeze and nominated the wildcard candidate by 34 votes to 14.[33] As soon as the decision was taken Unite began pouring resources into the left-winger's campaign. Suddenly, Corbyn was a contender.

• • • • •

If Unite's nomination was a shock, Unison's decision to follow suit three-and-a-half weeks later was an earthquake. To anyone *au fait* with union politics, the news was almost as astonishing as Corbyn winning the contest itself. Unison's bureaucracy was infamously paranoid about its own left wing activists. In the crude caricature of trade unionism, Unite was the big left wing union and Unison—the other giant with 1.3 million members—its mirror image on the right.[34] The depiction was unfair—in several of its policies Unison was actually to the left of Unite. Nonetheless, there was a legacy of Unison's leadership having once been close to New Labour, although its enthusiasm for the project had long since waned.[35]

"Let's be absolutely frank," says John McDonnell, "[Unison] made it clear from most of the leadership in the beginning... 'No way will you get this nomination.'" The story of how Unison changed its mind is one of grassroots pressure shifting the position of a union—but only in the most propitious circumstances. The tide of enthusiasm for Corbyn forced a sceptical union leadership to bow to the inevitable or risk being swept away.

The key decision that led to Unison's endorsement was taken before Corbyn was even in the race. The first post-election meeting of the union's Labour Link national committee agreed to make its nomination late, at the end of July 2015.[36] This delayed the choice until after Corbyn's candidacy had taken off and provided time for a grassroots campaign to get organised.

Three Unison activists—Andrew Berry, who sat on the Labour Link committee, Marshajane Thompson and Ed Whitby—quickly established an unofficial Unison4Corbyn group. Their aim was two-fold: to build momentum for the nomination of Corbyn by urging members and local branches to lobby their regional officials, and—seeing as that seemed a bit far fetched—to encourage people to sign up as affiliated supporters and vote. The activists immediately received support from unlikely quarters. When they stood outside the union's annual conference with homemade 'Jez We Can' placards in mid-June, "the people who were coming up were not exactly the normal left wing members of Unison," Berry remembers. A statement drafted by the group calling for the nomination of Corbyn attracted over 400 signatures from known figures within the union. "We had ex-presidents, ex-chairs and vice-chairs of the Labour Link committee, NEC members who wouldn't have normally supported," says Berry.

As Corbyn's campaign took off nationally, his support among Unison members surged. His decision to vote against the Welfare Bill in the House of Commons on 20 July, while the party was whipped to abstain, was, says Berry, "huge in Unison," an organisation largely made up of low-paid, predominantly female public sector workers, many of whom would be hit by the government's benefits cuts. Members inundated their officials with emails, asking what the union was doing to support Corbyn.

This pressure from below came at an opportune time. Unison general secretary Dave Prentis was facing an election later in the year. He was sure to be challenged from the left.[37] In McDonnell's opinion, "if [Unison] hadn't supported us it would have jeopardised [his] re-election." General secretaries do not get to the top without being attuned to the sentiment of their union. With a week to go until the meeting to decide the nomination, Prentis seemed to realise it would be unwise to push for an endorsement of Yvette

Cooper—thought to be his preference—or for the union to take no position.

But Prentis needed to take the rest of the union's bureaucracy with him—not straightforward given its hostility to the left. Unison had committed, before Corbyn entered the race, to consult its members about who to nominate. The task had been delegated to the union's 11 regions, but only one had competed it. Others seemed happy to let it slide. Were a genuine consultation to be undertaken, it would inevitably reflect the fervour for Corbyn. Although the consultation would not be binding, it would provide cover for Prentis to do a U-turn. Suddenly the regions were pressured to consult properly—and fast. The London region, for example, turned its exercise around in three days after receiving direction from headquarters. The results were unambiguous: nine of Unison's 11 regions supported Corbyn.[38]

A couple of days before the decisive meeting of the Labour Link national committee, Berry and Thompson received word that the leadership was going to recommend nominating Corbyn. They could barely believe it. But, Berry says, they still "couldn't be confident at all" that the vote was in the bag. Half the committee was not due to be appointed until the day of the meeting.[39] The left would certainly be numerically weak.

When the meeting convened on 29 July at Unison's headquarters on Euston Road, London, Berry was encouraged to see that all six of those he considered solidly pro-Corbyn were among the 16 committee members in attendance. Better still, with it being summer holidays, several less sympathetic members were absent.

Prentis opened the discussion by saying he thought the committee should go along with the wishes of the membership. He talked about how Corbyn's policies were in line with the union's, highlighting in particular their shared position on Trident. Soon it was Berry's turn to speak. He was more anxious than when addressing a conference of 2,000 people. "I was so keen I didn't say anything that would put people off in any way, because I have to say I'm to the left of a lot of the people on the committee," he recalls.

When it came to the vote, nine of those around the table backed Corbyn, six wanted Cooper, and one opted for Burnham. Unison, against all expectations, had nominated Corbyn for Labour leader.

Had Prentis opposed the move he would have been able to swing it. But the tide in the union—and in the Labour Movement—had turned. Prentis was not about to play King Canute.

The nomination was also a victory for activism. "Whatever the various politics behind it, I don't think it would have happened by accident," says Berry. "It's one of my proudest moments actually, to have nominated Jeremy on the Labour Link committee… Never in my wildest dreams…"

As soon as the meeting broke up Berry left the building and walked down the road to the TSSA office, where the Corbyn campaign was based. He strode in a hero. "Jeremy came in. I couldn't help myself, I just gave him a big hug. We were all just amazed… I got there and Dave Prentis was on the phone."

Thompson remembers the scene. "We were in the campaign office, me, Jeremy and Simon Fletcher," she says. "Dave Prentis rang Simon and he was like, 'We've just nominated Jeremy.' Simon had me and Jeremy sitting either side of him being really giggly, sort of, 'Oh my God, we've got Unison!'"

· · · · ·

The decision of Unison to nominate Jeremy Corbyn was a huge moment in the campaign. If even Unison had succumbed to the Corbyn juggernaut, his opponents feared, there might be no stopping him. "Disappointed, Unison. You fight the hard left so hard inside your union then capitulate to them on such an important vote," tweeted stalwart of the right Luke Akehurst in anguish when he learned the news.[40]

The situation looked so ominous for Akehurst and his ilk that when the GMB, the third largest union with 630,000 members, announced on the same day that it would be making no nomination, they greeted its abstention as a victory.[41] The GMB had been one of the big battalions behind Ed Miliband in the 2010 leadership contest. Along with Unite it had been on the frontline of the battle with Progress during the previous parliament. But politically the GMB was not aligned with the Corbyn and McDonnell strand of the left. It represented workers on the Trident nuclear weapons programme, for one. John McDonnell had previously incurred the wrath of general secretary Paul Kenny for defending a dismissed GMB official.[42]

The GMB was famed in the union movement for doing whatever it wanted and not giving a damn what others thought of it.[43] Its structures and traditions made it immune to peer-pressure. Although it justified its decision to make no nomination on the grounds of there being "no clear consensus" in the union "following consultations," members did not remember being consulted.[44] Like Unison, the GMB had a general secretary election coming up, but Kenny was not standing again, leaving regional secretaries to vie for the top job. The risk of the nomination becoming a divisive issue internally, combined with Kenny being unimpressed with the leadership candidates, led him to keep out of it.

The day after the Unison and GMB decisions, 30 July 2015, two more unions came out for Corbyn. The endorsement of the 20,000-strong TSSA was a matter of when, not if.[45] As a railway workers' union its main test for the candidates was whether they supported bringing the trains back into public ownership. Corbyn's campaign team had already been squatting in the TSSA's headquarters for a month at the discretion of its hugely supportive general secretary, Manuel Cortes. Now the union's executive gave the nomination the official seal of approval.

The endorsement of the postal and telecoms workers' union the CWU, the country's fifth biggest trade union with 200,000 members, was less predictable.[46] Its general secretary, Dave Ward, was an unknown quantity, having just displaced the long-time incumbent Billy Hayes. But much to Team Corbyn's delight, says Jon Lansman, Ward "went out on a limb" to back the left candidate. The story in the CWU was less like Unison's groundswell from below and more a decision from the very top.

Ward's politics and those of the CWU were shaped by the long and ultimately unsuccessful battle against the privatisation of the Royal Mail—a battle waged as much against New Labour as the Coalition government. This created an appetite for Corbyn's agenda. But the union also contained telecoms workers, mostly centred in the North West of England, among whom Andy Burnham was popular. The two sectors came together on what Lansman describes as a "reasonably factionalised" executive council, where it was

Ward's backing of Corbyn that made the difference. "Dave made his case very much for Jeremy," says James Mills, who worked as a press officer for the CWU before being seconded to the Corbyn campaign. "He met all the candidates and Jeremy was the person he liked."

If there was any danger of the CWU being seen as just another union following the crowd, the way Ward announced it saw to that. "We think that it is time for a change for Labour," he said in a statement: "The grip of the Blairites and individuals like Peter Mandelson must now be loosened once and for all. There is a virus within the Labour Party, and Jeremy Corbyn is the antidote."[47]

The comment appropriately went viral and provoked fury from the Blairites.[48] But Ward was not finished yet. An accompanying YouTube video was amusing for the sense of underworld menace it conveyed, completely unintentionally. Ward, a solid-looking man with a bald head and a working class London accent, delivered a message directly to camera sat in a darkened room with the blinds down. With no lighting on his face he appeared almost in silhouette, giving the whole thing the feel of a scene from a Guy Ritchie gangster film. "We think the Labour Party needs to be shaken up," he said, and it was possible to imagine Vinnie Jones sitting just out of shot waiting to be tasked with the job.[49]

· · · · ·

Six of the 14 Labour-affiliated trade unions—ASLEF, BFAWU, CWU, TSSA, Unison and Unite—nominated Jeremy Corbyn to be Labour leader. Their combined memberships accounted for the overwhelming majority of workers belonging to affiliated organisations.[50] Corbyn also had the backing of three non-affiliated unions. As well as the RMT and the FBU, he picked up the endorsement of the 30,000-strong Prison Officers' Association.[51]

As with the nominations of CLPs, the endorsements of trade unions carried no direct weight in the final result. But they were enormously important to Corbyn for three reasons. Two of them were tangible—votes and money; the other was more difficult to quantify—credibility.

The most prominent benefit Corbyn derived was the delivery of votes, although on a more modest scale than might be imagined. Individual trade unionists were free to vote as they pleased, but the recommendation of their union was thought to have some influence. In the event, 57.6 per cent of affiliated supporters backed Corbyn in 2015. But the big unknown was how many would take up the opportunity to vote. That number turned out to be relatively small. Corbyn ultimately won 41,217 votes—just a third of the number he received from party members and half as many as he got from registered supporters.[52]

The reason was that not enough trade unionists were eligible to vote, a consequence of the convoluted arrangements put in place by the Collins Review. In 2010 all 2.7 million affiliated trade unionists who paid into their union's political fund were entitled to vote for the Labour leader. The effect of the Collins measures—which required union members to not only 'opt in' to contribute money to Labour, but then to 'opt in' for a second time if they wanted to vote as affiliated supporters—slashed the number balloted to 148,182 in 2015.[53]

The Collins Review envisaged that unions would have five years to adjust to the new rules. But the 2015 election defeat and Ed Miliband's resignation meant the work of recruiting trade unionists to be affiliated supporters was crammed into a couple of months. Only Unite threw everything at it. "We probably spent over a million pounds from our political fund in quite an organised campaign," says Martin Mayer. "In a few short weeks we got 100,000 of our members to sign up."[54] That meant the bulk of all affiliated supporters were Unite members. "The truth is only Unite brought any real votes," says Jon Lansman.

There was a second factor that depressed the number of votes cast: low turnout. Only 71,546 people, half of those eligible, actually voted. As voting was still effectively free for affiliated supporters, it was not surprising that fewer of them made use of the chance than did those who paid £3 for the privilege.

Predictably, commentators seized on the low level of participation to question the union link.[55] For the first time, they pointed out, party members outnumbered union members in the final tally. The votes of the latter accounted for just 17 per cent of the total ballot, much less than the 33 per cent allocated to the unions under the old electoral college. But this was hardly an unforeseen consequence of the Collins Review—for the Blairites it was the intended consequence.[56]

Union nominations were not just about votes. The most concrete benefit was desperately needed money and resources. Corbyn's campaign was initially run on goodwill and his own credit card. But things became much easier when Unite offered a £50,000 loan. "Early on the underwriting of the campaign, a loan that Unite made, meant that you didn't have to raise every pound before you spent every pound," says a member of the team. "We were able to hire some staff or get some staff on secondment. They were all people who would have happily volunteered for Jeremy anyway, it just meant they didn't have to take unpaid leave and worry about their rent."

Corbyn's parliamentary register of interests shows that money soon came flowing in. Unite supplemented its loan with donations adding up to £100,000. The RMT contributed £25,000. There were thousands more from ASLEF, the CWU and the FBU. Unite and the CWU also seconded staff, and the offices used by the campaign in both the TSSA and Unite buildings were donations in kind.[57]

The total of the large donations from trade unions was £167,000.[58] That was a lot of money, but only around half of what Andy Burnham took in large donations from individuals and companies.[59] And it was not as much as the Corbyn campaign raised in small online contributions from members of the public, which brought in over £200,000.[60] One trade union source accustomed to being badgered for money knew the campaign had taken off when the calls stopped coming in. Suddenly Team Corbyn had ample funds and was taking out full-page ads in the *Guardian*.

Trade union nominations conferred upon Corbyn something even more valuable: credibility. To an outsider candidate this was gold dust. Burnham's decision to spurn the unions by declaring that he would not take their money was therefore extraordinary. As David Lammy MP said, "The general view was because Andy had the unions, [Corbyn's] was a very fringe candidacy... Andy then kicked off his campaign almost rebuffing the unions, and opened up a space." Remarkably, Burnham's campaign director, John Lehal (a professional lobbyist who went on to run Owen Smith's 2016 operation), has insisted that "Not taking the [union] funding I don't think damaged the campaign," and "Had [Burnham] won it would have meant he wouldn't have been labelled the union candidate."[61] But he lost, and no wonder.

The value of credibility to Corbyn's candidacy is illustrated by Unison's nomination. The union gave no material resources to the campaign at all. Neither did it contribute many votes.[62] Yet the prestige of having its support was everything. "The big unions historically have been the king makers," says Labour activist Michael Calderbank, "so when both Unite and Unison came out in support of him... that is what says: 'This guy is a serious player.'"

The effect was compound—Unite's nomination gave Corbyn's candidacy a plausibility which then drew in more grassroots support and, partly as a result, more union endorsements, including Unison's. And the impact was not confined to trade unionists— the legitimacy unions bestowed upon Corbyn gave confidence to party members and even to potential registered supporters who saw that their £3 would not be wasted. As soon as it began to look like Corbyn could win, the most powerful force of all was unleashed: hope.

9

DIVISION BELL

"We won't oppose the Welfare Bill, we won't oppose the household benefit cap, [we won't oppose] what they've brought forward in relation to restricting benefits and tax credits for people with three or more children."

—Harriet Harman

The House of Commons is four-fifths empty by 8.58 p.m. on 20 July 2015 as John McDonnell stands up to speak. MPs have been debating the government's Welfare Reform and Work Bill for three and a half hours, although 'debating' is perhaps too strong a word.

Under the proposals child tax credits will be limited to two children per family, child poverty targets will be abolished, and the benefits cap—the total amount of welfare payable to any household in a year—will be lowered by £6,000. That change could plunge 40,000 children into poverty, according to leaked civil service advice, and will increase homelessness.

The Bill piles the cost of austerity onto those in work on low pay—the very people Labour was founded to represent. But in her wisdom, acting leader of the party Harriet Harman has decided not to oppose it. Labour will first table a 'reasoned amendment,' an obscure parliamentary mechanism for setting-out objections, and when that inevitably fails it will abstain.

But back to McDonnell. He has been sitting on the backbenches seething at the debate he has heard. He sees the issue as one of moral principle. Now the Speaker has finally called him. With his first sentence he cuts through all the vacillation: "I would swim through vomit to vote against this Bill, and listening to some of the nauseating speeches tonight, I think we might have to."

He continues: "Poverty in my constituency is not a lifestyle choice; it's imposed upon people... This Welfare Reform Bill does as all the other welfare reform bills in recent years have done and blames the poor for their own poverty... I find it appalling that we sit here—in, to be frank, relative wealth ourselves—and we're willing to vote for increased poverty for the people back in our constituencies."

McDonnell winds up by addressing his fellow Labour parliamentarians: "I say to my own side that people out there don't understand reasoned amendments; they want to know did you vote for this Bill or did you vote against? I say tonight, I vote against."

When the division bell rings at the end of the debate, 48 Labour MPs—over a fifth of the parliamentary party—defy Harman to oppose the Bill. Andy Burnham, Yvette Cooper and Liz Kendall are not among them. John McDonnell and Jeremy Corbyn are.[1]

· · · · ·

'What was Harriet Harman playing it?' is a question that has been asked on all wings of the Labour Party since she used the opening words of an interview on the BBC *Sunday Politics* programme of 12 July 2015 to announce: "We won't oppose the Welfare Bill, we won't oppose the household benefit cap, [we won't oppose] what they've brought forward in relation to restricting benefits and tax credits for people with three or more children." Harman's rationale was that Labour had just lost the election and "what we've got to do is listen to what people around the country said to us," which was that "they didn't trust us on the economy and benefits."[2]

It was reported that Harman had been "traumatised" by her previous experience as acting leader after the 2010 election, when the Tories pinned the blame for the financial crash on Labour overspending.[3] The new benefits proposals looked like a classic Osborne set-up designed to cast Labour as the party of welfare. This time Harman was determined not to let it stick. But there was a flaw in her reasoning. The Conservative smear had been so successful in 2010 because Labour mounted no defence, tacitly conceding the Tories were right on public spending. Now Harman proposed mounting no defence again, explicitly conceding the Tories were right on benefits. Both moves involved surrendering ground to a Conservative agenda.

Whatever her thinking, Harman had a practical problem. As interim leader she had limited authority. Of the leadership candidates only Liz Kendall supported her stance. Jeremy Corbyn's reaction to Harman's *Sunday Politics* interview was unequivocal: "I am not willing to vote for policies that will push more children into poverty. Families are suffering enough. We shouldn't play the government's political games when the welfare of children is at stake."[4] Clear statements also came quickly from Yvette Cooper and Andy Burnham. "Labour should strongly oppose" the Tory plans, said the Cooper camp. "These tax credit changes are regressive, they are wrong, they hit families in work and Andy opposes them," announced Burnham's team.[5] Something would have to give.

Burnham and Cooper knew Harman's stance would provoke an outcry from Labour members that would cause problems for their leadership bids (Kendall had a different and unique electoral strategy, refusing to take any positions that were not deeply unpopular within the party). Following Harman's lead would leave an open goal for Corbyn to be the only candidate to vote against the Welfare Bill, while the others were bound by shadow cabinet collective responsibility unless they resigned.

It was extraordinary that Harman did not anticipate the consequences. She borrowed JFK-style phrasing in her interview to deliver a less than inspiring message to members choosing a new leader: "Think not who you like and who makes you feel comfortable, but think who actually will be able to reach out to the public and listen to the public and give them confidence."[6] Assuming this was a reference to Corbyn, and that preventing him winning was important to Harman, her actions seemed oddly calibrated to achieve the opposite.

"It's pretty basic stuff," says a member of Corbyn's campaign team. "Most Labour Party members do not like Tories. They do not want to do anything that in any way favours or agrees with the Tory government. That at times might lead to overly adventurous opposition but the mood was that this was not one of those times, that this was a very important thing for the core people that many Labour Party members regard themselves as doing their politics for."

The MP Cat Smith remembers travelling around speaking to CLP meetings at the time: "It was, 'We've got a Tory majority government, can you fight them?'... I could see that the majority of Labour Party members wanted us to vote against it." The sense of moral outrage was captured by Diane Abbott in an op-ed published the day after Harman's interview: "How did a party that once promised to end child poverty in a generation become one that will shrug and vote for measures which will force tens of thousands of children into poverty?"[7]

With anger mounting, Burnham and Cooper separately pushed for a change of position at a shadow cabinet meeting on 14 July. Both wanted to table a reasoned amendment, by which Labour could set out objections to the Bill without having to vote against it. The Burnham camp was furious that Harman asked Cooper—who according to later reports had privately threatened to quit the shadow cabinet if there was not a vote against the Bill—to address the meeting before Burnham, meaning she got to suggest the reasoned amendment first (such was the maturity of political discussion at shadow cabinet level).[8] When it was Burnham's turn he argued openly that when the reasoned amendment fell Labour should oppose the Bill. But Harman would not accept that. In the end an unsatisfactory compromise was reached whereby Labour would table the reasoned amendment and then abstain.[9]

The trouble for Burnham was that he had already made his preference public at a Westminster press gallery lunch on the same day. In what journalists described as a "half-challenge to Harman's authority" he said he wanted to vote against the Bill, but stopped short of pledging to defy the acting leader.[10] Cooper publicly matched his stance on 15 July with a clear rebuke to Harman. "Our job is to develop and champion alternative reforms based on Labour values and principles," she wrote in the *Huffington Post*, "not follow Tory plans because we lost the election."[11]

All this posturing failed to move Harman. When the vote came on 20 July Labour tabled its reasoned amendment, which was duly defeated. And then Harman led 80 per cent of her parliamentary party in abstaining, including Burnham and Cooper. They were the ones to give.

David Cameron had said in January 2015 that the proposal to lower the benefits cap "tells you everything you need to know about our values."[12] Many Labour members now felt it told them as much about their own leadership. "It was an indicator of how far wrong [Labour MPs] had gone, how far the party had gone to the right, and how distant they were from our own values," says a scathing John McDonnell.

> They were cut off. Absolutely cut off from our people, the real world... It was just staggering. Even I was shocked at that. You can talk about tactics, and tactically it was absolutely such a tactical error for them to vote that way, but more importantly you realised just how cut off they were from what was happening to people... I did that thing about 'I'll swim through vomit against this Bill,' but that's how I felt. I couldn't understand why they didn't.

There was a group from which Harman was certainly not cut off: political journalists. MPs' "understanding of politics is so determined by the media," says Labour activist Michael Calderbank. "If the media narrative is that Labour lost the election because it was profligate, that is the reality." It was easy to see from Harman's *Sunday Politics* interview with Andrew Neil how a politician could be seduced by such a media narrative. Demonstrating that political journalists are liable to mistake their own prejudices for the views of others, an uncharacteristically complimentary Neil told her: "If you'd stood [for leader] and said what you're saying to me this morning, you could have done pretty well."

In retrospect, the only way Harman's tactics can be viewed as anything other than a catastrophic blunder from her perspective is if she held a secret desire to see Corbyn elected leader of the Labour Party. Even her assertion that voters did not want Labour to oppose welfare cuts did not bear scrutiny. A YouGov poll conducted shortly after the vote found that more people thought Labour should have opposed the government's changes to benefits than thought it should have supported them, by 38 per cent to 34. Among Labour voters the figures were stark: 13 per cent backed the party's decision to abstain, 14 per cent thought it should have supported the government, but 61 per cent said the measures should have been opposed.[13]

· · · · ·

Although the abstention meant Yvette Cooper failed to vote against restrictions on child tax credits that she had branded "a shameful betrayal" just a week-an-a-half earlier, it was Andy Burnham who caught most of the flak from an incensed party membership.[14] As an ostensibly leftish candidate his supporters expected better. Having made it so obvious that he opposed the Bill, to then abstain was seen as cowardly. "Andy was showboating on this and then didn't follow through, so he shot himself in the head," said a source close to Cooper.[15]

The backlash against Burnham was ferocious. He was besieged by outraged comments on social media: "Shithouse! You should have shown some backbone. Lost my vote now!"; "Gutted you abstained!! I had faith in you"; "My vote is now in the hands of JC. It was Andy all the way but not now. That's some hole you have dug for yourself Mr Burnham!!!!"; "Andy the flip-flop man, that is what the Tories and press will say if you are elected as leader."[16]

The flip-flop accusation did stick. Burnham framed his decision as a matter of party loyalty, but he was still having to justify it over a month later. "There's no flip-flop at all," he insisted in an interview. "If people are saying I should have resigned and split the party, I could have done, possibly I would have won this contest if I'd done that. But it wouldn't have been me."[17] Privately he went further, saying he *would* have won in that scenario.[18] Ben

Sellers from the Corbyn campaign is not so sure. "It would have been more of a fight," he says, but "there was always going to be that New Labour politics… He would have had to have had such a big change."

The theory that Burnham could have won had he acted differently ignores the constraints upon him that meant it was never likely to happen. It was assumed he had secured the backing of Rachel Reeves by promising her the shadow chancellor job. Reeves was strongly in favour of backing the Tory plans and, as shadow work and pensions secretary, had reacted to the leaked report showing that lowering the benefit cap could push 40,000 children into poverty by moving Labour *closer* to the government's position [19] Had Burnham voted against the Welfare Bill he would have split not only the parliamentary party but his own campaign, putting him at odds with his putative chancellor and several other backers.[20]

Burnham's campaign director John Lehal has explained his boss' dilemma in a way that perfectly captures why so many people found the decision objectionable: "It's easy to resign and say, 'I don't support this, I've got to do what's right, this is a measure that's going to have a very punitive effect on people in poverty, people with families'… versus does he stay in and therefore have the respect of the shadow cabinet and the loyalty he wants as Leader of the Opposition?"[21]

But Burnham's failure to oppose the Bill finished him. As Cat Smith puts it, "once he talked the talk and didn't walk the walk I think he lost too much credibility to come back from."

• • • • •

The Welfare Bill controversy has sometimes been portrayed as the moment Jeremy Corbyn won the leadership. For some in the Westminster press this provided a convenient explanation, since the theatre for the drama was a venue they understood.[22] The grown-up politicians of the Labour establishment took a responsible if tactically unwise decision not to oppose the Tory measures; Corbyn, being an irresponsible protest politician, voted against; party members and supporters reacted with petulance and made him leader. No further examination was needed of the deep-seated historical phenomena that led to Corbyn's rise, or of the forces outside parliament that pushed him to the fore, or of the shifts within the party membership that were exposed by the reaction to the abstention.

There is no denying that the Welfare Bill episode was important, but its effect on the contest was more complex. The beneficial fallout was immediately apparent to Team Corbyn, indicated by a burst of small donations from the public, improved telephone canvassing results, the recruitment of more volunteers, and a spike in social media activity.[23] Yet it is clear from the chronology that the contest did not pivot on the Bill. Rather, the debacle served to consolidate and accelerate existing trends. On the evening after the 20 July abstention, the first opinion poll of the contest was released showing Corbyn in the lead. The coincidence of timing created the impression that Corbyn had surged ahead on the back of the furore, but most of the fieldwork for the poll was conducted before the vote.[24] Corbyn was already ahead according to CLP nominations and internal canvassing data. A buzz had been going around the trade union movement. Campaign events were growing in size.

But the fiasco did have a deep and lasting effect on party members. For many the vote was, as the Corbyn campaign's press officer James Mills says, a "whose side are you on?" moment. Burnham and Cooper's effort to split the difference with a reasoned amendment—a depressingly tokenistic gesture—failed to pass muster. As the Corbyn-supporting shadow cabinet minister Jon Trickett put it (despite having abstained himself): "Three trapped in the old politics, and Jeremy outside... I think people just said to themselves, 'We're not going to go back to that.'"[25]

The fallout had an important ideological dimension. Burnham's failure to take a stand finally put paid to the idea that he was the 'soft left' candidate. Among the membership—a large chunk of which could be characterised as loosely 'soft left' in its beliefs—Burnham's decision created a vacuum of representation. Into the void stepped Corbyn, the ideal candidate for the moment. He was able to bridge the historic divide between so-called 'hard' and 'soft' left party members (MPs were a different story). In so doing he freed the Bennite tradition from its historical ghetto and proved that it could have wide appeal. Admittedly the opportunity to do this was handed to him on a plate. Corbyn would always have opposed the Welfare Bill—he was just being consistent; it was the party establishment that had gone off on an expedition to the right. "You had Jeremy just straight as a die," remembers John McDonnell. "'Of course I'll vote against it, who wouldn't?' The contrast between that and some of them who were sweating, 'Which way do I go?' There shouldn't have been any calculation."

But uniting the left was also a personal achievement for Corbyn, much as he would downplay the role of personality in politics. He embodied the steel and adherence to principle of the left, yet combined it with personal warmth and humility. On what was a moral issue for so many Labour members, who believed that a government should not deliberately increase poverty, Corbyn's priest-like demeanour felt entirely appropriate. The MP Clive Lewis captures the key to Corbyn's intrinsic appeal when he says: "I don't think Jeremy Corbyn is 'hard left'... He's more of a Christian socialist without the Christian. He's an ethical socialist." A firebrand might have found it more difficult to pick up 'soft left' support, but Corbyn's manner removed barriers.

The Welfare Bill vote demonstrated just how important it had been to get Corbyn on the ballot. It vindicated the argument that the party needed a broad debate involving all of its wings—only one of which passed the big practical test thrown up during the contest. The upshot was a shift of loyalties within the party membership as the 'soft left' swung decisively behind the left candidate. As Michael Calderbank comments, "It couldn't have been scripted better for Jeremy."[26]

10

PANIC IN THE MEDIA

"People need to get a grip. Jeremy Corbyn is not going to be elected Labour leader."

—Dan Hodges, columnist

"Just before we came on air we got news of an astonishing poll in the Labour leadership election," says Kirsty Wark, the presenter of the BBC's *Newsnight* programme. It is late on 21 July 2015 and the results of a YouGov survey to be published in the following day's *Times* newspaper have just dropped. It is the first authoritative poll to be conducted during the contest—and it is a bombshell. It shows Jeremy Corbyn leading on first preference votes with 43 per cent, a whole 17 points clear of second-placed Andy Burnham on 26, with Yvette Cooper on 20 per cent and Liz Kendall languishing on 11.

"He's ahead by a ginormous amount," says a breathless Allegra Stratton, *Newsnight's* political editor. What is even more extraordinary, she says, is that after the less popular candidates have been knocked out and second and third preferences redistributed, Corbyn would beat Burnham by 53 per cent to 47. Jeremy Corbyn would become the leader of the Labour Party.

As the shockwaves from the news begin to rattle through the Westminster village, the challenge for Wark and Stratton at the epicentre of the earthquake is to keep their journalistic footing for five minutes of balanced analysis, even as the political terrain falls away beneath them. The adrenaline of the moment is manifest in the two journalists' nervous, excited laughs and quick, stumbling speech. "This latter figure, the actual eventual result, is scary for the Labour Party," asserts Stratton, temporarily forgetting that it is the expressed preference of the very same party.

For reaction they turn to their guest John McTernan, a former advisor to Tony Blair and chief of staff to Jim Murphy during the latter's epoch-making spell as Scottish Labour leader. "Let's just put this to John," Wark says, "this is YouGov doing a service to sleepy Labour voters to wake up and smell the coffee..."

"Or is it though?" interjects Stratton, suddenly conscious that the BBC's fabled impartiality might get lost in all the excitement. "I mean," she says, readying to say something truly outlandish, "there may be many people who want a left wing leader."

The idea does not impress McTernan, who has a different point to make. "The moronic MPs," he begins, eliciting a burst of laughter from Stratton, "who nominated Jeremy Corbyn to have a debate, need their heads felt... They're morons. Morons."

"But you do accept that there are Labour members, and indeed people in the country, who support Jeremy Corbyn?" asks Wark, who cannot avoid laughing as she says his name. McTernan concedes the point with characteristic grace: "Political parties are full of suicidally inclined activists."

He continues: "These figures are disastrous for the Labour Party. There's no other way of describing it. Disastrous. And the consequence is that the other candidates for leadership have to decide who is the ABC candidate—Anybody But Corbyn."

"Let's say they can't agree, well that *would* be a disaster," proclaims Wark, unable to help herself. The news is too intoxicating, the shared perspective of the three interlocutors too emboldening: the BBC's balance is tipped. McTernan is in his stride: "The election campaign has been a disaster from beginning to end. There's no debate. There's only one analysis, a failed Bennite analysis from the 1980s." Wark nods in apparent agreement.

Turning back to Stratton, Wark asks who is going to "shake this down." Stratton lets out a huge sigh. The pace slows. *Newsnight*'s political editor has some sad news to deliver. "The momentum appears to have gone from Liz Kendall's campaign," she laments. "She seemed to be the person who was the counterbalance to Corbyn. The other two are trying to scoop up second and third preferences and it seems to be a counsel for being very safe. The problem is in the fullness of time it's basically shifted the Labour Party contest to the left."[1]

$$\cdot \ \cdot \ \cdot \ \cdot \ \cdot$$

In such moments of political flux, when a sudden development cannot be made to fit into the standard patterns of reporting used to depict the world, underlying biases are revealed. The shock evinced in the *Newsnight* studio was reflected across the media; the shared assumptions and sympathies echoed in the vast bulk of the reporting and commentary that followed.

In fact, the segment on *Newsnight* was a relatively subtle example. In subsequent days the press went into a full-blown panic. Suddenly the Labour leadership contest, hitherto regarded by most journalists as dull, was front-page news. "The longest suicide vote in history?" asked page one of the *Independent*'s print edition of 23 July 2015. "Labour in turmoil as MPs turn on Corbyn," crowed the *Daily Telegraph*.

Some journalists were in denial. "I don't believe that YouGov poll," wrote Polly Toynbee in the *Guardian*. Displaying her famed political instincts, she reassured readers that "Labour people who spent years slogging round the doorsteps, only to lose a raft of seats they expected to win, aren't about to choose a leader who will ensure it happens all over again."[2] The reliably wrong columnist Dan Hodges tweeted: "People need to get a grip. Jeremy Corbyn is not going to be elected Labour leader."[3] Atul Hatwal, editor of the *Labour Uncut* website, was even more explicit. He titled an article on 22 July: "Sorry, that Labour leadership poll is nonsense. Jeremy Corbyn is going to finish fourth." Given that "members are normal people," he wrote, YouGov must have overlooked the "silent majority" that would ultimately swamp Corbyn's vote, and which "is also why Liz Kendall will surprise many people with her result."[4] She certainly did that.

Newspapers used their editorial columns to tell readers that Corbyn, in the words of the Conservative-endorsing *Independent*, "is not the answer to the Labour Party or the nation's problems."[5] Even the solidly Labour *Daily Mirror* joined in, saying "those who look to Labour to give voice to those most at risk from this Tory government... must be holding their heads in despair."[6] Meanwhile the *Daily Mail* took a brief break from its daily evisceration of Labour to express a new-found concern for the party: "A functioning democracy requires a strong opposition—not a fractious, irrelevant rabble."[7]

Topping even that for hypocrisy was the *Daily Telegraph*. Just a week earlier it had published an article headlined "How you can help Jeremy Corbyn win—and destroy the Labour Party." The piece instructed readers on how to buy a vote in the contest for £3: "Sign up today to make sure the bearded socialist voter-repellent becomes the next Labour leader—and dooms the party."[8] But eight days later on 23 July the newspaper pompously intoned: "Britain needs a grown-up opposition prepared to debate the issues of the day, not a populist rabble interested only in echoing the wealth-hating delusions of the disaffected left. It is quite possible to wish for a better Labour Party without wishing that party to be in power."[9] Readers who had followed their paper's instruction to "destroy" Labour might have been confused to learn that they must also wish for it to be "better."

The right wing press was shot through with such contradictions for the remainder of the campaign, caught between an impulse to laugh at Corbyn the unelectable joke candidate and an equally strong compulsion to terrify the public with forecasts of doom should he succeed. "Jeremy Corbyn's plan to turn Britain into Zimbabwe," read one memorable *Daily Telegraph* headline, epitomising the newspaper's now customary level of understatement. The author had to walk a fine line between writing-off Corbyn's chances as "remote" and convincing readers that his economic ideas were not just "dangerous" but would "almost inevitably lead to a collapse in the currency and eventually the kind of hyper-inflation that engulfed Weimar Germany... Zimbabwe and Argentina."[10]

The incoherence was perfectly encapsulated in a video by the *Daily Telegraph*'s assistant comment editor Asa Bennett. Entitled "Why should you care if Jeremy Corbyn becomes Labour leader?" it gave viewers three reasons. First, Corbyn "would destroy Labour as an effective opposition." Second, despite having destroyed the opposition, Corbyn would "warp the nature of political debate" as his theories "become the norm"—a remarkable achievement. And third, despite this incredibly influential opposition remaining destroyed, Corbyn might win! "It will only take one collapse... the government will fall, and you'll find Jeremy Corbyn as prime minister," Bennett warned. "Imagine that."[11]

It was said during the contest that right wing newspapers were holding back, waiting for Corbyn to become leader before attacking him in earnest. But although the level of hysteria would indeed go through the roof after his victory, the volume of personal intrusion, smears and accusations of guilt-by-association hardly suggested the press was going easy. The frenetic dirt-digging into Corbyn's personal life yielded no valuable finds. A revived allegation that his second marriage broke up over his wish to send his son to the local state school only enhanced his reputation as a principled MP.[12] The revelation that, when young, Corbyn "liked a night in eating cold beans with his cat called Harold Wilson" just made him seem more endearing.[13]

Since many of the scare-stories about Corbyn were fictional anyway, it did not seem out of place when the *Mail on Sunday* published an imaginary account of Corbyn's 1,000 days as prime minister. To evoke the full horror of this prospect, the piece opened with a scene of "rioters, looters and demonstrators fighting on the city streets" in the "hellish glow of the flames rising from a myriad burning buildings"—suggesting that the Britain of 2023 would be eerily similar to that of 2011 when there were riots under David Cameron. But it would also be just like the 1970s: the national debt would be £3 trillion, inflation 25 per cent and bread £5 a loaf. Casting all this into the shade, the unthinkable would have happened: "the collapse of the London luxury property market."[14]

A feature of the press' treatment of Corbyn was simple rudeness—more prevalent from the right but present across the political spectrum. Thus Corbyn became a "slightly less feral version of Ken Livingstone" for Suzanne Moore in the *Guardian*.[15] But the abuse bounced off a man scrupulous in not issuing insults in return. As Corbyn himself put it: "I do not engage in personal abuse, I do not name-call people, I am not particularly bothered if people name-call me because I don't bother to read it anyway. I don't care. It is the name-calling, the depoliticisation of serious political debate that drives people away."[16] Even Corbyn's fiercest critics had to concede that he was a man of principle and sincerity, a fact that some clearly found frustrating. "I've had enough of people describing him as 'principled' as if it were a synonym for 'holds opinions I agree with,'" wrote an angry Helen Lewis in the *New Statesman*.[17] Going several steps further, freelance columnist Christina Patterson said in an appearance on Sky News on 24 July: "Everyone talks about Corbyn being sincere, but Hitler was sincere, ISIS are sincere. It's not necessarily what you want."[18] Perhaps one day a candidate will run on a promise to be insincere, to test if the public wants that.

The publications that the leadership contenders were particularly concerned with were those that Labour members and supporters might read—the *Daily Mirror*, the *Guardian*, the *New Statesman*, the *Independent* and the smaller left publications. Among the latter Corbyn attracted support. Left newspaper the *Morning Star*—for which Corbyn had been a columnist— endorsed him, and its reporting of the grassroots campaign driving events was far more illuminating than the Westminster-bound media. Activist magazine *Red Pepper* came out for Corbyn, with an eye-catching cover mimicking the famous Obama 'Hope' poster.[19]

Corbyn received his most weighty media backing from the *Daily Record*, the second highest selling newspaper in Scotland.[20] But every other major title in the UK opposed his leadership bid (making his eventual win all the more remarkable). The *Daily Mirror* went for Andy Burnham. The *Independent* did not endorse a candidate but warned against a Corbyn victory.[21] The *New Statesman* endorsed Cooper, although it waited until 19 August before doing so, by which time it conceded that she would probably lose and, extraordinarily, hoped that her "moment may yet come" at the next leadership election.[22]

The sympathies of the *New Statesman's* top editorial staff had been clear all along, however. Its editor, Jason Cowley, staked out his position on 22 July in the *Daily Mail* of all places, writing that Labour should "come to its senses" and realise that the left would "doom the party to... absolute irrelevance."[23] Introducing an interview with Corbyn in the *New Statesman* on 29 July, Cowley wrote that "Three months ago, when Corbyn was deemed to be little more than a stubborn, if principled, relic of Benn-era Labour politics, he would have been an unlikely candidate for a *New Statesman* interview, so predictable seemed his oppositionism and so complete his irrelevance."[24] For some, this would constitute an admission of editorial failure—a magazine seen as an authority on Labour had not only missed the shifting sands within the party but apparently had a policy of wilful ignorance towards one section of it. For Cowley, however, it seemed to be a badge of honour.

The *New Statesman's* coverage was not monolithic. Its correspondent Stephen Bush, though a self-described Blairite (at least in the past), provided the most accurate and alert coverage of the contest found anywhere in the mainstream media. But he was the exception that proved the rule. Many of the magazine's other attempts to explain the Corbyn phenomenon were risible. The standout example came on 22 July from deputy editor Helen Lewis, for whom the entire thing could be understood as "virtue signalling." Lewis' theory, which bore the hallmarks of a little too much time spent on Twitter, was that those supporting Corbyn were just "doing it to signal that they are on the side of right and good." There were no economic or political forces at work, no historical processes to consider, no real causes for what was happening at all—beyond social media. Fortunately, this was a hypothesis that could easily be tested, and Lewis outlined how: "Ultimately, in the secrecy of the ballot, when there's no more virtue signalling to be done, Corbyn will fade away."[25]

• • • • •

The *Guardian* occupied a special place in relation to the left. Although the newspaper's daily print circulation was low, its online reach was wide and individual articles could have a huge readership when shared on social media. The *Guardian*'s own research demonstrated that the newspaper served a demographic that was crucial to the leadership contest. When its consumer insight team questioned a sample of its "core readership" in the UK in the midst of the campaign on 30 July 2015, it found that 15 per cent were Labour members and a further 9 per cent were registered supporters, meaning that nearly a quarter of the *Guardian*'s avid readers had a vote (a proportion that probably increased subsequently).[26] Labour elites clearly regarded the *Guardian* as an important medium for communicating with voters, as several of them—including David Miliband, Alan Johnson, Peter Hain and Tony Blair—chose to place anti-Corbyn opinion pieces in the newspaper.

In the *Guardian* these New Labour veterans found a reliable ally. While not a loyal Labour-supporting newspaper, it was the primary mainstream venue for leftish opinion-forming in the UK. In its choice of what was newsworthy, its framing of the news, and its selection of opinion writers, the *Guardian* wielded considerable influence over the terms of debate. It helped define the political field of play, and then acted as linesman on the left-side touchline. Or, to switch metaphors, it policed the boundary of acceptable opinion.[27] In usual times, this policing operation was low-level, almost implied. But just as the full force of the state becomes visible during an emergency, so the *Guardian*'s role in British political life was laid bare when an outsider MP threatened to overturn politics as usual.

In the beginning, when Corbyn was judged to pose no danger, the *Guardian* could afford to be generous. As his team scrabbled for MPs' nominations the newspaper even devoted an editorial to helping him. Titled "The *Guardian* view on Labour's leadership: don't narrow down a lacklustre contest," the newspaper argued that Corbyn "has a right to a place" in the election. Why? Because otherwise the Tories' battering of the welfare state "could be entirely obscured in an exchange of empty clichés about 'reform' if nobody does what Mr Corbyn will do, and vows to fight the cuts." The *Guardian* even welcomed the prospect that Corbyn's "opposition to Trident could spark an overdue debate about defence." This was all OK because "few—and perhaps not even the modestly mannered Mr Corbyn himself—would imagine [him] in No 10."[28]

Optimists could read in to the editorial hints of a hoped-for shift in the political stance of the newspaper. Just two weeks earlier Kath Viner had taken over as editor, the first woman to hold the post. Seen as having the backing of the paper's more left-leaning journalists, she was appointed by the *Guardian*'s owners after a landslide win in an indicative ballot of staff.[29] Could she be exerting her will over the *Guardian*'s executive editor of opinion, Jonathan Freedland, a man whose politics were viscerally opposed to Corbyn's?

Even Martin Kettle, the *Guardian*'s associate editor who would become Corbyn's coldest critic, echoed the editorial line after nominations closed on 15 June: "The good news is that there is a decent range of candidates to choose from... a spectrum of views from old left to Blairite." Burnishing his credentials as an astute reader of Labour politics, Kettle asserted that "Jeremy Corbyn's nomination has helped Burnham because it means he can't be so easily cast as the leftie" and Liz Kendall "has proved that there is a sizable level of support" for a Blairite analysis.[30]

The *Guardian*'s initial portrayal of Corbyn as an interesting no-hoper continued in its first long profile interview with him on 17 June. Despite treating the MP as someone who could be freely mocked—"He still has a touch of Citizen Smith about him (without the laughs)"—Corbyn nonetheless came across as warm, and was even afforded some policy credit: "The thing about Corbyn is that he is nearly always proved right—after the event."[31] The next day's paper carried an unambiguously positive mention from Seumas Milne, then the most senior voice within the *Guardian* from the left, who had a firmer grasp of the electoral dynamics than his colleagues. "Given that any Labour supporter can now sign up to vote for £3," he wrote, "the reluctant Corbyn is likely to do better than many media pundits imagine."[32]

But that was as far as Corbyn's *Guardian* honeymoon went. In the following weeks, as public excitement built behind the left candidate, applause at hustings got louder, and local party endorsements notched up, the *Guardian*'s response was a virtual blackout. In a later review of his paper's coverage, the *Guardian*'s readers' editor, Chris Elliott, admitted that "in the early days of Corbyn's charge, the readers rightly got a sniff that on occasions we weren't taking him seriously enough."[33]

The newspaper's interest picked up after revelations in mid-July that Corbyn was ahead in private polling. And then, when the YouGov poll landed, the coverage exploded—fuelled by Tony Blair's first clumsy intervention into the contest. Headlines from the *Guardian* website's front page on 22 and 23 July give a sense of the hysterical tone that took hold: "Blair urges Labour not to wrap itself in a Jeremy Corbyn comfort blanket"; "Think before you vote for Jeremy Corbyn"; "Labour can come back from the brink, but it seems to lack the will to do so." On these two panic-stricken days alone, the *Guardian* website carried opinion pieces hostile to Corbyn from Anne Perkins, Suzanne Moore, Polly Toynbee, Tim Bale, Martin Kettle, Michael White, Anne Perkins (again), and Anne Perkins (yet again). There was not a single pro-Corbyn column.[34]

In one of her three efforts, Anne Perkins dispensed with subtlety and simply pleaded: "Please, new associate members who will shape the party for the next five years, maybe forever: do a little research. Think what kind of country you want for you and your children and, even more importantly, think how you might get there. Now think, is Jeremy Corbyn in the middle of that picture? I don't think so."[35]

But the *Guardian* had a problem: its readers did think so. On 24 July the newspaper published the results of an initiative to get feedback from readers on who they were supporting. The group was self-selecting but the verdict was overwhelming: 78 per cent of the 2,500 respondents backed Corbyn.[36] More rigorous research conducted by the *Guardian*'s consumer insight team at the end of July found that of the newspaper's core UK readership, 51 per cent said Corbyn was their choice for leader, while 7 per cent supported Cooper. Kendall and Burnham had 6 per cent each.[37]

Such sentiment was often reflected on the letters page, an oasis amid the relentless negativity. And anyone brave enough to venture "below the line" into the netherworld of online comments could not mistake the strong feeling that Corbyn was being unfairly treated and his supporters patronised. On 3 August the paper's readers' editor, Chris Elliott, felt the need to respond to the backlash with a makeshift review. Of a sample of 43 pieces of journalism, he classed 16 as opposed to Corbyn, 17 as neutral, and 10 in Corbyn's favour. On those figures he implied that the coverage was fair, but he refused to release which pieces he had placed in which category. In any case, such a quantitative analysis obscured more than it revealed. Elliott argued that the *Guardian* "should not be a fanzine for any side"—but that was not the issue.[38] The charge was that the *Guardian* was effectively trolling one particular candidate—one who had the support of its readers.[39]

This trolling stretched across the dividing line between opinion and news. It was glimpsed in the headlines chosen by sub-editors and in the framing of reports. Elliott agreed that one example went too far: a 28 July item headlined "Jeremy Corbyn warns 'naughty people' to leave Labour Party alone" had "held him up to ridicule." But consider these other news headlines: "Jeremy Corbyn caught looking gloomy on night bus"; "Jeremy Corbyn suggests he would bring back Labour's nationalising clause IV" (in which the first line of the story read "Jeremy Corbyn has denied that he would reinstate clause IV..."); "View from Nuneaton on Corbyn: 'I can't imagine that he will go down well around here.'"

Another news headline from 4 August read: "Anti-austerity unpopular with voters, finds inquiry into Labour's election loss." The sub-heading of the article by political editor Patrick Wintour—long regarded by the Labour left as a cipher for Peter Mandelson—made clear the story was directed at Corbyn: "Independent review shows abiding concern over economic deficit, and may fuel doubt about policies of Labour leadership frontrunner Jeremy Corbyn." This framing was based on a poll commissioned by Labour MP Jon Cruddas as part of his own inquiry into the 2015 general election. Fifty-six per cent of participants agreed with the leading statement: "We must live within our means so cutting the deficit is the top priority." Wintour reported that the finding "shows Britain's voters do not back an anti-austerity message."[40] Yet the poll had not mentioned "anti-austerity"; nor had Labour offered an "anti-austerity message" at the election.[41]

By so explicitly linking the poll to Corbyn's programme, Wintour put a particular spin on news that may have had political consequences at a crucial time. His own opinion of Corbyn could be inferred through phrasing and throwaway lines elsewhere in his work—remembering that, as a news reporter, he was expected to maintain a greater degree of objectivity than an opinion columnist. In an article on 31 August he described Corbyn as having had "next to no experience of making difficult political decisions, preferring instead the safety of left wing protest politics." A victorious Corbyn would be "entitled to receive the levels of loyalty he gave previous Labour leaders—none."[42] When Wintour wrote of "the left's hermetically sealed belief that they have created a mass movement," many of his readers would have considered themselves part of that movement.[43]

On 13 August, the *Guardian* finally placed its cards on the table. The paper that was "not a fanzine for any side" endorsed Cooper for leader. The editorial announcing the decision was curious for being almost entirely about another candidate—no prizes. "The insurgent has breathed extraordinary life into the Labour leadership race," it read. "The party must harness the energy he has unleashed." But though one contender had shone, another should win. Just one paragraph was devoted to Cooper's qualities—she was a woman and good at economics—without mentioning any of her policies.[44] In a sense the situation facing the *Guardian* hierarchy mirrored that of the Labour elite. Their readers were for Corbyn, their attention was on Corbyn, and they could find no positive, inspiring reason for Labour supporters to vote for anyone else.

The Sunday sister paper of the *Guardian*, the *Observer*, had its own editorial line and, in keeping with its generally more conservative politics, took an even harder anti-Corbyn stance. It launched a Blairite-themed onslaught on 19 July with a long piece by political editor Toby Helm (taster: "The prospect of Corbyn being crowned leader in September has focused minds on a crisis that could destroy the party"); a focus group of voters who had switched to the Tories ("Labour's lost voters may never return again"); columns by Nick Cohen (Labour would become "a left-wing version of the Tea Party") and Andrew Rawnsley ("the hard left always betrays the very people it purports to care about"); a piece from Alistair Darling endorsing the "realist" Liz Kendall for leader (rather unrealistically); and a 1,800 word editorial on Labour sinking into "a warm bath of delusion."[45] The argument of the editorial was monotonous. Labour "must locate themselves in the centre"—that was the lesson of Tony Blair. "It is impossible to conjure a winning position if you are too far from the centre"—that was the lesson of Ed Miliband.

The *Observer* was nothing if not consistent. Two months later, despite the extraordinary happenings in the interim, all the newspaper could say in its begrudging editorial on the morning after Corbyn's victory was that the new leader must "reach out to voters in the centre."[46] The piece was so cheerless that it provoked a withering response from one of the *Observer*'s own journalists, Ed Vulliamy. "We let down many readers and others by not embracing at least the spirit of the result, propelled as it was by moral principles of equality, peace and justice," he wrote. "Why not embrace those principles, or at least show an interest in the fact that hundreds of thousands of people just did?"[47]

· · · · ·

The identity of a newspaper is not just determined by its editorial line but also by its star columnists. They are the ones with the freedom to speak out, to frame an argument in the most persuasive manner. With a few exceptions, the big names at the *Guardian* and *Observer* proved relentlessly hostile to Jeremy Corbyn. The following vignettes give a sense of the tone.

Polly's Journey

Polly Toynbee is the quintessential *Guardian* columnist. She recognised Corbyn's appeal earlier than most—noting on 23 June 2015 that he "wins on the clapometer" by using the crafty trick of "saying what no doubt many Labour members believe." He would never be leader. Toynbee's "hunch is Cooper is the one to beat." But "every Corbyn vote gives ammunition to Labour's enemies" because he is "a relic," "a 1983 man."[48]

She returned to the subject a month later, at the height of the panic following YouGov's first poll. "Suddenly the party that has been a reasonably friendly coalition through the Blair, Brown, Miliband years, begins to feel like the poisonous place it was in the early 80s," she wrote of Labour, whose members had presumably taken to calling each other "relic" and other insults. (A tendency to abuse the left for being abusive became ubiquitous among journalists and found its ultimate expression in eight words from the *Times'* Philip Collins complaining of "the stupidity and nastiness within the Corbyn campaign.")[49]

By 4 August it was clear to Toynbee that Corbyn really might win. It was also apparent that—remarkably—admonishing his supporters was not working. So in a dramatic change of tack she adopted the 'I'm with you, but...' method. "Free to dream," ran the headline of her column, "I'd be left of Jeremy Corbyn. But we can't gamble the future on him." Yes, Toynbee (who in 1983 stood as a candidate for the SDP, the rightist splitters from Labour) was Che Guevara without the beard, Rosa Luxemburg without the limp. "I'd go further than Corbyn," she declared. "I'd go for a windfall wealth tax to pay off the deficit, make the Queen be Elizabeth the Last, abolish faith schools, private schools and inheritance, tax millionaires at 70 per cent." But, she argued, it was best not to say such things out loud.

None of this had any impact. "Let me have one last try," Toynbee begged on 13 August, willing her readers to back Cooper (whom she later described as "a tough anti-austerity economist").[50] The call to arms was laced with violent imagery. Cooper would "lay into," "attack," "take on the Corbyn arguments, gloves off." "Could this be the knockout blow?"[51] Apparently not. "It's all over," she conceded two weeks later.[52]

Angry Andrew

The *Observer's* chief political commentator, Andrew Rawnsley, was genuinely angry at the "Piped [sic] Piper of Islington."[53] After all, he had been the "100/1 token candidate of the hard left" when he "threw his Lenin cap into the ring." It was sheer impertinence for him to be leading. "I am tempted to argue," Rawnsley wrote on 19 July, "that Labour should go right ahead, make David Cameron's day, choose Jeremy Corbyn and field him as its leader at the next election, so that the thesis that Labour loses because it isn't left wing enough is finally tested to the destruction that it so richly deserves."[54]

That Rawnsley should react with animosity rather than curiosity was understandable. Suddenly, the centre of gravity was moving away from the Labour elite to which he had unparalleled access, and from which he had mined the raw materials needed to fashion the books and journalism that had won him acclaim. "Any veteran Labour MP who has the temerity to question whether Jeremy Corbyn is a viable candidate for prime minister," he projected on 6 September, "is now vilified as a Tory, a fascist or worse by flash mobs of people who only declared their support for the party five minutes ago and might as readily find a different hobby five minutes later." Much better that democracy be left to the professionals.[55]

Even at the moment of Corbyn's victory, Rawnsley was complaining about the "leftwing bubble." He wrote on 13 September: "In the self-validating echo chamber of a leadership rally or when communing with the like-minded on social media, it is possible to trap yourself into believing that everyone thinks exactly as you do."[56] It was a strange line to take on the morning after a landslide victory in a contest involving half a million people. But with just two small changes, the sentence could be made more appropriate to the moment: "In the self-validating echo chamber of a *national newspaper* or when communing with the like-minded *in Westminster*, it is possible to trap yourself into believing that everyone thinks exactly as you do."

Jonathan's Woes

By far the most amusing reaction to the rise of Corbyn came from the *Guardian*'s art critic, Jonathan Jones. His first, little noticed intervention in late July was an article titled "Labour should win the Turner prize—it's a disastrous piece of performance art."[57] It appeared Jones was trying his hand at satire, although it was hard to tell. By the time of his second attempt in early August, obscure humour had been replaced by visceral anger. What had piqued his pique was a strike at the National Gallery that was disrupting his art time. "Seriously," he pleaded, "I've never voted anything but Labour in my life. Can't you at least let me alone when I'm looking at Titian? I have to be a socialist in the museum now?" The sacrifice of the striking staff was as nothing to Jones' suffering. And he knew who to blame—the union that was "throwing its weight about." The evidence? Union leader Mark Serwotka "appeared this week alongside Jeremy Corbyn." Caught red handed! Jones did not need to mention that the staff had voted overwhelmingly to strike; this was a technicality given his discovery of the illicit involvement of "anti-austerity ideologues in the trade union movement" engaging in a "cynical act of muscle flexing."[58] After all, in a dispute between workers and management, how could a gallery director "who writes books about Raphael" be at fault? "Whose side am I on?" Jones asked, to no one in particular. "Not Mark Serwotka's. Go on, call me a Tory. I am crying because the hard left is probably going to turn me into one."[59]

What readers did not yet know was just how deep were the roots of Jones' distress. A few days later, in an extraordinary essay that ranged across history, philosophy and ethics with the unhesitating confidence of the non-specialist, Jones revealed the traumatic personal story behind his decision to take on the Corbyn menace. It all began in Cambridge in the late 1980s—in Sainsburys, to be precise. It was there that Jones, a student at the university, was recruited into the Communist Party of Great Britain. Before he knew it, he was in Soviet Russia, confronted by the "actual existing, concrete and cardboard reality [of] one of the most inhuman and murderous follies ever dreamed up in the fevered minds of zealous thinkers." He ate "soup swimming with sausage fat in the decaying hostel of the Komsomol." He "queued for gruel ladled out from huge tubs at Moscow airport." This was "pure socialism," and it left a bad taste. (One concerned reader wrote to the *Guardian*: "I know that art critics are famous for their heightened sensitivity and Jonathan Jones writes movingly of his bad soup moment in 1980s Russia...")[60]

"I am not calling Corbyn a Marxist," Jones continued, after telling how 6 million Russians were murdered by Stalin. "But Marxist ideas live again in some spectral form in Corbyn's runaway campaign." For a man who had seen the brutal culinary reality of Stalinism, electing Corbyn looked like the first step on the road to serfdom. "You—we—have to face up to what was done," he wrote, before revealing why he was no longer a socialist: "Markets are human." Surprising as this finding seemed, "to believe otherwise is to indulge in the same folly that killed the hapless peasants who Stalin labelled capitalist 'kulaks' and saw fit to starve and shoot." Vote Corbyn, get liquidated. Jones drew his essay to a close on a portentous scene: "In Russia I came across [the magazine] *Marxism Today* in a news kiosk in Volgograd—that is, Stalingrad. And beside the vast silver emptiness of the Volga, the kulaks were nowhere to be found."[61] It was not clear what he meant.

· · · · ·

The *Guardian* was also home to some writers who supported Jeremy Corbyn. Providing a space to columnists from the left is crucial to the *Guardian's* identity. Without them, the newspaper would lose all credibility as the prime organ of the liberal-left. Contributing a minority of the paper's coverage, their dissenting voices actually bolster the legitimacy of the editorial line by creating the impression that their case has been heard but set aside. And in commercial terms they attract particular subscribers and generate advertising revenue when their articles are shared on social media, where strident arguments do well.

Owen Jones turned in five pro-Corbyn pieces during the contest. Seumas Milne penned two. Zoe Williams produced two broadly supportive articles, although one was preoccupied with why Corbyn's opponents were "coming at him with the wrong truncheon."[62] George Monbiot contributed one.

Scattered examples of open mindedness towards Corbyn could be found elsewhere in the newspaper. Interestingly, in the economics pages substantial figures Larry Elliott, Robert Skidelsky and William Keegan saw something in his anti-austerity policies. There were occasional one-off comment pieces from supporters, a few inquisitive accounts of campaign rallies, and a positive write up of Corbyn's housing policy from Dawn Foster. Space was afforded to Diane Abbott and John McDonnell, although this came nowhere near offsetting the acres of column inches granted to New Labour grandees. And a clutch of famous names chipped in, including Brian Eno, Stewart Lee and David Edger.[63] Comedian Frankie Boyle contributed the best line of the *Guardian's* coverage:

"It's worth remembering that in the press, public opinion is often used interchangeably with media opinion, as if the public was somehow much the same as a group of radically right wing billionaire sociopaths."[64]

But that was it, during three months. Set against this was a prolific group of *Guardian* and *Observer* big guns. What made the newspaper feel so claustrophobic was that most of them wrote essentially the same column, repeatedly. There was theological agreement around a shared article of faith. As Martin Kettle put it in typically deadening words on 23 July 2015, Labour must "compete in the centre, with a modern reformist agenda that can challenge the centre right." The political centre ground, in this view, appears as a clearing in a forest—a fixed location—and politics is a simple orienteering exercise where the parties are given a map and a compass and told to go and find it. Occasionally they inexplicably wander off into the woods and have to be scolded by journalists until they take their navigation task seriously again. The great, unpredictable, social and economic forces that constantly sculpt new historical terrain are, in this Duke of Edinburgh Award Scheme version of politics, merely gusts of wind that must not blow the parties off course. Nothing changes.

The trouble with such a static, ahistorical view is that it is unable to account for new phenomena, much less understand people's motivations for acting in unexpected ways. So when hundreds of thousands of people simultaneously decided they had other priorities than hopelessly trudging around looking for a centre ground that, mysteriously, kept moving further away, these professional political pundits could only dismiss them as either insane or self-indulgent. Rafael Behr epitomised this, using his own strained metaphor: "Corbynism is a festival on the beach of opposition, which appeals to many Labour supporters more than the choppy waters that must be sailed on the way back to power."[65] He even evoked the compass: "If Labour sets its moral compass by the mythologised conscience of this accidental saviour, it will abandon rational politics."[66] For Polly Toynbee, the surge of support for Corbyn could be explained as a mental health crisis. "This is summer madness," ran the diagnosis, the sole comfort being that she was sure it was not contagious: "I don't think a majority of Labour members will take leave of their senses."[67]

The only other explanation was a variation on the patronising notion of "virtue signalling" advanced by Helen Lewis in the *New Statesman*. On the single occasion that opinion editor Jonathan Freedland chose to wade into the debate under his own name, it was to argue that "the Corbyn tribe cares about identity, not power." Corbynism "is about being true to yourself," he declared, without evidence or experience. As such, it "is a form of narcissism."[68] Kettle expressed a similar idea when he wrote about "faith-based socialists." "There's nothing particularly wrong with being a faith-based socialist," he said, generously, "but please don't confuse it with politics."[69]

It was axiomatic for these commentators that moving an inch from the fabled centre ground would mean electoral oblivion (although some of them argued that Labour had no chance of winning the next election anyway). But there was no actual evidence that Andy Burnham, Yvette Cooper or Liz Kendall were electable—a fact implicitly conceded by the glaring lack of columns attempting to sell any of them (Toynbee's promotion of Cooper was an exception). Absent from journalists' deliberations was any reflection on the role of the media itself—that the manner in which journalism is practiced makes the media a player as well as an observer. By insisting in advance that Corbyn was unelectable, journalists were attempting to create a self-fulfilling prophecy.

Consider again the metaphor of the *Guardian* as the linesman on the political field of play. A detailed look at its coverage leaves no doubt that, as an institution, it decided that Corbyn was out of bounds. The precise location of the touchline was revealed—it ran right through the PLP. Yvette Cooper, Liz Kendall and Andy Burnham on one side of the line were supported, respected and accepted in turn, but the Labour left had to be stopped.

· · · · ·

Ask the Corbyn camp about the press coverage during the leadership contest and a surprising response comes back. "There are very few campaigns on the left that I've been involved in where we've had good press," says Jon Lansman, "but this is one of them." His definition of "good press" is unconventional, a variation on 'all publicity is good publicity.' "We always made the agenda. The others didn't get a look in. We were the story throughout." It was all about Corbyn.

Because of the scale of interest, the campaign's press team found that along with the dross came greater opportunities to place stories in the media than would normally be afforded to a left candidate. "The majority of things we tried to land landed, and in the ways we wanted them to land," says press officer James Mills. Whatever was being thrown at them, Team Corbyn pushed on with scheduled policy announcements, getting out a positive message that Mills believes cut through.

Even when the attacks came, a curious thing happened. The more the press lambasted Corbyn, the more his support grew. The onslaught may have been, in John McDonnell's view, "horrendous," but Corbyn's supporters were "immune" to it. The very tactics that, for a time, proved damagingly effective with the general public after Corbyn became leader—feigned outrage at some perceived slight to the nation or the deliberate misrepresentation of his words—fell flat with a Labour audience. As Clive Lewis, who was a journalist before becoming an MP, points out, members of a political party are "a more informed group of people who have gone out of their way to find out a bit." Castigating Corbyn as "the outsider, the long-shot, the maverick, the fruit-loop leftie, the man who couldn't tie his shoe-laces" only galvanised people to his defence. When these abominations came not from the right wing press but from the liberal-left media, many readers' reaction was one of anger that "the publications they had assumed shared their politics were so averse to what Corbyn represented."

Ironically, the volume of hostile coverage prompted broadcasters to give valuable airtime to the man of the moment. Broadcast media followed a journalistic agenda set by newspapers, despite the precipitous decline in their circulation. But broadcast had an inbuilt corrective missing from print—people could see and hear Corbyn for themselves. "They threw everything at Jeremy and it was so over the top that when he came on TV you expected him to be a combination of all sorts of villains," says McDonnell. "When he came across as just a nice bloke answering questions honestly, that was it."

The visual spectacle of young people flocking to mass rallies played well on TV. The coverage could not help but convey a sense of excitement. But some of the BBC's output did foreshadow what Sir Michael Lyons, the former chairman of the BBC Trust, later called "quite extraordinary attacks" on Corbyn once he was leader. An episode of *Panorama* on 7 September 2015 was a glaring example. Decried by the Corbyn camp as a "hatchet job," the programme amounted to a compilation of smears aired by the public broadcaster while voting was still underway.[70]

Perhaps the most important factor explaining why the press onslaught backfired was the existence of social media. Research carried out by YouGov in August 2015 found that 57 per cent of Corbyn supporters cited social media as "a main source of news," compared to around 40 per cent for backers of the other candidates.[71] On Facebook and Twitter ordinary people could critique and rebut journalists' output directly. "Every time the mainstream media attacked Jeremy the social media shield would go up around him," says Marshajane Thompson. One function of the online operation she helped run was to circumvent the press, both by publicising the explosion of grassroots activity and by curating the half-decent reports from the traditional media.

It was patently clear that some journalists felt threatened by the arrival of this new realm. A media narrative asserting that there is no alternative is much easier to sustain if there is no alternative media. The existence of a different point of view, forged among a network of people who would previously have been atomised, is what provoked the snobbish accusations of "virtue signalling" and "identity politics." Being continually challenged about their bias brought howls of exasperation from journalists that congealed into a collective feeling of offence. It contributed to the general sense of consternation at Corbyn's rise. Events were spinning beyond the media's control.

11

HUBRIS TO HUMILIATION

"When people say, 'My heart says I should really be with that politics,' well get a transplant because that's just daft."
—*Tony Blair*

The man stood in front of the purple Progress display boards looks like the Tony Blair of 1997 might look eighteen years later—if, in the meantime, he had helped launch an illegal war killing hundreds of thousands of people, shattered an entire region of the planet and given rise to ISIS—except a little bit worse.

How easily he slips into the old routine, lecturing the Labour Party on how it is "confused" about the "modern world"—but not to its face. Only the press and the Progress faithful are in the small audience. Journalists were not given the location in advance by email; they had to wait for a phone call—presumably for fear that if the address leaked out normal people could turn up, the kind of people who might mention the war.

The atmosphere in this controlled environment is hardly electric. There are echoes of the '90s but without the pizazz. The venue is the Institute of Chartered Accountants. Cool Britannia.

"I could make a speech to you about how to win," Blair begins in the familiar cadence, "but given the state of the debate in the party right now, I don't want to." He does really. He is just teasing his audience, reprising his famous "Today is not a day for soundbites, but I feel the hand of history upon our shoulders" shtick. Today is not a day for speeches about how to win, but "you win from the centre..." etc.

"We won not because we did what we thought was wrong as a matter of principle but right as a matter of politics," Blair reveals, "but when we realised that what is right as a matter of policy is right as a matter of principle." Clear as the Baghdad sky.

"We can win again next time," he says, still not making that speech about how to win, "but only if our comfort zone is the future and our values are our guide and not our distraction." Our comfort zone is the future? Perhaps that is genuinely how it feels, if the Green Zone is your past.

But Blair's central message is refreshingly clear: "I wouldn't want to win on an old-fashioned leftist platform. Even if I thought it was the route to victory, I wouldn't take it."

Blair would rather lose—which in practical terms means he would rather the Tories win—than for Labour to succeed from the left. There it is, from the warhorse's mouth. The Labour left has always suspected as much of the Blairites, but it is useful to have it confirmed by their commander-in-chief.

In the Q and A following the speech—conducted by Matt Forde, who describes himself as a comedian—Blair loosens up. The patina of faux-intellectual abstract claptrap is pulled away to reveal… a void. A leftist platform "wouldn't be right," he says, "because it wouldn't take the country forward, it would take it backward, so that's why it's not the right thing to do."

Blair then drops the cluster bomb he has been itching to drop all along: "When people say, 'My heart says I should really be with that politics,' well get a transplant because that's just daft."

It is an instant headline. *'If your heart is with Corbyn get a transplant, says Blair.'*

And then it is over. There are no tough questions from the journalists because they have been banned from asking any. It is almost as if there is some big, looming, unmentioned topic that Blair would prefer to avoid.[1]

· · · · ·

Why were the Blairites so inept? That was one of the big questions of the 2015 Labour leadership election. The political force that dominated Labour from 1994 to 2007, and debilitated it for a further eight years, was humiliated in the summer of 2015. Its candidate, Liz Kendall, could secure the backing of just 4.5 per cent of Labour members and supporters. The Blairites were revealed to be organisationally defective, ideologically bereft, and tactically hapless. Jeremy Corbyn's rise was in part a reaction to—and in whole a rejection of—Tony Blair and New Labour.

Blair's intervention at the Progress event on 22 July 2015 betrayed a chronic lack of self-awareness that proved to be a recurring theme. Coming in the immediate aftermath of the Welfare Bill vote and the YouGov poll bombshell, Blair presumably thought he could nip the Corbyn insurgency in the bud. His speech had precisely the opposite effect. At Team Corbyn HQ, the staff saw an immediate rise in donations and volunteer sign-ups.[2] Social media lit up. Clive Lewis remembers it as "a turning point." "All of a sudden a lot of people who were not particularly interested in internal Labour politics had their attention drawn to this individual who Tony Blair didn't like," Lewis says. "Tony Blair is news. He's instantly recognisable. 'Who's he talking about? What's he saying?'... It injected amphetamines into the whole debate."

Lewis puts Blair's error down to hubris. "I think at that stage he thought he still had some credits to cash in with Labour members. 'The public, the right wing media, the hard left might hate me, but good, decent New Labour members, they'll remember that I won three election victories.' But I think he came in for a bit of a shock."

Just an hour or so after Blair's appearance, in another central London venue, Corbyn gave his own speech at the launch of 'The Economy in 2020,' the major policy paper of his campaign setting out his anti-austerity platform. The timing could not have been better. "I don't think I've ever seen so many cameras at a Jeremy Corbyn speech," tweeted the BBC's assistant political editor Norman Smith.[3] John McDonnell remembers being worried the event might not get much coverage. But as he and the candidate emerged from the building where Corbyn had been speaking, all fears evaporated. "Tony Blair attacked us," McDonnell recalls. "He did his Cilla Black thing, 'Anyone who had a heart.' We had every media camera outside. Best thing he could have done for us. I felt like sending him a bunch of red roses."

Lewis recalls the moment vividly:

I was looking up at a News 24 screen and I remember Jeremy had just come out after launching his economic policy. The world's media were outside. You could see the shock on his face, he's come out and he's thought, 'They're not this interested in what I've got to say, surely!'... It was 'Mr Corbyn, Mr Corbyn, your comments on Mr Blair's comments on you.' To his eternal credit he was so dignified in his response.

Asked what he made of Blair's remarks, Corbyn responded: "It's perfectly OK, he's entitled to his opinions, but let's have a debate about policies."[4] When pressed, he delivered a nonchalant killer blow: "I think Tony Blair's big problem is that we are still awaiting the Chilcot report... Yes, we did win the 1997 election. We lost support consistently after that, and he led us into a disastrous illegal war." Finally, told that Blair had said he was the Tory choice for Labour leader, Corbyn dismissed the former prime minister: "I would have thought he could manage something more serious than those kind of rather silly remarks."[5]

For a man famous for proclaiming that "what matters is what works," Blair appeared to either not realise that his intervention did not work, or believed it did not matter. He was at it again three weeks later, penning a plea in the *Guardian* on 13 August under the rather pathetic headline: "Even if you hate me, please don't take Labour over the cliff edge." The man who had made a fetish of party unity when he was in charge now issued an open call for disunity. He ended with an appeal to "think about those we most care about and how to help them" before voting Corbyn, perhaps with his Davos friends in mind.[6]

By Blair's third attempt, an op-ed for the *Observer* on 30 August, the penny had dropped. Reflecting on his repeated warnings, he asked plaintively: "Anyone listening? Nope. In fact, the opposite. It actually makes them more likely to support him." If Blair's previous article had been a scream of defiance, this one was a whimper of bewilderment. "People like me have a lot of thinking to do," he admitted. "We don't yet properly understand this... So the question is: what to do?... I don't know." It was almost sad.[7]

Tin ear was a common affliction among Blairites in summer 2015. Blair's partner in crime Alastair Campbell popped up on 11 August with a long and windy essay demanding people vote "ABC: Anyone But Corbyn."[8] It was a misjudged call, if only because painting the other three candidates as interchangeable further differentiated Corbyn from the old politics. It was unclear why the UK's most infamous spin-doctor thought he was well placed to warn people off a politician they were drawn to for his eschewal of spin. Campbell's outburst, and the inevitable reaction, prompted the former Labour MP Bob Marshall-Andrews to write to the *Guardian*: "As a Jeremy Corbyn supporter may I suggest that Peter Mandelson joins Tony Blair and Alastair Campbell in publicly condemning his campaign?"[9]

Wishes do come true. Writing in the *Financial Times* on 27 August, Mandelson lamented that Blairism had been "caricatured" as "a sectarian creed alien to the party's values and history." But in a self-defeating move, he combined this with a veiled threat of a coup to overturn party democracy if Corbyn won.[10]

It seemed like all of the old Blairites came out of the woodwork to "sit the kids down and say: 'Look, you've had your fun,'" as the *Guardian*'s Jonathan Freedland patronisingly put it.[11] Jack Straw, Alan Johnson, David Miliband, Alan Milburn, David Blunkett—all approached the task in the expectation that their weight would swing it. All skulked off confounded, their pride wounded, when their words rebounded on them. It could only have been a form of strategic incontinence that moved Charles Clarke to describe Corbyn as the "continuity Benn/nutter candidate" whose supporters were "barking mad."[12]

The new generation of Blairites fared no better. The MP John Woodcock, then chair of Progress, urged his Blairite legions to be "passionately intolerant" of fellow Labour members succumbing to the "flawed logic of the cult"—an approach sure to win them back.[13] Tristram Hunt declared that "the party needs shock treatment."[14] Topping them all was Chuka Umunna. In an extraordinary temper tantrum he accused his own party of "behaving like a petulant child." He then achieved the remarkable feat of contradicting his own advice while administering it. "We're running around stamping our feet, screaming at the electorate, when ultimately what we need to do is meet people where they are at, not necessarily where we would want them to be," he said, apparently unaware of the irony that he was then in the midst of a leadership election in which he was stamping his feet, screaming at the electorate, and refusing to meet them where they were at.[15]

"I think there was a confusion," says Lewis. "They all thought that we've played around with Ed Miliband and dallied with the 'soft left' agenda, now it's back to business as usual... They've had a rude awakening. The country, the party, has moved on since 2008."

· · · · ·

"New Labour," Tony Blair once said, "is the newest political party on the scene and the smallest. It has about five people."[16] The roots of Blairism's humiliation in 2015 lay in the manner of its past success. As a clique in control of a party it maintained its position through the machine and the media. Its ideology, incessantly going against the grain of Labour traditions, never commanded wide enthusiasm among members, and became less appealing in the wake of the 2008 crash. As soon as New Labour was deprived of its powers of patronage, it was in trouble.

New Labour's reputation for control freakery was not incidental. Despite cloaking itself in the rhetoric of democracy and individualism, in practice the leadership tried to avoid involving the party membership in any meaningful way.[17] Avenues for dissent were closed down, alternative power centres brought to heel, and contentious decisions stitched up. The annual conference was emasculated, becoming little more than a backdrop for the leader's speech.[18] Policies—when not just handed down from on high—were determined by a National Policy Forum described by the MP Lisa Nandy in 2010 as "an insult to members because people felt their contribution was making no difference."[19]

It was possible to run such a managed party provided control was retained over all the important levers. New Labour relied on four interdependent power centres: the Leader's Office, the party machine, Progress, and sympathetic elements in the media. Losing the Leader's Office to first Gordon Brown then Ed Miliband was a catastrophic blow. The party machine, which had been the unseen enforcer of the leadership's will, was a much less formidable force when not working hand in glove with the leader, despite most party staff remaining fiercely loyal to the Blairite faith. Similarly, Progress—the "Militant Tendency of the right," in Jon Lansman's striking description—was exposed without the shelter of the leadership to work under. It functioned by taking people from student politics and moving them up through the party via patronage networks.[20] But after a damaging confrontation with the unions in the Miliband period, joining Progress looked less attractive to ambitious young politicians eager to get on. "They're dead, they just don't know it yet," one union leader said at the time.[21] Even the Blairites' access to a friendly media became less of an advantage as blogs and social media allowed alternative perspectives on party matters to gain wide currency.

However, the Blairites' biggest problem was ideological. Whatever dynamism Blairism had, it sprang from sources not available in the post-crash economy. The programme it offered was designed for the 1990s and had ossified into dogma.[22] The Blairite instinct always to move right squeezed its adherents into a shrinking political space. There were no more public services to be sacrificed to the market that the Tories had not already offered up. There were no more brownie points to be earned by sounding tough on the deficit that the Tories had not already banked. The Blairite agenda had reached the end of the line.

New Labour had been a unique departure in the party's history based on the collaboration of the 'soft left' with a new, neoliberal right.[23] That "consensus... began to erode piece by piece," says Clive Lewis. "Iraq, economic policy, the 2008 crash, neoliberalism, the dawning realisation that what we'd bought into as a party had ultimately caused our demise by 2010."

"The justification for the support for New Labour in the end was solely based upon their ability to win elections," observes John

McDonnell. "When they stopped winning elections that whole support edifice collapsed completely."[24]

The waning power of the Blairites was mirrored in the declining quality of their MPs. The first generation that rose with Blair and Brown were robust politicians who had battled the left to get to the top. Their successors had an easier journey, often moving effortlessly from university to ministerial advisor to parliament to the cabinet.[25] It was a career path that produced technocrats. They were "tram-lined, constrained politicians," says Luke Akehurst, secretary of Labour First, the organising group for the non-Blairite 'old right.'[26]

The Blairites also had a problem retaining people. Some of their number were perceived as a threat by Brown and taken out. Others were tempted through the revolving door between politics and the corporate world—most shamelessly, former health secretaries Alan Milburn and Patricia Hewitt sold their services to the very private healthcare firms their market reforms had benefitted. And others just wandered off—the likes of John Hutton, Ruth Kelly, James Purnell and David Miliband. Such a high rate of absenteeism suggested that Blairism was not an ideology people were prepared to make sacrifices for. As a result, the Blairites arrived at a situation in May 2015 where they had almost as many potential leadership candidates as nominators—not through a surfeit of talent, but because no one stood out among the clutch of nondescript politicians to which New Labour had been reduced.

· · · · ·

The remarkable thing about the humiliation of the Blairites was that they did not see it coming. An article published by Progress at the outset of the 2015 contest makes for amusing reading in retrospect. "On Monday the nominating stage of the Labour leadership race came to an end and we now know the overall shape of the race," it opened. "Three people who have a realistic chance of becoming leader of the Labour Party made it through. Jeremy Corbyn did also." The article went on to assess the candidates' prospects in the battle for CLP nominations. "Early feedback from members has been positive" for Kendall, it claimed, "which will please her team. However, I would still be surprised if she was able to better Andy Burnham's total." This proved correct—Burnham went on to win 111 CLP nominations; Kendall, 18. The candidate with no "realistic chance of becoming leader" won 152.[27]

As soon as the MPs' nomination phase was over Andy Burnham and Yvette Cooper joined forces to clobber Kendall by pronouncing the death of "Taliban New Labour." "The whole strategy for Liz was a Westminster strategy," a source from one of their campaigns told the *Daily Telegraph* on 15 June 2015, continuing:

> She played up to the media, to the right-wing commentators, to the Blairite Taliban MPs, made a few headlines by saying she was relaxed about free schools and committing to defence spending, and just took a chance that the momentum would carry her forward. But the trouble with that is that the fizzle and sparkle has gone already. Now the contest has moved on to the membership, who will not be interested in that kind of rhetoric or those policies, you will see her star wane very quickly.[28]

It proved a devastatingly accurate prediction. It was not long before Kendall was facing calls to withdraw from the race to enable the anti-Corbyn forces to gain focus. Valiantly she refused, asserting: "I'm the only candidate other than Jeremy Corbyn who is setting out an alternative from where we've been over the last five or eight years." Touchingly, or perhaps cynically, the Corbyn campaign concurred, commenting that Kendall "represents a body of opinion in the party that is as entitled as any to a voice in this contest... Liz should remain in the race."[29]

It only prolonged the agony. By August the Kendall campaign had become piteous. When a reporter for *Vice* went to a campaign picnic in Dulwich, London, he found only a smattering of people, many of whom explained that they would be voting for Corbyn but had come for the snacks as they lived nearby. "People will come literally tens of metres to hear Liz speak," the reporter noted.[30]

The Blairites' campaign strategy was "bizarre," according to Luke Akehurst. "Rather than try to build a coalition capable of reaching the 50 per cent needed to win the leadership they have run as the purest of the pure, setting the ideological bar so high that many people who would call themselves Blairites don't qualify."[31] Towards the end of the contest Kendall issued her own critique. "Modernisers" had "come across as technocratic and managerial," she said, "concerned with winning elections alone, rather than winning for a purpose—thereby ceding the mantle of principle to the far left."[32]

Even though it was apparent to everyone that Kendall was heading for a bad defeat, the scale of the rout when it came was almost as shocking as Corbyn's resounding victory.[33] The Blairites were confronted with an inescapable truth: there was no appetite for their message.[34] Moreover, their famed organisational prowess amounted to almost nothing in a big, wide-open contest. Their prior championing of the registered supporters system is all the more confounding in this context, and can perhaps only be explained by arrogance. It was their belief that a reservoir of centrist, Blairite voters existed beyond the party that led to its introduction. But from a potential electorate of 45 million people just 2,574 were prepared to pay £3 to vote for Kendall.

The puncturing of the Blairites did not happen in isolation. The exhaustion of Blairism and its refusal to either adapt or die was a major impetus behind Corbyn's rise. The years of managing the party with thinly veiled contempt for the members had sown the seeds of deep resentment. Presented with a candidate who aspired to sweep all that away in favour of party democracy, members seized the opportunity. Afforded a chance to cast a verdict on triangulating politics and neoliberal dogma, they did so unequivocally. The election of Corbyn was, in the words of Unite's Martin Mayer, "a massive 'vote no' to New Labour and everything it stood for."

12

THE CORBYN SURGE

"It's like when I saw Jagger come on stage at a Stones concert. Jagger in a yellow shirt, with his signature vest peeking through, a row of biros in his top pocket. The roar is deafening."

—Carole Cadwalladr, the Observer

The queue outside the Jeremy Corbyn rally stretches 500 yards along Euston Road and round the corner, and that is just for the overflow room. There is a second queue for the main hall, wrapping round the other two sides of the massive Camden Town Hall building in London. To ensure they get in, people have arrived an hour-and-a-half before the event begins. Nobody minds the wait. It is a warm summer evening in early August and something is in the air.

The queue itself becomes a giant meeting place for political discussion. Ordinarily reserved Londoners are *talking* to each other. It is such an unusual occurrence that people start taking out their phones to photograph the lines. For Labour activist Michael Calderbank, it feels like people are not just queuing for a political meeting but to experience "history happening." The sense of anticipation is so strong that the crowd could be waiting for a Beatles reunion concert, he thinks, "with John Lennon coming back to life."

Inside the building working class tube drivers sit next to middle class Hampstead radicals. Muslim university students squeeze past veteran trade unionists. There are young people everywhere, some of them still of school age. And there are Westminster journalists—this is their opportunity to witness the Corbyn phenomenon without having to venture out of London. "I've never seen anything like it!" one deputy political editor says to a colleague. "I covered the entire general election but this is… unbelievable."

So many people have turned up—over 1,500—that they are packing out not just the main hall, but also an overflow room, and even Camden Council chamber. Corbyn will personally address all three meetings in rotation. But still there are people who cannot fit in, and so the fire-fighters' union has parked a fire engine in the street outside equipped with a PA system. In one of the iconic scenes of the summer, Corbyn stands on top of the vehicle and addresses the crowd of several hundred supporters in the open air. "I hope the Dolphin does well out of our attendance here this evening," he says, referring to the adjacent pub.

The whole thing is a logistical nightmare for the team of volunteers shepherding Corbyn between venues. Everywhere he goes he is mobbed. The team cannot afford any delays but, as is his wont, Corbyn stops to chat to people anyway.

When Corbyn finally makes his entrance into the main hall to give his fourth and final speech of the night, the place erupts. The man who eschews the politics of personality and celebrity gets a rock star reception. For one of the journalists observing the spectacle, "it's like when I saw Jagger come on stage at a Stones concert. Jagger in a yellow shirt, with his signature vest peeking through, a row of biros in his top pocket. The roar is deafening."

As a member of the LRC, Calderbank has seen Corbyn speak on countless occasions. The man at the centre of the attention is still "the same old Jeremy in his ordinary work clothes, looking slightly dazzled in the stage lights." But the world around him has transformed. The atmosphere is that of a "religious revival meeting." There is a "sense of euphoria."

Some of those who could not get in are literally climbing the walls to be a part of it—four teenagers balance on a ledge on the exterior of the building to peer in through the window. Snapped by a photographer, the unlikely scene becomes another iconic image. John McDonnell will later joke that something must have changed—in the past, political meetings he attended were typically so boring that people would be breaking out of toilet windows to escape, not trying to clamber in.

For half an hour Corbyn does his thing. His speech is more honed than earlier in the contest but it is still delivered in his relaxed, informal manner, speaking without bombast and without notes. Towards the end he turns to the question that everybody has been contemplating: why is this happening?

> We had 1,500 people in Liverpool on Saturday night crammed into the Adelphi Hotel—it was probably more than the fire regulations allowed. We had 1,000 people in Birmingham yesterday. All over the country we're getting these huge gatherings of people. They're young, they're old, they're black, they're white, all ages, many outlooks, many people who have never been involved in politics before. Why have they come together? Why? It's an odd thing to do... Is it because they want to see something different in our society: real democracy, where everybody can contribute to the policy discussion? So we don't make policy at luxurious, obscure country hotels at weekends by consensus. Instead we have what may well be a very gritty debate in a community centre, in a school, in a college, at a place of work, in a canteen, around the water cooler, all kinds of places. And that then informs and expands our minds and brings about some real hope for the future.

When Corbyn winds up his speech the hall rises for a loud and fervent ovation. The crowd claps Corbyn; Corbyn claps the crowd; everyone claps everyone; the whole room stands clapping each other for two solid minutes. It is a bonding exercise, a way of acknowledging a shared experience, of fusing a collective spirit.

Spontaneous chants of "Jez we can!" burst out—the affirmative, inclusive, unofficial slogan of the campaign. People feel they are part of something.[1]

· · · · ·

What the press pejoratively labelled 'Corbynmania' was the emergence of a new political movement. An almost viral growth in support was triggered by the extraordinary three days in late-July 2015 when the Welfare Bill, the YouGov poll, Tony Blair's intervention, and a full-scale media meltdown followed one after another. It took the form of packed rallies, floods of people signing up to vote, an explosion of activity on social media, thousands volunteering their labour to the campaign, and uncounted, unheralded acts of evangelism—unofficial street stalls, informal gatherings, the unprompted recruitment of friends and family to the cause. These elements were mutually reinforcing and translated into huge jumps in the polls. It was not long before the inevitable declaration that, in terms of Google search frequency, Corbyn was "bigger than Jesus."[2]

The surge hit a peak around the 12 August deadline for people to register to vote, when Labour's website crashed under the weight of traffic.[3] The party received 167,000 applications in the final 24 hours. Around 100,000 were affiliated supporters submitted by trade unions *en masse*, but that still left a massive influx of registered supporters and new members.[4] James Schneider was a Corbyn volunteer fielding calls from people having trouble registering. "It was just like red lights going off constantly, can't possibly take enough calls," he remembers.

The energy was sustained for the rest of the contest as Corbyn made his way to all corners of the country. Jon Lansman believes the rallies were crucial in "helping Jeremy move on to the possibility of winning." Corbyn had not liked pestering his parliamentary colleagues for nominations in June; it was not his style. But getting out of Westminster and campaigning was. "It was predictable that he would enjoy it," Lansman says. "OK, we didn't know we were going to have rallies with umpteen overflows and a fire engine outside for him to speak from the top of, which of course will have been exhilarating, will have boosted his morale enormously and helped him get onto the next stage and be willing to do it. So during the whole process he grew into the role, though not in a conventional sense, perhaps."

The plan to hold campaign meetings separately from the official hustings was hatched from the very beginning. "Jeremy and I sat down," remembers John McDonnell. "I said: 'The nature of this campaign is that you've got to go on the stump all around the country.' He said: 'You'll come with me?' I did joke, I said: 'No, look, it'll be *Last of the Summer Wine*, you and me on tour. You go out there yourself. I'll help organise it, just get out there.'"[5]

The initial ambition for the meetings, McDonnell says, was a relatively modest one, to "raise people's consciousness... Then even if you don't win you get a reasonable vote but you've recruited, you've raised the politics." But it was immediately apparent that people's consciousness was already raised. "I did the traditional thing: book a hall for 100, no more than that, pull the chairs away if there's not many turn up. Unbelievable. The first one you get 500 people turn up. You know there's something going on."

Thereafter the pace was frenetic. Corbyn gave a sense of it when he reeled off his schedule to a reporter on 31 July: "Tonight Leicester, tomorrow Preston and Liverpool. Sunday, Coventry and Birmingham. Monday a big rally in London. Tuesday I think I am in Croydon. Wednesday, Belfast. Thursday, an event in London and a public meeting in Norwich. Friday, Bradford. Saturday, Sheffield and Doncaster and Leeds and so it goes on... do you need more?"[6] It was a "gruelling" programme, says McDonnell, adding: "His stamina is unbelievable."

On one visit to Wales Corbyn packed four meetings into one day. On 10 August in Llandudno, 1 in 40 of the small town's inhabitants squeezed into a hotel ballroom to hear him speak.[7] When Corbyn went to Scotland, where Labour was a gutted party, he addressed over 2,500 people in four cities on 13-14 August.[8] Huge demand forced events to be switched to larger venues at the last minute; in Glasgow a 300-capacity venue was swapped for the city's 1,200-capacity Fruitmarket, yet it still filled up.[9]

Organising the logistics of Corbyn's itinerary became a massive operation. It did not help that he was notorious for missing trains. "Once when he was travelling up north it was such a panic because he'd missed about three trains already that week," remembers Marshajane Thompson. She was on the phone to Corbyn while he was at the station. "I'm going: 'Right, don't miss the train, don't miss the train.' And he's going: 'No, I won't miss the train. Oh, it's just pulled away.'"

People started queuing in the rain two and a half hours before a 1,000-strong afternoon rally in Middlesbrough on 18 August. Afterwards, so many supporters wanted to talk and grab selfies with Corbyn that he was late for his next engagement in Newcastle, which was unfortunate because it was an open-air affair and the patient crowd of 500 was drenched.[10]

It was a rally in Nottingham on 20 August that convinced Corbyn he was about to become Labour leader. "You know Nottingham; normally we think that 50 or 60 people at a meeting is a good turnout," Corbyn said. But 900 packed into the elegant Albert Hall, with 300 more having to be addressed by loudhailer outside. "I thought then we might win this one."[11]

On 29 August Corbyn addressed nearly 5,000 people in three large rallies on the same day in Derby, Sheffield and Manchester.[12] Cat Smith was one of the speakers at the Manchester event, where around 2,000 gathered in a massive venue usually used for big Indian weddings. Actresses Maxine Peake and Julie Hesmondhalgh were also on the bill. "There had been about two days' notice and it had sold out in minutes," Smith recalls. "It was just electric... It wasn't like anything I'd ever done before. I almost had to pinch myself." Afterwards she was "buzzing" and told her partner Ben Soffa, who worked for the campaign: "It was amazing. These things are amazing. We have to go to more of them."

Incredibly, towards the end of the contest, Corbyn was able to take his message to areas where Labour was not strong at all—even Essex, where he addressed sold-out rallies in Chelmsford and Colchester on 2 September.

The tour concluded back on Corbyn's home-turf in Islington on 10 September for a rally that had the feel of a victory party (his 99th event of the contest—the announcement of the result would be the 100th). Corbyn's team calculated that he had addressed 50,000 people over the summer.[13]

"This was a mass campaign that was way beyond anything the left has done in my lifetime," says the veteran organiser Lansman. "I remember the [Tony] Benn campaign in '81... It was tiny in comparison." Corbyn was "astonished at the turnout" his events attracted.[14] The only reference point he could reach for was the groundswell against the Iraq War. "That was huge," he said. "But that, in a sense, was against the war and this is for something—for a programme—which is very different."[15] The experience had a powerful effect on him. "He's not a person with ego at all but what he came back with was the warmth of support that was there," says McDonnell. "Absolute confidence in the support for the ideas we were putting forward."

· · · · ·

The defining characteristic of the Corbyn phenomenon was that it was participative. People who showed up at a Corbyn rally felt they were making a movement. The campaign encouraged this sense of shared endeavour by incorporating an element of crowdsourcing into its policy development and emphasising the restoration of internal party democracy as an objective. But more immediate was the practical experience of building a force for change. The sudden realisation that here was a way to have a direct influence on national politics electrified the 2015 leadership contest.

Paradoxically, the grassroots vibe came right from the top. It was the essence of Corbyn's personal political philosophy. His line of libertarian socialism aspired to the radical democratisation of society and the economy, rejecting unaccountable power whether wielded by a corporation or a paternalistic state bureaucracy.[16]

This democratic ethos was the stuff of Bennism, yet Corbyn's leadership bid was more Bennite than a Benn campaign. No matter how many times Tony Benn said that what mattered was democracy and "the issues," he was a silver-tongued, charismatic communicator who inspired personal devotion.[17] Hero worship is an affliction to which the left has been prone throughout history around the world, partly as a function of the enormous odds facing anyone who dares to confront entrenched power. It is a trap, diverting energy that would be better focused elsewhere. It is usually unsustainable. Corbyn did begin to attract an element of hero worship. At the end of August a disposable cup from which he had drunk sold for £51 on eBay.[18] Such stories became more frequent after Corbyn assumed the leadership. Those close to him say it is something he is "baffled" by "because he's never wanted to be a cult hero figure."[19]

But in the 2015 contest it was a small concern. Although the press threw around the term 'Corbynmania'—suggesting irrational adulation of the leader—this revealed nothing of what made the movement tick. Corbyn was no demagogue. He excited people by offering them the opportunity to shape politics themselves. This was best expressed by a social media meme used by the Corbyn campaign—one fittingly created by a supporter—which said: "A movement, not a man."

Volunteers

The clearest evidence that the campaign was a collective endeavour was the sheer number of people willing to give up their time to help out. An incredible 15,800 people volunteered, doing anything from data entry to stewarding events.[20] This gave Team Corbyn a labour force equivalent to that of a large company, with a huge capacity to get things done.

At the volunteer centre in the Unite headquarters in London, the numbers went through the roof, almost literally. "We kept getting more and more rooms in the building as they kept overflowing," says James Schneider. "We'd have 50 people there by midday doing office work and having phone banks running for eight hours a day." By the evening there would be hundreds. "One week we had 700 different people come in, which was quite extreme."

More phone banks were established in other cities. And Ben Soffa, the campaign's tech wizard, built a piece of software called the 'canvassing app,' which allowed volunteers to make calls from home, with the data fed into the campaign's database. It contributed many thousands of calls to the total. The other candidates had nothing similar.[21] "We called the most people by miles which meant that we could construct the best get out the vote effort," says

Schneider. Once the ballot papers were distributed in August, the Corbyn campaign was "incredibly focused in finding and reminding lots and lots of people to vote."

The volunteers were predominantly young people, retired people, and teachers who were on school holidays. Schneider remembers a pep talk Corbyn delivered at the volunteer centre. "He said: 'We're seeing democracy in action, people coming together from different walks of life for a common purpose.' And I look around the room and it genuinely is—there's a middle-aged working class guy next to two young hijabi women." The prominence of young people "made it feel like it was young and fresh and couldn't be characterised as '80s." One regular volunteer, Lola May, says: "The stuff that happened when Blair was in power does seem like something I'd read in the history books... What year was the Iraq War, 2003? I was five."

Social media

The participative ethos of the Corbyn campaign synced perfectly with the technology of social media. Corbyn's social media team had a contrasting approach to that of the other candidates' campaigns. Ben Sellers has encapsulated the difference, writing that there is a "top down way to do social media (releasing news to your followers) and a grassroots way to do social media (using it as a forum for an activist-led movement)." The Corbyn campaign was the most spectacular example of the latter that British politics had yet seen. In Sellers' words: "It generated a real sense that this was a movement everyone could be involved in, discuss, interact with, get answers from... If people felt like actors in this campaign, rather than consumers of it, a large part of that was down to our social media operation."[22]

The scale of the online mobilisation was extraordinary. Corbyn received vastly more social media mentions than all the other candidates combined.[23] Most of this activity was spontaneous. But the team's strategy was to consciously encourage and, as far as possible, direct the "flowering of activism."[24] "There was an emerging democracy within the social media, and people setting up their own groups like 'We Back Corbyn,' 'Kittens for

Corbyn'—from the serious to the bizarre," says Sellers.[25] "None of it was very controlled, but our team of 15 people took responsibility for trying to funnel all that in through the main Corbyn For Leader page."

With their own content the team aimed to get people talking about the issues. This, they hoped, would overcome the so-called "echo chamber"—the tendency for people who agree to coalesce. This was more easily achieved on Facebook, where comments allowed for extended interaction, than Twitter. Sellers remembers a particular example: a picture of Corbyn holding a banner saying "Stop scapegoating immigrants" got 10,000 shares on Facebook. "The first few comments were quite positive because they were the core support," he says. "Then when people shared it, a percentage of their friends weren't in our bubble and they started commenting negatively. And then other people would react to that and argue against them... You could see there were those ripples, that it was going outwards, breaking outside of people that would normally be positive about immigration."

The social media team encouraged people to keep their interactions polite, putting out memes featuring quotes from Corbyn condemning abuse in politics. Supporters began to "do their own policing," according to Sellers. "If people said, 'I reserve the right to say what I like to Liz Kendall, she's a red Tory,' then other people would say, 'That's not helpful to our campaign, we want to win this campaign don't we? So stop doing it.'"

There was an interactive relationship between activity online and in the physical world. On the one hand, social media was, in Sellers' words, a "generator for the campaign on the ground"—pushing people to attend rallies and volunteer.[26] On the other hand, it acted as an alternative press to publicise what was happening, giving everything from humble street stalls to barnstorming speeches a far wider audience than they could have had in the past. "You literally just put out a photograph of a packed hall in Liverpool and you'd get an enormous amount of shares," says Sellers.

Social media enabled people to participate in another way: by giving money. The campaign raised more cash in small online donations than it did from trade unions—over £200,000, with the average contribution being £23.50.[27] "Every time I would put out an appeal our funding would jump £2,500 to £5,000 within the hour," says Marshajane Thompson. "Without social media I don't think we'd have had the money to run the campaign that we did." Thompson remembers appealing for money to fund a mailing to new recruits after the last-minute surge of sign-ups. "We raised £11,000 overnight," she says.

Another source of funding was an online shop selling Corbyn-branded merchandise, run by Thompson. Despite only opening for business half way through the contest it sold 75,000 items, including 10,000 'Team Corbyn' t-shirts at £10 each, beer mats, posters, badges and leaflets.[28] There were also traditional fund-raising efforts. A gig at the Union Chapel in Islington on 21 August raised over £12,000.

Jon Lansman believes Team Corbyn "spent more money than anyone else because we were able to raise more money than anyone else," a novel experience for a left campaign. Corbyn insisted that everyone who donated should get a signed thank you letter. He was evidently proud of his funding, boasting to a rally in Newcastle that he had accepted no corporate donations. "Before you get too excited" he added, "we were offered none, either."[29]

Policies

The construction of a policy platform was bound to entail centralised decision-making. But even here, Team Corbyn turned convention on its head. The ethos of participation permeated the campaign's programme from bottom to top.

For a start, actually having specific policies struck a blow for democratic engagement. The campaigns of the other candidates often felt like policy-free zones, with voters left to tease out the implications of press statements and coded speeches. Team Corbyn, in contrast, released 13 policy papers and made 10 significant announcements during the contest. These ranged from short, sharp pledges—like promising to scrap student fees—to more substantial policy papers on major topics—such as 'The Economy in 2020,' an encapsulation of Corbyn's anti-austerity economics.[30] The quality of the policy papers varied widely—some were produced in haste, others were more impressive—and they were released in a rather ad hoc fashion. Importantly, each was presented not as an edict but as a basis for discussion in a revived party democracy.

Pulling together the policies was the job of Corbyn's future advisor Andrew Fisher. His output was prolific. After some early press release announcements in June—sent into the ether when the media was not paying attention ("End austerity, have a living wage"; "Give private tenants the right to buy"; "Reinstate the Independent Living Fund")—the programme really started to take shape with a commitment to repeal the Trade Union Bill on 15 July and the announcement on student fees the following day. The economic strategy was the first of the big policy documents, released on 22 July. Before the month was finished Corbyn had outlined ambitious plans for a National Education Service (free learning from cradle to grave) and published a 'Working With Women' document (equal pay audits, universal free childcare, 50 per cent of the shadow cabinet to be women).[31]

Between 4-10 August the campaign released five chunky policy papers on the North, the housing crisis (build council houses, control rents, register landlords, tax land banking), peace and defence (scrap Trident and redeploy the workforce), protecting the environment, and improving life for young people.[32] In the second half of August Corbyn set out plans for the renationalisation of the railways, promised to apologise on behalf of the Labour Party for the Iraq War, outlined measures on mental health, proposed ideas to prevent the harassment of women, and called for an end to the private finance initiative (PFI) in the NHS.[33] Even as the contest was drawing to a close in early September, Team Corbyn released policies on widening access to the arts and reviving rural areas.[34]

Leadership campaigns are usually about style over substance. Corbyn tried to make his the opposite. "Jeremy doesn't get up and give speeches about vision and owning the future and the challenges of Britain and all that kind of awful fucking language that means nothing and you go, 'Mmm, can't disagree with it because I don't know what the fuck it means,'" says a member of Corbyn's team.

Of course, it is doubtful many voters took the time to read through all the policy documents. But they formed the backbone of the campaign. The sheer frequency of new announcements created a sense of forward motion. They gave Team Corbyn's press officers ammunition to counter relentless media negativity. They provided great raw material for the social media team to use to provoke discussion.[35] And, cumulatively, they amounted to a distinguishable political programme. As John McDonnell says, "At least people know where we're coming from. They might not fully support it but at least they know there's a clarity about the purpose other than just career politics."

There was some strategic thought behind the policies the Corbyn camp focused on. "There were a lot of issues where there was a clear grievance within the party," says a member of the campaign, mentioning railways, PFI and Iraq as examples. "We were picking up those issues where Jeremy could speak absolutely boldly and confidently... He just had a credibility that none of the other candidates could have."

The most overtly strategic of the policy papers was a 'Northern Future' document launched on 4 August. Team Corbyn knew Andy Burnham's support was strongest in the North and believed that eroding it was key to winning. "We were very, very exercised about the campaign focusing too much on an agenda that looks fine in London but really doesn't look fine in the North," says Lansman. "Too much time talking about multiculturalism and not enough time talking about class." McDonnell recalls: "It was important that we not only did policy on the North... but also that we had around us a whole group of northern MPs. So we had the youngsters there [at the launch] like Richard Burgon and Becky Long-Bailey... Jon Trickett... was a great advisor to us on all of that."

The campaign went further than just stating its positions. It explicitly invited engagement with its proposals. A typical passage—taken from 'Tackling the Housing Crisis'—explains: "This discussion document sets out some of the problems and attempts to outline some solutions. Your input would be welcome—in fact without it Labour will not get its housing policy right. As well as campaigning for a more rational housing policy, this campaign is about a more rational policy-making process. We want your ideas, experiences and suggestions."[36]

In some instances a crowdsourcing approach was used to gather ideas. The most successful example was the 'Northern Future' document. The campaign emailed supporters in the North asking what needed to be done in their part of the country. They were stunned to receive 1,200 replies. The best ideas were then woven into a policy framework. "That, I think, shows a different way," said Trickett at the time. "The alternative way to come up with a policy was to employ a thinktank, get a policy wonk or a panel of experts and announce a policy from on high. And that is not the form of leadership we are going to have."[37]

A similar approach informed the policy paper on young people, "compiled in discussion with more than 1,000 Young Labour supporters from across Britain... enabling them to have a say in the design of their own futures," according to the press release that accompanied it.[38] A member of Corbyn's team says:

> Whether it's housing benefit, minimum wage, benefits where the rates are lower for younger people if they can get them at all, college cuts, college places being cut, university grants being abolished... tuition fees being trebled to £9,000, cuts to educational maintenance allowance— all that kind of stuff we could talk about in a very clear way. And because we had so many young people enthused by the campaign we actually got them to drive it a lot of the time. They took on a youth mental health angle. I would never have thought of that. But then you look at it and think, 'Fuck, actually they've cut away at mental health services for the young as well.' All these things you could put into a manifesto, and they're the best people at sharing things on social media.

The crowdsourcing method was also responsible for the most unexpected policy intervention of all—a paper on 'Rural Renewal.' Buoyed by the support Corbyn was receiving in unlikely places, the campaign asked for ideas on how to build Labour in areas where it was almost absent. "The rural document was amazing because you think, 'It's a rural document, we're not going to get many responses,'" says Thompson. "We were inundated with all these comments."[39]

Corbyn's radical democratic spirit permeated the content of many of the policies too. For example, his preferred model of public ownership was distinct from both the market dogma of New Labour and the classic top-down statist approach. This was most clearly shown in Corbyn's plan for the railways. As he said: "I believe in public ownership, but I have never favoured the remote nationalised model of the post-war era... Public control should mean just that: so we should have passengers, rail workers and government too, cooperatively running the railways."[40]

This thinking was "far more Jeremy and John's kind of libertarian left," says a member of Corbyn's team. "It's the best of Bennism. There's a generation that has never heard of that sort of stuff." The campaign made it a rule that there would be "no Milibandisms; no old left talk... We were trying to present ourselves as radical, something new."

Overarching all of these positions was Corbyn's cherished aspiration to restore democracy to Labour's policy-making process. This seemed to be an alien concept to some of the other candidates. In a telling moment on LBC radio on 23 July, presenter Iain Dale asked Andy Burnham, Yvette Cooper and Liz Kendall whether they would serve in the shadow cabinet if Corbyn won. Burnham was a yes, Kendall a one-word no, and Cooper prevaricated. When Dale pressed Cooper, telling her "this is where I think you've got a problem, you equivocate too much," Kendall piled in, saying: "Oh come on, Yvette. Do you honestly think you could go out and make the case for the things that Jeremy calls for? Seriously?" At that point, having been talked about as if he was not in the room, Corbyn interjected: "Actually, we're just assuming everything is done by the leader. We've forgotten there are party members out there who are part of this election. Those party members have a right to influence and decide what the policies are."[41]

As Corbyn put it on another occasion: "Policy making... should not come from the top, passed down the food chain for the foot soldiers to go and knock on doors and release it on the unsuspecting public. I'd rather it started with the suspecting public putting their ideas forward... so that it works through and we end up with a very broad range of support."[42] For emasculated party members this was an appealing idea. Corbyn was offering them empowerment. There was no mistaking the message—every aspect of Corbyn's candidacy, from his own selfless demeanour to the specific form of rail nationalisation he was proposing, was about inviting people to take part.

· · · · ·

It is possible to oversell the extent to which the Corbyn campaign was, in the jargon, prefigurative—run in a way that foreshadowed its plans for wider society. Ultimately, in a leadership campaign, the candidate has to decide what the candidate is in favour of. For all the consultation on policy, no formal democratic mechanisms were established—there was hardly time. But when so much of the activity was self-organised, for so clear and limited an objective, that was largely by the by. The obvious desire to be inclusive gave a signal for people to get involved, triggering a chain reaction as their efforts galvanised others.

The informal, spontaneous side of the campaign is difficult to quantify. But the scale of it was significant. "Anecdotally I know loads of people who didn't technically volunteer in the campaign but sat down in their workplace or at home with their friends and explained who Jeremy Corbyn was, explained why it was important, and got five people to sign up," says James Schneider. "That swell of people was huge... You'd get people on the phone saying 'I've got 20 people to sign up.'" For Marshajane Thompson, the Corbyn phenomenon "reinvented word of mouth."

Once it had caught the wind, the campaign no longer had to be pushed along by the staff in the central office; rather, the office found itself being pulled along in the movement's wake. Corbyn's rallies in Essex, for example, were organised by an unofficial pop-up group called Essex For Corbyn. There were informal weekend picnics for supporters.[43] "You can sit there in an office in London but you won't necessarily know that there are 100 people meeting in Newcastle that are planning to do street stalls and events or comedy nights," says Ben Sellers. "There was all sorts of stuff like that going on all over the country." Sellers believes such grassroots activity was more significant to Corbyn's win than the high-level work done by the staff in the head office: "The idea it was very tightly managed from the centre, to some people that's what it would have looked like, but I actually think that some of the best work was done regionally and autonomously."

The campaign's 12 regional organisers sat between the central office and the grassroots upsurge. "There were people like Hannah Butler who ran the East Midlands region," says Thompson. "Hannah organised meetings all across the East Midlands... Some meetings we were having 800 people there and there wasn't even a big name speaker. She was at local events, she was making sure there were leaflets everywhere, she was making sure there were street stalls... she was making sure the fundraising was happening, that badges were going everywhere." Together, the regional organisers gave the campaign a valuable nation-wide infrastructure.[44]

To be fair to the central office, it too provided a framework, creating the iconography, campaign materials, and an administrative structure. There was a member of staff—Gavin Sibthorpe—coordinating the rallies. Plenty of vital work was done centrally—communicating with the press, honing the message, sending emails to supporters.[45] The campaign was not free of internal tensions: there were grumblings from the regions about HQ, and from one part of the office about another. But such was the head of steam behind Corbyn's candidacy that this made no real difference.

It was fortunate that the campaign had its own impetus because, according to Jon Lansman, there was not much strategy decided at the centre. In part, this was because "we had a USP.[46] None of the others did. So to some extent we didn't have to do [strategy]." The 'Northern Future' policy document was an exception; aside from that, the campaign stuck to its initial template. In contrast, the rival campaigns featured multiple relaunches, revamps, flip-flops and lurches.

Corbyn was playing an entirely different game. His campaign was not an exercise in political positioning, but a serious attempt to harness a movement. It could only be as successful as the movement was strong. "Yes it was a good operation but that wasn't why we won," concedes Lansman. "We didn't make it happen in my view... It happened because it caught the moment. It captured the imagination for political reasons, and the nature of Jeremy as a non-politician, as he was seen."

· · · · ·

The spectacular growth of the Corbyn movement could be seen in opinion polls. On 10 August 2015, YouGov published its second breath-taking poll of the contest. It had Jeremy Corbyn on 53 per cent of first preference votes, up 10 points in just two-and-a-half weeks. He was now 32 points clear. With a share of over 50 per cent Corbyn would win outright on the first round of voting.[47] His position was one of total dominance. He was miles ahead with every type of voter: women, men, the young, the old, working class, middle class, people from the North, the South, the Midlands and Wales, Scotland, London, trade unionists, registered supporters, and party members.

Digging down into the detail revealed what kinds of people made up Corbyn's support (although sub-samples within polls must be treated with caution). One of the many accusations thrown at the Corbyn phenomenon was that it was a middle class revolt, a takeover of a working class party by croissant-munching Islingtonians and hipster graduates. In fact, the poll showed that Corbyn had the backing of 57 per cent of "C2DE" voters (commonly characterised as working class), compared to 51 per cent of "ABC1s" (middle class). Further polling by YouGov, taken in the first week of August, showed a clear pattern differentiating the candidates. 36 per cent of Corbyn's backers were from the top social grade "AB," compared to 40 per cent of Andy Burnham's, 48 per cent of Yvette Cooper's, and 65 per cent of Liz Kendall's. On this evidence, Blairites were the real croissant-munchers.[48]

Also notable was Corbyn's popularity with women. He was the first choice for 61 per cent of female voters, compared to 48 per cent of men. Cooper's overt attempt to appeal to women with cringe-worthy reminders that she was a mother—in contrast to Kendall, who was apparently deficient by implication—did not work. Only 19 per cent of women backed her.[49] As for Kendall, her voters were heavily skewed towards men.[50] Geographically, Corbyn's support was strongest in London and weaker in the North and the Midlands and Wales—but in those areas he still crushed his rivals (Burnham was not nearly as strong in the North as the Corbyn camp had feared).[51]

Corbyn's support was more evenly distributed among age groups than might be expected.[52] But younger people were disproportionately attracted as the movement grew. Between YouGov's first poll of 21 July and the final result, Corbyn's overall standing improved by 17 points. Yet among the over-60s it climbed only 9 points, indicating they were less caught up in it all.[53] His support from 25-39 year olds, in contrast, jumped 22 points. It was this age group, and not the very youngest, that was most enthusiastic, although Corbyn made huge gains among every cohort under 60.[54]

It was reported that the influx of new members and registered supporters reduced the average age of a Labour Party member from 53 to 42.[55] The local parties with the biggest jumps in membership were often in university towns and cities, like Bath and Colchester.[56] Corbyn spoke proudly of his encounters with "very enthusiastic young people, who were written off as a non-political generation, when in reality they were a political generation that politics had written off."[57]

Corbyn's candidacy also attracted "a generation that's older who had walked away from Labour," says a member of his team, "people who had been members all the way through the '70s and '80s who were not necessarily 'hard left'... but who just didn't feel it was them any more and left over Iraq or foundation hospitals." They now flooded back to restore Labour to what they felt were its true values.[58]

The surge of people registering to vote at the last minute was so significant that YouGov had to update its 10 August poll four days later, saying Corbyn was now likely to win 57 per cent of first-preference votes.[59] "The final wave, the very late entrants, were very good for us," comments Jon Lansman. When the campaign tried phone canvassing registered supporters "it was really, really good," according to a member of the team. "So we did a few more, and then it just got to the point of, 'What's the point of canvassing? We're getting overwhelming support.'"

The impact of registered supporters was the subject of hysterical debate and wild claims of mass entryism.[60] The notion that outsiders distorted the contest subsequently congealed into conventional wisdom. So it is important ask whether the '£3ers' really were the driving force of the Corbyn movement. Certainly the system of £3 votes, which the left strongly opposed at its inception, played to the strengths of the Corbyn campaign—an outcome John McDonnell describes as "more than ironic." It was the involvement of non-members that expanded the contest beyond the usual bounds of an internal party election and created the sense of a mass movement. "The rallies were a really big thing," says a campaign source. "They were just so unlike the experience that anyone had had in the Labour Party... If it had just been Labour Party members that couldn't have happened."

The buzz also appeared to embolden existing members to vote for Corbyn. "The momentum was enormously helpful," says Lansman. "It was exciting. And the party was getting lots of members. What's not to like about that, even if you're a middle-of-the-road Labour Party loyalist? A bandwagon is attractive. You want to be on the winning side."

But this was not a one-way process. The chronology suggests registered supporters were only inspired to join in such large numbers after members had put Corbyn in pole position, raising the prospect that he could actually win. By 28 July, a week after Corbyn was revealed to be in the lead in the first YouGov poll, 21,000 people had registered for £3.[61] That was a large number, but over the following two weeks a further 92,000 signed up.[62]

Something profound was already happening within the membership. In fact, the most noteworthy figures in the 10 August YouGov poll were those concerning party members. 49 per cent of them said they intended to vote for Corbyn (in line with the final result). The left candidate had overwhelming support among members who joined after the 2015 general election and, more surprisingly, under Ed Miliband. But most remarkable was Corbyn's healthy lead among long-time party members from before 2010—people for whom Labour had been a political home when led by Gordon Brown and Tony Blair. Corbyn held a 13-point advantage over second-placed Burnham in this group. This was evidence of a sharp turn against New Labour politics. The shift was not only coming from outside, but from within.[63]

The three distinct processes underway in the party, the trade unions, and the broader left were entwining. Each had, up to then, taken its own political form and progressed at its own speed, although they were all ultimately responses to the same economic crisis. But now, as they wound together around a shared objective, the strength of each was reinforced by the others. That shared objective was to change the direction of the Labour Party by electing not a demagogue with a pre-prepared plan, but a self-effacing democrat offering people the chance to shape the future themselves. It was an offer that was sufficiently open to unite a broad coalition, yet radical enough to generate great excitement.

13

THE EMPIRE STRIKES BACK

"We have reason to believe that you do not support the aims and values of the Labour Party."
                                        —*email from the Labour Party*

The queue outside the Yvette Cooper rally stretches... there is no queue. Cooper is due to make the biggest speech of her campaign, billed as the moment she will take the fight to Jeremy Corbyn, and about 50 people have ambled into a function room in HOME, a shiny new steel and glass arts complex in central Manchester, to hear it. There are spare seats.

For the first half of the contest Cooper has been the comatose candidate. But she has returned from a family holiday in America with renewed vigour. At a meeting with her campaign team the question was asked whether they really wanted to win. They decided they did. So instead of playing it safe, Cooper will attack Corbyn over his anti-austerity economics. It may alienate his supporters, but Cooper hopes it will make her the standard-bearer for those dubious about the left candidate.

"The truth is that Jeremy is offering old solutions to old problems, not new answers to the problems of today," Cooper tells the room, reading a pre-released script from behind a lectern. Her strategy may have changed, but her rhetoric is still chronic. "We have to look the 21st century in the eye," she says. "Face up to the future. That is where we will find the new radicalism, the new answers in the modern fight for social justice."

Cooper's delivery is professional and polished and entirely unengaging. "What is more radical?" she persists. Is it to elect a man as leader, "or is it to smash our own glass ceiling and to get Labour's first woman leader?" Cooper's voice turns stern as she personalises the question: "Who is really the radical, Jeremy or me?" It appears Cooper is attacking Corbyn for not being a woman.

The logic certainly does not convince everyone in the audience, small as it is. "I would love to see a woman leader of the Labour Party, absolutely no question about it," says one woman from the floor, "but I still haven't heard you find your own voice." Another attendee asks bluntly: "You say there's a need for a radical but credible alternative. What is it? I've not heard it this morning."

Journalists who have not made the trip up to Manchester to hear the speech in person judge it to be a tour-de-force. It is "brave" (Dan Hodges) and "trenchant" (Polly Toynbee). From their columns, Cooper emerges as a Saint George figure slaying the Corbyn dragon. But those on the scene are not feeling it. The room is "not exactly fizzing with excitement," tweets the *Guardian*'s North of England editor Helen Pidd. A few hours later her newspaper endorses Cooper for leader—the timing likely coordinated with the speech. But after witnessing the "scanty enthusiasm" that Cooper is capable of whipping up, Pidd's tweeted response to the editorial decision is a diplomatic "no comment."[1]

· · · · ·

Once Jeremy Corbyn emerged as a threat the only question occupying the Labour establishment was: how can he be stopped? For reasons best known to themselves, they chose to attack on terrain contoured to Corbyn's advantage. This yielded the spectacle of an elite tainted by Iraq tackling Corbyn over foreign policy; Labour politicians going to the barricades to defend austerity; and proven election losers lecturing on electability. The blows not only failed to land, they strengthened Corbyn. The sight of a discredited old guard closing ranks against the lone rebel galvanised his support. Theirs was a rear-guard action on four fronts: attempted procedural stitch-ups, electability doomcasts, foreign policy smears, and domestic policy distortions.

Attempted stitch-ups

A shiver went through the Labour elite on the evening of 10 August 2015. YouGov's second poll of the contest caused consternation in the campaign teams of Corbyn's rivals. They had clung to the hope that YouGov's first bombshell in July had been a rogue poll. Now it was clear that, barring something extraordinary happening, something extraordinary was going to happen.

Over the following week there was tumult behind the scenes as panicked MPs and advisors tried to work out what to do. Plan A was to get two of the candidates to stand down to make it a two-horse race between Corbyn and whoever was best placed to beat him. That was obviously not Liz Kendall, so an idea took shape whereby Chuka Umunna, from her camp, would try to broker a deal between the other two. Andy Burnham was open to the offer, unsurprisingly as all the data showed he was in second. But Yvette Cooper would not withdraw, sparking anger from her rivals.[2]

The Cooper campaign instead proposed that Burnham, Cooper and Kendall publicly tell their supporters to use their second and third preference votes for the 'moderate' contenders. Kendall agreed. Burnham, whose strategy by this point was to tack left and praise Corbyn in the hope of peeling off some of his support, refused, to the fury of the others.[3] The acrimony boiled over into the press on 17 August. Burnham's campaign chief Michael Dugher accused the Cooper camp of being in "complete denial," eliciting a response decrying "old-style bullying from the boys."[4] Such squabbling was manna from heaven for Team Corbyn.[5]

Meanwhile, on 16 August, it was reported that Lord Mandelson had attempted to get all three of the frontbench candidates to withdraw from the race in order to stop it altogether. There was just one flaw in his plan, as the *Daily Telegraph* noted: "The peer is understood to have believed that the party might suspend the contest if there was only one candidate, but he had to back down when officials said it would mean Mr Corbyn won."[6]

All of these backstairs manoeuvrings paled in comparison to the big procedural story of the contest: the 'Labour purge.' From the moment Corbyn was revealed to be ahead there were lurid claims of entryists flooding in to take over the party. Initially this took the farcical form of an over-hyped 'Tories for Corbyn' campaign. Conservative MP Tim Loughton paid £3 to vote but was thwarted by Labour staff, with a spokesman saying: "We would like to thank him for his generous donation to the Labour Party—which we are keeping."[7]

The Tory scare was followed by an inevitable Trotskyist panic. "Hard left plot to infiltrate labour race," screamed the *Sunday Times* headline on 26 July.[8] The dependable John Mann MP popped up, calling on acting leader Harriet Harman to suspend the contest because it was "in danger of getting trumped by people who have opposed the Labour Party and want to break it up—some of it is the Militant Tendency-types coming back in."[9]

Under pressure, Labour HQ assigned party staff to vet the new recruits in a procedure known as 'Operation Icepick'—after the weapon that killed Leon Trotsky in 1940, an appropriately Stalinist moniker for a purge.[10] CLP secretaries and MPs were mobilised to screen applicants in their areas. Soon staff and officials were trawling through the social media posts of registered supporters, looking for any evidence of past political deviation.

This was a far cry from the ideal underlying the registered supporters system. Its very purpose was to bring in new recruits. "We want as many people as possible to take part," Harman had said in May 2015. "This is a new and innovative way of letting the public in on an important decision."[11] At that time it was assumed the scheme would favour the right. "It was never envisaged that we'd vet every single [applicant] and say, 'Oh, you were a member of such and such a party a year ago, you shouldn't have a vote,'" says Martin Mayer from Unite. Significantly, from someone who sits on Labour's governing NEC, Mayer has no doubt about the reason for the party's sudden assertiveness: "They did that because they were paranoid, they wanted to stop Corbyn winning."[12]

The Labour elite was just as worried about the tens of thousands joining as full members. By the sign-up deadline of 12 August, membership stood at 292,973, up around 100,000 on the pre-election level, with about half of the influx having arrived after Corbyn made it onto the ballot.[13] The party even monitored trade union recruitment drives. Forty-eight paid staff listened to calls made by unions to their own members encouraging them to sign-up as affiliated supporters.[14] The effort expended was "completely insane," in Jon Lansman's view.

As the number of recruits shot up in August, so did the level of hysteria. Members of the shadow cabinet reportedly demanded an emergency meeting to discuss pausing or ending the election, but Harman refused.[15] A joint letter from the non-Corbyn campaigns was sent to the Labour Party expressing concerns about the vetting process.[16] Burnham's team even started talking about a legal challenge if Corbyn won.[17]

On the morning of 20 August a significant number of people received an email beginning: "We have reason to believe that you do not support the aims and values of the Labour Party or you are a supporter of an organisation opposed to the Labour Party and therefore we are rejecting your application."[18] It was a message the party had communicated to others in dribs and drabs, but the bulk email generated a backlash. The hashtag #LabourPurge was soon trending on Twitter. High profile purgees like Ken Loach, Jeremy Hardy and Mark Steel ensured it was news. Horror stories of people excluded for petty or indecipherable reasons abounded. A woman was rejected because she criticised Labour's immigration mug, saying the Greens' mug was better, according to Diane Abbott.[19] A 90-year-old who had spent decades volunteering for the party—even putting up the local Labour MP when he stayed in the constituency—was refused a vote and given no explanation.[20]

The vagueness of the criteria for exclusion—for example, "people who have made public statements, usually on social media, which make it clear they do not share our aims and values"—guaranteed inconsistency in how they were applied.[21] In some areas the process was used to settle scores. "There was definitely the old guard within the Labour hierarchy structures, the paid officials, and also local CLP secretaries, who were seeing this as their last opportunity to have their revenge before Jeremy was elected," says Ben Sellers, who fielded appeals for help via the Corbyn campaign's social media accounts.

Although they did not say so publicly, Team Corbyn feared the party machine "would succeed in stitching up the procedures," recalls Lansman. They suspected Harman of wanting to scrap the registered supporters category all together—or worse. "At one point we were very worried that they'd call the whole election off."[22]

There was visceral anger among Corbyn supporters at what they saw as a blatant attempt to skew the contest. But for the campaign team this presented a dilemma. Their instinct might have been to rail against the unfairness, but they were wary of handing the party a pretext to suspend the contest. "We had to calm it down," says Lansman. "Actually we wanted to end the campaign against the purge because it was playing into the hands of the other camps."[23]

Not everyone agreed. The social media team, at the sharp end of the #LabourPurge backlash, wanted a more robust response. Ben Sellers proposed making a stand over the exclusion of PCS union leader Mark Serwotka, which he saw as particularly egregious, as a symbol for all the others.[24] But the campaign HQ was reluctant, so the social media team had to join the de-escalation efforts. "We put out messaging saying keep calm, and also suggesting that this was a deliberate strategy by the right and the other candidates to discredit the election," Sellers says. He was surprised at its impact. "People think of social media as this rabble, [but] actually people can be incredibly disciplined when they can see the prize."

Team Corbyn appointed volunteer James Schneider as its 'purge tsar,' responsible for responding to victims and recording their details "to see if there are patterns developing, what are the reasons, the scale of the problem," he says.[25] It was clear the outrage was out of proportion to the actual number of exclusions. This was confirmed on 25 August when Labour released hard figures. The total electorate had been reduced from the 610,000 announced after the registration deadline to 553,000.[26] However, most of those removed were either not on the electoral register or were duplicates—existing members who had also signed up through their union or paid £3. Just 3,138 people had been excluded for allegedly not sharing the party's aims and values.[27] By the end of the contest this total may have risen to 4,000, according to reports.[28] But as Mayer puts it, "out of the numbers involved this was peanuts."

Part of the reason the figure was so low was that the vetting process was indeed, as its critics alleged, chaotic and last minute. *Buzzfeed* even managed to obtain a vote for a cat named Ned.[29] "They didn't have the capacity," says Schneider. "Harriet Harman basically ordered CLP officers to go and try to root out people. Lots did and lots didn't." But the low number was also because there were not that many infiltrators to find. Schneider knows officials who "spent all day [trawling lists for impostors] and managed to get rid of one person." A retrospective poll analysis by YouGov suggested that even if every possible non-Labour voter in the 2015 general election had been excluded, Corbyn would still have won in the first round with 54 per cent.[30]

The impact of supporters of other parties was, as a subsequent academic evaluation by Jessica Garland concluded, "limited." Indeed, given that in past leadership contests millions of trade unionists had been entitled to vote with no checks, "the new process was far less open to influence by those whose support for the party might have fallen short of the standard."[31]

Moreover, the excluded applicants were not the bogeymen Trots of enduring fascination. Of the 3,138 people 'purged,' 1,900 were removed for being Green Party supporters and 400 for being Conservatives, leaving only around 800 others, or 0.14 per cent of the electorate. Some of those were likely to have been members of other mainstream parties, not to mention people excluded erroneously.[32]

Even if there were more reds under the bed than Labour's checks managed to uncover, the idea that Trotskyists could explain a surge of hundreds of thousands of people was risible. There were simply not enough of them about. The two main Trotskyist parties had memberships speculated to be in the low thousands.[33] "There are not 500,000 Trotskyists in Britain," jokes Young Labour activist Max Shanly. "If there were... the revolution would have happened by now because they would be bigger than the army."

The only substantial movement of people between parties came from the Greens. These were not sleeper agents waiting for the best moment to radicalise Labour's environment policy. Rather, they were the same community of left people that had fuelled the 'Green surge' around the beginning of 2015. Accustomed to a culture of political pluralism, many of them did not see why joining one party after being in another was inherently malicious.[34] YouGov's post-result analysis suggested that 10 per cent of voters in the Labour leadership election had previously voted Green.[35] It was strange that this dramatic success at attracting new supporters was regarded as a calamity.

Ultimately, the 'Labour purge' was the worst of all worlds. It created the impression of a fix while not excluding enough people to make any difference. Clear examples of injustice tarnished legitimate efforts to prevent members of other parties influencing Labour's internal election. It roused fury and suspicion to no purpose and may even have rallied more people to Corbyn's side.

· · · · ·

Electability doomcasts

'Jeremy Corbyn is unelectable.' That was the most persistent charge laid against the left candidate in the 2015 leadership contest. 'You might agree with Corbyn and you might like him,' his supporters were told, 'but you have to pick the person most likely to win a general election; anything else is an indulgence.' Every prominent Labour figure was lined up to deliver the message. Even Neil Kinnock was rehydrated to lecture members on how to win elections, based on his extensive personal experience.[36]

To prove their point, Corbyn's critics conjured the spectre of 1983: heavy defeat under Michael Foot was a historical demonstration that moving left would lead to carnage at the ballot box. But this was a misreading. Labour did not lose in 1983 because it was too left wing; rather, Margaret Thatcher won because of the Falklands War. The 'Falklands factor' could not have been clearer from opinion polls. Prior to the war, the Conservative Party was slumped at a consistent 27 per cent throughout late 1981, with a slight recovery in early 1982. But the Tories' popularity shot up spectacularly with the war of April-June 1982, hitting 51 per cent and remaining above 40 per cent right through to the general election.[37]

During the 2015 leadership contest Tony Blair insisted: "Those of us who lived through the turmoil of the '80s know every line of [Corbyn's] script. These are policies from the past that were rejected not because they were too principled, but because a majority of the British people thought they didn't work."[38] But at the time Blair drew a different lesson, as he reportedly told Robin Cook: "The thing I learned... is that wars make prime ministers popular."[39] It is easy to see how Blair came to that tragic conclusion. Before the Falklands, Thatcher was the most unpopular prime minister since records began.[40] But immediately after it she scored the highest satisfaction rating she would ever achieve.[41] Thatcher wrote in her memoirs: "It is no exaggeration to say that the outcome of the Falklands War transformed the British political scene... The so-called 'Falklands factor'... was real enough. I could feel the impact of the victory wherever I went."[42]

The Falklands War took place against the background of an economy recovering from a sharp, self-inflicted recession.[43] The Conservatives were clever in linking the statistical upturn and the war in a grand narrative claiming that Thatcher had reversed Britain's national and imperial decline. "The years of retreat are over," said Nigel Lawson, commenting on the Falklands, "and exactly the same is true in the economic and industrial sphere."[44]

The 'Falklands factor' may have been enough to win the 1983 election for the Conservatives on its own. But in case there was any doubt, Labour assured Thatcher victory by splitting in two and squabbling over second place. In 1981 right-wingers broke off to form the SDP. The new party won a negligible six seats in 1983, despite a strong showing in the popular vote. But the effect was to hand marginal constituencies to the Tories, who won 65 more seats despite receiving 700,000 fewer votes than they secured in the previous election.[45]

Those claiming a Corbyn victory would mean a replay of 1983 could certainly bank on one thing: Labour would face the wrath of the media and the establishment for moving an inch leftwards. Inevitably that would scare some voters away. But here is a surprising result: the high water mark for the Labour left in the 1980s—the point by which it had supposedly rendered the party unelectable—was the October 1980 party conference. At that time, amid a press onslaught against Tony Benn, Labour's poll lead was a massive 50 per cent to the Tories' 36.

Labour still enjoyed an advantage of 42 per cent to 28 a year later when Benn narrowly lost the deputy leadership contest to Denis Healey. But from then on the left was in decline—along with Labour's poll ratings. In September 1982 Benn said in his diaries: "Compared to last year, when the left was riding high with successes everywhere, this year the left is very much tail-between-legs." By February 1983 he was "very, very depressed."[46] Corbyn's critics usually elided this distinction between the Bennites and the Foot leadership. Of course, a correlation between the wane of the left and the party's fall in the polls does not mean there was a causal link. But if left supremacy alone was supposed to make Labour less popular, this chronology provided no evidence for it.

Doom-mongers could, though, point to Labour's 1983 election manifesto, which contained many left policies. The party did lose support between its publication and the ballot (although Labour was already well behind). But it is doubtful that the manifesto had more impact in those final weeks than hostile press coverage and a shambolically run election campaign. That it attained much greater notoriety in retrospect was due to the sharp wit of Labour MP Gerald Kaufman, who dubbed it "the longest suicide note in history." For those insisting Labour's left programme cost it the 1983 election, it must have followed that the party could have won had it moved right. There were test cases for this. Labour moved significantly rightwards for the 1987 election—and lost. It fought the 1992 election still further to the right—and lost again. It took until 1997 for the 'modernisers' to be 'proved' correct, and only once the Tories had been stripped of all credibility by the ERM debacle, endless scandals, infighting and John Major.

So much for 1983. What about more contemporary evidence? One difficulty Corbyn's opponents faced in making the 'unelectable' charge stick in summer 2015 was that he was right then in the middle of winning an election. Though his critics countered that the wider electorate was very different to the Labour one, their case was not helped by opinion polls taken at the height of the contest. A Survation poll found Corbyn was the most popular of the leadership candidates with the general public. 32 per cent said he would make them more likely to vote Labour, against 25 per cent for Andy Burnham.[47] An Opinium poll had Corbyn as top choice on 23 per cent, against 18 per cent for Burnham.[48] A YouGov poll of Londoners left no doubt that Corbyn was the most popular candidate in the capital, with an emphatic 46 per cent to Burnham's 21.[49]

The mere act of labelling someone unelectable renders them less likely to be elected. Yet among the Labour electorate this tactic did not work—because those deploying it misjudged their audience. YouGov asked Labour members and supporters which qualities were most needed in the next leader. "Being in touch with the concerns of ordinary people" was deemed most important, chosen by 62 per cent. "Understanding what it takes to win an election" was ranked only fifth highest, with 27 per cent. This was not, as some commentators spun it, evidence members did not care about winning elections. Rather, it indicated a rejection of the 'electability at any cost' credo that had become synonymous with New Labour. It was no coincidence that only Liz Kendall voters placed "understanding what it takes to win an election" as the most vital leadership quality.[50]

There were two good reasons why 'electability at any cost' could no longer convince. First, if the cost included disasters like Iraq, perhaps the price was too high. Second, the transaction looked fraudulent if electability was not, in fact, delivered. As James Mills, the Corbyn campaign's press officer, puts it: "If you've failed to win two elections you're specialists in failure. Turning around and saying to the membership, 'You've got to listen to us because we know what we're talking about'—well, you didn't know last time."

Burnham, Cooper and Kendall represented three subtly different hues of failure at a time when the party wanted to redecorate in primary colours. Unison activist Andrew Berry has a theory that Corbyn's constituency was made up of two groups of people, one that wanted a left wing leader, and another "whose response to 'Jeremy's not electable' was to look at the other three and say, 'Well nor are they.'"

$$\bullet \ \bullet \ \bullet \ \bullet \ \bullet$$

Foreign policy smears

Gordon Brown stomped from one side of the stage to the other like a caged gorilla as he delivered his speech on 16 August 2015. Billed as a decisive intervention into the leadership contest, Brown disappointed those hoping he would bring his big clunking fist down on Jeremy Corbyn by saying: "I'm not here to attack any individual candidate." But he was really. "If our global alliances are going to be alliances with Hezbollah and Hamas and Hugo Chavez's Venezuela and Vladimir Putin's Russia, there is absolutely no chance of building a worldwide alliance that can deal with poverty and inequality and climate change and financial instability."[51]

Brown's line of attack was indicative. Foreign policy was the terrain upon which the Labour elite and the media mounted their fiercest attacks on Corbyn. The onslaught was inevitable because many of Corbyn's positions were directly opposed to what the British state considered to be its interests. In the course of the campaign he said that he found it difficult to think of circumstances in which he would deploy military force, was against bombing Syria, opposed the renewal of Trident nuclear weapons, and was critical of NATO's "global role."

Historically Labour has always contained opponents of imperialism, but the party's top echelons, especially when in government, have been reliable servants of the state—pro-NATO, pro-nuclear, usually pro-war and, back when Britain ruled a quarter of the world, pro-Empire. The prospect of the party being led by someone with Corbyn's views genuinely horrified the establishment.

Thus Corbyn was ritually condemned for wanting to pull out of NATO. The fact that he proposed no such thing during the contest was immaterial. Being critical of the alliance—"I think NATO is a cold war product; it historically should have shut up shop in 1990 along with the Warsaw Pact"—was beyond the pale.[52]

A pan-media myth, started by the *Times*, asserted that Corbyn harboured treacherous pro-Russian sympathies. When he appeared with Polly Toynbee on the BBC's *Any Questions* programme on 21 August, she put the accusation to him directly. "When have I been soft on Putin?" asked a bemused Corbyn. "Well, appearing on Russian television," Toynbee replied.[53] Corbyn had indeed given an interview about his campaign to the state-funded English-language news channel RT. But when former New Labour home secretary Charles Clarke was interviewed on the same RT show shortly afterwards, the condemnations were curiously absent. Perhaps the difference was that Corbyn had gone so far as to ask: "What is security? Is security the ability to bomb, maim, kill, destroy, or is security the ability to get on with other people and have some kind of respectful existence with them?"[54] This man had to be stopped.

Corbyn was frequently misreported as wanting to campaign to leave the European Union. The furthest he actually went was to say that he "wouldn't rule it out" in advance of David Cameron's EU renegotiation so as not to give the then-prime minister a blank cheque to "trade away workers' rights… trade away environmental protection… trade away much of what is in the social chapter." "We should be making demands," he said on 25 July, "rather than saying blanketly we're going to support whatever Cameron comes out with."[55]

For his entire political life Corbyn had been an anti-war internationalist and a human rights advocate. In his parliamentary career he had carved out a role taking up international causes on which the government of the day was often on the other side, using his position as a backbench MP to try to redress the imbalance of power. For example, he was one of the very few MPs to protest the gassing of the Kurds in Halabja in 1988 by Saddam Hussein when the dictator was still a British ally, and led calls for the suspension of the arms trade with Iraq. Many of those who would later profess such horror at the slaughter, including Tony Blair, stayed silent at the time.

Anyone who engages directly in international issues has to talk to people whom they would not choose as comrades in a domestic setting. This reality applies to MPs who meet representatives of liberation movements as much as it does to prime ministers who meet Saudi kings (although there is a sharp difference between working for peace and endeavouring to sell arms). A nation, party or group may use illegitimate methods yet still have justice to its cause. People who are suffering do not forfeit their right to redress because of the ideological bent of their leaders.

It is in this context that the most enduring charge against Corbyn should be placed: that he regarded the Palestinian and Lebanese militant organisations Hamas and Hezbollah as "friends." He used the term in 2009 when announcing "an event in parliament where our friends from Hezbollah will be speaking, I'd also invited our friends from Hamas as well." Corbyn later expressed regret at his choice of words, explaining: "It was inclusive language I used which with hindsight I would rather not have used."[56] No one honestly believed Corbyn shared the political outlook of Hamas or Hezbollah, which are neither socialist nor secularist nor feminist nor in favour of LGBT+ rights. The purpose of asking them to parliament, as Corbyn said immediately after referring to them as friends, was "to invite people from other parts of the world so that we can promote that peace, that understanding, and that dialogue."

The most powerful smears deployed during the campaign worked by suppressing all context, isolating a particular comment or association, and presenting it as evidence of Corbyn's villainy. In its most grotesque form this involved pulling out examples from Corbyn's long history of advocacy for the Palestinian people in order to tar him as anti-Semitic.[57] The *Jewish Chronicle* newspaper led the charge, printing a front page editorial on 12 August 2015 that claimed "there is overwhelming evidence of [Corbyn's] association with, support for—and even in one case, alleged funding of—Holocaust deniers, terrorists and some outright anti-Semites."[58]

The particular allegation that gained most attention originated from a report a few days earlier in the *Daily Mail*, which claimed Corbyn had "long standing links" with a "notorious" Holocaust denier named Paul Eisen. It was alleged that Corbyn had donated to Eisen's organisation, Deir Yassin Remembered, which ostensibly existed to commemorate the massacre of a Palestinian village in 1948. Corbyn explained that he had attended "two or three" of the organisation's events "some years ago" and might, if he had given any money at all, have thrown coins into a collection bucket. But so had several other respected figures prior to Eisen's views being revealed. Had Corbyn been aware that Eisen was a Holocaust denier, he said, "I would have had absolutely nothing to do with him."[59]

Corbyn was bolstered by a letter published in the *Jewish Chronicle* on 18 August, sent by around 50 prominent Jews including the poet Michael Rosen, actress Miriam Margolyes, and professors Avi Shlaim and Ilan Pappe, which rejected the allegations.[60] The organisation Jews for Justice for Palestinians also came to Corbyn's defence, with a letter in the *Guardian* on 20 August decrying the "McCarthyite techniques being deployed to smear a prominent critic of Israeli policy."[61]

For his own part, Corbyn said in a radio interview on 19 August: "The idea that I'm some kind of racist or anti-Semitic person is beyond appalling, disgusting and deeply offensive. I've spent my life opposing racism. Until my dying day I'll be opposed to racism in any form."[62] The journalists trawling Corbyn's past for evidence of anti-Semitism did not need to go back far to find examples that contradicted the media narrative. Yet not one outlet chose to mention, for example, that as recently as 25 June 2015 Corbyn had been the lead signatory to a call to mobilise against a planned anti-Semitic neo-Nazi demonstration in Golders Green, a famous Jewish neighbourhood in London. "This sickening, fascist move is particularly repellent in the year that marks the 70th anniversary of the liberation of Auschwitz," read the call, made under the banner of Unite Against Fascism. "It is essential to say the Jewish community has every right to express its opposition to this demonstration... We need a big protest to show that Nazism is rejected by the vast majority."[63]

When fighting prejudice against Jews means going to the streets and putting bodies on the line, Corbyn—following in the footsteps of his parents, who participated in the Battle of Cable Street in 1936—has often been among the first to step forward. Falsely levelling the charge of anti-Semitism for political advantage, meanwhile, risks debasing the term and undercutting the threat posed by the scourge.

Corbyn's international worldview may have been an anathema to the establishment, inside and outside Labour, but not to many party members. The foreign policy record of his Labour accusers was one of unremitting calamity since 2001. The prospect of a radically different posture was integral to Corbyn's appeal. Sympathy for the Palestinians was pronounced in the party.[64] Most Corbyn supporters were opposed to Trident.[65] A big part of his constituency was made up of returning and existing members still sickened by the shame of Iraq. They were more interested in Corbyn's pledge to apologise on behalf of the Labour Party for the Iraq War than they were in the assorted smears. Through their votes they ensured that, on 6 July 2016, following the publication of the Chilcot Report, Corbyn could make good on his promise.

·····

Domestic policy distortions

Considering the sheer volume of domestic policies and ideas thrown out by Jeremy Corbyn during the contest, relatively few came in for sustained criticism. Of the handful that did, some were trivial, such as the suggestion that trains might feature women-only carriages. In the policy paper 'End Street Harassment,' published on 25 August 2015, Corbyn wrote tentatively: "Some women have raised with me that a solution to the rise in assault and harassment on public transport could be to introduce women-only carriages. My intention would be to make public transport safer for everyone... However, I would consult with women and open it up to hear their views on whether women-only carriages would be welcome."[66]

These anodyne words provoked a furious response. Corbyn was accused of advocating "gender segregation" and of signalling that "harassment against women [is] acceptable in mixed carriages."[67] All three of Corbyn's leadership rivals condemned him.[68] The *Guardian* was especially agitated, publishing a news story about the proposal at 7.37 a.m. on 26 August, a disingenuous attack on it by columnist Anne Perkins at 11.50 a.m., a news story about the backlash at 2.12 p.m., a collection of passengers' reactions at 2.55 p.m., a comment piece in favour of the idea (balance!) at 4.25 p.m., a video of Londoners' reactions at 4.47 p.m., and a summary of women-only carriages around the world at 5.35 p.m.[69] Demonstrating that the furore was rather overdone, social media soon uncovered that women-only carriages had been floated by no less than the government minister for transport just a year earlier, without any comparable outrage.[70]

But the main assault on Corbyn's domestic policies took aim at the big one: his anti-austerity economic agenda, dubbed 'Corbynomics.' Its central feature was the unashamed promotion of public investment rather than austerity cuts, using a National Investment Bank to stimulate growth and reshape the economy.[71] "You can't cut your way to prosperity, you have to grow your way to prosperity," was one of Corbyn's favourite refrains. To avoid the political stigma attached to borrowing and taxing the rich, 'Corbynomics' instead emphasised other mechanisms: cracking down on tax avoidance and evasion, cutting corporate subsidies, and 'People's Quantitative Easing.'

Corbyn's critics zoomed in on the last proposal. In the policy paper 'The Economy in 2020,' this idea was fairly marginal, allotted just a single sentence: "One option would be for the Bank of England to be given a new mandate to upgrade our economy to invest in new large scale housing, energy, transport and digital projects: quantitative easing for people instead of banks."[72] It was the brainchild of Richard Murphy, a tax specialist advising the campaign.[73] 'People's QE' was conceived to work in the same way as conventional QE, but with the money funding useful things instead of inflating asset prices to the benefit of the super rich.[74]

The attacks came first from the right of the party. Shadow chancellor Chris Leslie denounced the proposal, but was himself rebuked by a former Bank of England economist for the "poor grasp of economics" his comments betrayed.[75] Jack Straw then extraordinarily rendered himself part of the debate, going on the radio to condemn the "economic illiteracy" of 'People's QE' while demonstrating his own shaky understanding by bizarrely evoking Greece, whose problem was precisely that it could not print its own currency.[76]

When Yvette Cooper debuted her new aggressive strategy in her big speech in Manchester on 13 August, attacking 'People's QE' was one of her main themes. It would remain so for the rest of the summer. At the final TV hustings of the contest, hosted by Sky News on 3 September, she launched what was described as her most "impassioned" tirade, telling Corbyn: "You're offering people false hope, false promises, it's PFI on steroids, it's not fair and we'll let people down."[77]

Many of these critiques seemed to misunderstand what 'People's QE' was. "I don't think they had a clue what we were talking about," says John McDonnell. "Because it was relatively novel they didn't realise what we were actually saying about the overall economic policy: that QE was just one mechanism, one tool, at the appropriate time in the economic cycle... They didn't link it to a National Investment Bank."

While leading Labour MPs and political journalists could only defensively condemn or ridicule the proposal, a surprising range of weighty economic commentators were prepared to take it seriously, even as they expressed reservations.[78] Those included Martin Wolf in the *Financial Times*, Ambrose Evans-Pritchard in the *Daily Telegraph*, and Robert Skidelsky in the *Guardian*.[79] "Corbyn should be praised, not castigated, for bringing to public attention these serious issues concerning the role of the state and the best ways to finance its activities," wrote Skidelsky, a professor of political economy. "The fact that he is dismissed for doing so illustrates the dangerous complacency of today's political elites. Millions in Europe rightly feel that the current economic order fails to serve their interests. What will they do if their protests are simply ignored?" (They will vote to leave the EU, it turned out.)

As it happened, a strong Keynesian case against 'People's QE' did exist, but Cooper and company were too terrified to make it. This was simply that 'People's QE' was an unnecessary diversion when the cost of conventional borrowing was so low.[80] It is a measure of how tightly bound they were by an austerity consensus that fetishised deficit reduction that no senior Labour figures deployed this argument, even when they were in the fight of their lives for control of their party. The Keynesian critique did, though, influence the Corbyn campaign, for which 'People's QE' had become a political millstone it wanted rid of. Yet, as McDonnell recalls, "Even when we switched some of the arguments to say that we'd borrow instead of QE, they then launched the Tory attack on us about too much borrowing. It demonstrated to me just how incorporated they were in existing thinking."

It was difficult to sustain the charge that Corbyn's anti-austerity stance was, in Leslie's words, "starry-eyed, hard left," when Nobel Prize-winning economists Joseph Stiglitz and Paul Krugman were expressing support for it.[81] A further 42 economists argued that Corbyn's "opposition to austerity is actually mainstream economics" in a letter to the *Observer* on 23 August, which made a front-page splash.[82] Although 55 economists retaliated with a letter in the *Financial Times*, claiming that 'Corbynomics' had "not been seriously thought through," even they had to concede that public investment was "in many areas much needed."[83]

Corbyn was swimming with an intellectual tide. Neoliberalism had been stripped of the cloak of inevitability by the 2008 financial crash and the failure of the austerity experiments that followed. It could no longer explain events convincingly—a crippling condition for any ideology. 'Corbynomics'—the whole of it, not just 'People's QE'—represented a modest break from that orthodoxy.

In fact, the remarkable thing about Corbyn's economic programme was not that it was radical, but that it was so restrained. Throughout the contest Corbyn played against type by emphasising how conventional his proposals were. He frequently commented that his plans could only be considered new in Britain. "If I was putting forward these ideas in Germany I'd be called depressingly moderate, depressingly old fashioned as they have a national investment bank already and they invest in public services," he told a rally.[84]

Corbyn was frequently accused of being a throwback who had not changed his position in 30 years. But this was simply not so. As the academic Andrew Gamble argued, compared to the Alternative Economic Strategy promoted by Tony Benn in the 1970s, 'Corbynomics' was "a very pale reflection" advancing "quite modest" institutional reforms.[85] The economist James Meadway, who later advised McDonnell, contended that Corbyn's economic programme was to the right of that contained in the 1983 manifesto of the centrist SDP.[86] The reason was not that Corbyn had gone soft, but that the context had changed so profoundly. As Labour activist James Doran says, "Both John and Jeremy put forward a platform which they would have opposed at the start of their career when the Labour Movement was much stronger and able to make more radical demands."

McDonnell himself describes 'Corbynomics' as having "floated a number of ideas that weren't politically radical, but demonstrated how you could move the debate forward." He professes to have been "amazed" at the hostile reaction of some of his colleagues. "It did demonstrate just how far backwards the mainstream thinking had gone within the Parliamentary Labour Party," he says. "They'd adopted neoliberalism hook, line and sinker."

But the party outside had not. The attacks on Corbyn's anti-austerity platform entirely misread the mood of the Labour electorate. One senior campaign advisor believes the decision of Corbyn's opponents, especially Cooper, to go "really hard" on economic policy "backfired" because it showed "they were so wedded to austerity-lite." "OK, they may have got a nice write up in the *FT* or amongst a few wonkish, fairly orthodox economists, but really that's all they were appealing to," he says. "I don't think any of the other candidates had a clue who their base was... That's partially why they failed." After pausing to consider whether Cooper's strategy did any damage to Corbyn at all, he adds: "If it did work then Christ, what *would* we have won by?!"

14

TRIUMPH AND TRIBULATIONS

"I think Abraham Lincoln made a point. At the end of the American Civil War he said, 'with malice toward none and charity for all' we will go forward. I am sure that is the right way to do things."

—Jeremy Corbyn

Jeremy Corbyn and John McDonnell are at the table. Seumas Milne, Labour's future executive director of strategy, is down the line from France. Simon Fletcher and Anneliese Midgley, who have been running the Corbyn campaign HQ, are in the room, along with Jon Lansman. Diane Abbott and Jon Trickett are present too. Katy Clark, the former MP who will become Corbyn's political secretary, is in the surreal situation of being on the phone from Disneyland, Paris.

It is the beginning of September 2015, less than two weeks before the new Labour leader will be announced, and this is the first and only strategy meeting bringing together the key players in the future regime to work out what they will do if—when—they win. Except that strategy is not being discussed. There is only one issue dominating the conversation: should McDonnell be shadow chancellor?

The 'big four' trade unions—Unite, Unison, the GMB and the CWU—have decided he should not be. Steve Turner, the assistant general secretary of Unite and chair of the People's Assembly—an ally—has been sent to deliver the message. Some union top brass have never liked McDonnell despite his long history of campaigning alongside their activists. The fact that this has on occasion involved campaigning against the union bureaucracies themselves might have something to do with it. They fear he is too strident, likely to attract too much controversy. Having two out-and-out left-wingers in the party's most powerful positions will be a provocation to the PLP and a red rag to the media.

The demand from the unions means one thing: McDonnell has to be shadow chancellor. The leadership-in-waiting cannot be told what to do by the big four. Corbyn is adamant that he needs someone in the economic brief that he can trust: just look at Tony Blair and Gordon Brown for the paralysis that results otherwise; look at Ed Miliband and Ed Balls for the ideological drift that can take hold. It is a powerful case.

But while they are locking horns over who should be shadow chancellor, the small matter of how to pull off the almost unimaginable feat of leading the Labour Party from the left is not being discussed. There are just days to go.[1]

• • • • •

Jeremy Corbyn's victory on 12 September 2015 was a staggering achievement. Yet in no sense was he or his team ready for it. As a general rule, people who compete for the top job in a political party intend to win. Corbyn broke even this basic convention. The same all-consuming ambition that drives most leaders forward also compels them to prepare—to construct an infrastructure of alliances among parliamentary colleagues, power-brokers in business or the unions, professional advisors, journalists and editors. They have probably been thinking for years about their unique 'policy offer'; which combination of the words 'future,' 'Britain,' 'forward,' and 'together' they will adopt for their slogan; and how they will answer the question about whether they took drugs at university. Part of the reason Corbyn won was that he had done none of these things (including taking drugs, unlike his three competitors). But that also meant he was thrust into a nearly impossible situation.

Sweet as the moment of victory was, the surrounding days and weeks were more tense and stressful for Team Corbyn than at any other point in the contest. For three months nearly everything had been a breeze. But Corbyn was about to be thrown into a storm, and everybody knew it. "When we win, no matter what is said, there will be resistance within every area of the Parliamentary Labour Party," John McDonnell thought in the final weeks of the race. "In addition to that, in the [party] bureaucracy some will welcome us, some will just sit on their hands, and others will undertake sabotage."

Even with a clear strategy and a well worked out plan these challenges might have been insurmountable. But the Corbyn camp had neither. This was partly because for Corbyn and McDonnell one big prize took precedence: installing McDonnell as shadow chancellor. Their success in achieving this should not be underestimated given its central importance to Corbyn's leadership. "There was opposition to that from everybody," McDonnell remembers. "All round. Len McCluskey in Unite, people like Owen Jones even—I didn't realise at the time. Sound minds around us on the left as well. I could understand the argument."

The job of shadow chancellor was even more pivotal than usual after a campaign that had promised to transform Labour into an anti-austerity party. Corbyn had decided very early on that he wanted his friend in the role. "We needed a leader and chancellor of the exchequer who were absolutely unified," McDonnell says.

But they also had to fill the other ministerial jobs. Assembling a shadow team from an overwhelmingly hostile PLP was a daunting prospect. According to Jon Lansman, "John and Jeremy talked about it extensively." Their first priority was to identify enough MPs willing to co-operate, as a string of senior figures told the press they would not serve under Corbyn. "Basically they were desperate to find MPs who could do any job."

As early as the beginning of August Corbyn had signalled that he wanted to form a broad team. He used an interview with the *Observer* to invite the "great talents" of the PLP to "come in"—even

Blairites. "Of course there are differences of opinion and I have to be big enough to accommodate those differences of opinion and I understand that," he said.[2]

While Corbyn was travelling around the country addressing rallies, McDonnell was forging new connections. "Throughout August I was meeting with various people," he recalls. "I was meeting with Tom [Watson], Jon Ashworth and people like that, just to say to them: 'If Jeremy does win, would you be willing to serve?' That offer was out to them all. Some of them came back and said yes, some of them never came back at all. With the ones that said yes, people like John Healey and others, it was a case of saying 'What role do you want to play?'"

It was almost certain that Watson would triumph in the deputy leadership contest, meaning he would have to work with Corbyn should the left candidate win. It was in both camps' interests to talk. As a robust and canny politician, McDonnell was perfectly capable of negotiating with Watson, who at any moment might be pursuing multiple agendas. Watson dispensed advice on potential shadow cabinet appointments—who he thought should be in (chief whip Rosie Winterton, among others) and who ought to be left out (surprisingly, his friend Michael Dugher, who he predicted would be disruptive—a warning that was not heeded).

With his punishing schedule finally beginning to take its toll, Corbyn was allowing himself half-days off at weekends—only to fill the time in conversation with McDonnell. The two pondered how to maximise the political influence of the parliamentary left given its sorry state. "The plan that Jeremy and John agreed was that they'd have a lefty in every department," says Lansman. Bright prospects like Richard Burgon, Clive Lewis, Rebecca Long-Bailey, Kate Osamor and Cat Smith were too inexperienced to jump straight into the shadow cabinet; by spreading them out in lesser ministerial posts Corbyn and McDonnell hoped to give their team some political shape.

Another concern was the party machine. Asserting itself over the bureaucracy would be crucial to the new leadership's security and effectiveness. New Labour remained a "hegemonic force" at Labour HQ, where Tony Blair was still "the piper who plays the tune many party staff listen to," in the words of Young Labour's

Max Shanly.[3] From mid-August Lansman was "jotting down some ideas about what we needed to do in the party and the National Executive Committee." But he became frustrated as the plans were never properly discussed. "There was a terrible lack of strategy," he says. Corbyn would later be routinely accused of executing a dastardly plan to seize control of the party. The reality was he did not have one.

Within the campaign team there developed a distraction from the task of preparing for leadership. With the prospect of jobs being handed out in the new administration, a group of people brought together by nothing more than political conviction began jockeying for position. A couple of weeks before the result, Corbyn assured Simon Fletcher he would be chief of staff. Others were not so lucky. Lansman remembers this period as being "not pleasant," with "bad feeling afterwards from people who felt they'd been squeezed out or ignored."

Lansman made a bad mistake on 2 September in agreeing to be interviewed by BBC *Newsnight* about mandatory reselection, the mechanism to make MPs more accountable to party members, for which he had campaigned for decades. Although he made clear he was not speaking for Corbyn, he "hadn't appreciated the difference" being associated with the future leader would make. Fletcher was furious with him. MPs regarded mandatory reselection as a spectre haunting the PLP; the campaign had gone to great lengths to dampen their fears. "I was hung out to dry, persona non grata," Lansman says.[4]

· · · · ·

Team Corbyn still had to actually win the contest. Their internal data suggested they were on course for victory, but it was such a remarkable prospect that no one could be entirely confident. "Two or three weeks out it seemed the most likely outcome was that we were going to win," says a member of the team. "I still couldn't quite believe it, and wanted to do literally everything to not take the foot off the gas."

Meanwhile, some hostile MPs were finally realising the game was up. There had been talk that if Jeremy Corbyn won, the PLP would mount a coup against him "on day one," "before Christmas," or (getting warmer) after the May 2016 local, mayoral and devolved elections.[5] A different threat came from some of the party's big donors, who promised to withdraw their funding if Corbyn became leader.[6] Corbyn reacted to such reports by promising to bring people together: "I think Abraham Lincoln made a point. At the end of the American Civil War he said, 'with malice toward none and charity for all' we will go forward. I am sure that is the right way to do things."[7]

By early September the febrile talk of an instant coup had subsided. Tristram Hunt and Chuka Umunna, the leaders of a much-advertised group of MPs dubbed 'the resistance,' called on their colleagues to accept the likely result and unify.[8] Yvette Cooper was reportedly furious.[9] With less than two weeks of the contest remaining she was just hitting her stride. Indeed, in those final days a vociferous section of the press managed to convince itself of the existence of an 'Yvette surge.' Cooper's fortunes improved following her call for the UK to take in 10,000 refugees from the Middle East. She had finally articulated a policy that appealed to Labour members and supporters horrified by the catastrophe that had enveloped the region. Although the main difference between her position and Corbyn's was that he would go further, Cooper made her case with passion and humanity and won credit for her stance.[10]

For the first time since mid-July someone other than Corbyn was making the running. With Cooper turning in aggressive performances in televised hustings, and with strong backing from the *Guardian* and the *New Statesman*, it began to feel like Cooper was on the move. It was enough to get some commentators giddy with excitement. But there were two reasons to doubt the reality of the 'Yvette surge.' One was that voting had been underway since 14 August. By the time Cooper got round to competing, most of the votes had been cast. The other was a general rule: Westminster groupthink is usually wrong.

Voting closed on 10 September, two days before the result would be known. Corbyn's fate was now sealed—although, in light of the 'Labour purge,' cynics suspected his fate was then being sealed by the party's Compliance Unit.[11] The following day Jon

Lansman had the "horrible task" of drafting an email to be sent to supporters if Corbyn lost—the team still felt sufficient doubt for this to be necessary. That lunchtime the result of the contest to become Labour's London mayoral candidate was announced. Saddiq Khan, perceived as being on the 'soft left,' cantered to victory over the Blairite Tessa Jowell, the favourite. Diane Abbott exceeded expectations, finishing third. The results were hard evidence that Labour had shifted left, at least in the capital.[12] When he heard the news, Lansman decided not to bother writing the losing email.

• • • • •

"The result for the election of the leader of the Labour Party is as follows," announced Jim Kennedy, chair of the NEC, to the assembled audience in the QEII conference centre in London on 12 September 2015.[13]

"The votes cast in round one are—Andy Burnham: 80,462."

There was polite applause, but immediately people in the hall realised that of the 422,664 votes cast, that was a low number. As the clapping subsided, Kennedy confirmed:

"This represents 19 per cent of the votes in this round."

Just 19 per cent. Did this mean Burnham had haemorrhaged support to Cooper, as evangelists for the 'Yvette surge' had predicted?

"Yvette Cooper: 71,928, which represents 17 per cent."

No. Considering Cooper's media backing, and the fact that a portion of the Blairite vote had switched to her from the beleaguered Liz Kendall, this was an astonishingly poor result. And that meant only one thing.

"Jeremy Corbyn: Two-hundred and fifty-one thousand…"

Cheers erupted—but only from some sections of the audience. A couple of rows back, where Corbyn's campaign team was sat, George Aylett, regional organiser for the South West, jumped out of his seat and let out "an enormous squeal like a pig," according to Ben Sellers. It took Kennedy a full minute to get the room settled down.

"Jeremy Corbyn: 251,417 votes, which represents 59.5 per cent…"

More whooping and clapping. Corbyn had smashed through the 50 per cent threshold. He had won on the first round. But Kennedy had not finished.

"Liz Kendall: 18,857 votes, which represents 4.5 per cent of the votes."

There was "an audible intake of breath" before a sympathetic round of applause, remembers Martin Mayer of Unite. "Nobody believed she'd be trounced as badly as that."

4.5 per cent! "Barely statistically significant," jokes Labour activist Michael Calderbank, who was in the hall.

And then another shock. On the big screen behind Kennedy the breakdown of the votes by members, registered supporters and affiliated supporters flashed up. Corbyn had won the backing of 121,751 full party members, nearly as many as the others combined.

For all the hysteria about registered supporters, it was party members that dominated the decision. Their 245,520 votes accounted for 58 per cent of all those cast. This was the real story of the Collins Review rule change—it had massively empowered the membership, which under the old electoral college had been pegged at 33 per cent of the say over the choice of leader.

Corbyn won 49.6 per cent of the votes of members, within an inch of an absolute majority in a four-horse race—a crushing victory.[14] He was stunned. "I was predicted to be struggling in the membership," he said.[15] Had Corbyn lost among full members but triumphed overall due to the votes of registered supporters and trade unionists, he would have faced the same crisis of legitimacy that afflicted Ed Miliband—only many times worse.[16] John McDonnell was anxious to see the membership breakdown in particular. It was "much better than I thought possible," he says.

A few days after Corbyn was announced leader, YouGov released a final poll weighted to the actual result. It suggested that Corbyn was the first choice for a massive 62 per cent of members who joined the party between the 2015 general election and mid-July, before the Corbyn surge. 49 per cent of those who joined when Miliband was leader supported Corbyn too. Both results were consistent with the sense of a party moving left and attracting more radical recruits. But even among members who joined before 2010—party loyalists through thick and thin—44 per cent voted Corbyn, well ahead of Burnham and Cooper on 25 apiece. (Kendall won a miserable 6 per cent from these veterans of the golden era of Blairism.)[17] Had the Labour Party excluded everyone from voting except this group in an apocalyptic fit of Mandelsonian panic—severed the link with the unions, banned registered supporters, and disenfranchised anyone who had joined since New Labour lost office—Corbyn would possibly still have won on second preference votes.[18] This was not a victory; it was a rout.

The 105,598 votes cast by £3 registered supporters accounted for 25 per cent of the total ballot—a large wave, but not the flood to inundate the membership as was commonly portrayed. An incredible 83.8 per cent of them voted for Corbyn—88,449 people, more votes than Burnham amassed in total. It was such a one-sided result that it might have been assumed the registered supporter scheme had been designed specifically to encourage movement-style politics. The fact that its intended purpose was almost the opposite brings to mind Chairman Mao's order to exterminate all sparrows to stop them eating grain, resulting in a plague of locusts.

A troubling note for the Labour Movement was that affiliated supporters accounted for just 17 per cent of all votes cast. Of those trade unionists that did vote, 57.6 per cent chose Corbyn. That was a dominant display, but not as spectacular as his roster of union nominations might have suggested—proving trade unionists do not robotically vote in line with their organisation.[19]

YouGov's post-result analysis showed a similar demographic picture to that seen at the height of the Corbyn surge in August. Corbyn's support was skewed towards the younger end of the scale. Sixty-seven per cent of 25-39 year olds voted for him. He continued to do better among women (63 per cent) than men (57 per cent). Women had been hit hardest by austerity; they voted for the candidate promising to do something about it.[20]

The overall result was a super-sized endorsement for Corbyn. His 59.5 per cent beat Tony Blair's 57 per cent from 1994, although the two contests used different voting systems. "It is a huge mandate," said Corbyn on the day. "It is a mandate for the issues that

I have put forward during the election and a mandate for new democracy in the party."[21]

· · · · ·

At an unofficial victory party in Hyde Park screams and cheers greeted the moment of the result. Around a thousand gathered to listen to the announcement from two boomboxes incongruously blaring BBC Radio 4 coverage. There was dancing and fizzy wine, before the revellers headed off to join the 'Refugees Welcome' rally taking place in central London.

In front rooms around the country there was unbridled joy as Corbyn supporters watched the news break on TV. Michelle Ryan, the party member who had initiated the petition demanding an anti-austerity candidate back in May 2015, was waiting nervously with her family in Worthing. "We were all holding hands, all sat in a row on the sofa," she says. "I couldn't look at the telly. They announced the result and we were just screaming. Next door—I hope they're into politics because we were literally screaming and crying. It was magical. I'm getting tearful talking about it, reliving it. Monumental. Probably one of the happiest days of my life, up there with getting married and having kids."

Ryan's close collaborator on the petition, Rebecca Barnes, was living the same experience in Orpington. "I was sat with my two littleuns beside me and we absolutely just went mad," she recalls. "Leaping round the room and then we were in floods of tears. I just couldn't believe what was happening."

On social media a digital community forged over the summer held a virtual party. As the number of votes was read out, sitting three rows back in the QEII Centre was Ben Sellers, head down in his phone, desperately hoping the wifi held up so he could send out a 'Thank You' meme. "That was one of our biggest things," he says, "to actually thank people."

For many, the result was a reason to get involved in the Labour Party. 15,500 joined as full members in the first 24 hours of Corbyn's leadership.[22] Others, though, had a different response. The MP Jamie Reed, a little known shadow health minister, tried to make a name for himself by publishing his resignation letter while Corbyn was still giving his victory speech. A roll call of the distressed and dispossessed, many experiencing for the first time the inconvenience of an obstacle in their career path, presumptuously announced they would not accept jobs they had not been offered: Tristram Hunt, Chris Leslie, Shabana Mahmood, Rachel Reeves, Emma Reynolds and John Woodcock.[23] John Prescott aptly dubbed them 'Bitterites'. Their favoured strategy, if it can be called that—to anonymously whinge to the press in an incessant wrecking operation—began immediately, with one "former cabinet minister" defending their non-participation by predicting: "Anyone who sups with [Corbyn] will be permanently tainted. Their credibility will be destroyed."[24]

There were bad signs too at Labour HQ. Staff wore black for the day of the result, in mourning for the party they had lost.[25] There was minimal help for the new leader—the campaign's press officer James Mills had to organise an impromptu round of media interviews. There was no car arranged to transport Corbyn through the thronging streets.[26] When Corbyn and Mills arrived at Labour's head office some time after the result was announced, it was like "turning up to a wake." There were "mouldy crisps and a few cheap bottles of wine" strewn across the desks, Mills remembers. The mood was "really sombre, it wasn't polite or friendly." One member of staff approached Mills and said: "See those three files over there? That's how the Labour Party works. See you Monday morning."

Even at the Sanctuary pub, where the Corbyn campaign was toasting victory, there was apprehension as well as joy. "In situations like that you don't feel jubilant, you start thinking about other stuff like what do we need to do next," remembers Sellers. "There were rumours... that when Jeremy was announced at HQ there wasn't a single person that applauded. So it's weird to think we're the leadership now but we're going into a really hostile environment where nobody really wants us, so how do we manage that?"

But for all the troubles ahead, the political movement around Corbyn had just pulled off the upset of the century. "It was a day of celebration," recalls Jon Lansman. "It was a real high. We knew that the shit was going to hit the fan the next day."

· · · · ·

Building a shadow ministerial team is difficult at the best of times. Doing so as a new leader elected against the explicit efforts of most of the PLP, with no experience of being on the frontbench, with only shallow relationships with many senior MPs, having done very little preparation, being from a political tradition that has never led the party and is structurally weak, under extreme time pressure with little more than a day to complete the job, is what might be called a nightmare.

Jeremy Corbyn came to the task with one specific priority, one prior commitment, and a clear—but doomed—strategy to bringing the PLP behind him by constructing a broad shadow cabinet. His problem was that these goals tended to work against each other.

The specific priority was to install John McDonnell as shadow chancellor. This made it harder to secure the wide participation Corbyn sought. Some MPs told the press it would be a "declaration of war" if McDonnell got the job. Others said they would not join the shadow cabinet until Corbyn confirmed the economic brief would not go to his friend.[27]

The prior commitment was to create a shadow cabinet in which, for the first time, women held at least half the positions. This was accomplished, but was overshadowed by Corbyn's failure to appoint any women to the 'great offices of state': shadow chancellor, shadow foreign secretary, and shadow home secretary. It was a blunder that stemmed from Corbyn's preoccupation with the shadow chancellorship and the limited room for manoeuvre he had for other appointments.

The strategy of constructing a broad shadow cabinet—the so-called collegiate approach—was both a practical response to the weakness of Corbyn's position and a return to what he felt was an appropriate way of doing things. As McDonnell explains: "All traditional Labour leaders have appointed from across the political spectrum... left, right and centre. You get better politics that way... But the reality is we only had 20 people that had voted for Jeremy in the PLP. In principle that's what I agree with anyway but pragmatically it had to happen."

For Corbyn, the 1980s "taught me the formation of the SDP was catastrophic to the electoral chances of Labour," leading him to be concerned that no part of the parliamentary party should feel excluded.[28] The theory, as Corbyn's ally Cat Smith outlines, was that "by including people from across the party everyone's got a stake in it." She says Corbyn's strategy "surprised a lot of people" because it was so different from the custom under New Labour, where overt loyalty to a narrow political project was a prerequisite to getting on. Corbyn's approach, in contrast to the 'on-message' culture, was to encourage a 'new politics' that was tolerant of disagreement and debate.

To make this work the leadership had to attract prominent members of the old guard to stay on in the shadow cabinet. "I hope you're going to continue to serve," McDonnell said to Corbyn's defeated rivals immediately after being told the result. Of the three only Andy Burnham eventually would, although he did not commit there and then.

A few hours later, following Corbyn's victory speech, a scene played out that resembled *The Thick Of It* paying homage to *Spinal Tap* as Burnham and his campaign team got lost in the endless corridors backstage at the QEII conference centre while trying to find the way out. "We got in the wrong lift and ended up in the boiler room," Burnham's head of press Katie Myler told the journalist Rosa Prince. "We get back upstairs, walk down the hall and straight into the lobby journalists waiting to interview Corbyn... Then we ran into Corbyn. By this time we have arrived at the right lift... Corbyn's trying to get in the lift with us, pushing all the buttons, and then one of his people stepped in front of him... and he was kind of shouting over this guy's shoulder: 'Andy, I need you!'"[29]

Sunday 13 September was a gruelling day of negotiations and decisions as the shadow cabinet slowly took shape. It was exactly the kind of experience Corbyn disliked—reminiscent of the scramble for MPs' nominations back in June that he had largely left to others. This time it was mostly on him, with only the chief whip Rosie Winterton—whom Corbyn kept in position despite not fully trusting her—and Simon Fletcher for help. "That was extremely hard for him, I think," says McDonnell. "It was really difficult."

McDonnell was excluded unexpectedly from taking part by Winterton, who claimed official rules stipulated that the shadow cabinet must be appointed by the leader and the chief whip—although McDonnell says he "left them there to get on with it because I thought if I'd been hanging around if people were coming in it might put some people off."[30]

Corbyn and Fletcher had no experience of assembling a shadow ministerial team. Influential MPs would not simply accept the jobs they were offered, but would make their participation conditional upon their allies being given positions too—from seats at the top table right down to junior ministerial roles. In such ways MPs build networks of parliamentary support—mini-patronage systems based on favours. Corbyn had never bothered with this kind of politics.

Armed with lists and plans, Corbyn set to work, ensconced in the chief whip's office in parliament. His first priority may have been to appoint McDonnell as shadow chancellor, but that would have to wait. "What we wanted to do was get all the other appointments in," recalls McDonnell, "then, once people had signed up, announce me, because we didn't want that to deter anyone."

Corbyn desperately needed big names on board early. This he achieved, with Andy Burnham, Hilary Benn and Angela Eagle agreeing to serve, their participation used to reassure other colleagues. "Andy is IN, Hilary is IN, Angela is IN," Winterton said down the phone to potential appointees.[31]

With Burnham as shadow home secretary and Benn as shadow foreign, Corbyn had already erred in earmarking all the top jobs for men. Burnham, as the second-placed candidate in the leadership election, was an important inclusion. But his involvement came at a price. It was rumoured he agreed to serve on the understanding that Benn and Michael Dugher be given jobs too. Dugher, Burnham's campaign chief, became shadow culture secretary. Tom Watson had warned he would be disruptive; he made it to January 2016 before being sacked.

What ultimately proved to be the biggest disaster was the retention of Benn as shadow foreign secretary. Moving him would have made space for a woman and avoided a lot of trouble down the line. Perhaps there was a dash of sentimentality in Corbyn's hesitance to demote his great friend's son. There was also a policy rationale. According to McDonnell, it was envisaged that Corbyn would take the "leading role" in foreign policy decisions, and so could afford to keep Benn in place.

To speculate: it appears the new leadership chose to be conciliatory on foreign affairs—the arena of sharpest disagreement within the PLP—so as not to distract from the immediate goal of converting Labour into an anti-austerity party. Benn was pro-Trident and generally pro-bombing people. He was also fiercely pro-NATO and pro-EU. This had the benefit of reassuring the PLP.[32]

The shadow defence job proved the hardest to fill. Corbyn was open to appointing someone sympathetic to Trident. At one point it was offered to Chris Bryant, until he demanded "a 30-minute conversation about what would happen if we had to invade Russia."[33] Eventually Maria Eagle took it.

At 8 p.m. on Sunday evening Corbyn emerged from the chief whip's office to nip to the loo. When the journalists stationed outside asked him if it was going to be a late one he responded: "The night is but young." It was imperative that a shadow cabinet be in place by a meeting of the PLP the following day, both as a demonstration that the show was on the road and because there was urgent parliamentary business waiting.

With more positions filled Corbyn finally felt confident enough to appoint McDonnell—in the face of continuing resistance from trade union leaders as well as MPs. "Even until the Sunday night... there were people still phoning in lobbying," McDonnell says. (After McDonnell's successful first conference address as shadow chancellor a few weeks later, Len McCluskey privately apologised, saying the "historic" speech had proved him wrong.)[34]

At 10 p.m. the first batch of appointments was released to the press. The backlash over the lack of women in the top jobs was instant. McDonnell says it "came as a real shock... We didn't even classify them as senior jobs... In fact we thought the more important ones were education and health and DWP, the big spending departments." Should that explanation not convince, McDonnell's next sentence gets to the nub of it: "All that Jeremy was interested in was getting the shadow chancellor sorted out. Then after that all the rest were equal."

Unbeknown to those in the chief whip's office, the journalists huddled outside were listening through the door. Fletcher was reported as saying: "We are taking a fair amount of shit out there about women. We need to do a Mandelson. Let's make Angela shadow first minister of state. Like Mandelson was. She can cover PMQs [prime minister's questions]. Tom [Watson] knows about this. Do the Angela bit now."[35]

At 12.19 a.m. the press were sent an email confirming Eagle as shadow first minister of state. Corbyn, meanwhile, was finally heading home. "Are you tired?" he was asked on the way out. "We never sleep, sleep ended months ago," he replied. Minutes later he was followed by a Sky News cameraman and reporter as he walked through the late-night deserted streets of Westminster. His refusal to answer questions made for agonising viewing. He looked exhausted.[36]

The final shadow cabinet appointments were made the following day. Corbyn's team spanned Labour's political spectrum from Diane Abbott to original Blairite Lord Falconer. He had appointed more women than men. McDonnell was shadow chancellor yet the sky had not fallen in. Corbyn said to reporters: "We have a shadow cabinet of a majority of women covering all areas of policy and public life and I think it's a great team. And it reaches out to the entire party and I think that is a bit of an achievement, if I may say so."[37]

History went on to show that Corbyn's collegiate approach did not work. Most shadow cabinet members could only manage nine months of service before resigning in an attempt to subvert the democratic choice of the party. The desire to include all wings of the PLP may have been one that Corbyn shared with traditional Labour leaders, but there was a big difference. When, for example, Harold Wilson fostered a collegiate approach, he did so from a position of relative strength that allowed him to play the ringmaster while the different factions competed. Corbyn was acting from a position of weakness in which, ironically, most of his shadow cabinet was already united—against him.

Was there an alternative? Only four shadow cabinet ministers were from the left—Abbott, Corbyn, McDonnell and Jon Trickett— leaving them heavily outnumbered. Due to his overwhelming victory, Corbyn probably had the political space to include a few more. But, as Jon Lansman asks, "Who else was there who was left out who wanted to be in there? None of the [new intake MPs] did [because they felt too inexperienced]." Yet there were some longer-standing colleagues who could have bolstered Corbyn's position. And there was Emily Thornberry—not from Corbyn's part of the left, but supportive and highly capable—who was strangely overlooked until January 2016.

"Jeremy had a very difficult hand to play," says McDonnell. "He did the best he could with the resources that he had and in the position that he was in... Nothing's perfect. But to get to the PLP [meeting] with a shadow cabinet when he's only had 20 people vote for him in the PLP is a hell of an achievement... You could always improve things but that was the best we could do."

Corbyn had made it. He was Labour leader. He had appointed a shadow cabinet. He was heading to his first meeting with the PLP.

Now all the trouble started.

15

THE SUMMER COUP

"As plotters, they're fucking useless."

—*John McDonnell*

There is only one intention: "to break him as a man." That is the view of Diane Abbott as she watches her parliamentary colleagues take turns to spit venom at Jeremy Corbyn.

It is 27 June 2016, nine and a half months since Corbyn addressed his first PLP meeting as leader. MPs are determined to ensure this will be his last. There are so many of them crammed into Committee Room 14 in parliament this evening that Corbyn's staff have to wait outside in the corridor. In the room it is hot and cramped. The MP Stephen Kinnock says it is "like being in a pressure cooker." He is not just referring to the temperature.

The long-anticipated coup against Corbyn is in full swing. MP after MP stands up to attack their leader in "the most contemptuous terms possible, pausing only to text their abuse to journalists waiting outside," according to Abbott.

"You are not fit to be prime minister," the widely unknown Bridget Phillipson tells Corbyn.

"It's time to be honest with yourself. You're not a leader. You need to go for the sake of the party," remarks Ivan Lewis.

"You are a critical threat to the future of the Labour Party," chimes in Jamie Reed.

"You're not uniting the party. You've got no vision. The only person who can break this logjam is you by resigning," pronounces Chris Bryant.

"You're not just letting the party down, but the whole country," declares Labour's only Scottish representative, Ian Murray. When he claims—without evidence—that his staff in Edinburgh have been "intimidated" by members of Momentum, another MP shouts "Scumbags!" Murray tells Corbyn to "call off the dogs."

The branding of party members as dogs is echoed by Jess Phillips, who characteristically finds a way to make it all about her. "On social media I've been accused of taking Zionist money and other things," she says. "These are your people. Ian's asked you to call off your dogs. Yet you won't do anything, you won't resign."

The tirade continues for over an hour. Nobody talks about Corbyn's politics; everything is focused on his person. It is "a bloodbath, the worst I've ever seen," comments one parliamentarian; "brutal," says another. A non-Corbyn supporting MP has "never seen anything so horrible" and feels "reduced to tears." Lord Mandelson, at the scene of the crime as ever, says there has been no meeting like it "in the history of the Labour Party."

As the finale, Margaret Hodge and Ann Coffey propose a motion of no confidence in the leader, to be conducted the following day. "This is not just about the party members who gave you a mandate a year ago," Hodge says. Indeed, MPs do not want it to be about them at all. Hodge explicitly belittles them, saying the number of members is dwarfed by the millions of Labour voters whose interests MPs alone appear able to interpret. "I would urge you Jeremy to show the basic decency I know you have and step down," she says. "By that simple act you will have made the most important contribution you can make to the Labour Party." Hodge receives rousing applause.

With the meeting finally at an end, Corbyn leaves the claustrophobic environment of Committee Room 14, navigates the dark, gothic corridors of parliament, and emerges into the midsummer evening sun. He can hear the roars and chants of a crowd across the road in Parliament Square. From one centre of power, a private gathering of a couple of hundred people in a closed room, he is heading to another, a public rally of thousands under the open skies.

As he crosses the road and approaches the square he attracts people to him like iron filings to a magnet. It requires a police cordon to move him through the throng. His destination is familiar. He is heading for the fire engine; the same vehicle from which he spoke in Camden in August 2015, called into service again as an improvised stage.

Tonight's 'Keep Corbyn' rally has been called with just 24 hours' notice. As one shadow cabinet minister after another resigned their post on Sunday 26 June it became clear that a coordinated action was underway and that the leader's position would hang in the balance at tonight's PLP meeting. The coup has been taking place in the anti-democratic arena of the TV studios. To change the narrative, to exert some power from below, it was essential to provide a physical demonstration of Corbyn's support—and fast. When campaigner Marshajane Thompson called the event she expected a couple of thousand to turn out at best. There was double that even as the rally assembled at 6 p.m. and the number has since swelled with people arriving after work. Now the square is jam-packed. It has been announced from the stage that the police estimate 10,000 are here.

They have already listened to John McDonnell deliver the message they all came to hear. "Let me make it absolutely clear," he said. "Jeremy Corbyn is not resigning, he's..." His voice was drowned out by the crowd.

Now they are hearing from Dennis Skinner, who looks surprised to be there at all. His speech begins with the words: "Anyway, I didn't know about this until five minutes ago." He is visibly taken aback at the warmth of the reception he receives. "I see the greatest crowd since the miners won in 1974," he declares. "We've got a battle on to save Jeremy as the leader of the Labour Party and we're going to win!"

The proclamation sparks a spontaneous rendition of "Cor-byn, Cor-byn, Cor-byn, Cor-byn". As it continues, unbeknown to most of the crowd, Corbyn arrives at the back of the fire engine and begins to climb the steps up to the roof.

"By the time that we get to October," Skinner continues, "Dodgy Dave [Cameron] will have gone and Jeremy Corbyn will be back!" As if on cue, the man himself appears. The roar from Parliament Square is deafening. Skinner looks round to see what is happening. The two men shake hands. Skinner continues to speak but no one can hear him. Everyone has their hands above their heads clapping. Some are visibly moved. It is a moment of real collective emotion.

To the onlooker it might look like cult-like devotion to a leader—that is certainly what some in the media will report. But that is not it. To be sure, people want to salute Corbyn's fortitude in circumstances that must be horrific for him as a human being. But there is something more to it: his survival is necessary for their survival as a political force. When he refuses to let a small part of the Labour Party impose its will on the rest, he is defending the project that all those in Parliament Square and beyond came together to build just the previous summer.[1]

· · · · ·

At times of crisis the façade of everyday politics is ripped down, exposing the real structure of power behind. To see the pillars upon which Jeremy Corbyn's original election was built, and the forces weighing down on his leadership from day one, just look at the attempted coup against him in summer 2016.

The defining feature of the coup was that it was anti-democratic. It was an attempt by two power centres within Labour—the PLP and the party bureaucracy—with ample assistance from the media, to cancel the democratic choice that party members and supporters had made nine months earlier. Its objective was to exclude Corbyn from standing again for leader, either by forcing him to resign or keeping him off the ballot, in order to deny members the opportunity to cast judgement themselves. The coup was distinct from the subsequent leadership election. The latter only came about because of the failure of the former. But from the beginning that contest was tarnished as every effort was made to skew the race to the detriment of the incumbent.

That there would be a challenge came as no surprise to the Corbyn camp. In April 2016, in an interview for this book, John

McDonnell predicted it. "In terms of attempted coups they might want to chance their arm after the [EU] referendum but if they did Jeremy would be on that ballot paper and we'd win it again," he said. Asked about the possibility of Corbyn being kept off the ballot, he responded: "Legally they wouldn't be able to do it. It's quite clear what the rules are. He'd be on the ballot paper. And then I think people who want to chance their arm on a coup attempt or putsch need to think what would be the average Labour Party member's reaction to that, when they've just voted for a Labour leader on the biggest mandate that a political leader's ever had in the party?"[2]

Given that one of the main justifications for the coup was Corbyn's supposed incompetence, his opponents' ineptitude was ironic. It was hard to disagree with McDonnell when he later branded them "fucking useless" plotters.[3] For a start, there was not one plot but two. The first to break cover, on the day after the EU referendum, was Margaret Hodge's proposal of a vote of no confidence in the leader—a device with no basis in Labour Party rules. While that was gathering momentum, Hilary Benn was busy ringing fellow shadow cabinet ministers to coordinate their resignations, only for Corbyn to hear of the plan, call Benn late at night on 25 June, and sack him. That pre-emptive action stole Benn's thunder, and apparently brought forward the staged resignations of shadow minister after shadow minister on 26 and 27 June, each quitting live on-air, on the hour, every hour. The plan was transparently orchestrated to create as much political damage as possible, yet by the time of the PLP meeting on the evening of 27 June Corbyn had been able to appoint a new shadow cabinet. Hence MPs' desperate and unpleasant display of bullying. All of this happened before the motion of no confidence could even be tabled, making it seem a superfluous gesture when 172 MPs backed it (in secret, to evade accountability) the following day.

The timing in the wake of the Brexit vote, with the prime minister having resigned, the Tories attacking each other, the economy looking shaky, and racist incidents on the rise, seemed to many irresponsible and tactically indefensible. MPs' chosen pretext for action—the EU referendum result—did not stand up to much scrutiny. The idea that Corbyn's alleged lack of enthusiasm for Britain remaining in the EU had swayed a million people to choose to leave was unpersuasive. Immediately available polls showed around two-thirds of Labour voters cast a ballot for Remain, the same proportion found among SNP voters.[4] Yet Nicola Sturgeon was credited with leading Scotland to a firm Remain vote while Corbyn was blamed for Brexit. Analysis by the psephologist John Curtice concluded there was "little in the pattern of the results of the referendum to suggest that Mr Corbyn was personally responsible for Remain's defeat." Demography was more likely to determine a person's vote than party political allegiance.[5] Research from Loughborough University found that Corbyn was by a wide margin the most prominent Labour voice in the media in the run-up to the vote, appearing more than the rest of the shadow cabinet put together, while Alan Johnson, who ran the Labour In campaign, featured just 19 times.[6]

In reality the coup would likely have been triggered whatever the referendum result. The bulk of the PLP resented Corbyn's leadership because they did not share his left politics. There had been continuous hostile briefings and sniping since he was elected. McDonnell revealed in a speech on 29 June 2016 that the leadership expected the putsch to come as early as December 2015, after the Oldham West and Royton by-election. Media commentators had speculated that Labour would lose the seat to UKIP. In the event, Labour won handsomely with a 7-point increase in its share of the vote. The plotters had to wait.[7]

The next opportunity was expected to come after the local, devolved and mayoral elections in May 2016. So confident were Corbyn's opponents of Labour's dire performance that Neil Coyle MP went on BBC *Newsnight* to kick-start the coup before a single result had been announced. It turned out to be the world's most inconsequential political intervention. Labour beat the Tories in projected national vote share, more or less matched Ed Miliband's high-watermark in council seats, retained control of the Welsh Assembly, recorded its best ever performance in the London Assembly, and won all four mayoral contests including big gains in Bristol and London.[8]

The picture was mixed—the party slipped to third in Scotland as Labour's long-term collapse north of the border continued. The overall performance fell short of what was expected of an opposition on course for government. But it was not the meltdown Corbyn's critics had convinced themselves was coming. When the Labour leader made a slip shortly before polling day by predicting that his party would not lose any council seats, the *Daily Telegraph*'s Asa Bennett scoffed that "Jeremy Corbyn is betting he's smarter than every pollster and expert." In the event, Corbyn's prediction was much closer than theirs: Labour lost 18 seats, not the 150 forecast by psephologists Colin Rallings and Michael Thrasher or the 170 predicted by John Curtice.[9]

So, when the coup finally came, MPs' second favourite pretext, that Corbyn was a sure-fire electoral calamity, was not as convincing as they might have hoped. On the day the shadow cabinet resignations began, 26 June, a post-Brexit poll from Survation put Labour level with the Tories on 32 per cent, although on average it had been running slightly behind.[10] It was difficult to blame the subsequent tumble in the polls on Corbyn, when everyone could see that it was precipitated by the coup.

Labour MPs assumed they could force Corbyn to throw up his hands and resign. When he simply refused they were bewildered. They had no plan B because the entire scheme was designed to deny Corbyn the opportunity to participate in a democratic contest. There followed the farcical spectacle of nearly two weeks of prevarication. By the end of June the MPs' insurrection was being labelled a 'chicken coup' because of the failure of a candidate to come forward.

Angela Eagle did want to stand—but not against Corbyn, and so instead of formally triggering a challenge she issued chilling ultimatums threatening that if the leader did not resign she would ask him to resign again.[11] While she hesitated, Labour's deputy leader Tom Watson engaged in negotiations with trade unions, presumably hoping to weaken their support for Corbyn in one more desperate attempt to remove the leader without recourse to party members. Those talks failed on Saturday 9 July, prompting Eagle to announce that she would announce on Monday what she had announced that she would announce several times already. But her performance in a round of media interviews on the Sunday was so bad that any fizz left in her candidacy visibly flattened. "You can take a stalking horse to the studio but you can't make her perform," one Corbyn ally commented to a journalist.[12] Eagle's flop contrasted sharply with Corbyn, who turned in his most assured performance yet on the BBC's *Andrew Marr Show* on the same morning, looking intensely relaxed about the prospect of another leadership battle.

Eagle's troubles worsened when her campaign finally had its official launch the following day. After delivering a speech in which her awkward delivery was met with artificially enthusiastic applause, she was jilted by the press who ran off to cover breaking developments in the Conservative leadership contest, leaving Eagle to plaintively call out the names of journalists who were no longer in the building.

Eagle's candidacy was falling apart sufficiently for the PLP to consider an alternative: Owen Smith. This brought a new absurdity—a squabble between two 'unity' candidates. Smith quickly gathered momentum and swept up support from MPs. Eventually, on 19 July, Eagle was cast aside. The whole affair had been a humiliation for her.

By formally triggering a contest MPs had failed in their objective of forcing Corbyn to resign. The baton was handed on to the party machine, which moved to keep the leader off the ballot and, when that did not succeed, restricted the franchise and suspended all local party meetings. In taking these actions Labour Party officials exposed the role they had long been playing as a centre of resistance to Corbyn. Their ability to damage the leader had been seen periodically, as in the anti-Semitism furore in spring 2016 when the details of alleged cases were leaked to the press before the members involved had been informed that they were under investigation.[13] Party staff were responsible for inefficiencies that were blamed on Corbyn's office, according to his allies, for example by "delaying press releases on purpose, meaning they missed news deadlines." A source from Corbyn's 2016 leadership campaign told *Buzzfeed* that while "80 per cent of employees at Labour's HQ and regional offices do their job well, there are 20 per cent at the top who interfere politically with attempts to get Corbyn's message across."[14]

Upon assuming the leadership, Corbyn and his allies had chosen not to tackle the machine. "Really no one has been taking the restructuring of the party seriously," said Jon Lansman in January 2016. He was "very worried" about it.[15] The danger became all too obvious as soon as a leadership contest was triggered. Working hand in hand with elements of the NEC, the party bureaucracy used every trick in the book, plus a few more, to secure the ouster of the leader. The crunch meeting of the NEC on 12 July 2016—which was to decide whether Corbyn needed to secure 51 nominations from MPs and MEPs in order to be on the ballot, a feat he was not expected to manage having only just scraped 35 the year before (the required number was higher when there was no vacancy)—was unilaterally called at 24 hours' notice while two Corbyn-supporting trade union representatives were on holiday (they hurried back). Party officials had reportedly refused to communicate with Corbyn's office for several days prior. At the meeting there was an attempt to prevent Corbyn from voting—which was defeated, although he was excluded from taking part in the discussion. And the unprecedented step was taken of voting in secret, despite members of the NEC being representatives of the various sections of the party. The given reason was to prevent intimidation but it was suspected that the real purpose was to allow trade union representatives to discreetly vote against the agreed position of their unions.[16]

According to reports, Labour's general secretary, Iain McNicol, was "willing to put his job on the line" to ensure Corbyn would not automatically be on the ballot and believed that he could swing a majority behind this position on the NEC.[17] He had managed to obtain legal advice that interpreted the party rules as saying Corbyn needed to secure MPs' nominations afresh. This was wrong in law, as was later confirmed by the High Court, as well as being an affront to democracy. But at the NEC meeting, despite four separate sets of contradictory legal advice being circulated, McNicol only invited the author of his previously unseen guidance to make a presentation, prompting protests from some attendees.[18]

Following five hours of discussion, the NEC voted by 18 to 14 that the leader should be on the ballot automatically. There was as much relief as joy among Corbyn supporters. It looked like the coup had finally been defeated. But the machine had a fallback position. The rules could still be set in a way that made it more difficult for Corbyn to win. After some pro-Corbyn members had left the meeting, including Corbyn himself, the NEC voted through a six-month retrospective freeze date, meaning that only members who had joined the Labour Party before 12 January 2016 were able to vote. Since the onset of the coup Labour had experienced the most rapid membership surge in British political history, with 130,000 people joining in a fortnight.[19] It was widely thought that the majority had signed up to defend Corbyn. Any leadership challenge seemed futile unless they were excluded. The freeze date disenfranchised a quarter of the party membership.[20]

Two other important decisions were reached. First, the fee to become a registered supporter was hiked from the £3 it had been in 2015 to £25. This was an attempt to kill off the scheme in all but name.[21] As it turned out, people's desire to participate outweighed the cost: an incredible 180,000 applied to be registered supporters despite the party also restricting the sign-up period to just 48 hours.[22]

Second, the NEC took the extraordinary step of banning all CLP and branch meetings for the duration of the leadership contest, effectively shutting down the party.[23] This was justified on the grounds of preventing intimidation, but it seemed to be no coincidence that several local parties were in the process of passing motions of no confidence in their own MPs. Having provoked fury among the members, the Labour establishment's solution was simply to stop them talking to each other. The machine doubled down in subsequent weeks, putting Corbyn-supporting local parties Wallasey and Brighton and Hove into administrative suspension.[24] A 'Labour purge' mark two was soon launched. This time merely using the words "scab," "scum" or "traitor" on social media was grounds for exclusion.[25] It was reported that a member was denied a vote for an "inappropriate" post on Facebook reading: "I fucking love the Foo Fighters" (prompting one social media user to quip: "First they came for the Foo Fighters, and I did not speak out—because I was not a Foo Fighter").[26] In Croydon, members were told that the term "Blairite" constituted an insult.[27]

The legacy of pulling such blatant administrative manoeuvres was the branding of Corbyn's opponents as bad losers who placed little value on democracy. Their behaviour was "backroom chicanery," wrote the Labour blogger Phil Burton-Cartledge, driving long-term members like him to adopt "reluctant Corbynism" in protest at "an uncaring, selfish, stupid, and anti-democratic culture."[28] It was as if the coup had cracked open the casing around the party machine, making its inner workings visible for all to see.

Predictably, throughout these shenanigans, the media abandoned what little semblance of objectivity it had previously maintained. Corbyn supporters' ritual complaints of media bias had, by the time of the coup, been substantiated by academic studies. It was no surprise that newspapers with an established editorial policy of denigrating Corbyn continued to play what a report had described as "an attackdog, rather than a watchdog, role." But, more significantly, a study found that coverage of the coup on the BBC's evening TV news bulletins, watched by millions, was also skewed towards Corbyn's opponents. To show this was an editorial choice not a journalistic necessity, the academics compared the BBC output with that of ITV and found that the latter gave "considerably more equal attention" to pro- and anti-Corbyn voices.[29]

An alliance with the mainstream media was integral to the PLP's power. MPs found the press willing to amplify virtually any story they came up with however tendentious or trivial. They were particularly keen to establish the idea that Corbyn and his supporters were bullying them. For some MPs, this seemed to involve little more than channelling their playground memories. Conor McGinn, a Labour whip (a job reserved for tough arm-twisters), accused Corbyn of threatening to ring his dad over disparaging comments the MP had made in an interview.[30] Seema Malhotra, the former shadow chief secretary to the Treasury, said she was going to tell on Corbyn to the Commons Speaker over his office manager having attempted to enter her office—which she should have vacated after resigning. The Speaker decided not to give Corbyn a detention, telling Malhotra "there is nothing in your letter... which would justify regarding these events as a possible breach."[31]

The fiction that journalists are dispassionate observers of politics rather than actors in the drama became difficult to sustain at moments of high tension. On 27 June, the most febrile day of the coup, the *New Statesman*'s political editor George Eaton reported the damaging claim that he was "near certain that Corbyn voted Leave" in the referendum. The revelation turned out to be third-hand gossip: Eaton was told by the MP Chris Bryant who claimed he was told by a member of the public who alleged he was told by Corbyn, whom he professed to have met one night in a tapas restaurant in south London.[32] When, during an appearance on Sky News on 26 June, the journalist Rachel Shabi refused to conform to the media consensus view that Corbyn should resign, her exasperated interviewer Anna Botting declared that it was "totalitarian" for the elected leader to resist a coup aimed at overturning democracy. Topping them all was the *Financial Times* political columnist Janan Ganesh, who tweeted on 23 August: "You can do analysis of Corbyn and his 'movement' (I have done it) but the essence of the whole thing is that they are just thick as pig shit."[33]

· · · · ·

Mighty as the troika of the PLP, the machine and the media seemed, Jeremy Corbyn was able to see off the coup because his sources of power, in the membership, the unions and the movement, were greater than those of his opponents. Any conventional politician who had won the leadership by advancing through parliament and the press would have been unable to survive. But Corbyn's success was achieved in spite of those institutions. He was not playing by Westminster rules.

The issue at the heart of the coup concerned where power lay in the Labour Party. Was it with the PLP or the membership? And where did the unions, with the constitutional might to settle the matter, stand? Corbyn's survival made this clear: power now resided with the membership. Corbyn was only able to defy the coup because of the legitimacy he took from the members—hence his frequent reminders that he had been given a huge mandate by a greatly expanded party under a one-person-one-vote system.

In contemporary Western society individualised one-person-one-vote democracy commands greater legitimacy than any alternative. Collective arrangements, such as those that traditionally characterised the Labour Movement, are regarded as inferior, suspect, even corrupt. MPs and commentators regularly express their commitment to the ideal of individualised democracy. Yet on this standard, Corbyn's credentials were impeccable. Consequently, there followed the odd spectacle of the same MPs and commentators venting their outrage at Corbyn for sticking to the democratic principles in which they professed to believe. They were unable to clearly articulate what he was doing wrong in refusing to resign. All they could charge him with was constitutional impropriety, arguing that it was harmful for the country to not have an opposition in which the MPs were loyal to the leader.[34]

Behind this confusion lay two contending conceptions of the Labour Party. The Labour establishment was correct to say, as Neil Kinnock expounded in a speech to the PLP on 4 July 2016, that the party had been founded to represent the Labour Movement in parliament. Therefore, the argument went, it was a parliamentary party above all else, and the leader had to have the confidence of the MPs. "This is our party!" Kinnock exclaimed.[35] But when the Labour Party was first created it had no individual members. In the intervening 116 years it had transformed gradually, stutteringly, into a democratic membership organisation. Just two years before the coup it had taken the latest step along this road when it decided overwhelmingly—with the fulsome backing of the PLP—that all of its members and eligible supporters would have an equal say in choosing the leader.[36]

It was ironic that a rule change promoted as a solution to the split electoral college in 2010, when trade unionists secured Ed Miliband's victory, facilitated the opening of a much wider chasm between the PLP and the membership. But this was not solely a result of the new rules. In the aftermath of the 2008 crash the membership had adapted to the new political context. Its shift left under Miliband was then greatly accentuated by the influx of new recruits during and after the 2015 leadership contest, when the party doubled in size from 200,000 to nearly 400,000 members (before rocketing to over half a million during the coup).[37]

In contrast to the flexible, responsive membership, the parliamentary party was largely a relic from the New Labour era. The stitching up of parliamentary candidate selections over many years had resulted in a PLP that was unhitched from the values of the wider party. There was no quick mechanism to alter its composition in fast-changing times. This was a constitutional conundrum. Under first-past-the-post, where most constituencies are safe seats, many MPs can have what are effectively jobs for life if their party has no recall process in place, such as mandatory reselection. This creates a lag effect. At any one time the PLP is the product of a bygone age. This can work both ways—Corbyn's own presence in parliament was a legacy of the strength of the left in constituency parties in the early 1980s. But, as leader, Corbyn faced a far less politically diverse cohort of MPs than had Labour leaders of old, and certainly one less representative of the party at large.

MPs justified their defiance of the elected leader by emphasising their personal mandates from voters. They had a higher calling than to the party membership, they said, which was to their constituents. But this denied the reality of a party system.[38] Most voters look for their favoured party on the ballot paper when they go to the polling station, not for an individual. Candidates' electoral prospects often depend on the campaigning efforts and resources of their party.

Members had elected Corbyn in part because of his promise to empower them.[39] With its coup, the PLP explicitly attempted to void that promise. The lengths to which the Labour establishment was prepared to go in order to defeat Corbyn confirmed that if the left lost the leadership it would be "put in a box for 30 years or out of the party," as one former shadow cabinet minister put it.[40] Tom Watson's proposal to reinstate the electoral college, made in August 2016, was a clear indication that the PLP's first priority was to diminish the power of ordinary members.[41]

The one institutional base of support that Corbyn did enjoy during the coup (though it fragmented slightly in the subsequent leadership election) was the trade union leadership. For the unions, the coup put at risk a 10-year project to reshape the Labour Party, restore their position within it, and steer it away from Blairism.[42]

Having backed two successive leaders that a majority of MPs did not want, it was highly likely that had Corbyn been overthrown undemocratically a triumphant PLP would have sought their emasculation. On the other side of the coin, Corbyn's ouster would have created immense pressure within several unions, including Unite, to disaffiliate from the Labour Party.

For Corbyn, trade union support was vital. It undermined the notion that his inadequacy was self-evident to all but the Momentum "rabble." The trade unions were widely seen as pillars of the Labour Party. When they insisted—as 12 unions did in a joint statement on the day after the EU referendum—that "the last thing Labour needs is a manufactured leadership row... we call upon all Labour MPs not to engage in any such indulgence," it was hard to brush off their view as zealotry.[43] Significantly, the signatories to that statement featured five unions that had not nominated Corbyn for leader the previous year, including the third-biggest union the GMB.

In going ahead with their action anyway, MPs evidently hoped that by creating a crisis they would force a rethink. It did not happen. The unions restated their support on 29 June, urging MPs to "respect the authority of the party's leader."[44] Meanwhile, Unite general secretary Len McCluskey filled the airwaves and newspapers with an unambiguous message, warning that any attempt to keep Corbyn off the ballot paper would "lead to the break up of the Labour Party" and pillorying the plotters for "betraying not only the party itself but also our national interest."[45]

Of even greater importance than the unions' public support was their steadfast stance behind the scenes. Their refusal to budge on the issue of Corbyn's resignation led Watson to unilaterally break off negotiations he had opened with the unions, a move McCluskey described as "an act of sabotage."[46] The ultimate reason why the unions held so much sway became clear at the crunch meeting of the NEC on 12 July, when the votes of their 12 representatives spelt the difference between Corbyn being on the ballot or not. The whole gambit had been undertaken on the assumption that some unions, under the cloak of a secret vote, would swap sides. As was becoming a habit, the Labour elite had miscalculated.[47]

· · · · ·

It was the political movement that formed around Corbyn's candidacy in the 2015 leadership contest that propelled him to such a stunning victory. Yet the speed of Corbyn's rise left no time to build any kind of stable base. The skyscraper went up before the foundations were laid, leaving it vulnerable to buffeting winds.

This explains why the PLP expected Corbyn to be so easy to knock over. But the miserable failure of their attempted coup was both a consequence and a demonstration of their poor understanding of how Corbyn had come to be their leader in the first place. It sometimes seemed that the actions of Labour MPs were designed to galvanise a movement that had shown during the previous summer that it thrived on adversity.

The Corbyn movement overlapped with, but was distinct from, the party membership.[48] Its distinguishing quality was that it could exert collective power quickly to change the course of events. Corbyn's position was heavily dependent on the energy and people power embodied in this unprecedented burgeoning of support.

When the moment of crisis arrived thousands of people turned out for 'Keep Corbyn' rallies such as the one in Parliament Square on 27 June 2016. These events transformed the coup from a performance being staged by a closed politico-media clique to a live-action experience in which ordinary people could improvise the script. As the putsch dissolved into a leadership contest, the movement made itself visible at Corbyn rallies around the country that were far larger than those seen the previous summer: 7,000 assembled outside St George's Hall in Liverpool in the rain; 3,000 congregated in Hull for the city's biggest political rally in decades; 3,000 turned out in Leeds; 2,500 in Sheffield; 4,000 in Kilburn, London.[49] This was a genuine phenomenon that could not be faked, as Owen Smith found out when just a smattering of people attended his outdoor rally in Liverpool, despite the offer of free ice cream.[50]

The movement also came alive online. As a tool for quickly mobilising support in a coup-type situation social media was unsurpassed. The potential was demonstrated on the day after the EU referendum. In response to Margaret Hodge announcing her plan for a motion of no confidence, a "vote of confidence in

Jeremy Corbyn after Brexit" petition was started on the 38 Degrees campaigning website on the afternoon of 24 June.[51] Within two hours of the petition going live, 45,000 people had signed. By 9 p.m. the total had risen to over 100,000.[52] The following day, when Corbyn gave a speech, he was able to answer questions about his leadership by pointing to the 150,000 signatures to the petition, something the media could not avoid acknowledging as evidence for his support.[53] By 1 July over quarter of a million people had signed, more than had voted for Corbyn in the 2015 leadership contest.[54]

The advent of social media had a further impact on the course of the coup: as a platform for exposing and countering the old-school back-room manoeuvring of the PLP and the party machine. Skulduggery was more difficult to get away with when every twist and turn was being live tweeted. What might in the past have been a demoralising series of *fait accompli* was transformed into a spur for mobilisation. Although it ultimately failed, the best example of this was the crowd-funded legal action by five new party members challenging the six-month freeze date that meant they could not vote in the leadership contest. After their case was lost in the Court of Appeal and the Labour Party demanded its costs be paid by the five, £30,000 was raised online in a single evening.[55]

A movement is a spontaneous thing, but from the early days of Corbyn's leadership there was a conscious attempt to give it an organisational core: Momentum, the Corbyn-supporting group conceived as the "successor" to his 2015 leadership campaign.[56] With no expectation of winning, Jon Lansman had, from the outset, seen that contest as a means of building a new left hub. The campaign had been legally structured in a way that allowed all of its data and resources—including its 120,000-strong contacts list—to be retained by the new organisation.

From its inception, Momentum had a dual role. Some hoped it would be a left wing version of Progress, an internal Labour faction dedicated to bolstering the leadership's position. Ed Miliband had made an "enormous mistake" in "doing nothing to build up his own support network," Lansman believed, and Corbyn would be doomed if he repeated it.[57]

On the other hand, Momentum wanted to be an outward-facing approximation of a social movement, building alliances with other movements and campaign groups and establishing a presence in communities. Labour "must understand it does not have a monopoly on opposing vested interest," the MP Clive Lewis wrote announcing the organisation's launch on 8 October 2015, just a month after Corbyn's victory.[58] For Lewis, Momentum was an attempt to answer the question: "How do you become a mass social movement? How do you begin to capture all those people, all those in Avaaz, 38 Degrees, environment activists, tax avoidance activists, all those different groups that had fragmented into single issue campaigns?"

Momentum's two roles were immediately in tension. Because of its hasty launch—which Lansman says was "pressed on us by Jeremy and John because they thought they needed it straight away"—Momentum emerged without a proper structure of governance. Autonomous Momentum groups popped up spontaneously all over the country in true social movement style. But unlike in most nascent movements, the activists involved were immediately plunged into the boiling water of high-stakes politics. Any minor misdemeanour or political *faux pas* was seized upon by the press and blamed on Corbyn. Momentum was quickly painted as a conduit for entryism and an organisation dedicated to deselecting MPs, neither of which was accurate.[59]

It took a while for the central Momentum organisation to take shape and assert its authority on the spontaneous networks that had sprung up. In the process some of the initial buzz was lost. It became difficult to maintain a sense of forward motion when the focus of politics was on the daily grind at Westminster.

That all changed with the coup. Momentum's potential was revealed as it mobilised supporters, helped arrange 'Keep Corbyn' rallies, and upped its press operation. Once the leadership election got underway, it deployed digital tools to help people check their eligibility to vote, recruited thousands to become £25 registered supporters, and provided much of the backbone of the 2016 iteration of the Corbyn campaign.

· · · · ·

With Jeremy Corbyn on the ballot the outcome of the leadership contest was never in serious doubt. Polls showed he would beat all comers, although it helped that his eventual opponent, Owen Smith, was relentless in his determination to underperform expectations. Corbyn's dominance was underlined by constituency party nominations, of which he won 285 to Smith's 53. Interestingly, whereas in 2015 Corbyn's support had been strongest in London—allowing opponents to claim Labour had been taken over by cosmopolitan liberals—this time he did best in the north of England, while Smith did disproportionately well in the capital and in Scotland.[60]

That Corbyn's appeal within the party was undiminished explains why the PLP chose Smith to be its 'unity' candidate. Ostensibly from the 'soft left,' his initial strategy was to pitch himself as being just like Corbyn, only slicker. But this meant that, in the absence of a serious policy debate, there was not much Smith could do other than make increasingly ugly attacks on the leader and his supporters. This might have worked better had Smith not committed a series of scarcely believable gaffes, from suggesting Scotland's first minister Nicola Sturgeon should be silenced with a gobstopper ("banter," he said in his defence), to answering that yes, he would negotiate with ISIS, making him one of the few mainstream politicians ever to have been outflanked on the right by Corbyn. If Smith was the best the PLP had to offer, Corbyn supporters wondered, why had MPs spent months criticising their leader on the grounds of competence?

The only attack that troubled Corbyn came not from Smith but, oddly, from Richard Branson, who falsely accused the Labour leader of staging a video in which he sat on the floor of a packed Virgin train.[61] In what had become a familiar pattern, a poll found the "traingate" scandal only made Corbyn more popular with his supporters.[62]

Meanwhile, the Corbyn camp calmly honed the policy agenda it had outlined the previous year. Corbyn's platform was largely the same, but was given more coherence, neatly organised into '10 pledges' covering all areas of policy.[63]

The story of the contest was encapsulated in a moment at the end of a TV debate between the candidates on the BBC's *Victoria*

Derbyshire programme on 17 August 2016. After what seemed an interminable two-hour debate focused predominantly on accusations of abuse within the party that were somehow held to be Corbyn's fault, Derbyshire asked the undecideds in the audience to vote with their feet by moving to where either Corbyn's or Smith's supporters were seated. The vast majority joined the Corbyn block, to an eruption of cheers and applause.[64]

As nothing Smith did seemed to work, he ended the contest with what Sam Tarry, Corbyn's campaign director, described as a "scorched earth strategy." "In the last six weeks [the Smith campaign] essentially gave up on winning and they just sort of decided to burn the party to the ground," he said. "'Let's just smash it to pieces and hope it just takes Jeremy Corbyn out.' I just think that's unforgivable."[65] Smith likened Momentum to a parasite "trying to use our movement as a host body, seeking to occupy it, hollow it out, until it's outlived its usefulness, when you throw it aside like a dead husk."[66] Neither Andy Burnham, Yvette Cooper nor Liz Kendall had insulted a section of the party in such a way.

The only unknown of the contest concerned how many non-members had signed up to vote for Smith. The opaque pop-up anti-Corbyn group Saving Labour claimed it had recruited 70,000 registered supporters and 50,000 trade unionists, making the race "too close to call."[67] Though reported seriously, these figures turned out to be pure fiction—Smith won the votes of only 37,000 registered supporters and 40,000 trade unionists in total.

The result was announced at the Labour Party conference in Liverpool on 24 September. Corbyn not only triumphed again but increased his mandate from the 59.5 per cent he won a year earlier to 62 per cent, amassing 313,000 votes. Among full party members his share of the vote rose by 10 points to 59 per cent. Amusingly, the Corbyn campaign was "kind of disappointed" by the outcome, according to Tarry, having hoped to clear 65 per cent.[68] With thousands having been denied a vote, there was no doubt that the result understated Corbyn's true support.

The ironic consequence of the coup and the leadership challenge was to cement the leader's authority. In the process, it was revealed just how emphatically Corbyn and his supporters had won the argument on domestic policy. Corbyn's opponents had not even tried to challenge his anti-austerity agenda. During her brief sortie, Angela Eagle went to great lengths to open no policy rifts with the leader at all. Smith's programme was self-evidently a watered-down version of Corbyn's—albeit supplemented with a pledge to hold a second referendum on the EU while also saying there were too many immigrants in parts of the country. Smith even promised £200 billion of borrowing for investment. It would have been unimaginable for any of the 2015 leadership candidates—bar Corbyn—to stand on such a programme, illustrating how dramatically the political terrain had been reshaped. When Smith released a list of 20 policies early in the contest, the Corbyn campaign responded sardonically: "We welcome Owen's focus on equality of outcome, reindustrialisation and workers' rights—and his support for policies announced in recent months by Jeremy Corbyn and John McDonnell... Owen's speech today shows the leadership that Jeremy Corbyn has demonstrated in placing economic justice and fairness back at the heart of Labour politics."[69]

16

THE SNAP ELECTION

"This election campaign, it's like two stories. One is, from many of our national media, deeply cynical, a series of calculations... Then on the other side of it is an amazing sense of unity... There is nothing inevitable about this election."
—*Jeremy Corbyn*

What could possibly go wrong? A 67-year old politician going on stage at a Libertines gig... in front of 20,000 young people... on a Saturday night in a tough Northern town... in the middle of a general election.

It is 20 May 2017, just over a month since Theresa May shocked the political world by calling a snap election. There are 19 days until polling day. Jeremy Corbyn is in the Wirral. He has just addressed a rally of thousands of Labour supporters on the beach in West Kirby. In nearby Prenton Park stadium, the home of Birkenhead's Tranmere Rovers Football Club, a music festival is underway. Rumours are buzzing around social media that Corbyn is going to appear with the headliners. "If Corbyn comes out with the Libertines then this could possibly be the best gig ever," tweets one attendee. "Gonna vote Tory if Jeremy Corbyn comes out with Libertines. Not even joking," posts another.

As it happens, whether Corbyn will appear is yet to be decided. The idea, devised by a team of young advisors working on Labour's election campaign, is for him to appear not with the Libertines but during the set of one of the support acts. But the proposal has faced opposition from various quarters. The Special Branch officers assigned to protect the Leader of the Opposition are not happy about the security risk. "That can't happen," they told Corbyn's chief of staff, Karie Murphy, when they learned of the plan.

"Not a problem," she said.

"So you're not going to do it?"

"I'm absolutely going to do it," she replied. "I'll get private security in Liverpool."

Labour's press team has a different concern: the Libertines' frontman, Pete Doherty. He and his band have been very helpful, but people who are paid to worry about bad headlines are worrying about bad headlines should Doherty, whose reputation precedes him, do something unpredictable. Nerves are allayed when they learn that the singer is running late to the gig.

Then there is the question of the reception Corbyn will receive. What if the crowd boos him? What if they bottle him off? This is Birkenhead, not Glastonbury. A crowd of mainly working class Northerners has paid to get into Prenton Park for a concert, not an election rally.

Ordinarily, any one of these risks would be enough to keep a politician away. But the Labour leadership is doing things differently. If the opinion polls are to be believed, they started the election campaign up to 25 points behind the Tories. There was never any point in being cautious. They have broken every political rule. When they outlined a strategy designed to mobilise young people, non-voters and marginalised groups, all the experts and pundits— and even top officials in the Labour Party—laughed. Yet the gap to the Tories has since halved. Labour is on the up.

Corbyn will do the gig.

"There's someone special who's come here to talk to you," says Jon McClure, singer of Reverend and the Makers, interrupting his band's set. "Please welcome Mr Jeremy Corbyn!"

The crowd erupts instantly. This is a good sign. There is even the sound of girls screaming. Unexpected.

"Look here," says Corbyn after 30 seconds of applause, "we've got football and music all in the same place." The crowd has not stopped cheering so Corbyn speaks in short bursts to make himself heard. He has simplified his message for the occasion: "I love football! And I love sport! And I want it for everybody! Those very wealthy clubs in the Premiership, pay your 5 per cent so we've got grassroots football for everybody!"

The crowd likes it. Corbyn looks out on thousands of hands raised above heads, clapping. This is going well.

"And it's also about young people and music," he continues.

Some way back in the crowd on the right hand side a chant has started. It is just a few singing at first, but it spreads like wildfire. Soon it is audible from the stage.

Corbyn is still speaking. "In every child…"—he repeats himself, competing with the noise and glancing to the origin of the chant—"in every child there's imagination and there's hope, and tha…"

His speech stumbles. The chant is louder. The whole front section of the crowd has joined in.

"…and so what I want," Corbyn persists, "is every school… every school… to have the money for every child to earn… learn… musical instruments."

They are not listening to him. The chant is drowning him out. Corbyn stops speaking. It is difficult for him to tell from the stage what they are singing. He thinks they might be having a go at him. This could be a disaster. "I'm looking at these guys chanting," Corbyn will later recall, "and I realise they're smiling. So I paused and realised what they were chanting."

The melody is familiar. It is the White Stripes song 'Seven Nation Army,' a tune appropriated by fans in football stadiums around the world. But it has never before been sung with these words.

"Ohhhh, Je-re-my Corrr-byn."

As it dawns on him that they are singing his name, Corbyn feels "quite moved." For 20 seconds he says nothing as the chant envelops the stadium, getting louder and louder, gaining rhythm as people start clapping along. Sections of the crowd are jumping up and down as they sing it. Some are perched on others' shoulders, arms stretched up to the heavens as they belt it out. Something magical is happening. From the left to the right, at the front and even right back at the bar, Prenton Park pays musical tribute to the politician who has come to speak to them.

To the side of the stage, the staff accompanying Corbyn cannot stop laughing. They think it is "absolutely amazing." This is not a Corbyn rally. It is not even a protest. It is 20,000 mostly young music fans. Labour has somehow found itself a leader who can turn up on stage unannounced at a big outdoor concert, and instead of the crowd lobbing pints of beer at him, they chant his name.

"Thanks guys," Corbyn finally interjects. He tries to press on with the rest of his 5-minute speech. "I'm going to upset the Coral otherwise because they'll be delayed coming on." But the chant rumbles on, increasing in volume again as Corbyn winds up. "Thank you for giving me a few minutes, and remember: this election is about you!"

By the time Corbyn leaves the stage, footage of the crowd's reaction is already setting social media alight. It is one of those spontaneous moments that turns received wisdom on its head. The notion that young people are unreceptive to political ideas is wrong. The notion that Corbyn is universally derided is wrong. The notion that Labour is headed for a crushing defeat is—suddenly a little less certain. One of the staff greeting Corbyn as he comes off stage has been saying for weeks that "something subterranean is going on." Now it is clear: the ground is shifting.[1]

ACT ONE

It is possible that Theresa May saved the 'Corbyn project' on the day she called a snap election. Things were not looking good for the embattled leader. The coup in June 2016 had been like a neon sign advertising to the electorate that Labour was a divided party. After winning his second leadership contest that September, Jeremy Corbyn did not receive a polling bounce. Instead, Labour continued on a gradual decline that had begun with the coup, sinking to the 25 per cent mark by the time May made her announcement outside Number 10.[1] Although the Parliamentary Labour Party professed to have taken a vow of silence after Corbyn's re-election, the anonymous briefings did not stop, and MPs from outside the shadow cabinet seldom showed any enthusiasm when defending Labour's positions in the media.[2]

Despite being leader, Corbyn had never been in control of the party. His efforts to chart a new course had been met with continuous internal obstruction. The Labour establishment maintained a powerful presence in every area of the party bar the Leader's Office—not only in the PLP but also on the National Executive Committee, at the top of some trade unions, in the party's regional offices, and among the staff at Southside, the name of the building housing Labour's London HQ, dubbed 'the Dark Side' by supporters of the leader. This omnipresent establishment was the product of cultural and political affinity, rather than conspiracy (although it did also conspire). But it was structurally entrenched. Party staff were appointed by the general secretary, Iain McNicol, who was elected by the NEC. Corbyn supporters were in a minority on the NEC, and there was no easy way to change that since only six of the 35-person committee could be elected by the membership. When the left seemed to make a breakthrough by winning all six of those places in a one-member-one-vote ballot in summer 2016, two more seats were suddenly added to the NEC at the behest of the Scottish and Welsh party leaderships, tipping the balance back to the right.

Within the party, Corbyn set three objectives for his leadership: to have a left policy platform; to democratise the party; and to make it more like a social movement. A year and a half into the job he had only made progress on the first. Efforts to advance the others were met with bureaucratic defiance. Corbyn's wish for the party to become a social movement was particularly radical in Labour terms, a direct affront to the traditional parliamentary perspective in which the wider organisation was little more than an electoral machine dedicated to perpetuating the PLP. Corbyn instead wanted a party that could begin to transform society even as it forged the alliances needed to win elections. Practically, that meant local parties involving themselves in community campaigning. To push the process along, the leadership instructed Labour HQ to employ an executive director of organising. Southside protested that it would make the party's structures unsafe. In reality, the bureaucracy was evincing its customary horror at the idea of grassroots organisation, which threatened its stranglehold on power.

The determination of the Labour establishment to frustrate the left had a direct impact on the party's effectiveness. The day-to-day experience of the Leader's Office, based in parliament, was one of "trench warfare" with Southside, located down the road on Victoria Street. Precious time and energy were diverted into bureaucratic battles, such as over the appointment of staff and the allocation of resources. During the most intense period of press hostility throughout the coup the leader's media team was threadbare. It took four months to secure four members of staff. "I was the only person dealing with the press lobby," recalled Corbyn's former spokesman, Matt Zarb-Cousin. "Some days I was getting 80 to 100 calls or texts from journalists, mostly with stories that were leaked by people on our own side."[3]

The leadership had grown used to routine leaking from Corbyn's first frontbench team. Sometimes details of shadow cabinet discussions would be reported in the press while meetings were still in progress. This dysfunction came to an abrupt end with the mass resignations in June 2016, when all of Corbyn's most dangerous critics took the interesting decision to voluntarily relinquish their positions of power, forcing the leader to assemble a shadow cabinet far more to his political advantage. That group of allies proved watertight. The leaks resumed after the shadow cabinet was broadened out slightly following Corbyn's second leadership victory, but at a much lower frequency.

Other parts of the party were more than capable of filling in, however. The leaking to the *Sunday Times* of the results of an internal focus group conducted to test the reaction of northern voters to Rebecca Long-Bailey and Angela Rayner, which made the front-page in February 2017, was a particularly nasty example.[4] The data was only available to a select group of top Labour Party officials and the intention of publicising it, in the view of a member of the leader's team, was to break the two women's confidence.

Most outrageous of all was when obstruction crossed over into outright sabotage of Labour's electoral prospects. A leak of internal canvassing data showing that the party was on course to lose a by-election in the Cumbrian constituency of Copeland, reported in the *Daily Telegraph* in January 2017, could only have weakened Labour's chances. The leak was accompanied by a quote from a "senior Labour source" blaming Corbyn's "incompetence" for the bad returns. Who knows if the source considered whether a competent bureaucracy would leak damaging information to a hostile newspaper before a by-election?[5]

On top of this internal obstruction, the early part of 2017 saw the first serious divisions open among those sympathetic to Corbyn. The issue was the leadership's decision to whip the PLP to vote for the triggering of Article 50, beginning the process of leaving the European Union. Four shadow cabinet members resigned, including prominent supporters of the leader Clive

Lewis, Dawn Butler and Rachael Maskell. They joined a rebellion of 52 Labour MPs. "It wasn't comfortable," says one of Corbyn's advisors (like several of those quoted hereafter, the source requested anonymity).[6] "We had a few resignations with MPs in very Remain seats thinking, 'I have to do this to save my seat.' In hindsight they didn't, but you could understand it at the time, given the polling and their own concerns."

Unlike on previous occasions, this schism in parliament reflected rifts in Corbyn's base. Many of the leader's supporters had campaigned vigorously to Remain and thought the referendum result was a disaster. Some wanted Labour to block Article 50 by whipping MPs to vote against it. This was a practical impossibility—it would have resulted in the disintegration of Labour as a parliamentary unit with a rebellion of more like 152 than 52, since two-thirds of Labour MPs represented Leave-voting areas.[7] More realistic were those who argued that Labour should abstain or allow a free vote on Article 50, keeping the movement together by effectively having no position on the big issue of the day. Although these two positions were not really compatible, they cohered on social media to create the impression of a flood of anger, especially when Corbyn critics and vociferous Remainers joined in. Commentators delighted in talking up the disagreement as a catastrophic split in the movement.

In fact, most supporters of the leadership recognised that Corbyn was in a tricky position over Article 50, and many agreed with him that parliament had a democratic duty to ratify a decision it had asked the public to make.[8] But the saga contributed to a sense of demoralisation afflicting the movement. It did not help that a nasty fight had recently taken place within the Corbyn-supporting Momentum organisation, raising the prospect of the left embarking down its usual path of sectarian splits and bureaucratic manoeuvres.[9]

The last thing the party needed amid this strife and poor polling was to have to fight two brutal parliamentary by-elections. Having been voted-in less than two years earlier, Blairite MPs Jamie Reed and Tristram Hunt had apparently grown bored of sitting in parliament for a party in which they were out of favour. Suddenly the honour of representing their constituents could not compete with lucrative job offers and the chance to cause maximum disruption for a leader they reviled, and so they resigned their seats. This was a particularly extraordinary move for Hunt, who in 2015 had felt so devoted to the party that he had put himself forward to lead it.

The battle in Hunt's former seat of Stoke-on-Trent Central was fierce. UKIP's new leader, Paul Nuttall, threw his hat into the ring, claiming that his right-wing party would "replace Labour" in the north. The commentariat duly took him at his word. "Stoke-on-Trent is the Brexit heartland that could be Corbyn's Waterloo," declared John Harris in the *Guardian*.[10] But Nuttall was a fantasist whose claim to have a window into the soul of the northern working class should have been taken as seriously as his false assertion that he was a professional footballer for Tranmere Rovers, or that he had a PhD, or that "close personal friends" of his had died in the Hillsborough disaster, at which he said he was present.[11] As Nuttall's campaign descended into farce, Labour and Momentum mobilised their members and flooded the city with hundreds of volunteers. This massive effort proved to be enough to grind out a victory on 23 February 2017, delivering a near-fatal blow to UKIP.

The attention given to Stoke partly obscured a disaster for Labour in Jamie Reed's former constituency of Copeland. The leadership's favoured candidate to stand for the seat—local hospital campaigner and former 'Cumbrian Woman of the Year' Rachel Holliday, an embodiment of Corbyn's community campaigning vision—was passed over by the CLP in favour of a councillor. As a geographically isolated constituency, and without the draw of the UKIP leader as an opponent, far fewer volunteers made the trip to Copeland. Long-term trends were not propitious: Labour's share of the vote had declined in Copeland at every election since 1997. But whatever the mitigating circumstances, losing the constituency to the Tories on a 7 per cent swing was a shocking defeat for Labour. It was the first time a governing party had gained a seat in a by-election since 1982. The result was brandished as evidence that Corbyn was leading his party to ruin.

Whereas Labour's performance in by-elections in the first period of Corbyn's leadership, before the EU referendum and the coup, had been very good, the Copeland result—together with that in Stoke where, despite winning, Labour recorded a slight decline in its vote share—suggested something had changed. It was easy to guess what: the referendum had transformed the political landscape. The Conservatives' reinvention as the party of Brexit looked to be working—in Copeland the UKIP vote fell by 9 points while the Tory vote rose by 8.5, unifying the right. For Labour things were much tougher. Brexit drove wedges into all the party's fissures. Across the country two-thirds of its voters had favoured Remain in the referendum and a third Leave. The line that Labour was a national party that sought to represent 100 per cent of the people, rather than the 52 per cent on one side of the referendum or the 48 per cent on the other, was met by sneers from commentators who joked that it risked representing 0 per cent.

With the picture looking bleak, some of the small band of media commentators who had previously expressed sympathy or support for Corbyn buckled. Owen Jones said after Copeland that Corbyn's leadership would result in a "catastrophic" defeat that would be "blamed on the left" and argued the leader should do a deal with the Labour right to allow another left candidate a shot at replacing him.[12] Jones' journalistic colleagues George Monbiot, Ellie Mae O'Hagan, Abi Wilkinson, and Zoe Williams all publicly expressed a loss of faith.[13]

The ubiquitous hostility of the rest of the commentariat was by now so complete that in order to get noticed Nick Cohen was reduced to disgracing himself with an expletive-strewn, intelligence-free diatribe in the *Observer*. "In my respectful opinion," Cohen told an imaginary Corbyn supporter, "your only honourable response will be to stop being a fucking fool by changing your fucking mind."[14] Things were not much better over on the news pages where May was enjoying an open-ended honeymoon. There was more scrutiny of the opposition than the government as journalists fearlessly held the powerless to account.

With local elections fast approaching in May 2017, speculation mounted about the possibility of another Labour coup following an expected poor showing. By mid-April the Tories were over 20 points ahead according to some polls. With turbulence over Brexit likely to increase as the negotiations got under way, and with a weakening economy, Conservatives wondered if they might ever get a better chance to win a landslide majority. This was the political backdrop against which May took her fateful decision.

·····

"I'm not going to be calling a snap election," said Theresa May on 4 September 2016.[15]

"I have just chaired a meeting of the cabinet where we agreed that the government should call a general election to be held on 8 June," said Theresa May on 18 April 2017.[16]

In the Labour Leader's Office there was shock. The party had been on an "election footing" for months, and Seumas Milne, Corbyn's executive director of strategy and communications, was convinced that an early vote was looming. But the most likely date for it was 4 May, the same day as local elections, and the deadline for that had passed. "We were all: 'Wow, didn't see that coming,'" says one of Corbyn's lieutenants. "The very first day I was totally down... It took all of us 24 hours, but that was it. Then we were like, 'OK, what do we need to do?'"

The prospect of an election was so terrifying for some commentators that they believed Labour should block it in parliament, even though willingly keeping a Conservative government in power would have been politically indefensible. "Corbyn is rushing to embrace Labour's annihilation," wrote the *Guardian*'s Polly Toynbee on 19 April. "Was ever there a more crassly inept politician than Jeremy Corbyn, whose every impulse is to make the wrong call on everything?" He was "wrong, wrong and wrong again," she declared, in a column in which nearly every sentence—from her insistence that the election would not be about policy to her prediction of a Lib Dem revival—was ultimately proved wrong.[17]

But trepidation did run deep among Corbyn supporters. Many dreaded that the election would spell the end of their dream. Even Len McCluskey felt acute anxiety waiting for May's appearance after news broke that she was going to speak to the nation: "I was desperately hoping that she was going to make an announcement that maybe Prince Philip's dead or something! But no. I felt pretty downhearted then." Opinion polls seemed to bear out his fears. May's U-turn on calling a snap election was initially seen as a gamble, but she was quickly vindicated by a clutch of surveys showing the Tories soaring to around 48 per cent. One particularly ominous ComRes poll had the Conservatives on a whopping 50 per cent of the vote, precisely double Labour's share of 25 per cent.[18] How could there be any way back from that?

Yet amid the gloom there were early rays of hope. In his public appearances an upbeat Corbyn gave confidence to a movement temporarily frozen with fear. Taking questions from journalists after his first speech of the campaign on 20 April, the leader received a spontaneous standing ovation for his passionate response to the suggestion that he had made Labour a "tainted brand": "Keir Hardie was vilified—vilified beyond belief—when he was elected as the first ever Labour MP... Anyone who stands up to create a better, fairer, more decent society gets vilified. Our party gets vilified. But I tell you what: we're bigger than we've ever been, we're stronger than we've ever been, and we're more determined than we've ever been!"

A correspondent for ITV asked: "You say that you want to speak for the many, not the few, but your poll ratings suggest that only a very few people believe you. You've attacked the elite but aren't you just part of an Islington elite that doesn't reflect the views of people around the country?"

"You very helpfully mentioned the opinion polls," Corbyn replied. "All I can say is: in 2015, almost exactly two years ago, I was given 200/1 as an outside chance."[19]

Snap elections are supposed to favour the governing party—forewarned is forearmed—but it was Labour that hit the ground running. The first few days of the party's campaign could scarcely have gone better. Labour dominated broadcast coverage while the Tories went to ground having taken themselves by surprise. There was a reason Labour was able to make such a sharp start. Desperate to improve the party's position ahead of the local elections, Corbyn's team was already running what looked like a mini-general election campaign. Over Easter they had released a string of well-packaged, eye-catching policies. Some of these, such as a £10 living wage and a plan for free lunches for primary school children paid for by charging VAT on private school fees, were snappy ideas that perfectly communicated what Corbyn's Labour was about. They resonated so well, in fact, that they went on to become signature policies of the general election campaign.

The Easter offensive marked a step up in the effectiveness of the Leader's Office operation, which had been dogged by accusations of incompetence ever since Corbyn's election. It is a charge that staff vociferously reject, arguing that they were working in a near-impossible situation. Having come to the task with no experience of running a Leader's Office, and receiving little help or guidance from Labour HQ, Corbyn's team had to cope with unprecedented levels of hostility from both the press and sections of their own party. On top of it all, they were chronically understaffed.

This began to be remedied after the appointment of a new chief of staff in June 2016. Simon Fletcher was replaced by Karie Murphy, who had been the candidate at the centre of the Falkirk furore in 2013 (without which, ironically, the job of chief of staff to Jeremy Corbyn would never have existed). Whereas Fletcher did not like confrontation—not ideal in the circumstances—Murphy was a street fighter. "Karie coming in definitely accelerated things," says a colleague. "She gets things done."

Together with Milne and policy advisor Andrew Fisher, Murphy completed a trio of aides—all with the same rank of executive director—who ran the leader's operation. They quickly became a tight-knit team. "It's a unique combination of characters and skills," says Murphy.

> Seumas is the strategic brain, he has incredible vision. Andrew is the political soul, whose politics are so close to Jeremy's. I'm the vigour, I drive things through. I don't want to be conceited but I really do think that combination is important. And we all like each other. We respect each other, but it's more than that—we really care about each other. That kind of relationship is only found on the left where as comrades we are completely committed to the cause and to each other.

Visible improvements in the performance of the Leader's Office were not immediate. After Murphy's arrival it took six months and countless battles with Southside before the team was fully staffed. It was then plunged into the Article 50 controversy. Only with the Easter policy launches was the Leader's Office finally able to show what it could do when running on all cylinders. Murphy installed a new grid system plotting out the local election programme—what would be said on each day, where it would be said and what the intended aim was—and enforced "grid discipline," ensuring everyone stuck to the plan. As soon as May made her surprise announcement the grid was adapted for the general election campaign. Labour was off.

The discipline of an election demanded that Labour's more overt displays of infighting be put on hold—a necessary condition for its subsequent rise in popularity. But this newfound unity was superficial. Below the surface the waters were as turbulent as ever. On the second day of the campaign an email was sent to all CLP secretaries that began: "The National Executive Committee has agreed an exceptional selections procedure for candidates in the general election." All sitting MPs would automatically have the right to stand again, but even where there was a vacancy candidates would be "selected directly by panels of the NEC and regional board members." "It is with the greatest regret," the email insisted, "that local party members will not be able to select parliamentary candidates." Behind the scenes Corbyn had personally tried to secure what an aide describes as "a process that would allow local parties some input into selecting candidates," but had been met by a wall of opposition at a meeting of NEC officers.

The justification given for the move was that there was no time for selections in a snap election. One of Corbyn's close advisors, however, describes this as part of "another coup" by the Labour establishment. In retrospect, the outcome of the process was not as bad for the leadership as it feared. Trade unions were given huge leverage. "There was no great pressure from the right wing saying we want this or that," says Len McCluskey, who wonders whether a decision had been taken to let the unions get their way in order to keep them—and their money—on board after the election. "Parachuting" candidates, McCluskey agrees, was "not the best way of doing things," but it meant that, while those pushed by the unions were not all left-wingers, they were at least steeped in the Labour Movement. Unite itself overtly favoured candidates of the left. "We got quite a number," McCluskey says, "which means there's now a new wave of MPs... who'll begin to change the nature of the Parliamentary Labour Party." (Ultimately the election saw around a dozen MPs enter parliament who were strongly pro-Corbyn, with others expected to be generally supportive.)[20]

Meanwhile, some long-standing MPs were testing how far they could push their luck without forfeiting their automatic selection. John Woodcock was allowed to stand on a Labour ticket despite announcing on 18 April: "I will not countenance ever voting to make Jeremy Corbyn Britain's prime minister."[21] Although his remarks provoked fury in the party (not only from the left), the NEC spared him any sanction when it considered the matter on 3 May, with Tom Watson and Kezia Dugdale, the Scottish Labour leader, reportedly phoning in to support him.[22]

While Woodcock went furthest in distancing himself from Corbyn, a parade of Labour MPs followed in his wake.[23] Some gave their constituents the bizarre message that they should vote Labour because the party would lose. "When I knock on doors I tell people they can vote for me if they like me and not have any fear of Jeremy becoming prime minister, because there is absolutely no chance of that," one of them told ITV's Robert Peston.[24] Another informed his voters that re-electing a 'moderate' was the only way to get rid of Corbyn after the election—a line that must have had very niche appeal.[25] On the other hand, ultra-Blairite Ben Bradshaw wrote to his constituents to tell them they were *not* electing a "party leader."[26] Even Tom Watson mused that "Sometimes the most important question isn't what makes the best PM, it's who makes the best MP."[27]

In the background, Yvette Cooper was limbering up for a leadership challenge to follow the coming defeat, and was promoting herself via sponsored ads on Facebook.[28] The Leader's Office was "100 per cent" certain that Cooper was planning to run, according to a high-ranking source, having heard from "four or five different areas" that she had lined up funding, staff, a campaign manager, and was likely to get the support of Unison.

What all this reflected was a widespread conviction that the election was going to be a disaster. It was a sentiment shared in Labour HQ. Sources briefed the *Times* that party staff were planning to strike if Corbyn stayed on as leader after defeat.[29] It would be the first strike they had ever supported, joked Corbyn supporters.

Southside's private data painted a bleak picture. One early list produced for internal use ranked constituencies by how likely Labour was to lose them. Polling commissioned from the pollster BMG had Labour on 27 per cent at the time, 18 points behind the Tories. Forty Labour-held seats on the list were marked as category 1, which meant, according to a source, "they're beat." These were not just the most marginal 40 seats—top of the list came Hornsey and Wood Green, where the Liberal Democrats were projected to overturn a healthy Labour majority on a vast swing, suggesting Southside was expecting a dramatic Brexit effect. A further 21 seats were marked as category 2—likely to be lost. These included constituencies such as Tynemouth, with a Labour majority in excess of 8,000. In all, the model suggested Labour would lose 80 seats, although those in category 3 were all to play for.[30]

The data helped determine where the party spent its resources. Why waste money on category 1 seats that were lost? Category 2 would get limited support. Officials advised Corbyn's team that the leader should visit constituencies where a Labour incumbent was in with a shot. There was no point targeting too many Tory-held marginals. The Leader's Office had other ideas. "We said, 'No, we want an offensive strategy,'" recalls a key lieutenant. Murphy and Niall Sookoo, Corbyn's campaigns director, plotted out an itinerary for the leader's visits based on very different criteria: they would go to the constituency of any MP who had been supportive—none would be abandoned, no matter how imperilled their seat—and then branch out to any Tory or Labour-held marginals in the vicinity.

Staff in the Leader's Office are critical of Southside's defensive strategy. While it could be justified on the basis of Labour's poor polling at the time, it reflected a particular conception of politics that the leadership did not share. Labour HQ was "locked into a mindset of historical trends in voting, historical modes of campaigning, and historical organising that didn't embrace everything we had learned from Jeremy's leadership elections," says one aide. Instead, Corbyn's team would offer to transform people's lives with bold policies designed to appeal to those suffering under a "rigged" economic system. Crucially, they would reach out to people who did not usually vote. This had strong echoes of Corbyn's 2015 leadership bid, in which the very first leaflet had aimed to get non-members to vote for £3. That summer Corbyn was asked how the party could advance under his leadership when an analysis by the Fabian Society had asserted that four out of five voters that Labour needed to gain had to come direct from the Tories. Labour, he responded, should appeal to:

> Young people who didn't register, who didn't vote... Secondly, the numbers of reliable Labour voters who disappeared into the arms of UKIP or non-voting because they didn't feel the Labour Party represented anything they wanted to hear, do or say. I think we can grow our support that way. Do we have to win back people who voted for other parties? Yeah, but we have to say to people, in a very clear way, what we're offering.[31]

When a refined version of this strategy was discussed with the Southside top brass at a meeting on 4 May 2017, tensions boiled over. "They all sat around the table all fucking churlish saying 'we don't understand what the strategy is,'" an aide recalls. Murphy then blasted: "You fucking do understand the strategy, you don't like the strategy, you don't want the strategy, but you know the strategy."

In fact, the strategy had been outlined in a paper by Jon Trickett, formerly the election coordinator. It said Labour should put forward "a transformational offer... which offers hope to the different groups who at the moment feel abandoned and alienated from politics."[32] When Trickett presented the paper to the 4 May meeting he argued, the aide recalls, that Labour must appeal to "young people who we needed to get registered to vote, black and ethnic minorities, public sector workers, and working class post-industrial left behind communities... If we combine these groups together we will get 40 per cent. They all scoffed."

The Southside contingent simply did not believe it could work, remembers another advisor who was present:

> They said there are two things we know about national campaigns. One is you can only shift the vote by two or three per cent during the campaign, which, to be fair, is historically true. We were quite confident we could shift it more than that with a different approach... Secondly, this idea that voter registration drives don't work, non-voters don't vote, there's no point trying to appeal to them. Actually, they do vote if there's something worth voting for.

Behind these divergent approaches lay different aims. Southside's concern was to weather the storm and emerge with a party intact, if a bit battered—or, as the Corbyn aide speculates, "It was just: 'Let's get to the finish line and then let's get them fuckers [the leadership] out of here.'" But the leadership needed to advance. To keep the 'Corbyn project' alive they felt they had to exceed the share of the vote won by Ed Miliband in 2015—30 per cent. If they did that, they could argue that the party was rebuilding its support and heading in the right direction, even if the Tories' absorption of UKIP meant that Labour was likely to lose seats.

· · · · ·

The general election very quickly settled into a pattern. The Conservatives based their campaign on a soundbite—"strong and stable leadership"—and very little else. Theresa May used the phrase three times while announcing the election; 11 times in her first stump speech of the campaign; it was deployed 16 times in the final prime ministers questions of the parliamentary session; and countless times in media appearances. Asked by an interviewer "Do you know what a mugwump is?"—after Boris Johnson had used the term to insult Jeremy Corbyn—the prime minister replied: "What I recognise is that what we need in this country is strong and stable leadership."[33]

May began with sky-high approval ratings and a vast lead over Corbyn when the public was asked who would make the best prime minister.[34] Seeking to exploit this advantage, the Tory campaign was built entirely around her. "Every vote for the Conservatives will make me stronger," she said.[35] Tory hopefuls were "my local candidates," or part of "Theresa May's team."[36] But the public image did not match up to the reality of a flawed politician, as was clear to anyone paying attention—including, it seems, to Tory campaign managers. A risk-averse approach was adopted to hide the truth. May was kept away from direct interactions with the public. Her events were held in factories with workers replaced by pliant Tory activists.[37] There were attempts to restrict the opportunities for journalists to question her.[38] When she did take questions, she developed a reputation for not answering them, to the extent that she seemed incapable of giving a straight response.[39] Despite her selling point being strong leadership, the Conservatives immediately made clear that May would not debate Corbyn on TV.

The Tories wanted the campaign to be about Brexit and Corbyn to the exclusion of all other issues—they did not even make the traditional attacks on Labour over the economy (although that was probably because May was determined to sideline her chancellor). The prime minister's justification for calling the election was that her approach towards Europe faced too much obstruction in parliament.[40] Suddenly Tory supporters who had spent months disingenuously complaining that Labour was a weak and ineffective opposition flipped to arguing that it was over-mighty. The *Daily Mail* crystallised the message with the front-page headline "CRUSH THE SABOTEURS."[41] Things became even more surreal when May accused European politicians of trying to meddle in the election.[42] Yet all of this seemed to work a treat. While Brexit was the dominant theme, May maintained her polling highs. The former Remainer was now Leave personified, ruthless in her pursuit of the 52 per cent. UKIP was sent into a precipitous decline.

But however strong and stable the strategy looked, it had dangers. The hard rhetoric alarmed those who wanted a less confrontational approach to Brexit. May's dramatic attacks on parliament sounded a touch hysterical given that Labour had voted for Article 50. In fact, although it was not immediately obvious, Labour's Article 50 stance proved to be an electoral masterstroke. With the party saying that Brexit was going to happen, the Tories were left angrily punching at thin air. Setting aside issues of principle, Labour had a clear slogan with "jobs-first Brexit"; a matter-of-fact line on freedom of movement ending when Britain left the EU; a humane pledge to guarantee the rights of EU citizens in the UK; and a reasonable-sounding desire to approach the negotiations in a spirit of cooperation.

It was a position that alienated only the most fervent Leavers and Remainers. Though it has been described as a political fudge for a party with voters in both camps, and as the ultimate triangulation strategy from a leader famed for not triangulating, according to one of Corbyn's close advisors it was simply "pragmatic." Contrary to the notion that the leadership team were secret Brexit zealots (an allegation lent weight by Corbyn's historical voting record), the advisor insists that in the context of the referendum: "They're not on the wing that says Europe is the root of all evil, not even the left version of that... And they're not on the wing that says Europe is the root of all enlightenment and wonder in the world... Even around the shadow cabinet, Keir Starmer, Diane Abbott, they're not hard Remainers or Brexiteers. To be honest I think most people come down on that position."

The great advantage of Labour's stance was that it largely neutralised Brexit as an election issue, enabling the party to talk instead about its domestic agenda.[43] While supposed strategic wise men from Labour's past, like Tom Baldwin and Alastair Campbell, toured the TV studios complaining that Labour should make the abstract issue of Brexit its focus, the leadership set about convincing people it could transform their everyday lives.

Labour's campaign looked like an inverted version of the Conservatives': open, upbeat and policy-rich. "Jeremy's input and design was extremely important," says a member of his team. "He wanted positive messages. If we were going to attack the Tories it was going to be about their record and always coupled with what we were going to do instead, being positive."

> Most days we would have a story of the day, which would
> be a policy. We'd have the relevant shadow cabinet min-
> ister go and do the morning round of broadcast. We'd

have briefed it the day before so we'd have some write up in the printed press—a much better write up in the *Mirror* than anywhere else. Then all the images of the day would be Jeremy at rallies. He would do an interview on the issue generally mid-morning, so his voice would be running on the story throughout the day. That was how we structured our media grid.

Given the hostility of the press, Labour focused on broadcast coverage, especially music radio. "If we're getting the first 30 seconds of a 90 second news bulletin at the top of drive time on music radio that's actually getting into the public imagination much more than some argument in the pages of the *Times*," says the aide. Labour's punchy, discrete policies were ideally suited to this medium. Occasionally one of them would take off and achieve 'cut through,' such as the plan to create four new public holidays on the home nations' patron saints' days, or the pledge to scrap hospital car parking charges paid for by taxing private health insurance. Corbyn's policy team was surprised that it was the relatively inexpensive ideas that seemed to fly.

As for Corbyn, he was back on the road doing what he did best: campaigning. "Jeremy became more confident because he was out all the time," says one of his lieutenants. "Instead of being out one day a week and then being dragged back to parliament to be demoralised and undermined by the PLP, he was out there amongst his people, feeling it." His easy manner with the public provided a stark contrast to his Conservative opponent. And freed from parliamentary fetters, Corbyn's rhetoric was again radical and engaging. A speech delivered on 29 April to young people, urging them to "step up" and register to vote, marked a shift in his message. Instead of focusing, as he had previously, on the "left behind," he asked people to consider how they, personally, were "being held back"—a theme that would recur throughout the election. Unusually, he talked about himself and his understanding of leadership. "And now for a sentence I've yet to utter in my political life," he joked, "enough about you, what about me?" He told the story of being arrested for protesting against apartheid. The audience loved it.

Yet anyone watching TV news in these early weeks would have come away with the impression that everyone—*everyone*—hated the Labour leader. The format became wearily familiar: a reporter would devote a sentence to the latest Labour policy before interviewing a selection of three people in a town centre somewhere. Two of them would say they were lifelong Labour supporters but would never vote for Corbyn, while the other would say she was not sure about him. As BBC journalist Jonny Dymond later admitted, the selection of vox poppers was not scientific, the choice reflecting the editorial judgement of the reporter.[44] In reality, although the media appeared not to notice, Corbyn's personal approval ratings were creeping up. He was, in fact, the only leader who was improving. Polls by Opinium showed Corbyn's approval rating climbed 3 points between 19 April and 2 May. The prime minister's, in contrast, fell 8 points. There was still a huge gap between them, but it was narrowing. Meanwhile, all the other party leaders went backwards. Tim Farron of the Liberal Democrats did worst—his rating fell by 11 points as the public realised that the liberals had managed to find a leader who was not a liberal on social issùes. The much-talked-of 'Lib Dem surge' did not materialise, and the party was barely seen again.[45]

Labour, in contrast, was on the up. That expectations were at rock bottom was turned into an advantage. Any improvement in Labour's score lifted the morale of members and generated a sense of momentum. There was huge excitement on the evening of 29 April when three separate surveys put the party on or above 30 per cent. Not only did this suggest Corbyn's Labour would match the result achieved by Ed Miliband—a huge relief—but the party appeared to have gained five points in a single week. "According to tonight's Opinium poll, Corbyn is only set to lose 1 point from 2015. That's a pipe dream," tweeted the *Mail on Sunday*'s "election guru" Dan Hodges, who predicted that Labour would in fact get 20 per cent. "Labour melting down is the story of the election," he wrote.[46]

· · · · ·

Dan Hodges need not have bothered trying to demoralise Corbyn supporters; the local and mayoral elections were on hand to do that. Coming as an awkward interlude two weeks into the general election campaign, the results were disastrous for Labour. The party lost 382 council seats across Britain, while the Tories made over 500 gains—remarkable for a party in government. Of the six metro-mayor contests, the Conservatives won four, including surprise victories over Labour in Tees Valley and the West Midlands. The only consolations were wins in Liverpool for Steve Rotherham and in Greater Manchester for Andy Burnham, who then snubbed Corbyn when he travelled to the city to celebrate. There was a hint of Labour's latent support in the West of England mayoral contest covering Bristol and Bath, where the party scored an unexpectedly strong second place that could have been first had the campaign not been starved of resources.

The projected national vote share put the Tories on 38 per cent and Labour on just 27. Although the 11-point gap was narrower than most polls were then showing, pundits pointed to historical patterns demonstrating that the government's share of the vote was sure to increase at the general election, while the opposition would slip back. For Labour "this is as good as it gets," warned the *New Statesman*.[47] Had there not been a general election looming, the results would have provoked a bout of intra-party conflict and recrimination, although staff in the Leader's Office doubt it would have amounted to another coup.

How could a party just five weeks away from winning 40 per cent of the vote in a general election have fared so badly in the locals? Answering that question reveals some of the distinctive features of Corbyn's later success. First, turnout was low—as low as 21 per cent in the Tees Valley mayoral contest. The reliable voters who go to the polling station come what may tend to be older—the segment of the population most enamoured with the Conservatives.[48] The non-voters Labour was hoping to engage, in contrast, did not come to its aide—the deadline to register had long passed, and those who did not usually vote in general elections were unlikely to participate in a local one. The kind of people Labour was appealing to—especially the young—were simply not as interested in local politics. "It's just councils, bins and shit, but I'll vote in the general election," was one reported response.[49]

Second, Labour had not yet published its manifesto. The policies it launched ahead of the local elections were neat and popular, but they did not add up to a programme. The general election would present a stark choice between the status quo and a radical plan to transform society. There was never any chance of such a transformation being delivered by the local council.

Third, broadcasting rules in a general election guarantee the opposition equal airtime, but these did not kick in until after the dissolution of parliament on 3 May. The legacy of 20 months of negative reporting cast a long shadow. With the big day still a way off, most voters had probably not yet engaged with politics closely enough to question received wisdom and revise their perceptions. The big set-piece TV events of the general election, in which millions of voters got to see Corbyn unmediated, had not yet happened.

Finally, the lower stakes in a local compared to a general election were reflected in a lower level of mobilisation of the Labour membership. Having hundreds of thousands of people to knock on doors and deliver leaflets was a great potential advantage for Labour—but in many areas it remained just potential. It was reported that Corbyn requested data on the amount of canvassing done in places where the results were disappointing.[50] The leader's supporters were not blameless in this—it was often the newer members who were less active.

It was, perhaps, a worrying characteristic of the Corbyn movement that it seemed to require an emergency for it to come alive. Although Labour's campaign had been gathering momentum before the local elections, it had not yet become the viral phenomenon seen in Corbyn's 2015 and 2016 leadership bids. It was still an open question whether the movement had the capacity to recreate that kind of energy outside of an internal party battle. Corbyn supporters were briefly knocked off balance by the disappointment of the local elections. It would take a dramatic event to kick-start their movement again. They were about to get one.

ACT TWO

At 9:04 p.m. on Wednesday, 10 May 2017, the *Telegraph* published a story on its website headlined "Exclusive: Jeremy Corbyn's left-wing Labour manifesto leaked." Somebody had passed the newspaper an entire 43-page draft of Labour's electoral programme.[1] Nothing like it had ever happened before. And there was more: the *Mirror* had also obtained the document. Suddenly details of the party's policies, not due to be unveiled until the following week, were all over the internet.[2]

Who did it? Matt Zarb-Cousin, Jeremy Corbyn's former spokesman, quickly tweeted: "Hearing the whole manifesto has been leaked by Labour HQ. Helpful of them to continue their tradition of undermining the leadership."[3] But sources in Southside hit back, briefing that the document had been "leaked by the Leader's Office itself in a bid to blame Labour HQ for damaging the party's election campaign."[4] Others speculated that the leadership had leaked it as part of a guerrilla media strategy to draw attention to its policies. But there was consternation in the Leader's Office when they learned of the leak. "Allies of Corbyn appeared genuinely discombobulated... and initially suspected figures on the party's right wing, including the deputy leader, Tom Watson," reported the *Guardian*.[5]

The plot thickened: Labour's 'Clause V' meeting, at which the various components of the party come together to finalise the manifesto, was due to take place the following day. Had someone within the leadership put out the document in order to bounce the meeting into accepting Corbyn's radical policies? Or was it leaked in the expectation that there would be such a backlash against the left wing prospectus that the leader's critics would take the chance to water it down? The latter seemed the most plausible theory, but no one really knew.

An internal investigation conducted after the election eventually traced the leak to a member of Kezia Dugdale's team in Scotland. "I'm sure the intent was malicious," says an aide to Corbyn. "Normally parties don't try to sabotage themselves." But if the aim was to discredit the manifesto the plot backfired spectacularly.

The media, always excitable about any kind of leak, was consumed by the story, propelling Labour's plans into the public consciousness. The fact that costings for the programme were not leaked along with the draft meant that all the focus had to be on the policies themselves, rather than how they would be funded. For all the predictable sneeriness about Corbyn wanting to "take Britain back to the 1970s," journalists conceded that this was a bolder manifesto than anything seen from a major party in decades.[6] "This will be an election where voters will not be able to say 'they're all the same,'" observed the BBC's Laura Kuenssberg.[7] Social media was immediately abuzz. For Corbyn supporters the drama of the leak created a powerful emotional cocktail of fury at the sabotage but exhilaration at the audacity of the radical blueprint. Even for Corbyn-sceptic Labour members, the news was like a shot of adrenaline.

Perhaps as a consequence, there was no attempt to dismember the manifesto at the Clause V meeting the following day. The gathering of more than 80 people—including the NEC, the shadow cabinet, representatives from the PLP, Scottish and Welsh Labour, the National Policy Forum, and the trade unions—heard first from the leader. "Jeremy Corbyn said he was extremely disappointed [about the leak], which in Jeremy's language means very cross indeed," reported NEC member Ann Black.[8] According to another attendee, shadow foreign secretary Emily Thornberry then made "the most fantastic contribution," declaring: "I've never seen such treachery in all my life."

When the meeting got down to business there was some dispute over the proposal to ban fracking, but it was not pushed to a vote. Changes and additions were suggested but overall the manifesto sailed through intact. It got a far easier ride than the Leader's Office had initially expected, although a source says that by the time of the meeting "we'd done a fair bit of management." In Len McCluskey's opinion, "a number of the right wing had decided, 'We're going to get smashed, by all means if you want to do another even longer suicide note [than in 1983] be our guest, and we'll be here to pick up the pieces.'" But for McCluskey the lack of opposition also reflected how thoroughly Corbyn and John McDonnell had transformed Labour into an anti-austerity party. "The right wing had nothing to offer, " he says. "How could they argue against it? What are they going to say, 'I think we should have austerity and I do support the pay freeze and I don't agree with investment banks'? They didn't have any alternatives or solutions. That's why it went as smooth as anything."

That evening the *Mirror* published a poll revealing that the policies were wildly popular. Renationalising the railways, the Royal Mail and the energy industry, which the journalistic clique gleefully paraded as proof of a return to the bad old days, each had the support of roughly half the public, with only a about a quarter opposed. Seventy-one per cent wanted zero hours contracts banned. Sixty-three percent supported the radical idea of requiring any company bidding for public contracts to adopt a maximum pay ratio of 20:1 between their highest and lowest paid staff. Taxing the rich, for so long taboo in British politics, turned out to be a big hit. Sixty-five per cent liked the idea of raising the income tax of those earning over £80,000, including an absolute majority of Tory voters. And so it continued, with policy after policy attracting vast support.[9]

The leaker "miscalculated badly," says one of Corbyn's top team. "It was a torturous 24 hours but it makes me smile, because that's what you call karma. You release that for no other reason than you want to cause trouble... and as a consequence we're positioned further to the left as a party than we would otherwise have been. I'm thrilled. I would like to shake the hand of the person that leaked it."

What emerged from the Clause V meeting was a Swiss army knife of a manifesto, containing policies fashioned for all sections of the population: ending tuition fees for the young; lifting the pay cap for public sector workers; protecting the pension triple lock for older people; requiring equal pay audits from big companies to close the pay gap afflicting women and Black and Asian workers; scrapping the hated work capability assessments for those with disabilities. But the whole was more than the sum of its parts. Taken together it painted a picture of how society could be organised on fundamentally different lines. Its distinctive themes were collectivism and universalism, after years of individualism and means-tested entitlements.

This was Corbyn's vision—an evolution of the platforms set out in his 2015 and 2016 leadership campaigns. The legacy of the policy papers thrown together in a rush by Andrew Fisher in the summer of 2015 was impossible to miss in the new prospectus by the same author—a National Education Service, universal free childcare, rent controls, a National Investment Bank and more. "It was very similar, with more development, more detail," says an advisor to the leader.

The '10 pledges' upon which Corbyn stood in the 2016 leadership contest provided an important source of legitimacy. "The 10 pledges were endorsed by the NEC and went through conference unanimously in 2016, not because every delegate believed in every one of them but because Jeremy had just won 62 per cent of the vote and they had to accept that was a mandate," says the advisor. "We had those as a base. They were party policy, so you could shape the manifesto around that agenda."

It was this consistent direction, developed over two years and unwittingly cemented by an unsuccessful coup, that gave the manifesto its coherence. Extracted from the context of British politics the programme could be described as social democratic rather than socialist, and in some respects quite mild. But as a live political intervention it represented a radical break from Thatcherite orthodoxy.

One feature of the 2015 experience that did not recur in 2017 was the emphasis on participative policy making. In his first 20 months in charge Corbyn had been unable to do much to democratise the party without a majority on the NEC or at conference. The National Policy Forum remained unreformed. Although a last-minute electronic survey of the membership was carried out to inform the manifesto, it was "incredibly limited—but what can you do when there's a snap election?" While Fisher and his small policy team undertook the drafting in close collaboration with the shadow cabinet and the unions, and despite the formality of the Clause V meeting, the 2017 programme was no more democratic in its construction than its predecessors.

In fact, the early election gave the Leader's Office even more leeway than usual. "The National Policy Forum is designed to be this process that builds over a five-year period towards writing a manifesto," says the advisor. "It doesn't have a system in place if there's a snap election. We had more of a free hand in some ways than we would otherwise have had."

Yet there were areas where the manifesto diverged substantially from Corbyn's leadership campaigns. The most obvious was the retention of Trident nuclear weapons. "Trident is Labour Party policy," the advisor says. "We were able to push a lot of things into the manifesto without too much dissent. We couldn't change Labour Party policy. We haven't got a majority at conference on Trident because of where the unions [representing workers in the defence sector] are. It's a compromise to the extent that it's not Jeremy's view but it's not like we had a negotiation and had to back down, that's just where party policy is." Similarly, it was party policy to comply with the NATO requirement to spend 2 per cent of GDP on defence.

The manifesto position on Brexit was the product of a long process of evolution in the shadow cabinet. Many left wing party members saw the line on immigration—"Freedom of movement will end when we leave the European Union"—as a serious defeat.[10] For months shadow Brexit secretary Keir Starmer and shadow home secretary Diane Abbott had been saying different things on the issue in public, with the latter reluctant to give up on free movement.[11] It seemed Abbott had lost the battle. But the line left open possibilities. "The position we ended up with was just saying: 'Look, if you come out of the European Union then you lose free movement,'" recalls the advisor. "It's not to say you couldn't negotiate something that had an element of free movement or preferential treatment for European citizens."

In the 2015 general election Labour supported freedom of movement while giving the impression it would be tough on immigration; in 2017 Labour's statement that freedom of movement would end was accompanied by some of the most positive language about migrants seen from a major party.[12] "Labour values the economic and social contributions of immigrants," the manifesto said. "We will not denigrate those workers... We will not cut public services and pretend the cuts are a consequence of immigration." Labour's criteria in Brexit negotiations would be the inverse of the Conservatives': "Our priorities favour growth, jobs and prosperity. We make no apologies for putting these aims before bogus immigration targets."[13]

Given the importance of the Welfare Bill controversy to Corbyn's rise to the leadership in 2015, the most surprising section of the manifesto was on social security. While promising to end "the worst excesses of the Conservative government's changes" such as the bedroom tax and the sanctions regime, there was no commitment to reverse all of the welfare cuts, something the media and think tanks were quick to notice.[14] According to the advisor this "wasn't a compromise" but rather a failure on the part of the policy team to communicate their intentions. They believed they could make substantial savings in welfare spending through wider measures on the labour market and housing, which would reduce the extent to which the state had to subsidise low-paying employers and private landlords. That money could be "recycled" in the welfare budget. But such a sweeping transformation was impossible to cost in a hurry. "What we didn't want to do was say we're going to reverse everything with the costs attached and not be able to bank the savings," explains the advisor. "We were trying to find a way of saying 'Look, we can restructure this and it'll all be alright,' without making too explicit a commitment on it. We didn't articulate that well. That was the only bit of the manifesto that was probably a bit of a mess."

Shortcomings were inevitable—the manifesto was written in just three and a half weeks. Remarkably, it was nevertheless the first Labour manifesto in living memory to be sent to the printers on time—a fitting repudiation of the charge of incompetence levelled against the Leader's Office and a proud achievement for Fisher.[15] The party could be thankful that he had survived an attempt by MPs Caroline Flint and Siobhain McDonagh to have him expelled in 2015.[16]

Titled 'For the Many, Not the Few,' the manifesto was officially launched on 16 May in the bright and cavernous atrium of Bradford University—which guaranteed a huge cheer when Corbyn announced that Labour would scrap tuition fees. Rather than detracting from the occasion, the fact that everyone already knew most of what was in the prospectus seemed to generate heightened interest. The leak had enabled Labour to present its proposals twice in consecutive weeks, with extensive coverage during the days in between. Parties work hard to ensure their manifesto launch is not just a news story but an event; Labour's had gone beyond that—it was a saga. A simple link to the finished document even went viral on Facebook.[17] The manifesto received 5 million hits on the Labour Party website during the election.[18] Seldom, if ever, can a manifesto have attracted such attention.

The manifesto had a powerful impact on the Labour Party membership. At canvassing sessions across the country vociferous critics of the leader could be heard saying that it encapsulated everything they believed in. There was a palpable sense of pride in the programme. Here were policies members could promote with feeling. The effect was to mobilise the membership and galvanise campaigning activity.

But not everyone was impressed. The usual brigade of fearless Labour MPs was on hand to provide anonymous briefings to the press, branding the manifesto "childish," "an expensive wish list," and "like a 10-year-old's letter to Santa Claus." "Those of us who are realistic about this know we can't stand on the manifesto that has been produced by the party so we won't mention it on leaflets and on the doorstep," said one heroic figure. "You could promise unicorns for everyone, none of this is going to happen," declared another political colossus. "It's a ludicrous document, it won't serve Labour MPs well on the doorstep and the public have largely stopped listening and taking us seriously anyway."[19]

Savvier critics had a better attack line, enthusing that the policies were very popular and would do well—if it were not for the leader. "Are they fucking stupid?" asks one of Corbyn's lieutenants in response. "We would never have had that manifesto without Jeremy. Never in a million years. I don't know anybody else who could have created the circumstances that led to that manifesto."

If the Conservatives were hoping their offering would generate the same level of interest as Labour's then they should have been careful what they wished for. Universally regarded as a disaster in hindsight, the 'manifesto of misery,' as it was dubbed on social media, mimicked the Blairite propensity to take the core vote for granted.[20] In a fit of hubris the Tories decided to attack the home-owning pensioners who made up their base by announcing that their houses would be used to pay for their social care after they died, their pensions would no longer rise by at least 2.5 per cent each year, and their winter fuel allowance would be means-tested with no hint at what level.

Not content to stop there, the Conservatives set about dismantling their reputation as a low-tax party by refusing to rule out income tax and national insurance rises. (In an extraordinary act of political ineptitude, defence secretary Michael Fallon later did rule out income tax rises—but only for high earners!)[21] And to complete the job the Tories went out of their way to reclaim the 'nasty party' tag by suggesting fox hunting could be legalised. That policy enjoyed tremendous 'cut through' with the public—which was unfortunate for the Conservatives as 78 per cent opposed it.[22] Barely mentioned in the traditional media but ubiquitous on social media (people shared more stories about fox hunting than Brexit on Facebook), this was the kind of issue that motivated a layer of the population to vote specifically against the Tories.[23] Similarly, the plan to scrap free school lunches for infants came across as callous—even before it emerged that the proposed replacement, free breakfasts, had been budgeted at 6.8p per meal. "How many Cornflakes does six point eight pence buy you Karen?" shadow trade secretary Barry Gardiner asked Conservative minister Karen Bradley during a TV appearance, with a look of intense seriousness. "Not very many."[24]

If there was any discernible political strategy to the Tory manifesto beyond a desire to self-harm, it was to win working class voters in traditional Labour areas that had voted Leave in the referendum. The venue for the launch on 18 May signalled as much—a gloomy former mill in the marginal constituency of Halifax (where Labour subsequently increased its majority from 428 votes to 5,376). But the actual policies targeted at workers were patronising. One measure, proudly briefed in advance of the manifesto, was to give workers the right to take a year off—unpaid—to care for sick relatives.[25] It was not clear if it had occurred to the manifesto drafters that workers might not be able to afford a year without pay, and might not regard the state offloading its responsibilities onto them as an act of beneficence.

Although May overtly positioned herself as the Brexit champion, she appeared to regard working class Leave voters as having been motivated solely by immigration and patriotism. There was no recognition that many had voted believing Brexit would mean higher public spending—£350 million a week for the NHS—and so there was nothing for them in the manifesto. There would be no retreat from austerity. "They were going to carry on cutting corporation tax down to 17 per cent and at the same time they were saying 'There's no money for this, no money for that,'" recalls Corbyn's advisor. "That really resonated." A general sense of arrogance was compounded by the failure to publish costings for the proposals, as Labour had done by the time of its official launch. This gave Labour spokespeople a ready retort to any Tory attacks on their numbers. While the Institute for Fiscal Studies disputed some of the assumptions behind Labour's figures, at least the party had provided them.

The flagship policy of the Tory manifesto, their plan to tackle the social care crisis by making anyone with assets over £100,000—the vast majority of home owners—pay an unlimited amount for their own care, was immediately branded a "tax on dementia" by Corbyn in his response to the launch of the document on 18 May.[26] As soon as the 'dementia tax' label stuck, the policy was finished. The *Daily Mail*'s valiant attempt to put a positive spin on it with the front-page headline "AT LAST, A PM NOT AFRAID TO BE HONEST WITH YOU" could not quell a tsunami of criticism from natural conservatives. They found themselves in an unusual alliance with shadow chancellor John McDonnell, afforded a rare chance to display his passionate belief in the inviolability of Tory voters' property rights.[27] Not only was the policy electorally inexplicable, it had barely been thought out. "It was really amateur," says a member of Labour's policy team. "There was an immense amount of complacency there."

After a weekend of political pain, on Monday 22 May the prime minister took the fateful decision to U-turn on the policy. It was simply unprecedented for a major political party to row back on a manifesto pledge *before* an election—let alone on a flagship policy. The Labour campaign team could scarcely believe it: "We were talking in the office saying, 'Has anyone ever done this?'"

Worse still, it was not even a proper U-turn. Under hostile questioning from journalists, a rattled May bellowed: "Nothing has changed! Nothing has changed!" Apparently the PM *was* afraid to be honest—everyone could see the policy had changed. There would now be a maximum amount any individual would have to pay for social care. But as May refused to say at what level this cap would be set the Tories were left with the worst of all worlds: defending a discredited policy they had half-abandoned, without offering reassurance to those who saw it as a threat to all their worldly possessions.

May had been found out, and at the worst possible time. Reflective Tories might have rued the easy ride she had received from a pliant media since inheriting the top job. "A key aspect of the campaign that we knew going into the election was that Theresa May is very bad in a crisis situation," says a Leader's Office source. "That was the experience from the whole Muslim ban fiasco [when President Trump issued a controversial decree shortly after May had visited the White House in January 2017], where they couldn't get ahead of the story and they looked terrible. Whereas we're very good in a crisis because we'd had almost two years of perpetual assault."

At a stroke, the contrived image of May as a "strong and stable" leader was in tatters, the slogan a national joke. She was now the "weak and wobbly" prime minister. The danger of attempting to build a personality cult without a personality was revealed. May's media appearances became excruciating ordeals—her set-piece interview with the BBC's Andrew Neil, falling with unfortunate timing on the evening of the U-turn, was so lamentable that not even the Tory press bothered to dress it up.[28]

The publication of the manifestos had been a triumph for Labour and an unparalleled disaster for the Conservatives. Labour edged up to 34 per cent in the polls after their launch while the Tories would never again hit the 49 per cent they recorded on the eve of theirs. A survey revealed that Labour's ideas enjoyed greater recognition from the public with one exception—more people had heard of the dementia tax than any other policy.[29]

. . . . .

There were already 3,000 people gathered by the time the Labour battle bus pulled up outside the Brudenell Social Club in Leeds. News that Jeremy Corbyn would address an event in the venue had gone out just the previous day, but so many had turned up after word spread on Facebook that organisers had to switch the rally to the car park. That space was quickly filled by the swelling crowd, which spilled over into Queens Road—causing the police to close it to traffic. A grassy bank by the side of the street was soon lined with people, lending the place the feel of an amphitheatre. Some stood on the roof of a building to catch a better view. Others perched in trees. All chanted Corbyn's name as the Labour leader got off the bus and made his way through the throng to deliver a speech stood on a bench, surrounded on all sides by people.

It was 15 May 2017, the day before the official launch of Labour's manifesto but after the leak that had created such excitement. The crowd was young—the Hyde Park area in the constituency of Leeds North West was popular with students. Corbyn began by asking all those who were registered to vote to put up their hands. "If you know somebody who isn't registered, get them registered," he said. The Electoral Commission would later report that Leeds North West was one of three constituencies where the electorate increased in size by over 15 per cent between December 2016 and the election (not just because Corbyn held a rally there, of course, but it can only have helped).[30] Labour went on to take the seat from the Liberal Democrats.

After running through Labour's policies on health, education and housing, Corbyn reflected on an emerging gulf between the way the election was being portrayed and what he was experiencing. "This election campaign, it's like two stories," he said. "One is, from many of our national media, deeply cynical, a series of calculations... Then on the other side of it is an amazing sense of unity—look around you in this crowd today... There is nothing inevitable about this election." As he reached the finale of his speech, Corbyn turned to do a 360-degree sweep of the rally punctuated with the words "We. Can. Do. This. Thing. Together!" A roar went up. It looked like a scene from a movie.[31]

The "two stories" that Corbyn identified were indeed irreconcilable. In the press Labour was still cast as universally unpopular, constantly in 'meltdown,' and on course for certain annihilation. But out in the country the Labour campaign was taking off. The rally in Leeds, together with an event earlier the same day in the small town of Hebden Bridge that featured people standing in a river to watch Corbyn speak, recaptured the feel and excitement of the 2015 leadership campaign. This was visible proof of a resurgent movement. "No," the pundits said, Corbyn was merely "preaching to the choir"; the attendees represented a tiny fraction of the population; Michael Foot had addressed big crowds, too. Such arguments, usually advanced in the most contemptuous tone possible, reflected an odd determination not to understand the phenomenon. Rallies gave confidence and solidity to the movement. They fortified supporters and inspired them to go out and campaign. Footage and images of the crowds spread far and wide online and on TV—including on regional TV news—undercutting the dominant narrative in which Corbyn was an isolated figure. This was what it looked like when an electoral strategy was aimed at mobilising the base in order to reach new people.[32]

As in the 2015 and 2016 leadership contests, there was a symbiotic relationship between activity in the physical world and online. Social media was where this movement cohered; where ties of solidarity were forged, morale was boosted, and ideas were shared. Social media's utility for building a movement was probably its least discussed attribute—it was far more common for journalists to write about how it was replacing the press as a source of information. But it was by providing a space for the movement to grow that social media played its most important role in the general election. With a common aim and an apocalyptic sense of urgency, tens of thousands of individual pro-Labour social media users became a swarm sweeping through the digital landscape. They fought with political opponents and scrutinised the coverage from the mainstream media. By working collectively they were able to shift the political agenda to an extent never before seen in Britain.

Labour dominated the election on social media, but how that was achieved cannot be grasped unless it is understood that it did so as a movement, and not as a result of its official output, still less paid advertising. A roiling, pulsating, bubbling online community was constantly cooking up its own content, spitting out memes and videos, stirring together new slang terms and in-jokes. As the election progressed, the movement expanded beyond anything experienced in the leadership contests of the previous summers. But at its core was the same band of Corbyn supporters—toughened by the intra-party battle, now fighting for the party as a whole.

This group contained within it a spontaneous division of labour. This could be seen clearly on Twitter, a battlefield of conflicting narratives where political momentum could be won or lost. There were the educators, like Dr Éoin Clarke (@ToryFibs)—ranked as one of the most influential election-related accounts on Twitter by one analysis.[33] He used his vast reach to push out summaries of Labour's policies and rebut attacks from the Tories. There were the videographers, like 'EL4C' (Ealing Labour for Corbyn), which published punchy, witty videos made by filmmaker Simon Baker; and the clippers, like 'I was a JSA claimant,' who grabbed useful snippets from TV to ensure they were widely seen on social media; and the performers, like Mark McGowan, the 'Artist Taxi Driver,' with his hilarious video rants. There were the memers, such as Rachael Swindon, who had a talent for homemade graphics with blunt messages, and 'The Agitator,' with sharp Photoshop skills. There were the in-house commentators, like Aaron Bastani and Liam Young, framing the arguments. There were the pugilists, like Matt Zarb-Cousin, cutting down the commentariat for fun. And there were the unofficial news outlets for the movement, like 'Jeremy Corbyn for PM,' an evolution of the 'Jeremy Corbyn for Labour Leader' account, now run by activist Sarah Henney. What was remarkable was the extent to which these diverse talents—and many more besides—functioned as one body, with a high level of voluntary coordination.

On Facebook the pro-Corbyn movement was centred more around 'groups,' 'pages,' and networks of friends than individuals. Tens of thousands congregated in groups such as We Support Jeremy Corbyn and Labour Party Forum, sharing and discussing news in long, threaded conversations. Stories and posts would spin out from these groups and pages onto the timelines of individual Facebook users, to be seen by their friends and family who were not necessarily Labour voters. As a genuine network, Facebook was a far more powerful platform than Twitter for reaching the uncommitted.

The growth of a new school of left news sites, such as the *Skwawkbox*, the *Canary* and *Evolve Politics*, was enabled by this technological ability to reach vast audiences. The stories they produced were far more viral, on a per-article basis, than those of well-resourced, fully staffed newspapers.[34] One piece from the blog *Another Angry Voice*—"How many of Jeremy Corbyn's policies do you actually disagree with?"—was the most viral article of the whole election, attracting over a million hits in three days.[35] The success of these emerging left media outlets, along with others like *Novara* producing quality content of a more analytical bent, buttressed the confidence of the movement.

Unsurprisingly, 'opinion formers' in the press recoiled in horror at this challenge to their monopoly. It was common to hear them blame social media for the interruption to normal service. It was true that a significant function of social media was as an alternative means of curating information, and that this weakened the influence of press barons and editors. But the reason why the new left news outlets were such a runaway success was not primarily because of the technology, but because of the presence of a ready movement eager to promote coverage that reflected its worldview. New media and the movement were mutually reinforcing.

Partly because of the way Facebook's algorithm worked, stories sank like a stone without a critical mass of people willing to share them—as the right found out. Analysis by *BuzzFeed* showed that "people on Facebook only want to share pro-Corbyn, anti-Tory news stories."[36]

Yet much of the journalistic profession dismissed pro-Corbyn social media as just an echo chamber, full of conversations between people who already agreed with each other. The political implications were endlessly hammered home: social media might be useful for winning a Labour leadership contest decided by like-minded political activists, but it was no use in a general election—in fact, it was counterproductive. "Labour's dangerous safe space," wrote the *Economist*, "gives activists a skewed impression of what most voters think."[37] There was an entire genre of commentary like this, all of which turned out to be completely wrong. What it described as an echo chamber was in fact the sound of an online movement in motion—a force capable of pushing an alternative perspective of the world onto millions of timelines. It was not an echo chamber; it was an amplifier.

The example of *Double Down News* illustrates the point. When Theresa May called the election, it did not exist. By polling day, half of Facebook users in the UK had seen one of its posts.[38] The outlet was set up as a simple Facebook page to publish a select number of videos by guests speaking direct to camera, well filmed with slick editing. "Our whole aim was to make politics accessible and to not preach to the converted," says Bobby, one of the founders of *Double Down News*. Its very first video, posted on 19 May, was a four-and-a-half minute monologue by the rapper Lowkey explaining why he was supporting Corbyn. It went viral, accruing 4 million views. Shared initially by the Corbyn-supporting crowd and Lowkey's fans, it soon took on a life of its own. "The best thing about Facebook, why it's the best place for reaching people, is that's where everyday Joes are," Bobby says. "People were tagging their friends in the comments. People were tagging 10 of their friends. It went organically by people saying to each other 'I relate to this.'" *Double Down News'* second video, featuring the comic Guz Khan talking about terrorism in the wake of the Manchester attack, did even better, exceeding 8 million views.

The Lowkey video was significant because, unlike a generic political endorsement from a celebrity, it came from someone with genuine influence with a particular community. The video fed into an extraordinary, spontaneous cultural phenomenon that was taking off on social media at the time: 'Grime4Corbyn.' Many of the biggest artists in the genre of grime—a British evolution of hip hop—including Stormzy, Novelist, AJ Tracey and Akala, announced their support for Corbyn on Twitter and Snapchat.[39] A grassroots campaign was set up, initially to get grime fans to register to vote.[40] #Grime4Corbyn soon became a top trend on Twitter. Corbyn was interviewed by grime star JME for *i-D* magazine. The video of them talking about the importance of voting was watched by 2 million on Facebook plus more on other platforms—a bigger audience than most political interviews get on TV.[41] Moreover, the people it reached were precisely those that the leadership's electoral strategy was aiming to win over—young people and BAME communities.

Grime4Corbyn became a movement within the movement. The combination of a 67-year-old veteran politician and Britain's edgiest underground music scene might have seemed incongruous, but for Bobby from *Double Down News* there was a "correlation between the rise of Corbyn and the rise of grime." Grime artists eschewed corporate record labels, instead releasing material themselves and promoting it on social media. "Ten or 20 years ago there couldn't have been a Corbyn, just like there couldn't have been a grime," Bobby says. "Corbyn has been able to do it just like grime. Use social, create value, put it out there and it will grow on its own terms without you having to compromise."

By mid-May Corbyn himself seemed to be going viral with young people. Somehow he was tapping into key cultural milieus. He managed to unite the music world, winning support from the indie and rock scenes as well as grime and featuring on the covers of *NME* and *Kerrang*. He was endorsed by a whole host of artists including Lily Allen, MIA and Rag N Bone Man. His love of football, together with Labour's policy of investing 5 per cent of the Premier League's TV income into the grassroots game, made a connection with sports fans. On FA Cup Final day Corbyn tweeted out memes and videos of football legends like Brian Clough talking about socialism, and conducted a relaxed interview with

Copa90, a young, fan-centred online football channel.[42] One of the most popular memes of the election had Corbyn's face photoshopped onto the body of former Newcastle United manager Kevin Keegan during his infamous rant declaring "I will love it if we beat them, love it."[43]

The memes were a defining feature of the social media election, bringing humour and creativity to politics and making the burgeoning movement look like an attractive thing to be a part of. A clip of Corbyn turning to look confidently into the camera, breaking the fourth wall, became ubiquitous whenever an opinion poll showed Labour gaining. An image of Corbyn in a white fur-style coat and tux in a supercar, taken from a sketch on comedy show *The Last Leg*, was endlessly repurposed with whatever witty caption fitted the moment. The Grime4Corbyn movement adopted a picture of the leader—who was never afraid to muck in—holding aloft a speaker so a crowd could better hear Rachael Maskell MP, although she was talking policy rather than spitting bars over sick beats. But in a widely-watched video from the entertainment website Joe.co.uk, Corbyn *was* spitting bars, his words about food banks, homelessness and corporate tax cuts clipped from an interview and somehow made to flow over Stormzy's song 'Shut Up,' with Corbyn's head superimposed onto the rapper's body.

Corbyn became a kind of folk hero. He was "the absolute boy." But this status only worked precisely because he was not a lad or a demagogue. There was a mildly ironic—but still admiring—undertone to it all. "corbyn ate a pringle tonight" was the matter-of-fact comment tweeted along with footage of the Labour leader taking a salt and vinegar crisp from a supporter, holding it up to a crowd and then eating it. The internet went wild. The tweet appeared on over a million timelines. "Hahaha!!! Just Watch this!!" posted the Artist Taxi Driver in response. "Jeremy Corbyn man of the people absolutely smashing it with a Pringle 'Crisp'." Another Twitter user revealed she had "honestly never related to anything so much in my life." The drama of the incident moved the *Radio Times* to ask: "Could Jeremy Corbyn eating a Pringle be the turning point in the election?"[44]

Corbyn's idiosyncrasies, which any spin doctor might have considered weaknesses, were embraced by the movement and transformed into strengths. "For once young people could look and see there's a dude who in every way is different from them, but wow, he's like them as well," says Bobby. "He makes jam but he's cool in his own way. Jeremy's cool because he's himself." The traditional press was still labouring under the misapprehension that everybody hated Corbyn, while in the other of the "two stories" of the election an increasingly large number of people felt deep affection for him.

It was into this living, unwieldy, spontaneous online movement that Corbyn, the Labour Party and Momentum posted their official output. It was not, as some journalists seemed to imagine, that all the excitement was conjured by the messages put out from the centre. This error betrayed a tendency to confuse social media with a simple broadcast medium, when what mattered was how messages from official channels interacted with wider online networks. For example, the Facebook and Twitter accounts of May and the Conservative Party spewed out invective against Corbyn, Diane Abbott and Labour, but received relatively few shares and retweets because they were shouting into a void—there was no substantial online congregation of Conservatives to pick up and amplify their content.[45] But as a result of being part of a movement at home on social media, Corbyn's personal accounts were by a wide margin the most influential of the election.[46] Every Facebook post, tweet or Snapchat update published by the Labour leader had vast reach. The further the posts travelled, the more new people were brought into the fold, and the better future posts did as a result. On both Twitter and Facebook Corbyn increased his number of subscribers from around 800,000 to 1.2 million during the campaign (despite being the prime minister, May lagged far behind, with 420,000 likes on Facebook and 350,000 followers on Twitter).[47]

Some of Corbyn's greatest online successes came with real-time campaign interventions, especially those involving humour or audacity. When May took part in a Facebook Live Q & A hosted by Robert Peston on 15 May, Corbyn was one of the viewers to post a question from his Facebook account. "Now, perhaps surprisingly, I've got a question in from Jeremy Corbyn of Islington," Peston announced. "Hello Theresa May, as prime minister you have served your elite friends by giving them tax cuts while wages have stagnated, house building is at its lowest since the 1920s, there are 20,000 fewer police on our streets since 2010, and the NHS is in crisis. Do you not think the British people deserve to see us debate live and on TV?" The stunt was devastatingly effective, not only because of its cheekiness, but because Corbyn's social media team quickly followed it up by posting their own video of the encounter on social media. The clip delighted Labour supporters, was shared in their orbit, quickly reached escape velocity and rocketed out into wider cyberspace. It attracted 4.5 million views.[48] A few days later Ben Sellers, a member of the team who helped execute the manoeuvre, was having his hair cut in Durham by a hairdresser who said she was sick of the election because "they all talk crap," but then added: "I tell you what was brilliant though, when Jeremy Corden [sic] surprised that Theresa with his tweets—when she was on live. Not many politicians would do that. I loved that!"

The power of videos shared on social media was something the leadership learned from the Bernie Sanders campaign in the US. Over the course of the general election, 20 of the films published by Corbyn's accounts exceeded a million views. These ranged from simple clips of news coverage, to messages spoken direct to camera by Corbyn, to smartly edited fly-on-the-wall footage from events and rallies, to high quality emotive films. Challenging May to a TV debate was a sure-fire winner. As well as the Facebook Live stunt, four more videos on that theme notched up 2 million views each. In the final week of the campaign, Corbyn's accumulated Facebook videos received 22 million views.[49]

With such a huge audience Corbyn's personal accounts were an invaluable campaigning tool. The leader's social media team saw their primary purpose as explaining Labour's policies in simple, accessible language—to make an emotional connection. The fact that it was Corbyn speaking (even though, at the risk of ruining the magic, not all the posts were drafted by him) humanised sometimes dry issues. "If you are a pensioner, I have this message for you," began one Facebook post in which Corbyn promised to protect the pension 'triple lock' and the winter fuel allowance. "I pledge these things not as an act of generosity, but because you have paid into the system all your life, and this is no more than you deserve. I pledge these things because Labour stands for the many, not the few."[50]

The numbers reached by Corbyn's missives speak for themselves. A post stating "We've just looked through Theresa May and the Conservatives' Facebook and Twitter pages, and they have not put out a single message encouraging people to register to vote," reached 5 million people on Facebook and was seen 3.7 million times on Twitter.[51] Another, declaring that "Foxhunting is barbarous," reached 3 million on Facebook, as did a post using the prevalence of Tory donors in the *Sunday Times* Rich List to reinforce Labour's message on inequality.[52] Corbyn also made good use of Snapchat, a newer social network with younger users, where he had 100,000 friends. The deadpan style of his behind-the-scenes campaign-trail snaps played to his quirky image.

Whereas Corbyn's personal online team worked on the assumption that the leader and the membership were Labour's greatest assets on social media, the party's official output suggested it took a different view. As a project of Southside, the Labour Party's social media presence kept its distance from the pro-Corbyn online movement, thereby restricting its own reach. Its content rarely used footage of rallies, or of members talking about issues, or even of Corbyn himself. Initially it featured hardly any humans at all—posts were dominated by bland graphics. At an early stage of the campaign, Corbyn's team decided they needed to produce their own material in lieu of the party's efforts, despite their vastly smaller budget. In fairness, there were constraints on what the party's official accounts could achieve—they could never match Corbyn for personal engagement, or be as daring as independent groups. And the quality of the Labour Party's output did get noticeably better as the campaign progressed. The party's number of 'likes' on Facebook increased by 75 per cent (with a spike around the manifesto launch) and in the later stages it was reaching a significant audience.[53]

But the main focus of Southside's digital operation was social media advertising. Having been massively outspent by the Conservatives in 2015, Labour poured £1.2 million into this new science. Southside was proud of the sophistication of its methods, which included using information gleaned from canvassing data to target the Facebook profiles of specific voters in specific seats with messages on specific issues.[54] At the very end of the campaign

Labour invested heavily in Snapchat advertising to reach younger voters with "staggering" results, according to Labour's co-campaign coordinator Andrew Gwynne: 7.3 million of Snapchat's 12 million UK users saw an "I'm voting Labour" image filter.[55]

During and after the election there was a deluge of press reports ascribing critical importance the use of "dark" and "targeted" online advertising by the parties, as if social media could be conquered by conspiratorial cunning backed up by million-pound budgets.[56] It is not easy to evaluate how effective these methods really were. The Conservatives reportedly spent £1.2 million on negative online ads attacking the Labour leadership.[57] These surely helped to propagate smears about the IRA and other issues, although most of the British press was on hand to do that for free. But they patently failed to win over many younger voters, the heaviest users of social media. While online advertising undoubtedly had an impact, it was not how the battle was won. Big spending was no substitute for a legion of committed supporters eager to spread the word. As Bobby from *Double Down News* explains, "Targeting an ad doesn't mean people are going to share it, like it, talk about it. It just means there's an annoying video in their timeline that they want to get past."

One Tory attack video, a montage of clips of Corbyn speaking about NATO and the IRA, his words stripped from their context, was widely hyped as "the most-viewed online campaign advert in British political history."[58] Paid promotion helped it achieve 6.6 million views on Facebook in two weeks. But Momentum's biggest video, a spoof Tory ad depicting a Conservative-voting dad telling his young daughter that he hated her, raced to 5.4 million views in just two days—and at minimal cost.[59] As a non-party organisation, Momentum could afford to be edgier in what it published. It concentrated heavily on video as the best way of communicating its message, and heavily on Facebook as the best way of disseminating it. But it owed its success to the amplifying effect of the wider movement that it was a part of.

According to one Labour campaign source talking to *BuzzFeed*, content shared "organically"—without paid promotion—could "mobilise people who are engaged with what you're doing, but you can only guarantee the people who need to see your stuff are reached through paid advertising."[60] Momentum's experience suggested otherwise. Ninety-eight per cent of its reach during the election came as a result of organic sharing; the organisation spent less than £2,000 on Facebook advertising in total. Yet in the final week of the election, 9.8 million UK Facebook users viewed a Momentum video—including 28 per cent of users in Cardiff, 27 per cent in Plymouth and 23 per cent in Derby, all areas with marginal seats. While some of its films were aimed specifically at activists to get them campaigning, the most prominent videos were consciously "designed to go beyond left-wingers to have mass reach," according to Joe Todd, Momentum's communications officer. Facebook statistics show how successful the strategy was: of the millions of Facebook users who watched a Momentum video in the final week of the campaign, only 5.3 per cent were subscribers to Corbyn's own page. "These people are more likely to follow 'Maximum Respect for the British Armed Forces and the RBL,' 'Ant and Dec' and 'Match of the Day' than Jeremy Corbyn, the Labour Party or Momentum," the organisation said. So much for the echo chamber.[61]

· · · · ·

Each Sunday a tight group of MPs and advisors would meet privately to discuss election strategy. Labour's two campaign coordinators Andrew Gwynne and Ian Lavery would be present. The coordinator role had been split in two to create a division of labour: Lavery wrestled with the party machine while Gwynne oversaw campaigning. John McDonnell and Jon Trickett would be in the room (Jeremy Corbyn was usually on the road somewhere), as would the trio of executive directors: Andrew Fisher, Seumas Milne, and Karie Murphy.

After the dissolution of parliament at the start of May 2017, the Leader's Office staff had to move out of their suite on the parliamentary estate and into the enemy territory of Southside. When they got there they found that no one was working on mobilising each of the voter groups the leadership wanted to appeal to—young people, BAME people, disabled people, women. So at one Sunday meeting it was decided to bring over to Southside a team of mainly young, left, shadow ministerial political advisors and set them to work on specific projects such as voter registration, cultural outreach, and mini-manifesto launches for different groups. But even this was only achieved after a fight with party bosses. "They wanted to pay them to sit at home," says a high-ranking source in the Leader's Office. "It was our campaign, be under no illusion. Southside did not contribute any of the vigour, imagination, flair, dynamism."

In its look and feel, the campaign was far from the amateur left wing production that cynics expected. The quality of some of Labour's videos was outstanding. It helped having a Palme d'Or-winning director in Ken Loach to make election broadcasts. The presence of actors, comedians and bands like Maxine Peake, Julie Hesmondhalgh, Steve Coogan, Clean Bandit, Wolf Alice, and Reverend and the Makers created a stark contrast with Theresa May's dour, joyless events. "Having the Farm play at Jeremy's gigs and not having innocuous piano music," recalls Murphy, "that was one of the first times it dawned on me: we're running this now. It was invigorating. In the local elections we were being told what to do because we didn't really know. By the time it came to the general we were learning all the time."

Labour HQ never bought in to the leadership's approach. According to a Corbyn aide, at a daily 7 a.m. meeting of senior officials one of the party's top brass exclaimed: "This voter registration is a fucking farce! What's the point? By the time of the election universities will have broken up." While not every member of staff was as hostile, many undertook small acts of resistance—"little things where they just hold you up," recalls one of those working in Southside, such as when Loach supplied some footage and it went missing for a week.

"We knew we were getting blocked," says a Leader's Office source. "We knew there were decisions being taken that they were ignoring." Feeling they needed assistance, the leader's team turned to Len McCluskey. "They had been battling through this horrible period and were beginning to pull it together but had to constantly fight in the trenches," says McCluskey. "All of a sudden, bang! There's a general election. None of them had run a general election before. So they asked, 'Is there any chance of somebody coming to help us?'" McCluskey seconded his chief of staff at Unite, Andrew Murray, to work on the campaign from 14 May, despite the inevitable headlines provoked by his recent membership of the Communist Party. "Karie had been like Boudicca fighting—and gradually winning the respect of—Southside," McCluskey says. "Andrew Murray was able to pull things together in a less confrontational fashion." Murphy agrees that Murray's role was "to ensure that the relationships between both sides merged... He was able to troubleshoot for us, break down some barriers and get things moving."

Almost as soon as Murray arrived, McCluskey caused some difficulties by saying in an interview that if Labour could hold 200 seats it would constitute a "successful campaign."[62] The press and Labour MPs leapt on the comments as evidence that the Unite general secretary was "lowering the bar" on behalf of the leadership.[63] In fact, the Leader's Office had nothing to do with McCluskey's intervention; his concern was to manage expectations within the trade union movement. But his words were, he admits, "ill judged," not only because they provoked negative headlines on the day of Labour's manifesto launch, but also because some inferred that Unite was backing away from Corbyn by setting him a target he was not expected to meet.[64]

The truth was that McCluskey was "not optimistic at all" about Labour's chances. "I thought we were going to be in some difficulties," he says. His job, as he saw it, was to prepare for the aftermath of a likely election defeat in order to "to protect the left project." Behind the scenes he was working to persuade the leaders of Unison and the GMB to "support a position where Jeremy wasn't forced to resign immediately. He'd have six months, nine months, in the hope that we'd be able to get another candidate." He was "deeply in conversation with John McDonnell about all of this." Even as Labour's position in the polls improved, McCluskey remembers, "I pinched myself. Other people can float away; I've got to concentrate on 9 June... We've got to buy Jeremy some time."

McCluskey's commitment to the "left project" was evidenced by the £4 million Unite ploughed into the campaign—far more than was contributed by other unions, which said their coffers were still empty after the 2015 general election. Unite offered loans to enable them to give more, but there were no takers.

Nevertheless, Murphy insists, in the heat of the general election "a new relationship with the unions was born," helped by the presence in the leadership team of Lavery, a former president of the NUM. Labour knew it would be at a massive financial disadvantage to the Conservative Party. The Electoral Commission later revealed that the Tories received £25 million from wealthy individuals and private companies in the second quarter of 2017—more than was raised by all the other political parties combined.[65] Anticipating a shortfall, Murphy appealed to TULO, the body bringing together affiliated unions, saying, "We have dismissed high value donors, they will no longer buy patronage in this party. This is your party, it is a trade union party, and you had better fund it if we are to win."

Murphy says the party was "overwhelmed with union support." In addition to Unite's £4 million, which "made it all possible," the CWU, which gave £1 million, was "unbelievable" and "the smaller affiliates were solid behind us." The GMB and Unison donated £1.25 million and £900,000 respectively, and even if their leaderships "perhaps had a Plan B" in mind for after the election, "their members were solid." USDAW committed £400,000.[66] In all, trade unions gave £8.2 million of the £9.5 million Labour took in large donations.[67] And it was not all about money—unions also contributed to campaigning, urging their members to get involved and to vote.

Labour did have other sources of funding. Subs from the enlarged membership were a boon. Gwynne has praised the "patient marshalling of Labour's finances" by party HQ and the NEC, which meant that "for the first time ever, we were able to draw on significant financial reserves at the beginning of the campaign, allowing us to get off to a flying start."[68] The £25 registered supporters who collectively paid over £3 million to vote in the 2016 leadership contest might also take some credit. According to an aide to Corbyn, "The party had £3.5 million and it was spent early doors, allocated in the first two weeks."

Although Labour did not have the millionaire donors and corporate backers of the New Labour era, it could rely on hundreds of thousands of individual contributors forking out around £20 each. During the campaign the party raised over £5 million in small donations, including nearly half a million on 1 June in what Labour called "the biggest day of online fundraising British politics has ever seen."[69] This was testament to the enthusiasm generated by Labour's programme, but Corbyn's advisors praise Southside for the way it was executed.

The Leader's Office was much less impressed with how Labour HQ allocated the resources it had. As the polls turned, the party machine resisted recalibration. A list of constituencies produced a few weeks out from election day, its contents not intended for public consumption, provides a fascinating glimpse into Southside's thinking. Certain seats were earmarked for additional spending on social media and direct mailings—invaluable assets to any local campaign. The collapse of the UKIP vote was by this stage causing anxiety. For each constituency on the list, UKIP's 2015 result was recorded, as well as whether the party was standing a candidate in 2017—it was feared its supporters could transfer wholesale to the Conservatives if there was no UKIP option on the ballot.

The list was ordered by size of majority: at the top was Labour's safest seat, Liverpool Walton. The party hardly needed to pour in money there, and so the "social media," "wide DM" and "target DM" columns were marked "NO." The same was true for the other constituencies at the safer end of the scale—with a few intriguing exceptions. One stood out in particular: Wallasey, the 39th safest seat, represented by Angela Eagle. Unlike all the constituencies above it on the list and the next 19 below, Wallasey was marked "YES" for all three types of additional help. Despite Eagle enjoying a bumper majority of over 16,000, the seat was categorised as "Looking marginal." Yet the UKIP vote had been just 5,000 in 2015, less than in many comparable constituencies, and Paul Nuttall's party was standing a candidate again, making it less likely that the second-placed Conservatives would inherit all of their voters.

The next safest seat set to receive all three forms of support because it was "looking marginal" was Barnsley Central (majority: 12,435), the constituency of Dan Jarvis, sometimes talked of as a challenger for the leadership. Corbyn-critics Kevan Jones, Bridget Phillipson and another leadership hopeful, Yvette Cooper, came next (all had majorities of over 12,000). Further down the list, as the majorities became tighter, many more candidates were earmarked for extra resources—even some who were not planning to oust the leader. But of those with the larger cushions, most were well-known sceptics, including Rachel Reeves, Tom Watson and Chris Bryant.

If it was assumed that Labour was going to do very badly on polling day, an argument could be made that most of these seats were under threat. The trouble was there were many more candidates, apparently in similar or more parlous situations, who were not granted additional support. Stoke-on-Trent South, with a 2,500 Labour majority but a UKIP vote of over 8,000 and no UKIP candidate standing, was not categorised as "Looking marginal," but merely as "Watching eye—social only," meaning it would receive social media help but not direct mailings. It went on to become one of only five seats that Labour lost on 8 June, the Tories taking it by 663 votes. It was the same story for Walsall North, marked "Watching eye—social only," and subsequently lost.

Why the disparities? There may have been particular local circumstances. Angela Eagle, for example, had a strained relationship with her local party, which remained suspended since the coup. Perhaps it was feared that members would not campaign for her. In some seats particularly bad canvass returns might have raised an alarm. An alternative explanation is that the candidates who were able to secure resources were those skilled at navigating the party machine, who enjoyed the best relationships with decision-makers, or had the most clout. A Leader's Office source suspects, although cannot prove, that some decisions were driven by a political affinity between the candidates and the staff at the top of the bureaucracy—who were supposed to be neutral party 'civil servants,' and strictly not factional operators.

It is likely that varying combinations of these motivations were at play. Neither of the candidates denied full support and then defeated in Stoke-on-Trent South and Walsall North were Corbyn supporters, suggesting they were not selected for political punishment. But other choices appear difficult to explain without reference to politics. The case of Bridget Phillipson in Houghton and Sunderland South is fascinating because a comparison can be made with the neighbouring seat of Washington and Sunderland West, represented by Sharon Hodgson. The two constituencies were almost identical. Both had virtually the same Labour majority of 13,000, the same total Labour vote and the same Labour vote share. The UKIP vote in Phillipson's seat was 8,280; in Hodgson's 7,321; both had UKIP candidates standing; both had the same percentage of Leave voters. Both seats had identical demographics.[70] Both were represented by female MPs first elected in 2010. Both came under the same regional party structure. Yet Houghton and Sunderland South was deemed to be "Looking marginal" while Washington and Sunderland West was not considered at risk—not even enough to be kept under a "watching eye." Phillipson, who attacked Corbyn in the venomous PLP meeting of 27 June 2016, was singled out for extra resources. Hodgson, a shadow minister who resigned in the coup but returned to the frontbench after Corbyn's re-election, was not.

When the Leader's Office learned that Southside was channelling funds to hostile MPs in safe seats, a member of Corbyn's team sought a meeting with one of the party's most senior staffers: "I said, 'Don't spend one fucking penny on these people.' He said, 'You write me a list of who you don't want me spending money on.' I said, 'What, so you can put it in the *Times*?'"

The Leader's Office did manage to redirect some resources, but "only when we demanded it was changed," according to the aide. For example, Chris Williamson, the left wing candidate in the extremely marginal constituency of Derby North, "wasn't getting any money at all until we intervened." According to another high-ranking Leader's Office source, Southside's preoccupation with defensive seats and its "caution in where the money went" started to become "obstruction" as the election wore on. There was no "justifiable basis for that later in the campaign."

Part of the reason why Labour HQ remained in such a defensive posture was that the polling company it hired, BMG, was the most pessimistic of all the pollsters about Labour's chances. It later finished bottom of the pollsters' election league table, having predicted in its final public poll that Labour would win 33 per cent.[71] If the countless gloomy forecasts of candidates and party workers were to be believed, Labour's 'voter ID' canvassing operation also failed to pick up any improvement in the party's standing.[72] This was probably because it had become too narrowly focused on reaffirming the support of people who had previously expressed an interest in voting Labour rather than identifying new voters and converts—a tendency accentuated by the time constraints of a snap election.[73] This data was more than enough to confirm the prejudices of those in the party who had always said Corbyn would lead them to disaster. But from mid-May there was plenty of evidence that sentiment was changing—for those that wanted to see it.

"The turning of the Titanic took forever at a crucial time when people were desperate for resources," says one of Corbyn's lieutenants. Believing that opportunities were being missed, Murphy went to Len McCluskey. "We're asking you to fund this," she said. "However, will you fund it our way, if we tell you where we want the money spent?" McCluskey agreed. £500,000 was transferred from Unite on 24 May that was, McCluskey says "effectively directed by Karie Murphy and Andrew Murray rather than going to the Labour Party, who of course were wanting to shovel all kinds of money to safe 'soft left' or right wing seats."

> It's something that we've done consistently—we haven't just given money over to the Labour Party, I've said to [Iain] McNicol 'I want to know where it's going.' We used to pay £3 million a year to the Labour Party to employ 150 people in Labour HQ, half of whom were engaged in attacking my union... So when Karie and Andrew raised that with me I said 'Yeah, absolutely'... I understood the initial defensive position [of Southside]... but it became clear that something was happening out there and they still were reluctant, bluntly in my view because quite a number of them didn't want Corbyn to win.

Frustration at the party's defensiveness went beyond the allocation of money. There were even more complaints about how it chose to use Labour's greatest resource: people. This was the domain of the party's regional structures, beyond the reach of the Leader's Office. "We had no control over human resources, we had no control over where organisers were being sent to work, we had no control over what regional directors were saying," says a source from Corbyn's team. The regional bureaucracies tended to mirror the predilections of Southside. Anecdotal reports suggested they were afflicted by the same pessimism. Two professional organisers were assigned to Leeds North East, a seat with a 7,000 majority that was later more than doubled; none was afforded to nearby Pudsey, which the Tories went on to hold by just 331 votes. Campaigners in the North West complained that volunteers were disproportionately deployed to the Wirral South constituency of Alison McGovern, the chair of Progress. McGovern was defending a majority of 4,599, with no UKIP candidate standing, and all the party's models suggested (wrongly) that she was in trouble. But this focus meant there was minimal help for marginals Wirral West, City of Chester and Weaver Vale (all of which Labour won anyway). In London there were persistent reports that volunteers were diverted to the defensive seat of Tooting (which Labour held with a majority of 15,000) instead of offensive seats like Battersea.[74]

"I'm furious," says a Leader's Office source, reflecting on the results. "All we needed was different decisions made in 12 seats and it'd have been a game changer." Asked if there were people within the party machine endeavouring to make the outcome worse than it could have been, the source says: "Our collective feeling on it is yes, that's probably the case... Can we prove it? It's attitudes as much as anything else." In the opinion of McCluskey, "Had Southside and the general secretary been more alert, had they been sharper, had they been wanting to look for a light at the end of the tunnel... it could have tipped it to Labour and Corbyn could be in Number 10."

Staff at Southside have disputed such assertions. In comments to the *Guardian* a source doubled down, saying: "We lost six seats that we held in 2015. If the defensive strategy had been stronger, perhaps we could have held those seats, and the Tories wouldn't have been able to form a government."[75] This may seem a curious argument in light of the revelation that at least two of those constituencies were denied the level of resources earmarked for much safer seats.

If the party was not willing to throw everything into marginals, another organisation was: Momentum. The Corbyn-supporting group ran what was, in effect, an alternative ground game. An internal Momentum strategy document, dated 13 May, confirms that this was deliberate: "Elements of the Labour Party HQ have appeared to be focusing on a defensive campaign, which overlooks the possibility of Labour changing the narrative over the election period, as well as sending out a negative message to activists by asking them to focus solely on defensive seats."[76] Instead, Momentum would concentrate on mobilising Labour members to campaign in marginal constituencies, both defensive and offensive.

In its most hands-on form, this strategy meant running campaign days and training sessions in 30 selected seats. Constituencies were chosen by whether they were deemed winnable, then according to whether Momentum's efforts were likely to leave a "sustainable legacy"—meaning priority was given to areas where there was an activist base that could be built up and a candidate who reflected the organisation's politics. This did not exclude Momentum helping candidates who were not on the left, however. One of its biggest campaign days, attracting hundreds of people to canvass in the constituency, was in Croydon Central, where the candidate, Sarah Jones, was associated with Progress, but where the local Momentum group was dynamic and the party's paid organiser was open to collaboration.[77]

Momentum organised more than 50 campaign days in seats such as Plymouth Sutton and Devonport, Battersea, and Crewe and Nantwich. Promoted online and through texts and emails to the organisation's members, the days put thousands of extra people onto the streets. Momentum also arranged over 30 activist training sessions, which included talks on 'persuasion canvassing' by organisers from the Bernie Sanders campaign. A session in Derby North "attracted more than 80 supporters, many of them having never knocked on a single door before," according to Lewis Bassett, who helped manage Chris Williamson's campaign in the seat.[78]

In some areas Momentum filled holes left by the Labour Party. In Nick Clegg's seat of Sheffield Hallam the CLP was "twinned" with next door Penistone and Stocksbridge, meaning members were told to go there to defend the fiercely anti-Corbyn Angela

Smith. As a result, Momentum had to do "everything" in Hallam, according to local activist Max Munday, "from the official campaign photos to making the memes for social media, to just arranging the printing of election materials... It didn't look slick, to be honest. It was a really scratch campaign—one that without Momentum wouldn't have existed."[79] It ultimately proved enough to overturn Clegg's 2,000-vote majority. "Our strategy was more optimistic," says Joe Todd, Momentum's communications officer. "We thought more seats were winnable than the regional Labour parties did. We would send people to Battersea or Sheffield Hallam, whereas the regional Labour parties were directing people away. We had to step in."

Momentum's most visible contribution to the ground campaign was its 'My Nearest Marginal' website, a tool that allowed users to enter their postcode to find their five closest marginal seats, together with information about upcoming campaigning sessions and a facility for arranging a carpool for travel. The site was launched to controversy as critics alleged that it excluded the seats of Corbyn's critics.[80] In fact, it was built to show every marginal with a majority of less than 7,000, and the temporary omissions were due to the difficulty of getting information from some CLPs. As a simple tool fulfilling an obvious need—over 100,000 people used it during the election, or a fifth of Labour's membership—the real question was why nothing similar was provided by the party itself (or, for that matter, by the organisations of the Labour right, given their frequently-voiced concern for winning elections).[81]

Indeed, it was remarkable that it was left to Momentum, a non-party organisation with a relatively small budget, to provide the encouragement and technology needed to begin to unlock the electoral potential of Labour's newer members. As Bassett observed in Derby North, "Momentum was fundamental to organising the crowd of support for Corbyn, something the party itself has shown little interest in."[82] By providing some fairly rudimentary campaigning infrastructure, Momentum exposed deficiencies in Labour's supposedly formidable ground game, from the choice of target seats to the absence of any systemic training for the party's army of volunteers. In some areas there was even a baffling nervousness about receiving help at all. In Gower, the most marginal seat in the country, constituency representatives complained about their inclusion on My Nearest Marginal.

It is difficult to quantify the impact of Momentum's efforts. In some seats where it did a lot, such as Middlesbrough South and East Cleveland, Labour lost. In others where it had no official involvement, such as Canterbury, Labour won. Of course, most of Labour's campaigning across the country was the self-organised work of the party's enormous base of members and supporters. But although correlation does not imply causation, there was a string of constituencies from the south to the north where Momentum was very active and Labour went on to see a larger than average increase in its vote share, including Brighton Kemptown (19 point rise), Hampstead and Kilburn (15 points), and Lancaster and Fleetwood (13 points). Momentum contributed something else, too. By not sinking into a defensive strategy, by looking as if it wanted to win, its campaigning gave a psychological boost to the movement on the ground. The polls might have looked bad, but all these young people were being mobilised. Perhaps they could swing it. Perhaps it was worth joining them.

ACT THREE

Suddenly there was a sense of the impossible becoming possible. It was the evening of Saturday 20 May 2017. The manifestos had transformed the dynamic of the election. Thousands of enthused Labour members had spent the day on the streets canvassing. Jeremy Corbyn had addressed a very large rally on the beach in Margaret Greenwood's marginal seat of Wirral West, one of those written off by the party. A few hours later he was stood in front of 20,000 music fans in the Tranmere Rovers stadium as the 'Oh Jeremy Corbyn' chant was sung for the first time. Footage from the scene electrified social media. "Something is definitely happening," tweeted John Prescott.[1] Then a new YouGov poll showed Labour on 35 per cent. The party under Corbyn was matching the result achieved by Tony Blair in 2005, the last time Labour won. YouGov had given the Tories a 24-point lead when Theresa May called the election. Now, for the first time in the campaign, the gap was down to single figures.[2] The excitement was infectious.

The impetus was with Labour. Two days later, as the prime minister made her catastrophic non-U-turn over the dementia tax, a poll revealed a massive swing to Labour in Wales. Earlier surveys had suggested the Conservatives were on course to win the most Welsh seats for the first time in over a century. But in the space of a few weeks the Tories had lost 7 points and slipped back to a distant second, while Labour had surged by 9 points—in spite of the efforts of the Welsh Labour leadership to distance itself from Corbyn.[3]

The timing of Labour's resurgence could not have been better. 22 May was the last day to register to vote. It was obvious that massive numbers were applying for a ballot—later confirmed as over 600,000 in the final 24 hours alone. In total 2.9 million applications were made in the election period, 69 per cent of them (over 2 million) by people under the age of 34. Although a significant proportion were duplicates by people already registered, the figures were unprecedented. Constituencies with lots of students—Canterbury, Cambridge, Bristol West, Leeds Central—saw their electorates increase in size by over 10 per cent.[4]

To an extent this was the fruit of voter registration drives run by various groups including the Labour Party. But the numbers signing up were on a scale far beyond anything any organisation could take credit for. Registering to vote had become a viral phenomenon fuelled by frustration at the reality of life for young people—few opportunities, student fees, extortionate housing costs and poor wages—and the fact that, for once, a political party was speaking directly to these concerns. Corbyn's own contribution to encouraging registration had been huge, and in the final hours before the midnight deadline his social media posts counted down: "7 hours to register to vote for a £10 living wage." "3 hours to register to vote to open a National Investment Bank instead of foodbanks." "1 hour to register to vote to save your grandparents or parents' universal winter fuel allowance." "30 mins to register to vote to bring back the Educational Maintenance Allowance."

And then, just before the deadline, news broke that a man had walked into the Manchester Arena, where the pop star Ariana Grande had just finished playing, and detonated a bomb packed with nuts and bolts.

When 22 people are killed in an act of terrorism, politics does not carry on as normal. The election campaigns of all the parties were suspended. For anyone who was not at the concert, comprehending the full horror of the incident was impossible. It was much easier to grasp the political implications. For those involved in politics, there was no way to stop their thoughts leaping ahead to what the attack might mean for the election, even as such calculations were accompanied by a sense of guilt for considering the question at all.

What every Labour supporter feared, but could scarcely say, was summed up by a conversation outside Number 10 on the morning after the atrocity between two journalists, unaware that their words were being broadcast live on Sky News' Facebook page.

"It changes everything really, doesn't it?" said one.

"As much as it sounds disgusting and awful, this plays in [May's] favour," the other replied. "The whole kind of social care stuff is now dead, and you know, who's been portrayed as a terrorist sympathiser for the last...? And particularly obviously with the Manchester connotations as well, given the fact that the last major attack on Manchester was by the IRA."

"They don't even need to play that."

"No, that narrative is already, you know. All she needs to do is be prime ministerial."[5]

In the preceding days, attacks on Corbyn over his history of contacts with Sinn Fein had stepped up in what looked like an orchestrated campaign. On the morning after the Manchester atrocity the *Sun*'s front page—composed before the bombing—read "BLOOD ON HIS HANDS: Ex-IRA killer's Corbyn verdict" (it was curious that the *Sun*'s political editor Tom Newton Dunn gave such credence to the "verdict" of a former terrorist previously described by a High Court judge as a "practised deceiver").[6] In this context the Leader's Office even had to make a judgement on whether Corbyn should go to Manchester for an open-air vigil on the evening of 23 May. "People were saying shy away, it's Manchester, it's bombing, it's the very day 'blood on his hands' is on the front page of the *Sun*," says one of Corbyn's aides. "We could either hide Jeremy away or get right out there and do it." Corbyn was minded to go, but Andy Burnham, the mayor of Greater Manchester, did not want him there. Despite an ongoing tussle behind the scenes, Corbyn headed north. He later said he was "deeply moved" by the vigil, which saw thousands gather in Manchester's Albert Square. "I saw a people defiant, refusing to be divided, refusing to give in to hatred," he wrote on Facebook. "I felt so proud to be among those people, as I've felt so proud of the way Manchester and our whole country have responded to this attack."[7]

With campaigning suspended, fear stalked the Corbyn camp that Labour's impetus was lost. The atmosphere in the country had changed. The government had ordered troops onto the streets. The Conservatives reportedly wanted the campaign pause to last for six days, meaning Labour would have to be silent while May attended international conferences and looked, as the Sky News journalist had put it, prime ministerial.

What happened next was one of the key moments of the general election. Many in the Labour Party believed that Manchester had put them on the defensive, and that when politics resumed Corbyn would have to walk on eggshells. But instead, the leader and his closest advisors made probably the biggest call of the campaign. They decided Labour would restart the election on Friday 26 May, four days after the bombing, with an unflinching speech from the leader on terror and security. They would wrest the agenda by placing acts of terrorism in the context of foreign policy and austerity.

"It was bold, it was risky," says one of Corbyn's advisors. "There were people within our campaign team who were like, 'Fuck, are you sure about doing this?'" But the choice, as they saw it, was between getting out in front or passively waiting to be pummelled by the inevitable onslaught from Tory strategist Lynton Crosby. "If you say nothing on it you're on the back foot and are being asked to respond without a clear line to take," says the advisor. "In a general election campaign there's no point in meekly going along with things, that doesn't get you anywhere from a tactical point of view."

"Seumas [Milne] made the decision to do the security speech after Manchester," says Karie Murphy. "We were fucking terrified." When selected lines from the speech, shaped by Milne, Andrew Fisher, Andrew Murray, the academic Jem Bendell, and Corbyn himself, were briefed to the press the night before its delivery, the reaction was predictable. "Corbyn: UK wars to blame for terror," was the headline on the front page of the *Daily Telegraph*. The journalistic clique went into paroxysms of excitement, believing Corbyn was about to make the slip-up they had all been waiting for. Many in the Labour Party thought the same. The Leader's Office could not find an MP willing to introduce Corbyn for the speech. "I got phone calls from Labour MPs the night before saying 'If he says this we are fucked,'" recalls Murphy. "I didn't sleep and felt ill because it was such a small group making the decisions... There's insecurity because it's an overwhelming responsibility. Are we going to let the left down? Are we being too honest at such a sensitive time? Will this be seen as an attack on the Blairites?"

The speech that Corbyn delivered at 11 a.m. on 26 May was far more carefully argued than listeners could have anticipated from the brouhaha that preceded it. Corbyn did say that it was essential to understand the "causes" of terrorism, but was clear that "those causes certainly cannot be reduced to foreign policy decisions alone. Over the past 15 years or so, a sub-culture of often suicidal violence has developed amongst a tiny minority of mainly young men, falsely drawing authority from Islamic beliefs... And no rationale based on the actions of any government can remotely excuse, or even adequately explain, outrages like this week's massacre."

But, Corbyn argued, the shattering of a region had created conditions in which jihadism could grow. "Many experts, including professionals in our intelligence and security services, have pointed out the connections between wars that we've been involved in or supported and fought in, in other countries such as Libya, and terrorism here at home," he said.

The second objective of the speech was to place the issue of security in what Corbyn's advisor describes as "our wider austerity frame." May was vulnerable here, having presided over a 20,000 reduction in police numbers while home secretary. "Austerity has to stop at the Accident and Emergency ward and at the police station door," Corbyn said. "We cannot be protected and cared for on the cheap."[8]

As the content of Corbyn's intervention was not as controversial as expected, the Tories—who reportedly cleared their schedule in order to focus attention on the Labour leader—simply attacked the speech they wished he had made instead.[9] From the prime minister down, their response was flagrantly dishonest. "Jeremy Corbyn has said that terror attacks in Britain are our own fault," claimed May. "I want to make something clear to Jeremy Corbyn and to you: there can never be an excuse for terrorism, there can be no excuse for what happened in Manchester."[10] Boris Johnson called the speech "absolutely monstrous," and pretended it was an "attempt to justify or to legitimate the actions of terrorists."[11]

But Tory attack dog Michael Fallon, when interviewed on Channel 4 News that evening, was embarrassed by host Krishnan Guru-Murthy, who put to him the proposition that while the Iraq war had not created Islamic fundamentalism, it had given jihadists a pretext. Fallon condemned the idea, only for Guru-Murthy to reveal that he was quoting from an old Boris Johnson article. "It's exactly the same as what Jeremy Corbyn is saying now," Guru-Murthy exclaimed. "No, I think it's more, it's more is what he's saying that um, of what I've said," muttered a startled Fallon.[12]

The Conservative condemnations were matched by a blizzard of outrage from the press. But the media and the Tories were being played. By straying from the political consensus on terrorism, Corbyn had goaded them into attacking—and publicising—a view that was widely shared. An instant YouGov poll on 26 May found that 53 per cent believed that "wars the UK has supported or fought are responsible, at least in part, for terror attacks against the UK"; only 24 per cent disagreed.[13] An outright majority of the public supported a position the politico-media clique deemed beyond the pale.

This was not an accident but an object lesson in how to manage a hostile media. Corbyn's press team called it "the Capoeira strategy." "Capoeira," a source explains, "is a Brazilian martial art where you use the weight of the other person's attack to floor them." The idea dated back to January 2017, when Corbyn raised the notion of some kind of cap on high earnings. "The absurd response from much of the media and commentators and large sections of the political class served to underline our meta-narrative of the many against the few," the source recalls. As with the terrorism speech, a poll then found big support for what Corbyn had said. "By inviting their ridicule, especially on things we knew would be popular, we would strengthen our position. We saw it time and time again." For instance, it played out over the nationalisations proposed in Labour's manifesto. "We knew public ownership of the utilities would be an extremely popular policy, and the controversy around it would help people know about it," says the source.

If radio shows are holding phone-ins and you've got someone from a think tank talking about how awful it would be if you didn't have a monopoly increasing water bills by 50 per cent above inflation, skimming off £18 billion over 10 years in dividends, well that's an argument that we're perfectly happy to have, even if they're calling us the worst people on earth because of it... We played controversy, but controversy about ideas and power and policy. It was our main approach.

For the terrorism speech there was another feature of the media landscape which Corbyn's press team was able to exploit. After the dissolution of parliament on 3 May, election broadcasting rules meant that equal airtime had to be given to the two major parties. News channels carried speeches from Corbyn live and discussed their implications seriously. This changed the way that news narratives were created. In normal times, the source explains, "the printed press has a large influence on what the broadcast priorities are... So confected personalised tittle-tattle and bullshit posing as analysis takes greater precedence." But, adds another advisor, "It's different during an election. Seumas perceived that well." The speech was a risk, but Corbyn's inner circle was confident that it would be extensively covered. Sure enough, the public heard their message through the din. And with all the attention on Corbyn, May was reduced to a sideshow, carping at the Labour leader while he was the one communicating with the public—looking, dare it be said, prime ministerial.

The Corbyn camp had always insisted the polls would turn once broadcasters were required to show more of the Labour leader and that was proving true.[14] Labour's policies, too, were being reported "fairly straight on broadcast, and at the top of the bulletins," knocking the usual negativity "way down the order," says a Leader's Office source. "It was there, but we had positive stories to put on top of it."

The discipline of an election campaign also enabled Labour to keep its message far more focused than usual. "We had much tighter control of who a Labour voice was," recalls the source. "Our control over our message and our message carriers was heightened." The day-to-day job of defending Labour on the airwaves was performed with flair by Emily Thornberry and Barry Gardiner. Whether by design or not (one aide to Corbyn says the two were "exhausted" and would have appreciated others sharing the load), this gave the Labour Party a strong identity—most voters do not recognise more than a handful of politicians. Thornberry shone, earning a place in political history for an all-time great on-air ambush on the hapless Michael Fallon. Responding to the usual IRA smear while sat next to Fallon on the Andrew Marr sofa, Thornberry said: "I suppose if you judge people by who it is you spend time with the question has to be, do you remember where you were on 27 May 2007?"

"I'm sure you're going to tell me," Fallon replied.

"Yes I am! You were in Syria, and you were celebrating, at a reception, the re-election of President Assad with 99 per cent of the vote."

When Fallon tried to bring the subject back to "Corbyn's quite open support for the IRA," Thornberry interjected, "It's not open support for the IRA. You really can't go around making this stuff up... You've just said, for example, that I want to negotiate the future of the Falklands. That is..."—here Thornberry stopped making any noise, but mouthed the word bollocks.[15]

As for Gardiner, he became a cult hero of the movement. As Len McCluskey puts it, "Oh my God, he's the find of the century!" (This raises the question of why it took the unlikely blossoming of Corbyn to unearth Gardiner, whose roots are not on the left of the party.) Dubbed 'The People's Gardiner' by Corbyn supporters, the mild-mannered former philosophy student transformed into a human flame-thrower during media interviews. "Why did you let him off the hook?" were his first words of a Sky News appearance with presenter Adam Boulton, critiquing the previous interview with a Conservative. "If that had been a Labour minister... You didn't skewer him! You're supposed to be the tough guy of Sky News and you let him off the hook!"

"I didn't!" protested a flustered Boulton in a high-pitched voice.[16]

Labour's prioritisation of broadcast coverage reflected both the negativity of the printed press and its declining influence in an age of social media. Corbyn's press team broke with tradition by restricting newspapers' access to the leader on the campaign trail. "Why would you have a travelling band of people, who broadly speaking work for publications that are extraordinarily hostile to you and haven't been fair, snarkily tweeting?" asks an aide to Corbyn. Instead, access was granted on a rota basis, provoking bouts of entitled grumbling from the likes of Steve Hawkes of the *Sun*.[17]

Labour could only count on the *Mirror* to report remotely positively. Since Corbyn's election as leader, the *Guardian* had continued on the course it set during the 2015 contest. As Professor of Journalism Angela Smith has commented, "Even Corbyn's detractors (disclosure: I was one of them) couldn't fail to feel uneasy about the way in which the *Guardian* blindly followed the right wing news agenda—helping to demonise, rather than understand."[18] But as Labour rose in the polls the *Guardian* began to panic. Most of its readers were enthusiastically backing Corbyn's party (a post-vote poll confirmed that 73 per cent of *Guardian* readers that voted chose Labour, up 11 points on 2015 despite Ed Miliband having enjoyed the paper's fulsome support).[19] Tell-tale signs began to appear that, deep within the bowels of the *Guardian*, things were churning. In the wake of Corbyn's "sober and carefully caveated" security speech, even the obsessively hostile Jonathan Freedland managed to write a column that did not slander him.[20] Something was up.

Sure enough, on 2 June the newspaper gave its official endorsement. "Labour deserves our vote," it said. Corbyn had "generated an unfamiliar sense of the possible; once again, people are excited by politics"—a happy development for which the *Guardian* could thank its own declining influence.[21] After two years of denigrating Corbyn, the newspaper's big guns were lined up to blast him with praise. Having experienced an "epiphany" in a barber shop in Wolverhampton, John Harris revealed that "talking in plain-spoken, moral, essentially socialist terms about the fundamental condition of the country need not entail political disaster" (so not the "Waterloo" he had predicted just five months earlier).[22] The "received wisdom of the past 15 years was wrong," Harris concluded, and "most of the people charged with making sense of what is going on have barely begun to understand" (no comment).[23]

The *Guardian*'s abrupt change of tack infuriated the editor of the *New Statesman*. "The *Guardian* thriving in its role as the

Corbynite *Pravda*—the English press is so ludicrously partisan," said Jason Cowley in a tweet posted, then quickly deleted, on 5 June.[24] His rage at the *Guardian*'s betrayal was understandable. The *New Statesman* had gone all in just prior to the general election with a front cover proclaiming: "WANTED: AN OPPOSITION. The Labour Party has collapsed."[25] Cowley was not about to fold now. He had just penned an article asserting that Labour was "engaged in a dance of death," in which he dedicated five paragraphs to the wisdom of *Labour Uncut* blogger Atul Hatwal, the sage who in 2015 had insisted that Corbyn would finish last in the leadership race. Hatwal's forecast this time? Labour was "falling towards extinction levels."[26] Back in 2015 Cowley himself had asserted that Corbyn's leadership would "doom" Labour to "absolute irrelevance." But it was the *New Statesman* under his editorship that now risked meeting such a fate.

Right wing newspapers poured out venom of unprecedented toxicity in unparalleled quantity. However, the effect of their poison varied with age. It likely did help the Conservatives retain their vote with older people who still bought newspapers, even as Tory policies attacked their interests. It was notable, though, that the *Sun* had lost its potency. Its relentless campaign of hatred against Corbyn had little resonance—only 28 per cent of the paper's readers eventually voted the way they were told to (the majority did not vote at all).[27] Among younger people the hysterical front pages were mercilessly mocked and critiqued online. Many simply did not believe the traditional press any more, and were turning to alternative sources of news. An analysis by *BuzzFeed* found "Conservative-supporting newspapers continue to dominate the mainstream British news agenda, but their stories have failed to impact upon social media."[28] As an advisor to Corbyn comments, "The newspapers worked for the Tories' demographic and social media worked for ours. It's two different worlds."

It became apparent that, for all their vitriol, the press had nothing new to throw at Corbyn. Many of the stories may as well have been reprints of articles written during the leadership contests. "I would be sitting there on a Saturday expecting to have to deal with difficult Sunday newspaper attack stories," remembers a member of Labour's press team, "and in the end it's: 'Oh,

I remember that. Yeah, that's from last summer. I'll just go and look at what we said then. Done.'" The volume of hostile coverage over the previous two years meant that many voters were inured to it. And the more they saw Corbyn speaking directly on their TV screens, the more ludicrous the press' portrayal appeared.

· · · · ·

"There is nothing in this manifesto about getting rid of the monarchy," sneered Jeremy Paxman as if he had uncovered a scandal.

"There's nothing in there because we're not going to do it!" replied Jeremy Corbyn, smiling. The audience at the Sky News and Channel 4 *Battle for No. 10* programme broke into laughter and applause. "Listen," Corbyn continued, "it's not on anybody's agenda, it's certainly not on my agenda, and do you know what? I had a very nice chat with the Queen."

Corbyn's performances in a string of set-piece TV events during a packed penultimate week of the election campaign surpassed expectations. They should not have done. It had been clear from the very first televised debate of the 2015 leadership contest in Nuneaton that he had a talent for answering questions in an engaging manner and was at home in front of an audience. Having spent the previous two summers involved in a never-ending marathon of hustings he was well practised in the format.

But the Paxman interview on the evening of Monday 29 May 2017 was Corbyn's biggest televised test yet. The stakes were high. Labour members were nervous. Anything could happen. Two years earlier, on the same programme, Ed Miliband delivered his cringeworthy line, "Hell yes, I'm tough enough." In a subsequent *Question Time* special he half tripped as he left the stage. Such slips could define a leader.

If Corbyn was nervous, it did not show. The Labour leader that strode out onto the set was more confident and polished than ever. He was evidently well prepared, an in-house job by Andrew Fisher and Seumas Milne. He even looked smarter, dressed in what David Cameron might call a proper suit. This was Karie Murphy's doing. "Part of me has got my dad in my head saying: 'But he's got to look the part, Karie.'" Contrary to press speculation that Milne was in charge of 'Operation Suit,' Murphy says: "Seumas has never raised it with Jeremy in his life, it's all me. I say: 'Jeremy, that suit's fucking horrible. It has to go.' I phone his wife and say, 'Lose that suit.' I bought suits, I bought shirts. Laura Parker, his private secretary, has been a great influence too. We empower each other. It drives him mad."

The programme kicked off with Corbyn, alone, facing audience questions. He was surprisingly assertive, not giving an inch to a businessman complaining at the prospect of having to pay his staff a £10 living wage. But he also displayed his natural rapport with the public. When an audience member questioned his leadership skills, Corbyn replied:

John, people have perceptions about each other. But do you know what? In life I meet lots of people. Some I agree with, some I disagree with, some I profoundly disagree with. But I always want to get to know them because everybody I meet and everybody you meet knows something we don't know. You should never be so high and mighty that you can't listen to somebody else and learn something from them. For me, leadership is as much about using this [gesturing to his ear], as using this [gesturing to his mouth].

It was not the kind of answer people were used to from a politician. The audience visibly warmed to him. When Paxman took over the interrogation, firing off theatrically aggressive questions in an apparent attempt to parody himself, the "seductive power of Corbyn's astonishing good humour," as journalist Robert Peston described it, won out.[29] "Well JC had the better of that encounter with Jeremy Paxman," tweeted Sky's own Adam Boulton.[30]

When her turn came, Theresa May did not crumble, and was helped by some abnormally excited Brexit supporters in the audience. But her manner was cold, remote and dull. Her most memorable moment involved being jeered and laughed at when she said "the figures don't add up" in Labour's manifesto. Members of the audience reminded her that the Tories had provided no costings for theirs.[31]

The event was a triumph for Corbyn. As Barry Gardiner put it, "Jeremy got the audience laughing with him; May had the audience laughing at her—seven times!"[32] It was Corbyn's best media performance of the election, but far from his only good one. In interviews with the likes of Peston and Andrew Marr he managed to remain serene—"Monsieur Zen," as he branded himself—even while being berated by Andrew Neil about the IRA for a solid eight-and-a-half minutes.[33] Indeed, these interviews tended to feature an incessant focus on his past associations—Ireland, the Falklands, Palestine, magazines for which he had written three decades earlier. Had the election been taking place in 1983, the public would have been extremely well informed about Corbyn's views on current affairs. When former BBC political editor Nick Robinson offered his verdict on the *Battle for No. 10* programme—"Tonight confirmed what we already knew: Corbyn vulnerable on his own past, May vulnerable on her party's policies for the future"—Twitter user Andrew Evans responded: "So now we just need to find out if time is currently moving forwards or backwards."[34]

There was one glitch. Interviewed on BBC Radio 4 *Woman's Hour* on the morning of Tuesday 30 May, Corbyn was unable to say how much it would cost to provide 30 hours a week free childcare for all two to four-year-olds. There were agonising silences as Corbyn attempted to look up the answer on his iPad, harried all the while by presenter Emma Barnett. "You don't know the figure," she snapped. "It hardly inspires the voters... You don't know the cost... Hopefully someone's emailing it to you." The objective of this journalistic inquisition was not, in fact, to elicit information—Barnett knew the figure all along, and finally read it out after three minutes—but to make Corbyn squirm. In this it was successful.

Murphy recalls that she was "devastated" by the interview "because as a team we failed Jeremy." "He felt he wasn't prepared. He felt he didn't know enough about the type of interview, he didn't have a briefing in the format that he would have wanted, he didn't know he was going to be filmed in the radio station, he didn't have a press person with him to recover when he came out of it... We were driving him too hard, too much... That interview wasn't Jeremy's fault, it was our fault."

Murphy later had to apologise to staff for her reaction to the incident, having shouted at them. She remembers, "I was upset. Jeremy said, 'Karie don't get upset.' I'm upset now thinking about it, because he was embarrassed. He said 'I'm embarrassed, Karie.'"

Corbyn went some way to rescuing the situation a few hours later at the launch of Labour's 'race and faith' mini-manifesto, where he apologised for not having known the figure. Told by a reporter that Barnett had been "subject to abuse online, including anti-Semitic abuse, by people purporting to be your supporters," Corbyn gave an unequivocal condemnation. "Under no circumstances whatsoever should anyone throw personal abuse at anyone else because they're doing the job that they've been employed to do," he said. Asked if it was too much to expect politicians to have every statistic at their fingertips, Corbyn joked: "There is no such thing as being unfair to politicians."[35]

That evening the Labour leader was a guest on the *One Show* on BBC 1 for a quirky non-political interview covering allotments, jam and manhole covers. Going by the size of the audience it was among Corbyn's biggest engagements. His performance drew wide praise, with the *Radio Times* reporting that he "charmed viewers."[36] By the end of the show, the *Woman's Hour* disaster was a bad memory. "What could have been a two or three day story ended up a two or three hour story," comments an aide.

The following day Corbyn's team made another of the big calls of the campaign: a dramatic, last minute decision to join a 7-party TV debate on the BBC. May had been steadfast in her refusal to engage Corbyn head-to-head. When she was a popular leader with a giant poll lead her stance made sense. Why debate Corbyn when there was nothing to gain? Expectations of the Labour leader were rock bottom; he was sure to exceed them. For May the reverse was true—her advisors were no doubt aware of her weaknesses. But this calculation no longer worked once the public had come to view her as evasive, unable to answer questions, unwilling to submit herself to scrutiny. All Corbyn needed to do was challenge her to a debate to score an easy win. He did so repeatedly.

Corbyn himself sat out a debate of opposition leaders on ITV on 18 May, saying he would not take part without May. His team felt there were more potential risks than benefits. The spectacle could animate the Tories' "coalition of chaos" slogan; it could give the impression that Labour was on the same level as the smaller parties; as the only potential prime minister on the panel, Corbyn would be a target for the others. For the same reasons, Corbyn was not due to participate in the 7-party debate scheduled for the evening of Wednesday 31 May. But the context had changed for Corbyn, too. He was on the ascendant. There was a chance to embarrass May in a way that was sure to resonate.

Shortly after midday, Corbyn made the surprise announcement that he would attend the BBC event that evening. Commentators speculated that the move was a long-planned ploy. In fact, the decision had been taken an hour or so earlier by just three people: Corbyn, Milne and Murphy. The choice, for Murphy, was simple: "We're getting beat right now, we're not winning. We can either be delighted that we're going to get 37 per cent of the vote or we can be bold." Not even Fisher, who was travelling on the tube at the time, could be consulted on the decision, leaving him "cross because he had no time to prep Jeremy." "That was a very stressful day," remembers Murphy. "It was the one and only time that Andrew, Seumas and I disagreed on something."

May was thrown by the move. She looked flustered responding to journalists' questions at a campaign event that afternoon. If she was so strong and Corbyn was so weak, asked Sky News' Faisal Islam, why not debate him? May laughed unnaturally before delivering an inexplicable comeback: "I'm interested in the fact that Jeremy Corbyn seems to be paying far more attention to how many appearances on telly he's doing, and he ought to be paying a little more attention to thinking about Brexit negotiations, that's what I'm doing." She looked as if she was expecting a laugh, but there was silence from the audience, who may have been wondering why, if Brexit meant there was no time for debates, she had called an election.[37]

In the event, the actual debate in Cambridge that evening was not spectacular. Seven people talking over each other did not make great TV. But what mattered was the story surrounding it: May had bottled it. "Why is she such a coward?" asked Emily Thornberry when she gate-crashed a live interview with a Conservative minister afterwards.[38] The supposedly slick Tory campaign had been exposed as flat-footed, outmanoeuvred by the much-maligned Labour operation.

The scenes broadcast on *BBC News at Ten* were a dream for Labour. "Look who came after all, and what an entrance," said the reporter over cinematic footage of Corbyn stepping out of a car to be greeted by hundreds of cheering Labour supporters lining the road. He could have been a film star arriving for a premiere at Cannes.[39] One of his advisors remembers driving "slowly through the cobbled streets" of Cambridge on the way to the venue. "Jeremy had the window down, which really annoys the Special Branch staff... People walking past were going 'Jeremy!' Everyone. 'It's Jeremy Corbyn! It's Jeremy Corbyn!' No abuse... Admittedly, Cambridge is a Labour-Lib Dem marginal, but it's not the centre of the revolution. I thought there's something weird going on here."

Corbyn was in less friendly company at a BBC *Question Time* leaders' special two days later on Friday 2 June, which featured just the two main party leaders taking questions consecutively, not together. For seven excruciating minutes he fended off members of the audience demanding he show a willingness to use nuclear weapons. Three times host David Dimbleby interjected to pin Corbyn down. One man asked if Corbyn would "allow North Korea or some idiot in Iran to bomb us?" The crowd began to heckle. When another man in the audience said, "I'd rather have [Trident] and not use it than not have it at all, especially in today's day and age," Corbyn made no response. There was an awkward silence. "Do you want to comment on that?" Dimbleby asked. "No," answered Corbyn. To Len McCluskey, watching at home, Corbyn looked "down and wounded."

Dimbleby looked for another questioner. "The woman there. Let's just stick with this," he said. The friendly-faced young woman began: "I actually have a question about human rights." Corbyn stood up straight, no doubt thinking 'Thank God.' The woman continued: "But just before, I don't understand why everyone in this room seems so keen on killing millions of people with a nuclear bomb!" Half of the audience erupted in woops and applause. All the tension was swept away in an instant. Corbyn supporters watching TV in front rooms around the country punched the air. It was "the line of the night," tweeted the BBC's Jeremy Vine.[40] With just one sentence, the impression viewers took away from the discussion was transformed.[41] Whoever the woman was, her intervention had saved Corbyn's skin.

The *Daily Mail*, of course, did not agree. "CORBYN'S NUCLEAR MELTDOWN," ran the next morning's headline, "Labour leader humiliated in calamitous TV debate." But the *Mail* was out of step with public opinion. In a snap poll (commissioned, ironically, by the *Mail on Sunday*), 36 per cent of people said they were more likely to vote Labour as a result of *Question Time*, with 24 per cent less likely. For the Conservatives the story was reversed. Only 24 per cent of people were more likely to vote Tory and 32 per cent less likely after May's performance—the highlight of which was telling a nurse who had not had a pay rise since 2009 that "there isn't a magic money tree that we can shake that suddenly provides for everything that people want."[42]

Broadcast exposure did wonders for Corbyn's personal ratings. At the end of his intense week of appearances an Ipsos MORI survey showed Corbyn had nearly drawn level with May, while for the first time more people were dissatisfied than satisfied with the prime minister.[43] Amazingly, Corbyn's net satisfaction rating had risen by 16 points in just two weeks, while May's had collapsed by 27 points.[44] This was certainly one of the most dramatic reversals in perceptions of party leaders in British political history. The Conservatives had tried to make the election all about Corbyn, thinking he was their secret weapon; it turned out that May was Labour's. The turnaround was an astonishing personal achievement for Corbyn in the face of such venom, smears and bias.

Things were looking up for the party, too. Labour's fear of losing momentum after the Manchester atrocity had been unfounded. Even during the hiatus following the attack a YouGov poll had placed the party on 38 per cent, just 5 points shy of the Tories.[45] On 30 May, the night of Corbyn's *One Show* appearance, YouGov generated shockwaves when it unveiled a model that estimated the election outcome by seats. The results were startling. The forecast was for a hung parliament. "Shock poll predicts Tory losses," said the front page of the *Times*. The paper may only have been reporting on a projection, but even the existence of the headline was testament to the remarkable campaign Labour was running. Nearly every professional political pundit had regarded such a development as impossible—and they had not been shy in saying so. Unsurprisingly, their response to the new information was to mock it.[46] In this they were joined by Jim Messina, the former Obama advisor now working on the Tory campaign. "Spent the day laughing at yet another stupid poll from YouGov," he tweeted.[47]

The Tories and their media allies could take some comfort from the fact that the polls were diverging wildly. Some pollsters still had Labour over 10 points behind. This was speculated to be due to polling companies taking different views on whether young people would turn out to vote, which mattered because they were so heavily pro-Labour—68 per cent of 18-24 year olds backed the party according to an ICM poll released on 3 June; the Tories, in second place, were on just 16 per cent.[48]

There was more good news for Labour. A poll of Londoners released on 1 June had the party on an incredible 50 per cent—up 9 points in a month.[49] On 2 June, the day of *Question Time*, Labour hit 40 per cent in a nationwide poll for the first time.[50] Such a level of support astonished Corbyn's supporters almost as much as his critics. It was beyond the realms of what had been considered possible.

The following evening, 3 June, a Survation poll put Labour just one point behind, on 39 per cent to the Conservatives' 40 per cent.[51] Better still, Labour was gaining on the Tories hand over fist. With four days of campaigning to go the party could yet take the lead. This was dreamland for Labour activists.

And then, around 10:30 p.m., news broke that a van had driven into pedestrians on London Bridge.

· · · · ·

The political fallout from the London Bridge terror attack, which killed eight people, was like a replay of Manchester but on fast forward. Labour Party members were again subject to dual emotions—shock and horror at the violence; fear that it would hurt their party's chances. This was the second terrorist attack in less than two weeks. People were angry. There was bound to be an appetite for the knee-jerk solutions always offered by the right. For some, the urgency of the election and the inescapable fact that the agenda would now be wrenched back to security triggered alternating waves of desperation and resignation.

The parties suspended their national campaigns on the Sunday morning after the attack, although Labour, anxious not to lose the advantage of its army of volunteers on the last weekend before polling day, decided to continue its local canvassing. With the election so close nobody advocated another long pause. Proceeding with the democratic process was the best response to the terrorists, it was argued. The Tories would restart their campaign on Monday 5 June 2017; Labour, again worried about being pushed onto the back foot, announced that Corbyn would make a speech in Carlisle on Sunday evening. Until then, the prime minister was at the steering wheel. Labour was a passenger.

At 10:30 a.m. on Sunday morning Theresa May walked out to make a statement in Downing Street. As prime minister, people expected her to speak for the nation. Immediately after Manchester she had discharged her duty without making overtly political points. The first half of her speech in the wake of the London attack conformed to the same pattern: tributes to the emergency services, thoughts and prayers with the victims. But then she changed tack. "There is," she said, "far too much tolerance of extremism in our country." Steps had to be taken to tackle the "evil ideology of Islamist extremism": more powers for the police and security services, military action in Iraq and Syria, longer sentences for terrorism offences, curbs on internet freedom, and an end to "separated, segregated communities." "Enough is enough," she announced.[52]

Labour supporters were furious. In their view, May had agreed to suspend campaigning and had then made a campaigning speech. The measures she outlined were matters for legitimate debate, but not while the other parties were muzzled. She had chosen to politicise a tragedy while emotions were raw. It was ruthless.

Officially, Labour could say nothing. But this was the moment when the movement on social media came into its own. If May was making it political, so would they. It began with an explosion of anger at the speech itself. What did she mean there was "far too much tolerance of extremism in our country"? Who, exactly, was tolerating extremism? If what she said was true, why had she done nothing about it for six years as home secretary? Was she not just dog-whistling for votes? Had she considered the consequences of stoking prejudice in a country experiencing a spate of race hate crimes?

But the online movement could do more than just critique. It had learned over recent weeks how to shift the political agenda. With remarkable discipline and cohesion, it zeroed in on the issues of police cuts and Britain's relationship with Saudi Arabia. How could May pose as the person to keep the country safe after accusing the Police Federation of "crying wolf" over the impact of cuts?[53] How could she call out others for tolerating extremism while her government suppressed a report on alleged Saudi funding of extremist groups?[54]

When Peter Kirkham, a former senior investigating officer with the Met Police, was interviewed by Sky News that lunchtime, he slammed the government for "lying" about armed police numbers and not addressing the "urgent" need to reverse cuts to ordinary police. Usually a few hundred thousand people might have seen the encounter, but it was 'clipped' by the pro-Corbyn group EL4C and republished on social media. Their 2 minute edited video immediately went viral, accruing a staggering 6.5 million views on Facebook and 1 million on Twitter (the total number who saw it will have been higher as the clip was reused by various prominent people).[55] Kirkham's interview was ubiquitous—probably viewed more times than the famous Tory attack ad, but in the space of a day. EL4C had invested £2 to promote it.

It was extraordinary that such a focused online strategy could be executed without the guiding hand of the official accounts— there were no political posts from Jeremy Corbyn, the Labour Party or Momentum during the day. But having already been through the security debate in the wake of Manchester, the arguments were well rehearsed. Better-known pro-Corbyn social media users— some of whom reported that their online reach went through the roof at this time—provided direction, setting an example for others to follow. But this was largely a spontaneous phenomenon.

The online movement also had to do an important job of rebuttal. That afternoon the fourth most-watched video on the BBC News website was an old 2015 clip of Corbyn saying he was "not happy with the shoot-to-kill policy in general." The interview from which it was taken was notorious. When originally broadcast, Laura Kuenssberg had used Corbyn's answer to a general question about shoot-to-kill and falsely presented it as a response to whether police should be allowed to shoot terrorists in the midst of an attack. Even the BBC Trust judged that her report broke accuracy and impartiality rules.[56] Yet, despite the Trust's finding, the text accompanying the clip being shared that Sunday still contained the same falsehood.[57] Corbyn supporters regarded this as a serious threat. They leapt into action, re-sharing news stories covering the Trust's ruling.

All of this meant that by the time Corbyn made his speech in Carlisle that evening he could echo the narrative established on social media about police cuts and Saudi Arabia without appearing to go out on a limb. And to counter the distortion of his view on shoot-to-kill, he explicitly said that as prime minister he would give "full authority for the police to use whatever force is necessary to protect and save life."[58]

May had attempted to fix the agenda on the powers of the state with her speech in the morning; Corbyn, thanks in part to the battle waged on social media, successfully dragged it back to resources with his. Somewhat surprisingly, the traditional media followed in his wake. Next day May was hammered by journalists over the issue of police cuts at a campaign event. "Prime minister, you accused those who were concerned about police cuts of crying wolf, do you accept now that you were wrong to say that?" asked one. "On your watch as home secretary the number of armed police officers fell... the number of officers fell in total by 20,000... Would it not be leadership to say that you would reverse those cuts?" said another. "There have been cuts to community policing, cuts in exactly the place where you need to stop this ideology growing... What are you going to do about it?" demanded a third.[59]

Labour piled on the pressure with a hastily arranged press conference of trade union officials representing emergency service workers, testifying to the impact of cuts. "Everybody said it'll be crass, it'll be bad taste," remembers Karie Murphy, who organised the event. "It landed beautifully. Mark Serwotka [general secretary of the PCS union] was a star... It was another risk that paid off."

To the astonishment of political pundits, Corbyn was winning a debate on security. Police cuts became the national topic of conversation.[60] It demonstrated what could be achieved when a Labour leader actually argued the point instead of giving ground—although it was playing against type, and verging on ruthless, for the left to portray itself as so fervently pro-police. Desperate, May tried to change the subject back to Brexit, but in vain. "It is interesting that just when the focus of the campaign is on issues that you'd think the prime minister is comfortable talking about," reported ITV's political correspondent Emily Morgan, "she is forced on the defensive and unable to engage in the debate."[61]

May finally made a countermove on the evening of Tuesday 6 June. "If human rights laws get in the way of tackling extremism and terrorism," she tweeted, "we will change those laws to keep British people safe."[62] Though her meaning was vague, the line pressed all the right buttons for the reactionary sections of the press and was widely popular with the public.[63] It undoubtedly helped shore up the Tory vote, but it could not dent Labour's. "The right response to the recent attacks is to halt the Conservative cuts... and protect our democratic values, including the Human Rights Act," Corbyn retorted.[64] An advisor recalls: "That line, 'You can't keep people safe on the cheap,' resonated. It weakened anything the Tories said because they couldn't answer it... Crime and anti-terrorism is not home turf for the left but we made it ours."

· · · · ·

"Tonight, here in Gateshead, in the rain, we've shown just how much support there is," said Jeremy Corbyn to the 10,000 people filling the space outside the Sage arena on 5 June 2017. "Thank you for putting hope over fear! Unity over division!"[65]

The "traditional advice" at the end of a campaign, says a member of the Leader's Office staff, is to refocus the message onto the dangers of electing the opponent—in Labour's case, to "pivot into negative Tory risk." Corbyn "absolutely insisted" that the party would do no such thing. Instead, the source says, "We kept ascending with a hopeful message."

If the aim was to project an uplifting vision, the scenes from the final stretch of Corbyn's election tour were ideal. Whereas most of the leader's events had been publicised at very short notice, limiting the number of attendees, now caution was thrown to the wind as Labour went for big, Bernie Sanders-style rallies. "We never pulled crowds like this in 1997," tweeted John Prescott over a picture of the gathering in Gateshead.[66] Next day, in Birmingham, Corbyn was again surrounded by thousands, with footage of his speech beamed to five other rallies taking place simultaneously around the country (the original idea was to have him appear as a hologram, but there was no time).[67] Heavy rain had threatened to ruin the spectacle. Party staff even suggested it should be called off (Karie Murphy refused). But as Corbyn spoke—in what can only have been an act of God—a perfect rainbow appeared behind him.

It was difficult for the Conservatives to pivot into negativity at the end of their campaign since they had offered nothing else throughout. But they gave it a good go. The targeting of Diane Abbott, in particular, reached a new intensity in the final days. Abbott's campaign had been uncomfortable ever since she fell victim to Nick Ferrari's trademark cheap gotcha journalism in a "car crash" radio interview at the start of May. Her failure to recall the cost of Labour's policy to recruit more police was one of those election moments that pass into the national consciousness—for a while it was the main reason cited for people changing their view of the parties, until fox hunting came along.[68] (Curiously, white male Tories caught out by similar journalistic tricks, including even the chancellor of the exchequer, garnered only a tiny fraction of the attention.)[69] After another poor interview on the Andrew Marr programme on 28 May—which Abbott had done despite being asked not to by colleagues—the Leader's Office insisted she be less prominent. "We didn't think she was performing very well," says one of Corbyn's aides. "We didn't think she was herself, because we've all known and loved her for a long time, but we weren't sure what the circumstances were."

Abbott remained a prime target for the Conservatives and their media allies. The prime minister took to name-checking her at every campaign stop. Abbott was the subject of frequent attacks from Boris Johnson (a classy look for a man who had previously referred to black people as "piccaninnies" with "watermelon smiles").[70] She was singled out in vicious online Tory attack ads. All of this fanned the flames of a firestorm of racist abuse that Abbott was receiving on social media. It was bullying of the nastiest kind. On 6 June Abbott pulled out of two election events. The following day it was announced that she had temporarily stood down as shadow home secretary due to ill health. It later transpired that she was suffering from type 2 diabetes.[71]

The contrast with Labour's tactics could not have been greater. "We have refrained from personal abuse because I do not believe that gets us anywhere," Corbyn told a rally in the Tory-held marginal of Weaver Vale on 7 June. "I understand, because my neighbours tell me, that some people have said some very unkind things about me. I forgive them all!"[72] The front page of that day's *Daily Mail* screamed "APOLOGISTS FOR TERROR" over pictures of Corbyn, Abbott and John McDonnell, and inside there were 13 pages of invective.

Weaver Vale was the second of six rallies Corbyn addressed on a marathon final day of campaigning. It was telling that the red battle bus on which he travelled was emblazoned with the words "For The Many Not The Few, Vote Labour" while the Conservatives' battle bus was plastered with "Theresa May: For Britain." The Tory campaign had been all about May while Corbyn's had been all about Labour. Yet during the course of the election it was the self-effacing Labour leader that the public warmed to.

Labour's final video, released that afternoon, was indicative. It featured Lily Allen singing over a simple montage of footage skilfully edited to convey meaning and emotion. Portraits of Britons in all their diversity gave way to clips of Corbyn surrounded by people, by the movement seeking to transform society. That the film's story could be so easily grasped without a single word of dialogue was testament to the clarity of the message that Corbyn had communicated. The video raced to 2 million views.[73]

Whether all this positivity would translate into votes was still unknown. The pollster hired by the Labour Party, BMG, was not optimistic. Late that afternoon three of Corbyn's most senior aides were sat in the 'northern room,' their small private space in the Southside building, when one of the party's top officials burst in, eyes wide. "You'll never believe it!" he said.

"What?" replied the aides as one, hearts racing.

"We're 13 points behind!"

According to one of those present, the official was "fucking orgasmic at the thought that we were 13 points behind in the polls. It was brutal."

The final figures from other polling companies painted a brighter picture, although the wide variation between them made it impossible to tell what was really going on. Labour was either trailing by 12 points on 34 per cent, according to ICM, or it was 1 point behind on 40, according to Survation. YouGov, which throughout the campaign had placed Labour higher than most, copped out at the last minute. A change in its methodology dropped Labour down to 35 per cent (polling companies are commercial organisations with reputations to protect, after all).[74] Generally, the final polls suggested that Labour was falling back as the vote neared.

This did nothing to dampen the enthusiasm of those gathered outside the Union Chapel on Upper Street, Islington to welcome Corbyn home that evening. The Labour battle bus rolled up to the venue of his 90th and last campaign event to be met by several thousand cheering supporters. Islington resounded with chants of 'Oh Jeremy Corbyn.'[75] There was electricity in the air. Traffic came to a standstill as the crowd swelled onto the main road. Police were powerless to hold back the tide.[76] There was nothing but the arrival of the bus to see—the rally itself was an indoor event—but people wanted to be part of something.

Inside, Corbyn supporters danced in the aisles—literally. There was a sense of euphoria. Whatever the result the following day—all the experts still said it would be a bad defeat—everyone in the chapel and hundreds of thousands beyond felt enormous pride in the campaign Corbyn had run. For once, their politics had been done right. The ideas they really believed in had been offered to the nation and instead of being obliterated, they had raised the political horizon. That was something to celebrate. It was a joyous occasion.

"We've all been here at Union Chapel over many decades at protest meetings to protect this, defend that," Corbyn reflected when he spoke. "Tonight it's different because we're being totally positive. We're not defending." His voice became quiet as he repeated, "We're not defending. We don't need to. We are asserting. Asserting our view."

Corbyn was more confident and relaxed on the podium than ever. He was still not a great orator, but he was an outstanding communicator. The flaws in his style, the wonky sentences that drifted on after the point was made, were part of his appeal. He was a human, not a robot, with an unusual ability to tap into a deep sense of collective morality in his audience.

"We're not the party of the billionaires," he declared. "We're not the party of the corporate elite. We're the party of the people." He recited the final stanza of Percy Shelley's poem about the Peterloo Massacre, 'The Masque of Anarchy.'

> Rise, like lions after slumber
> In unvanquishable number!
> Shake your chains to earth, like dew
> Which in sleep had fallen on you:
> Ye are many—they are few!

The crowd lifted the roof. Corbyn was taken aback.[77]

From the first days of the campaign when he seemed alone in his optimism, to the final weeks riding a wave of support, Corbyn had done all he could. He had earned the gratitude that most Labour Party members now bestowed upon him. Their feelings were expressed most powerfully by shadow foreign secretary Emily Thornberry. Posting on Facebook on 7 June, she described Corbyn as:

A man who has taken more criticism and pressure than any of us could stand, but has stood up to it all. A man who has embraced every challenge in this campaign with enthusiasm and courage. A man who refuses to engage in personal abuse or deceit, no matter how politically convenient it would be.

A man who for three decades has stuck by the principles that brought him into politics, and has done so with an integrity, honesty and steadfastness that shames Theresa May. If anyone has proved themselves strong and stable during this campaign, it is him.[78]

· · · · ·

The polls were open. One last push. For all shifts and swings of the campaign, nothing was decided until 8 June. There were two sides to the story of Labour's election day experience. One was of a massive 'get out the vote' operation as the party reaped the benefits of a mobilised mass membership. The other was of a whole new block of the electorate appearing from nowhere to vote Labour, without having had any contact from the party.

Labour's formal 'get out the vote' efforts were crucial to maximising the turnout from its regular supporters. The information recorded on canvassing sheets during the weeks of campaigning was turned into lists of people intending to vote Labour. Teams of volunteers were dispatched to knock on their doors, remind them to vote, and offer help such as a lift to the polling station. Meanwhile, others were busy telephoning constituents, crossing off those who had already voted.

It was a labour-intensive system dependent for its effectiveness on the volunteers available. With over 500,000 party members—almost four times as many as the Conservatives—this is where Labour had an enormous advantage. The huge membership was, of course, a unique consequence of Jeremy Corbyn's leadership, and now it was put to work.

The most spectacular phenomenon was the thousands of volunteers who poured into marginal constituencies, often travelling from far afield. The controversy of regional party bureaucracies directing members to defensive seats with comfortable majorities persisted, but many ignored these instructions. A large contingent of the active membership in Putney, for example, went to help in neighbouring Battersea—where Marsha de Cordova was attempting to overturn an 8,000 Tory majority—rather than the constituency they had been "twinned" with, Tooting. (In hindsight they should have stayed in Putney—Labour missed out on taking the seat and unseating cabinet minister Justine Greening by 1,500 votes.).[79]

Many activists were guided as to where to go by Momentum, either indirectly thanks to its My Nearest Marginal tool and the calls it put out on social media, or, in the case of the organisation's own members, directly by text message. 10,000 people used a Momentum website, Election Day Pledge, to offer their assistance, resulting in 1.2 million doors being knocked on, according to the group.[80]

In some seats the number of volunteers was overwhelming. A local organiser in Cambridge called Momentum's membership coordinator Beth Foster-Ogg to complain: "You've sent me too many people! We've sent out all the [canvassing] boards and there's still loads of people flooding in, we don't know what to do." Foster-Ogg said that in Leeds North West "they had so many activists that they went, 'Right, let's scrap our whole strategy, we're going to just print off the electoral register instead,' and rather than focusing on likely Labour voters... they knocked on all the doors on the electoral register. That's unheard of." In Croydon Central, another Momentum target, Labour had 700 to 800 volunteers on the streets. Similar numbers were reported in other battlegrounds.[81]

Other than in Leeds North West, all these volunteers were talking to people who were on the party's radar, which was vital work. But more than 5 million people cast a ballot for Labour in June 2017 who had not done so in 2015.[82] In many cases, the party had no idea who they were. As Jenny Lennox, an experienced activist on the Labour left, explained to *New Socialist*:

> For Labour (at least the machine) this campaign started as a defence of the status quo, and not an attempt to win... [In Chingford] we concentrated on areas where we had won councillors in 2014, and had more recent information, but we hadn't made enough contacts. This was a surge all on its own, which was what was so amazing. I guess the national campaign must have really resonated. Activists reported lots of young people and black and ethnic minority voters turning up at polling stations and queuing out the doors.[83]

There were official efforts to reach new supporters, especially young people. Labour's Snapchat advertising directed over 780,000 to a tool for locating their polling station.[84] Momentum initiated a "WhatsApp cascade" by sending its members a reminder to vote which recipients could pass on to all their contacts, ultimately reaching an estimated 400,000 people.[85]

But more significant was the spontaneous buzz in communities and on social media, where people announced they had voted and urged others to do the same. "There were loads of people that you've never seen go to a polling station taking part," says Bobby from *Double Down News*, reflecting on the impact of the Grime4Corbyn movement in London. "The mandem were out."

These new Labour voters did not need to be reminded to cast a ballot because, anecdotally at least, they were inspired to do so by the campaign that Corbyn had run. The winning candidate in Croydon Central, Sarah Jones, who hails from the Progress wing of the party, was in no doubt:

> In Croydon there were people putting out leaflets to young people, and putting things on social media, that were nothing to do with the Labour Party. But they were supporting the Labour Party because of Corbyn, and because of this huge new membership, and because their friends in Momentum [were] talking to them about politics. There was a reach beyond what the Labour Party would normally be capable of.[86]

The formidable combination of Labour's 'get out the vote' operation and a spontaneous surge had its effect. The psephologists working on the broadcasters' exit poll could see the party's vote share steadily improving as the day wore on. But the campaigners on the streets did not know that. Even in the final minutes before polling stations closed at 10 p.m., thousands of Labour activists were still at it, desperate to secure every last vote. To zoom in on just one scene: as late as 9.30 p.m. a platoon of 30 volunteers was marching around the Doddington estate in Battersea in the gathering dusk, looking for doors to knock on.

Meanwhile, Corbyn, his wife Laura Alvarez, and his aides Seumas Milne and Karie Murphy gathered at the leader's Islington house, arriving only minutes before the fateful exit poll was going to be released. Corbyn asked everyone to write down a prediction. Murphy forecast Labour would win 39 per cent of the vote. Corbyn's was the second highest prediction. They knew, says Murphy, that they had been "feeling something" on the campaign trail that commentators had missed. But if that turned out to have been a mirage, if the true picture really was as bad as the Labour Party's private polling told them, they would be fighting off another coup before morning.

"He's got a tiny television," recalls Murphy. "None of your big fancy screens on the wall. Forget all that. A tiny TV on piled-up books. Seumas and Jeremy were standing right in front of the telly, it's that wee."

David Dimbleby spoke from the small set: "There are just over 20 seconds to go till Big Ben strikes 10... By the magic of psephology we're able to predict what we think has happened tonight." He stopped talking and turned to face a giant image of the Big Ben clock face. The hyperactive background music tailed off. Everything stopped. There was silence.

In that one-second pause Jeremy Corbyn's leadership—and with it the fate of a movement—hung in the balance. All the extraordinary happenings since the day in May 2015 when the unambitious MP ventured, "What about if I stand?" could have come to zilch. All the effort poured in by hundreds of thousands of committed supporters over two years could have been for nothing. The left's dream of transforming the country through the Labour Party might have been dashed.

Big Ben bonged. The clock face on the screen dissolved into a picture of Theresa May. A graphic read: "Conservatives largest party." Dimbleby elaborated: "They don't have an overall majority at this stage."

There were gasps in Corbyn's house.

"Fuck!"

"Hung parliament!"

"Oh my God!"

EPILOGUE

Although Labour did not win the June 2017 general election, its result was astonishing. The party increased its share of the vote by 9.5 points, the biggest gain between elections since 1945—all the more impressive as it had only been two years since voters last went to the polls. Jeremy Corbyn became the only Labour leader other than Tony Blair to break the 40 per cent barrier since 1970. A dizzying 12.9 million people voted for the party. Apart from the 1997 landslide, Labour had not won so many votes since 1966.

Instead of losing seats, Labour gained a net 30 (the first time the party had added to its tally since 1997), while the Tories lost 13 along with their overall majority. The resulting hung parliament—with the Conservatives occupying 317 seats and Labour 262—gave Corbyn's party great political clout in the House of Commons, reflected in the immediate dropping of noxious parts of the Conservative manifesto such as grammar schools and a vote on fox hunting.

Labour did fantastically well in England, where it won its second-highest number of votes ever, and in Wales, where it defied early predictions of doom to record its best result in a generation.[1] Scotland experienced a completely different election. Scottish Labour focused on attacking the SNP instead of the Tories, who sailed past into second place. Although Corbyn's campaign was credited for a late rescue of Scottish Labour from polling catastrophe, that only took the party to a vote share slightly better than the abysmal result of 2015—although it gained six seats thanks to the SNP's reversal of fortune.[2]

Theresa May called an unnecessary election to increase her majority and ended up losing it altogether. Understandably, the political fallout focused on the failure of her gamble and the dreadful campaign she ran. The Tories slipped by around five points in the polls between the publication of their manifesto and election day. But this obscured what was still a remarkable Conservative performance. They scored a 42 per cent share across the UK and won 13.7 million votes, more than they had managed at any election since 1992, largely by absorbing more than half of UKIP's support.[3] That would usually have meant a massive majority. It took something spectacular from Labour to stop them.

The big story of the election was not that the Conservatives imploded, but that Labour pulled off the most stunning surge in British political history. To the bewilderment of the election analysts, whose rules were broken into tiny pieces, all of Labour's success came in the campaign itself. It gained somewhere between 11 and 16 percentage points in just seven weeks.[4] This was all the more remarkable against the backdrop of two horrendous terror attacks and an ongoing civil war inside the party, although it was significant that certain things that could have happened during the campaign did not: neither the state nor business attempted to intervene, perhaps because they expected Corbyn to lose, or possibly because they disliked the Tory position on Brexit.

There was simply no precedent for a party coming from so far back in such a short time. It was a spectacular vindication of the unorthodox campaign run by the Labour leadership. Their conscious attempt to expand the electorate paid off, defying all the experts who had scoffed that it would be impossible. A post-vote poll found that 38 per cent of the voters Labour gained in June 2017—a whopping 2 million people—had not voted in 2015 (about 1.5 million had been non-voters, the rest were newly eligible).[5]

There was a giant swing to Labour among young voters. This cannot be credited solely to the campaign—voters' choices were already diverging by age at the 2015 election, a reflection of how conditions had become much harder for young people.[7] But the swing in 2017 was on a different scale. Labour won more than 60 per cent of the vote among the under-30s—a staggering number—compared to 36 per cent two years earlier.[8]

A less pronounced pattern was seen among BAME people. The Tories had cut Labour's lead with this section of the electorate at the 2015 election, causing Labour strategists to worry. But that trend was reversed—turnout rose, Labour's vote rose and, unlike among the general population, the Conservative vote shrank.[9]

The picture was less clear when it came to the working class base that Labour aimed to rebuild, particularly in "post-industrial communities." There was a swing to the Tories in some Labour heartland areas, particularly in the Midlands and the North East—although, interestingly, not in Wales. This provoked some commentators and MPs to lambast the leadership for having lost touch with the working class. In fact, even in these traditional areas, Labour piled on votes under Corbyn, going some way towards reversing a decline that had actually occurred in the New Labour era. But the Conservative Party piled on even more, likely due to its position on Brexit, which allowed it to envelop UKIP. This was the story in all of the constituencies Labour lost to the Tories, but Labour's strong showing meant that these numbered just five seats.[10]

Nevertheless, there seemed to have been a shift in the voting habits of the classes. The profiles of the two parties' supporters looked broadly similar through the prism of the pollsters' beloved social grades (AB, C1, C2, DE). The Tories had considerably improved their position with C2 and DE voters, while the shape of Labour's support was not much different to that won under Ed Miliband, except more people of every social grade voted for the party in 2017. But social grades, which are determined by types of occupation, are an imprecise proxy for class. If Labour's voters were instead categorised by their income a radically different picture emerged. Suddenly, it was clear that, compared to its performance in 2015, Labour had won significantly more support from the lower paid, and around the same amount from the better off (the Tories, however, also increased their support towards the bottom end of the scale, boosted by UKIP converts). Moreover, when social grades were broken down by age, it transpired that Labour's problem among C2 and DE voters was specific to older people, while those under 64 favoured the party—reflecting the startling fact that the only employment category among which the Conservatives won was retirees.[11]

Under the surface, a process of change was occurring within the working class. The Tories had made inroads into predominantly white, former manufacturing communities, but Labour had increased its support from a diverse so-called "new working class" of people employed in precarious jobs and the service industries. Combined with the overlapping categories of the young, the well educated, and a still-significant base in the 'old' working class, this was Labour's coalition of voters.[12]

Of course, the Labour leadership's strategy was about much more than targeting specific voter groups. They went to the electorate with a vision of how the whole of society could be transformed. "In the last 20 years, who has run a campaign that has put forward such policies that have created a real choice?" asks one of Corbyn's top advisors. "Doing that makes people sit up and say, 'OK, what are you offering?' I was very confident we'd shift the opinion polls."

The energy and excitement created by Labour's programme animated a movement and created a momentum which drew others in. The importance of the snowball effect was underlined by Labour's unusually impressive performance among those who decided late. Conventional wisdom suggests that undecided voters end up splitting roughly the same way as everyone else, but this time Labour won more than half of them. The party also picked up 54 per cent of those who switched allegiance during the campaign, while the Conservatives attracted only 19 per cent.[13]

The claim of Labour MPs such as Joan Ryan that people were only likely to vote Labour if they thought Corbyn would lose, and therefore the party's improvement in the polls in the final weeks was "scaring off the undecided," was nonsense. The better Labour's chances looked, the more people wanted to join the bandwagon, analysis subsequently confirmed.[14] Just as his team had predicted, when people saw Corbyn with their own eyes instead of through those of a hostile media, they liked him. His ease on the campaign trail and assured performances on TV transformed perceptions. He became Labour's great asset.[15]

All of this was rather embarrassing for the party machine in Southside and the regional offices. Because Labour effectively ran two campaigns in parallel—one designed by the leadership with help on the ground from Momentum and thousands of members, the other directed by the party's top officials—the election offered a unique historical opportunity to test both approaches under the same conditions. There can be little doubt about the outcome. Southside's defensive operation looked like a rational response to bad polls at the outset, and no doubt helped shore up some threatened seats, but it was the leadership's strategy that changed the dynamic of the election. Given the Labour right's unshakable belief that it alone knew the path to electoral success, it was ironic that on this occasion the 'unelectable' left showed it the way.

For Corbyn's team, delight at being vindicated competed with frustration that Labour's riven campaign had prevented the party reaching its full potential. "My overriding sensation at the end of the election was that we didn't let anyone down," says Karie Murphy. "But it soon turned to reflecting on what could have been if the party had believed in what we had, if we hadn't wasted a year before employing community organisers."

There was a competing explanation for Labour's good showing, taken up with gusto by some commentators. This held that the election was actually all about Brexit. Labour's large vote, it was said, was not down to Corbyn but to Remainers flocking to the party to thwart May's plans. It was true that Labour's biggest advances came in places that had voted to stay in the EU. The Conservatives gained most in constituencies that had voted to leave. More than half of Remain voters plumped for Labour. Sixty per cent of Leavers opted for the Tories.[16] These were striking correlations, but they did not prove causation. People who were less bothered about immigration, for example, were more likely to support Labour anyway, and more likely to vote Remain anyway. The election did see the gap widen between such voters and those more hostile to immigration, who backed the Tories in increased numbers. But this was the latest stage in a long-term shift that pre-dated the referendum, even if it had been accelerated by it.[17]

Although most people, when asked for the number one issue facing the country, said Brexit, it did not necessarily decide their vote. The importance and effect of the issue differed markedly between supporters of the two parties. Brexit unquestionably motivated Conservative voters. Polls found it was their main concern. But only 8 per cent of Labour voters named it as the single most important factor in their decision.[18] If the Labour surge was powered by people attempting to stop a hard Brexit then it would be reasonable to expect the more than 5 million voters the party attracted anew, at least, to rank it number one.[19] Instead, they ranked it fourth, after jobs and pay, education, and miles behind the NHS.[20] Contrary to the narrative that young people were motivated by a desire to revenge their elders for the referendum result, the importance of Brexit to voters decreased markedly the younger they were.[21] In short, leaving the EU undoubtedly was on the minds of Labour voters, but it was one issue among several.

May's rebranding of the Tories as the party of Leave was the reason they secured such an extraordinary number of votes, although the Conservative converts were not concentrated in the right constituencies for the party to gain seats as a result. However, the positioning was not cost-free: the Tories lost some ground among Remain voters. In contrast to May, Corbyn spoke about Brexit as little as he could get away with and, when he did mention it, said the referendum result had to be respected. This attempt to neutralise Brexit was successful. While Labour fared best with Remainers, gaining around 10 points on 2015, it was still able to advance by 5 points among Leave voters. The party's stance enabled it to pick up significant chunks of support from former UKIPers as well as Lib Dems; Conservatives as well as Greens.[22]

Labour's ability to gain votes from all over the place was the "clearest sign" of a "Corbyn factor," ventured the *Financial Times*.[23] Corbyn's liberal attitudes on social issues—a defining characteristic of the much derided "loony left" since the 1980s—were attractive to a growing swathe of the electorate that now identified with such values.[24] Meanwhile, after seven years of austerity there was a large audience primed for Corbyn's economic message. "At a time when people's living standards are falling, inflation is going up, wages are falling, it's a popular thing to say there are people at the very top who genuinely have got the broadest shoulders," says an advisor to Corbyn. Despite the protestations of the 'elections-are-won-on-the-centre-ground' zealots, it turned out there was not a fixed formula for winning votes. What worked depended on the circumstances. A pronounced anti-establishment sentiment had taken hold in the country. Seventy-one per cent of the voters Labour gained in June 2017 believed the establishment had let them down.[25]

Labour Party members and supporters had felt that sentiment in 2015. It was a major reason why they had chosen Corbyn to be their leader. For their act of insubordination they were ridiculed, patronised and insulted by a confederacy of commentators and politicians. These professionals had a habit of viewing Corbyn's Labour as if it was a controlled experiment. Strange phenomena could be observed, unusual results recorded, but these contained no wider lessons. Corbyn and his supporters were an anomaly unworthy of explanation because they were doomed to electoral oblivion anyway. "Everyone who is going to vote for a Corbyn-led Labour Party is already a member of it," sneered a talking head on Sky News early in the general election campaign.[26]

Back in the real world—as should have been obvious when talking about an organisation that grew to half a million members—the Labour Party was not a controlled experiment but part of society, made up of people experiencing the same pressures and frustrations as the communities in which they lived. If they believed the best response to those conditions was to elect Corbyn, it was always possible that a significant proportion of the general population would come to the same conclusion.

June 2017 showed that what happened to Labour two years earlier was not a freak result but a symptom of a deep, ongoing process. This helps to explain the striking features in common between Corbyn's leadership bid and the general election campaign: the ballooning movement, the prominence of young people, the sense of insurgency. Most tellingly, both campaigns featured essentially the same policy platform. Those policies had resonance in the context of a country still living in the shade of the 2008 crash.

The result shredded the credibility of the commentariat and much of the news media. The duty of journalists was to explain politics to the public. By and large, they failed, preferring instead to indulge their personal political commitments or those of their employers. Barring a few exceptions, it was difficult to find evidence that any of them had a grasp of how politics worked beyond the insular world of Westminster.

But the pundits were not the only ones to get it wrong. Most Labour MPs had attempted to overrule the party's choice of leader, insisting that they knew best the ways of the electorate. The general election was a stonking vindication of the members' judgement, while that of the MPs was found wanting. It was also just reward for the trade unions that helped propel Corbyn to the leadership, especially those that had not wavered. "I'm not someone who believes in false modesty," says Len McCluskey. "We sustained him through difficult times and that wouldn't have happened if someone else had been general secretary of Unite. I'm dead proud of that. But the real hero of it is Jeremy."

It was not necessary to resort to counterfactual history to show that if the MPs had got their way Labour could have been in trouble. There were salutary lessons from other social democratic parties in elections just across the Channel. The Dutch Labour Party suffered a complete meltdown in March 2017, falling from second place to seventh and losing over three quarters of its seats while parties to its left advanced. In France, the first round of the presidential election in April saw the Socialist Party candidate record a miserable 6 per cent, while the independent leftist Jean-Luc Mélenchon surged to nearly 20 per cent, missing out on a place in the run off by less than 2 points. Even allowing for the very different electoral systems and contexts, the fact that Labour bucked this trend suggested the British experience—in which the left had taken leadership of the established social democratic party rather than challenging it—was preferable.

Inside the Labour Party the election result destroyed the three pretexts used by Corbyn's opponents to justify their recalcitrance: that he was unelectable, incompetent, and not a leader. It was no longer plausible to claim that a man who took his party to 40 per cent of the vote was unelectable. Having headed a campaign that ran rings around the Tory operation, the charge of incompetence had lost its bite. As for leadership, Corbyn had not only inspired millions of new voters, he had changed the political weather. The only remaining grounds on which to oppose him were over his politics—the true source of disagreement all along. But Owen Smith's 2016 challenge on a Corbyn-lite platform had already demonstrated that the leader's critics did not want to go there. Although foreign policy divisions remained, Corbyn's domestic agenda was unassailable.

Seeing Labour stand on a left manifesto had been one of the leader's ambitions; he now set about achieving his other objectives of democratising the party and making it more of a social movement-style campaigning force. He had help. Emboldened activists made rapid advances through the structures of the party, winning internal elections and securing an overwhelming majority of delegates at a jubilant annual conference in September 2017.[27]

For the British left, the historic achievement of the June 2017 general election was to remove the albatross of 1983—the defeat that had weighed it down for three-and-a-half decades. "All my life I've been listening to people say you can't win popular support with a left programme," says McCluskey. "That's what Corbyn has given us. Something we'll be able to hang on to in future generations. It will live on."

There was nothing complicated about how it was done. As one of the leader's aides puts it, "Our whole campaign was just true to our politics." This had been Corbyn's way ever since he threw his hat into the ring for the leadership in 2015. Instead of ceding ground to the right as part of an elaborate political game, or searching for the mythical centre ground, Corbyn simply stood up for what he—and apparently millions of others—believed in. By leading opinion, rather than following it, he boxed out a new space for progressive politics. Corbyn's spectacular insurgent campaigns stand as vivid demonstrations that, as he said upon taking leadership of the Labour Party in September 2015, "things can, and they will, change."

REFERENCES

The references have been hosted online. They can be viewed or downloaded at: orbooks.com/catalog/the-candidate/endnotes

An archive of all the references can be found at: https://archive.org/details/CandidateReferences

Note on the referencing of interviews

Most of the direct quotations used in this book are taken from first-hand interviews conducted by the author. These quotations are not individually referenced except where it is necessary to do so for clarity. In general, where speech is quoted in the present tense—for example, "McDonnell says" or "Thompson remembers"—this signifies that it is sourced from an original interview, whereas quotations derived from a third party are rendered in the past tense—"Cooper said"—and are referenced. In instances where the tense is not clear, if a quotation is not otherwise referenced then it is derived from an interview with the author

Original interviews were conducted with: Luke Akehurst (31 January 2016); Rebecca Barnes (2 January 2016); Andrew Berry (16 December 2015); Bobby from *Double Down News* (3 July 2017); Michael Calderbank (2 December 2015); James Doran (14 December 2015); Billy Hayes (3 November 2017); Owen Jones (11 February

2016); Jon Lansman (19 and 27 January 2016); Clive Lewis (11 April 2016); Lola May (19 February 2016); Martin Mayer (12 January 2016); Len McCluskey (22 July 2017); John McDonnell (19 and 27 April 2016); James Mills (19 April 2016); Karie Murphy (28 and 29 June 2017); Michelle Ryan (11 December 2015); Ben Sellers (5 February 2016); James Schneider (19 February 2016); Max Shanly (27 January and 19 February 2016); Cat Smith (4 February 2016); Marshajane Thompson (3 March 2016), Joe Todd (22 July 2017).

A further four interviews were conducted between December 2015 and February 2016 with sources who wished to remain anonymous. Where quoted, these interviewees are usually referred to as "a member of the campaign team" or similar. Following the 2017 general election more interviews were conducted in June, July and August of that year, including three with sources who wished to remain anonymous and are typically referred to as "an aide to Jeremy Corbyn."

ACKNOWLEDGEMENTS

The bulk of this book was researched and written after Jeremy Corbyn's election as leader of the Labour Party in 2015 and first published in November 2016. Showing scant regard for my publication schedule, Labour MPs decided to launch a coup against Corbyn while I was finishing the manuscript, nearly making the book irrelevant. An Afterword covering their gambit, included in the first printing, appears here as chapter 15. Following the June 2017 general election I drafted a new prologue and final chapter for this updated edition. The original text has been streamlined. The only significant revisions to the substance of the earlier edition concern the accounts of the Collins Review and Unite's 2015 leadership nomination.

Thank you to all those who agreed to be interviewed for this book. Particular thanks to Jon Lansman, John McDonnell, and Karie Murphy for being so generous with their time. I am hugely grateful to everyone I spoke to (in alphabetical order): Luke Akehurst; Rebecca Barnes; Andrew Berry; Bobby from *Double Down News*; Michael Calderbank; James Doran; Billy Hayes; Owen Jones; Jon Lansman; Clive Lewis; Lola May; Martin Mayer; Len McCluskey; John McDonnell; James Mills; Karie Murphy; Michelle Ryan; James Schneider; Ben Sellers; Max Shanly; Cat Smith; Marshajane Thompson; Joe Todd.

I conducted a further seven interviews on the basis that any comments would appear unattributed. Anonymous quotes in newspapers drive me mad but I understand why some people could not speak on the record and I appreciate them taking the time.

As well as those on the inside, I set out to interview some of the activists and party members who have powered the Corbyn phenomenon. Given time I would have spoken to more of them.

Thank you to Byron Taylor for enlightening me on the recent history of the trade union movement. Thanks to Seumas Milne for his help. I am hugely grateful to Liz Davies for reading a draft of the original manuscript and sending encouraging comments. I owe one to Max Shanly, Marshajane Thompson and Ben Sellers for checking over chapters, and to Jamie Stern-Weiner for suggesting edits. I am thankful to Andrew Dolan for his research on the general election. Thank you to Norman Finkelstein for being so supportive.

I am very grateful to Allyson Pollock for not being cross with me for writing this book while I should have been editing hers on the NHS.

Thank you to Hilary Wainwright, especially for cajoling me into writing articles on the Labour Party for *Red Pepper*, and to Tom Walker and everyone else at the magazine.

Thanks to John Oakes, Colin Robinson and all at OR Books, with whom I have worked since 2011. I am particularly grateful to Alex Doherty for his help streamlining the manuscript and for getting publicity for the book. Thanks to Juliet Weis for her work on the endnotes. Thank you to Jen Overstreet and Justin Humphries for turning around the production so fast. I am grateful for the efforts of Emily Freyer, Shuja Haider, and Emma Ingrisani. I would like to thank Colin in particular for trusting that I could write this book, for the advice he gave on the manuscript, and for his patience.

ABOUT THE AUTHOR

Alex Nunns is a writer and editor. He is the co-editor of *Tweets from Tahrir: Egypt's Revolution in the Words of the People Who Made It* and has written for *Le Monde Diplomatique* and *Red Pepper*.